THE SOCIAL
AND POLITICAL
PHILOSOPHY OF

Jacques Maritain

194
M342N

THE SOCIAL
AND POLITICAL
PHILOSOPHY
OF

Jacques Maritain

SELECTED READINGS

by Joseph W. Evans
and Leo R. Ward

UNIVERSITY OF NOTRE DAME PRESS
NOTRE DAME, INDIANA 46556

University of Notre Dame Press edition 1976
Copyright © 1955 by Charles Scribner's Sons
First U.S. edition 1955 by Charles Scribner's Sons
Printed in the United States of America

Library of Congress Cataloging in Publication Data

Maritain, Jacques, 1882–1973.
    The social and political philosophy of Jacques
Maritain.

    Reprint of the ed. published by Scribner, New York.
    1. Philosophy—Collected works. I. Evans, Joseph
William. II. Ward, Leo Richard, 1893–   III. Title.
[B2430.M32E5   1976]   194   76-7587
ISBN 0-268-01674-7

ACKNOWLEDGMENTS

With exceptions noted below, the editors have made new translations from the French editions and, in a few instances, from texts carefully revised by Mr. Maritain. Some of the translations are at certain points quite similar to earlier ones, whereas others are widely different.

Man and the State first appeared in English, and we have taken passages directly from it. Passages are also taken directly from *The Range of Reason* (1952) because Mr. Maritain felt it inadvisable to have two translations appearing so close together. Ch. 10, "The Mystery of Israel," also appears in its original translation.

On our own behalf and Mr. Maritain's we are happy to express our appreciation and thanks to the publishers listed below who hold the English and American rights, for their cooperation in making this book possible.

George Allen & Unwin, Ltd., London, who hold the rights in the British Empire of:

> Ch. 2, "The Conquest of Freedom" from *Freedom: Its Meaning,* edited by Ruth Nanda Anshen.

> Ch. 25, "Confession of Faith" from *I Believe,* edited by Clifton Fadiman.

Geoffrey Bles, Ltd., London, who hold the English language rights of:
> *True Humanism,* translated by M. R. Adamson (1938), which was published in Paris by Fernand Aubier under the title *Humanisme intégral* (new edition, 1947; first edition, 1936). From this book the following sections [1] are taken:

>> Ch. 18, "Need of a New Humanism," pp. xiv–xvii, 20–26 (pp. 12–15, 36–42).

>> Ch. 19, "Sacral and Lay Civilization," pp. 128–147 (pp. 141–159).

---

[1] The first series of page references appearing after titles of chapters refer to the edition in English; the second series in parentheses refer to the recent edition in French.

51112

Ch. 20, "The Roots of Soviet Atheism," pp. 27–42 (pp. 43–61).

Ch. 21, "Concrete Historical Ideal of a New Christendom," pp. 121–122, 156 (pp. 134–135, 168–169).

Ch. 22, "Positive Construction," pp. 157–161, 169–201 (pp. 169–173, 181–212).

Ch. 24, "The Reintegration of the Masses," pp. 222–234 (pp. 232–244).

Charles Scribner's Sons hold the rights in the United States.

Harcourt, Brace and Company, Inc., New York, who hold the English language rights of:

Ch. 2, "The Conquest of Freedom," which first appeared in English in *Freedom: Its Meaning*, edited by Ruth Nanda Anshen (1940). This chapter appeared in *Principes d'une politique humaniste* (New York, 1944), pp. 13–42, published by Éditions de la Maison Française. Our translation is made at Mr. Maritain's request from this revised and corrected edition.

Charles Scribner's Sons, New York, who hold the English language rights of: *The Person and the Common Good*, translated by John J. Fitzgerald (1941), which was published by Desclée de Brouwer in Paris under the title *La personne et le bien commun* (1947). Geoffrey Bles, Ltd., hold the rights in Great Britain. From this book the following passages are taken:

Ch. 1, "The Individual and the Person," pp. 21–34 (pp. 25–36).

Ch. 8, "The Person and the Common Good," pp. 39–53 (pp. 44–56).

Ch. 4, "Human Rights," from *The Rights of Man and Natural Law*, translated by Doris C. Anson (1943), pp. 64–114. This chapter appeared in *Les droits de l'homme et la loi naturelle*, Éditions de la Maison Française (New York, 1942), pp. 84–138.

Ch. 6, "Human Equality," which appeared in *Ransoming the Time*, translated by Harry Lorin Binsse (1941), pp. 1–29. This chapter appeared in *Principes d'une politique humaniste* (New York, 1944), pp. 95–131. *Redeeming the Time* was published in England by Geoffrey Bles, Ltd., in 1943.

Ch. 15, "Gospel Inspiration and Lay Consciousness," from *Christianity and Democracy*, translated by Doris C. Anson (1941), pp. 42–56. This chapter appeared in *Christianisme et démocratie*, Éditions de la Maison Française (New York, 1943), pp. 49–64.

The following chapters are taken directly from *The Range of Reason* (New York, copyright 1952 by Jacques Maritain).

Ch. 11a, "The Pluralist Principle in Democracy," pp. 165–171. (Appeared originally in *The Nation*, April 21, 1945.)

Ch. 11b, "The Possibilities of Co-operation in a Divided World," pp. 172–184.

Ch. 13, "Christian Humanism," pp. 185–199. (Appeared originally in *Fortune*, April 1942.)

Ch. 14, "The Meaning of Contemporary Atheism," pp. 103–117. (Appeared originally in *The Review of Politics*, July 1949.)

Ch. 23, "The End of Machiavellianism," pp. 134–163. (Appeared originally in *The Review of Politics*, January 1942.)
The Range of Reason was published in England by Geoffrey Bles, 1953.

Ch. 16, "The Mystery of Israel," from *Ransoming the Time* (1941), pp. 141–176. This chapter was translated by Harry Lorin Binsse, seemingly from a manuscript and not from any published volume. *Redeeming the Time* was published in England by Geoffrey Bles, Ltd., 1943.

Sheed and Ward, London, who hold the English language rights of:

Ch. 5, "Person and Property," from *Freedom in the Modern World*, translated by Richard O'Sullivan (1936), pp. 193–214. This was published by Desclée de Brouwer in Paris under the title *Du régime temporel et de la liberté* (1933), pp. 229–255. Charles Scribner's Sons hold the rights in the United States.

Ch. 10, "Solitude and the Community," from *Three Reformers* (1929), pp. 119–140, which was published by Librairie Plon under the title *Trois réformateurs* (Nouvelle édition, Paris, 1930; first edition, 1925), pp. 170–200. Charles Scribner's Sons hold the rights in the United States.

Ch. 12, "Primacy of the Spiritual," from *The Things That Are Not Caesar's*, translated by J. F. Scanlan (1930), pp. 85–110, which was published by Librairie Plon under the title *Primauté du spirituel* (new and revised edition, Paris, n.d.; first edition, 1927), pp. 132–165. Charles Scribner's Sons hold the rights in the United States.

Ch. 17, "Religion and Culture," from *Religion and Culture*, translated by J. F. Scanlan (1931). This was published by Desclée de Brouwer under the title *Religion et culture* in Paris (2nd edition, 1946; first edition, 1930), pp. 11–24, 67–75. The English translation appeared also in *Essays in Order* (New York, 1931), pp. 3–13, 44–49.

Simon and Schuster, Inc., New York, who hold the English language rights of:

Ch. 25, "Confession of Faith," which first appeared in English in *I Believe*, edited by Clifton Fadiman, copyright 1939 by Simon and Schuster, Inc. A revised text was published as *Confession de foi* (New York, Éditions de la Maison Française, 1941). Our translation is made at Mr. Maritain's request from his own revised text.

The University of Chicago Press, who hold the English language rights of the following chapters from *Man and the State* (1951). (French translation, *L'homme et l'état*. Paris, Bibliothèque de la science politique, Presses Universitaires de France, 1953):

Ch. 3, "Natural Law," pp. 84–94.

Ch. 7, "The Body Politic," pp. 9–19.

Ch. 9, "Problems Concerning Authority," pp. 126–139.

Ch. 11c, "The Democratic Secular Faith," pp. 109–114.

Ch. 11d, "The Political Heretics," pp. 114–119.

Pp. 248–251, in Ch. 19, "Sacral and Lay Civilization," pp. 159–162.

Pp. 282–291, in Ch. 22, "Positive Construction," pp. 171–179.

J. W. E.
L. R. W.

FOREWORD

Jacques Maritain has been philosophizing about social and political life for a long time. *Primauté du spirituel,* his first major political writing, appeared in 1927. This remarkable "first work" was occasioned by Pius XI's condemnation in 1926 of Charles Maurras' *L'Action Française* party—a party largely imbued with agnosticism, and with political naturalism, monarchism, and strong nationalist tendencies. Although the Pope was only exercising the right of the Church to intervene whenever the spiritual is involved, the condemnation was bitterly opposed by party members and by others on the supposition that he was dictating to the temporal order as such.

Maritain had once shared with Father Humbert Clérissac, his spiritual director, certain sympathies for some of the nationalist and monarchical aspirations of *L'Action Française.* Yet he viewed the condemnation with great interest and with filial respect. Happily, it was the occasion for his serious study of Maurras' doctrines and for his own painstaking work on social and political problems.

"Today more than ever," Maritain wrote in his diary several years ago, "I bless the liberating intervention of the Church which, in 1926, exposed the errors of the Action Française, following which I finally examined Maurras' doctrines and saw what they were worth. There began for me then a period of reflection devoted to moral and political philosophy in which I tried to work out the character of authentically Christian politics and to establish, in the light of a philosophy of history and of culture, the true significance of democratic inspiration and the nature of the new humanism for which we are waiting."

This "period of reflection" turned out to be a lengthy one. It was enriched by Maritain's continued study of the metaphysical and theological questions which at an earlier date had been his almost exclusive intellectual interest, and it bore abundant fruit in the several books on social and political philosophy that are among Maritain's most notable works. From *Primauté du spirituel* to the recent *Man and the State* and *The Range of Reason,* Maritain has progressively fashioned a social and political thought that has come to grips with Communism, Fascism, and other forms of totalitarianism, and with present-day forms and remnants of nineteenth-century individualism. His arguments have such an incisiveness about them, his insights and intuitions such a freshness and originality, that it is a real intellectual experience to read any of his works.

Our purpose is to bring together in one volume those passages in Maritain's writings that are both representative and expressive of his social and political philosophy.

Joseph W. Evans
Leo R. Ward

NOTRE DAME, INDIANA
APRIL, 1955

PREFACE

In this brief preface I should like to make a few remarks about the subject matter of the book, namely, political philosophy.

Political philosophy does not claim to supersede and replace either sociology or political science. But, while being more abstract, and less bound to "the detail of phenomena," it raises the material scrutinized by sociology and political science both to a higher degree of intelligibility and to a higher degree of practicality, because it sees this material in the light and perspective of a more profound and more comprehensive, a *sapiential* knowledge of Man, which is Ethics and deals with the very ends and norms of human conduct.

I just alluded to the practical character of political philosophy. Does not this seem to be rather paradoxical indeed, since political philosophy—though it is and must be deeply and constantly concerned with experience and reality, with the facts of life, with *what exists*—winds up nevertheless, as more generally moral philosophy does, in considering not only *things as they are*, but also *things as they should be?* Hegel refused to admit the distinction between *should be* and *to be*, and in so doing he sanctioned all the crimes of history. But on the other hand is not this very distinction (or rather, in actual fact, this terrible gap) between *devoir être* and *être, should be* and *to be*, a sign of the inefficacy, not of the practical character of political philosophy? This objection comes from a quite superficial view of human matters. It disregards the fact that man is an intellectual agent, and, weak as flesh may be, has spirit in him. Man betrays his ideals but is prompted by them and cannot act, cannot do without them. And how could it be possible to betray a *should be* if this *should be* were not an incentive to make something *be,* an incentive to action? Not only is political philosophy "practical" in the sense that it deals with human actions, and with their ends, norms and existential conditioning: but it is, despite the jokes of so-called practical men, efficacious and eminently efficacious; for hope has to do with things as they should be, not with things as they are, and man cannot live or act without hope. Political philosophy is efficacious and eminently efficacious, because it deals with the terrestrial hopes of the human community.

Finally I should like to observe that, as a matter of fact, one of the problems with which I was mainly concerned while I wrote some of my essays in political and social philosophy was the problem of the situation of the Christian in the world and of the temporal mission of the Christian; and one of the purposes I had in mind was to look after the possibility which the philosophical approach to the truth of the matter might offer to delineate a concrete historical ideal for the social and political activity of Christians in the present world, and thus to maintain and foster among them, especially in Christian youth, terrestrial hope in the Gospel. Of course I am inclined, now more than ever, to think with Plato in his old age that philosophical reason is always disappointed if it tries to act *hic et nunc* upon the affairs or the rulers of the human city, and that the most important thing for a philosopher is to "turn toward the internal city he bears within himself." [1] But this is not the point I want to make. What I want to point out is the fact that, as a result of the circumstances I just mentioned, my essays in social and political philosophy have a particularly manifest relationship to the concept of "moral philosophy integrally considered," or moral philosophy as taking into account—in its own order, and while remaining genuine philosophy—theological data concerning the existential condition of man. I have discussed this problem in other books. [2] Here I wish only to express the hope that the excerpts gathered together in this volume may prove to be not too defective an instance of such Christian moral philosophy.

I wish, in concluding, to tell Reverend Father Leo R. Ward and Dr. Joseph W. Evans of my gratitude for their interest in my philosophical work and for the pains they have taken in selecting these excerpts and composing with them a book endowed with a unity and internal development of its own. They were even so kind as to re-translate a great many pages. I feel deeply indebted to them for such friendly devotion. I feel also indebted to the publisher, Messrs. Scribner, and particularly to Mr. William Savage, who spent much care and labor in the preparation of the volume, and I thank them cordially, as well as the various publishers who have been gracious enough to permit use of the material appearing in their books. The editing and publication of this volume is another token of the courtesy and generosity extended to a French philosopher by this great country, a country which he has loved for a long time and in the cultural life of which he is proud to participate.

Jacques Maritain

---

[1] *Republ.*, IX, 591 e.

[2] Cf. *An Essay on Christian Philosophy* (New York: Philosophical Library, 1955) and *Science and Wisdom* (London: Bles; New York: Scribner, 1940).

CONTENTS

THE SOCIAL
AND POLITICAL
PHILOSOPHY OF

Jacques Maritain

PART I

The Human Person

1 THE INDIVIDUAL AND THE PERSON*

Is NOT THE *person* THE SELF? Is NOT *my person my self?* Let us consider the singular contradictions to which this term and notion of *self* give rise.

Pascal tells us that "the self is detestable." This expression is a commonplace of Pascalian literature. Then, too, when we say in everyday language that someone is "self-assertive," do we not mean that he is self-centered, imperious and dominating—scarcely capable of friendship? A distinguished contemporary artist once remarked, "I do not like *others*"; a remark that reveals a strongly asserted personality. In this sense, we might construe personality to consist in self-realization at the expense of others. So construed, personality would always imply a certain selfishness or imperviousness, because no place remains for anything or anyone else in the man who is busy with himself and with all that concerns himself.

On the other hand, is it not a serious reproach to assert of a man that he has no personality? Do we not regard heroes and saints as men who have reached the heights of personality and, at the same time, of generosity? Nothing great is accomplished in the world save through a heroic fidelity to some truth which a man who says "I" sees, and to which he bears witness; a heroic fidelity to some mission which he, himself, a human person, must fulfill; of which, perhaps, he alone is aware and for which he lays down his life.

---

* *La personne et le bien commun* (Paris: Desclée de Brouwer, 1947), pp. 25–36.

But let us turn to the Gospel. No personality is more magnificently asserted than that of Christ. Revealed dogma tells us that it is the very personality of the Uncreated Word.

Here, in contrast to the expression of Pascal that "the self is detestable," the words of St. Thomas come to mind: "the person is the most noble and most perfect being in all of nature." [1] Whereas Pascal teaches that "the self is detestable," St. Thomas teaches that whosoever loves God must love himself for the sake of God, must love his own soul and body with a love of charity. Concern for self—or what contemporary psychologists call introversion—can cause much damage. Many of those reared in a strict Puritanism are said to complain of a suffering, a kind of interior paralysis, created by *self-consciousness*. On the other hand, philosophers, above all St. Augustine and in modern times Hegel, teach that self-knowledge is a privilege of the spirit, and that much human progress consists in the progress of consciousness of self.

What do these contradictions mean? They mean that the human being is caught between two poles—a material pole, which, in reality, does not concern the true person but rather the shadow of personality or what, in the strict sense, is called *individuality*; and a spiritual pole, which does concern *true personality*.

It is to the material pole, to the individual become the center of all, that the expression of Pascal refers. It is to the spiritual pole, on the contrary, to the person, source of liberty and bountifulness, that St. Thomas' expression refers. Thus, we are confronted with the distinction between *individuality* and *personality*.

This is no new distinction but a classical distinction belonging to the intellectual heritage of mankind. Its equivalent in Hindu philosophy is the distinction between the *ego* and the *self*. It is fundamental in the doctrine of St. Thomas. Contemporary sociological and spiritual problems have made it particularly timely. Widely different schools of thought appeal to it; the Thomists, certain disciples of Proudhon, Nicholas Berdiaeff, and those philosophers who, even before the invasion of the young existentialist group, already called themselves "existentialists." Hence it is all important to distinguish between the individual and the person. It is no less important to understand the distinction correctly.

---

[1] "Person signifies what is most perfect in all nature—that is, a subsistent individual of a rational nature." *Sum. Theol.*, I, 29, 3.

Let us consider individuality first. Outside the mind, only individual realities exist.[2] Only they are capable of exercising the act of existing. Individuality is opposed to the state of universality which things have in the mind. It designates that concrete state of unity and indivision, required by existence, in virtue of which every actually or possibly existing nature can posit itself in existence as distinct from other beings. The angels are individual essences; the Divine Essence, in Its sovereign unity and simplicity, is supremely individual. Pure forms or pure spirits are, of themselves or by reason of that which constitutes their substantial intelligibility, in the state of individuality. For this reason, St. Thomas teaches, each angel differs from any other as the whole species of lions differs from the whole species of horses or from the whole species of eagles. In other words, each angel differs specifically from every other; each is an individual by the very form (absolutely free from any matter) in which its being consists and which constitutes it in its species.

The situation of terrestrial things, material beings, is quite different. According to the Angelic Doctor, their individuality is rooted in matter, so far as matter requires the occupation in space of a position distinct from every other position. Matter itself is a kind of non-being, a mere potency or ability to receive forms and undergo substantial changes; in short, an avidity for being. In every being made of matter, this pure potency bears the impress of a metaphysical energy—the "form" or "soul"—which constitutes with it a substantial unit and determines this unit to be that which it is. By the fact that it is ordained to inform matter, the form finds itself particularized to such and such a being sharing the same specific nature with other beings likewise immersed in spatiality.

According to this doctrine, the human soul, together with the matter which it informs, constitutes one substance, which is both carnal and spiritual. The soul is not, as Descartes believed, one thing—namely, thought—existing on its own as a complete being, and the body another thing—namely, extension—existing on its own as a complete being. Soul and matter are two substantial co-principles of the same being, of one and the same reality, called man. Because each soul is destined to animate a particular body

---

[2] And also collective realities constituted of individuals, such as society (*unum per accidens*).

(which receives its matter from the germinal cells, with all their hereditary content, from which it develops), and because, further, each soul has or rather *is* a substantial relation to a particular body, it has within its very substance individual characteristics which differentiate it from every other human soul.

In man, as in all other corporeal beings, the atom, the molecule, the plant, the animal, individuality has its first ontological roots in matter. Such is St. Thomas' doctrine on the individuality of material things. This common characteristic of all existents, namely, that in order to exist they must be one and distinct from every other existent, does not in corporeal beings, as in pure spirits, derive from the form which constitutes them at such and such a level of specific intelligibility. In them, this common characteristic is realized below the level of that intelligibility in act which is proper to the separated form—whether it is separated in real existence, or separated by the abstractive operation of the mind. Corporeal beings are individual because of *materia signata quantitate*. Their specific form and their essence are not individual by reason of their own entity, but rather they are individuated by reason of their transcendental relation to matter understood as implying position in space.

We have characterized matter as an avidity for being, having of itself no determination and deriving all of its determinations from form. In each of us, individuality, since it is that which excludes from oneself all that other men are, could be described as the narrowness of the ego, forever threatened and forever eager *to grasp for itself*. Such narrowness in flesh animated by a spirit derives from matter. As a material individual, man has only a precarious unity, which tends to be scattered in multiplicity. For matter tends of itself to disintegration, just as space tends to division. As an individual, each of us is a fragment of a species, a part of this universe, a unique point in the immense web of cosmic, ethnic, historic forces and influences—and bound by their laws. Each of us is subject to the determinism of the physical world. Nonetheless, each of us is also a person and, as such, is not controlled by the stars. Our whole being subsists in virtue of the very subsistence of the spiritual soul which is in us a principle of creative unity, independence and liberty.

We have sketched briefly the theory of individuality. Personality is a still deeper mystery, and to probe the depths of its meaning is considerably more difficult. Perhaps the best approach to the philosophical discovery of personality is to consider the relation between personality and love.

"We never love the person, but only his qualities," Pascal has said. This is a false statement, and exhibits in Pascal a trace of the very rationalism against which he strove to protect himself. Love does not go out to qualities. They are not the object of our love. We love the deepest, most substantial and hidden, the most *existing* reality of the beloved being. This is a metaphysical center deeper than all the qualities and essences which we can find and enumerate in the beloved. The expressions of lovers are unending because their object is ineffable.

Love goes out to this center, not, to be sure, as separated from its qualities, but as one with them. This is a center inexhaustible, so to speak, of existence, bounty and action; capable of giving and of *giving itself*; capable of receiving not only this or that gift bestowed by another, but even another self as a gift, another self who bestows himself. This brief consideration of love's own law brings us to the metaphysical problem of the person. For love does not go out to qualities or natures or essences, but to persons.

"Thou art *thyself* though, not a Montague . . . Romeo, doff thy name, and for thy name, which is no part of thee, take all myself."

To give oneself, one must first exist; not only as a sound which passes through the air, or as an idea which crosses the mind, but as a thing which subsists and exercises existence by itself. Such a being must exist not only as other things do, but eminently, in self-possession, holding itself in hand, master of itself. In short, it must exist with a spiritual existence, capable of containing itself thanks to intellect and freedom, capable of super-existing in knowledge and in love. That is why the metaphysical tradition of the West defines the person in terms of independence, as a reality which, subsisting spiritually, constitutes a universe unto itself, a relatively independent whole within the great whole of the universe and facing the transcendent Whole which is God. And that is why this same philosophical tradition sees in God the sovereign Personality, since the very existence of God consists in a pure and absolute super-existence of intellection and love. Unlike the concept of the individuality of corporeal things, the concept of personality is related not to matter but to the deepest and highest dimensions of being. Personality has its roots in spirit, inasmuch as spirit holds itself in existence and superabounds in existence. Metaphysically considered, personality is, as the Thomistic school rightly holds,[3] "subsistence," that ultimate achievement by which the creative influx seals within itself a nature facing the whole order of existence, so that the existence which it receives is *its own* existence and *its own* perfection. Personality is the subsistence of the spiritual soul communicated to the human composite. Because, in our substance, it is an imprint or seal which enables it to possess its existence, to perfect itself and to give itself freely, personality bears witness in us to the generosity or expansiveness of being, which in an incarnate spirit derives from the spirit, and which constitutes, in the secret depths of our ontological structure, a source of dynamic unity and unification from within.

Personality, therefore, signifies interiority to self. But precisely because it is the spirit in man which makes him, in contrast to the plant and the animal, cross the threshold of independence properly so called, and of interiority to oneself, the subjectivity of the person has nothing in common with the isolated unity, without doors or windows, of the Leibnizian monad. It requires the communications of knowledge and love. By the very fact that each of us is a person and expresses himself to himself, each of us requires communication with *the other* and with *others* in the order of knowledge and love. Personality, of its essence, asks for a dialogue in which souls really communicate. Such communication is rarely possible. This is why personality in man seems to be bound to the experience of affliction even more profoundly than to the experience of creative effort. The person has a direct relation with the absolute, and only in the absolute is he able to have his full sufficiency. His spiritual fatherland is the whole universe of the absolute and of those indefectible goods which are as an introduction to the absolute Whole which transcends the world.

Finally, we turn to religious thought for the last word and find that the deepest value of the human person's dignity consists in his property of resembling God—not in a *common* way, after the

---

[3] Cf. my work *Les degrés du savoir*, Annexe IV (*The Degrees of Knowledge*, Appendix IV).

manner of all creatures, but in a *proper* way. He is *the image of God*. For God is spirit, and the human person proceeds from Him having as principle of life a spiritual soul capable of knowing, of loving, and of being uplifted by grace to participation in the very life of God so that, in the end, it may know and love Him as He knows and loves Himself.

If our description is adequate, such are the two metaphysical aspects of the human being, individuality and personality, together with their proper ontological features. It is evident that it is not a question here of two separate things, but we must emphasize this, in order to avoid misunderstandings and nonsense. There is not in me one reality, called my individual, and another reality, called my person. One and the same being is an individual, in one sense, and a person, in another sense. Our whole being is an individual by reason of that in us which derives from matter, and a person by reason of that in us which derives from spirit. Similarly, the whole of a painting is a physico-chemical mixture by reason of the coloring stuff of which it is made, and the whole of it is a work of beauty by reason of the painter's art.

Let us note, moreover, that material individuality is not something evil in itself. Obviously, since it is the very condition of our existence, it is something good. But it is precisely as related to personality that individuality is good. Evil arises when, in our action, we give preponderance to the individual aspect of our being. No doubt, each of my acts is simultaneously the act of myself as an individual and the act of myself as a person. Yet, by the very fact that it is free and engages my whole being, each act is linked in a movement towards the supreme center to which personality tends, or in a movement towards that dispersion into which, if left to itself, material individuality is inclined to fall.

2 THE CONQUEST OF FREEDOM*

FREEDOM OF INDEPENDENCE AND FREEDOM OF CHOICE

IN THIS ESSAY I SHALL NOT TREAT OF FREE WILL OR freedom of choice. The existence and value of this kind of freedom are, however, taken for granted in all I shall say. That is why I shall first give a few brief indications in its regard. The freedom I shall treat of subsequently is the freedom of independence and of exaltation, which can also be called—in a Paulinian but not Kantian sense—the freedom of autonomy, or even the freedom of expansion, of the human person. It supposes the existence in us of freedom of choice, but it is substantially distinct from this latter.

A badly constructed philosophical theory that falsifies the second operation by which the mind of man knows itself explicitly, can counteract and paralyze the primary and natural operation of spontaneous consciousness. As long as we are not victims of this accident, each of us knows very well *that* he possesses freedom of choice; that is to say that if we betray a friend, risk our property to aid an unfortunate man, decide to become a banker, monk or soldier, these kinds of acts are what they are only because we have involved therein our personality and have arranged that they be this rather than that. But each of us knows very poorly *in what* freedom of choice consists. This obscurity of spontaneous consciousness, incapable of anything more than implicit knowledge in

---

* *Principes d'une politique humaniste* (New York: Éditions de la Maison Française, 1944), pp. 13–42.

this matter, enables philosophers, and especially savants who philosophize without knowing it, frequently to becloud the question.

Philosophers professing an absolute intellectualism cannot understand the existence of free will, because for them intelligence not only precedes will, but precedes it in the manner of a divinity apart, which would influence will without being influenced by it and without receiving from it any qualifying motion. Hence, the domain of formal or specifying determinations (the *ordo specificationis,* as it is called) can never itself depend intrinsically upon the domain of efficiency or existential effectuating (*ordo exercitii*), and the will is reduced to the function by which the intelligence would realize ideas which, in virtue of the mere object they represent, would appear best to the subject. Such was the position of the great metaphysicians of the classical age.

Pure empiricists likewise cannot understand the existence of free will, because, recognizing only sequences that are knowable by the senses, the idea of a causality exercised by a spirit upon itself has no meaning for them. Hence, when they voice an opinion on a question which, like that of free will, is essentially of the ontological order, they cannot, metaphysicians in spite of themselves (and bad ones at that), fail to interpret the empirical results of observational science in the framework of the classical mechanism inherited from Spinoza; they cannot fail to give themselves over, without knowing what they are doing, to the most naive extrapolations. In proportion as science reveals dynamic elements working in our psychical activity, they see in the mere existence of these elements the proof that they operate in a necessarily determining fashion— which is precisely what remains to be proved.

In our times it is Freudism that offers this empiricist pseudo-metaphysics the greatest possibilities for illusion. I have shown elsewhere [1] that it is very important to distinguish most clearly between the psychoanalytic method, which opens for investigation into the unconscious new roads of the greatest interest, and the philosophy (unaware of itself) that Freud, leaving the field of his competence and giving full rein to his dreams, sought in a crass empiricism. The fact, revealed by psychoanalysis, that there are unconscious motivations which the subject obeys without knowing

---

[1] Cf. *Quatre essais sur l'esprit dans sa condition charnelle,* Chapter I (*Scholasticism and Politics,* Chapter VI).

them furnishes in no manner, as some imagine, an argument against free will, for free will begins with intellectual judgment and consciousness. To the extent that these unconscious motivations make us act automatically, there is no question of free will; and to the extent that they give rise to a conscious judgment, the question is to know whether or not at this moment they themselves fashion this judgment, or are only rendered decisively motivating by this judgment (and therefore by means of a free choice). In other words, the question is to know whether they are necessarily determining or simply inclining, and it is clear that the mere fact of their existence is not sufficient to decide the issue.

More generally, free will in man does not exclude but rather presupposes the vast and complex dynamism of instincts, tendencies, psycho-physical dispositions, acquired habits and hereditary charges, and it is at the top point where this dynamism emerges into the world of spirit that freedom of choice is exercised, to give or not to give decisive efficacy to the inclinations and thrusts of nature. It follows from this that freedom of choice, as well as responsibility, admits in us a multiplicity of degrees of which the Author of being alone is judge. It does not follow from this that freedom of choice does not exist—quite the contrary! If it admits of degrees, then it exists.

The efforts of eminent scientists, like Dr. Arthur Compton, to link up our natural belief in free will with the indeterminist theories of modern physics may be highly significant and stimulating to the mind and efficacious in eliminating many prejudices, but I do not think that a strict proof providing this belief with an unshakable intelligible basis can be found in that direction. The direction to be followed is a metaphysical one. It leads us to formulas like those of Bergson: "Our motives are what we make them"; "Our motives have determined us only at the moment when they have become determining, that is, at the moment when the act is virtually accomplished." But it is not by a philosophy of pure becoming, it is by a philosophy of being and intelligence, as is the philosophy of St. Thomas Aquinas, that such formulas receive both their full significance and their demonstrative value.

Spirit, as such, implies a sort of infinity; its faculty of desire goes out of itself to a good which completely satisfies it, and therefore to a good without limits, and we cannot will anything except in the willing of happiness. But as soon as reflection occurs, our intelligence, confronted with goods which are not the Good, and judging them so, brings into actuality the radical indetermination that our appetite for happiness possesses in regard to everything which is not happiness itself. The efficacious motivation of an intelligent being can only be a practical judgment; and this judgment is efficacious only by reason of the will; it is the will which, proceeding by its own unpredictable initiative towards the good presented to it by such a judgment, gives to this judgment the power to specify the will efficaciously.

The free act, in which the intelligence and the will involve and envelop each other vitally, is thus like an instantaneous flash in which the active and dominating indetermination of the will is exercised in regard to the judgment itself which determines it; the will can do nothing without a judgment by the intellect; and it is the will which makes itself to be determined by the judgment, and by this judgment rather than by another one.

Far from being a simple function of the intelligence, by which the latter would realize the ideas which in virtue of their mere object would appear best, the will is an original spiritual energy of infinite capacity which has control over the intelligence and its judgments in the order of practical choice, and makes what it wills appear as being *here and now* best for the subject. What constitutes the proper mystery of free will is that, while essentially needing specification by the intellect, the exercise of the will has primacy over this specification and holds it under its active and dominating indetermination, because the will alone can give it existential efficacy.

After this preliminary and necessary explanation of freedom of choice, I shall now discuss freedom of independence.

FREEDOM OF INDEPENDENCE AND
THE ASPIRATIONS OF THE PERSON

Human personality is a great metaphysical mystery. We know that an essential characteristic of a civilization worthy of the name is the sense of and respect for the dignity of the human person. We know that we must be ready to give our lives to defend the rights of the human person and to defend liberty. What values, then, deserving of such sacrifice, are enveloped in the personality of man? What do we mean precisely when we speak of the human person? When we say that a man is a person, we do not mean merely that he is an individual, in the sense that an atom, a blade of grass, a fly, or an elephant is an individual. Man is an individual who holds himself in hand by intelligence and will. He does not exist only in a physical manner. He has spiritual super-existence through knowledge and love; he is, in a way, a universe in himself, a microcosm, in which the great universe in its entirety can be encompassed through knowledge; and through love he can give himself completely to beings who are to him, as it were, other selves, a relation for which no equivalent can be found in the physical world. The human person possesses these characteristics because in the last analysis man, this flesh and these perishable bones which are animated and activated by a divine fire, exists "from the womb to the grave" by virtue of the very existence of his soul, which dominates time and death. Spirit is the root of personality. The notion of personality thus involves that of totality and independence; no matter how poor and crushed he may be, a person, as such, is a whole and subsists in an independent manner. To say that man is a person is to say that in the depths of his being he is more a whole than a part and more independent than servile. It is to say that he is a minute fragment of matter that is at the same time a universe, a beggar who communicates with absolute being, mortal flesh whose value is eternal, a bit of straw into which heaven enters. It is this metaphysical mystery that religious thought points to when it says that the person is the image of God. The value of the person, his dignity and his rights belong to the order of things naturally sacred which bear the imprint of the Father of being, and which have in Him the end of their movement.

Freedom of spontaneity is not, as is free will, a power of choice that transcends all necessity, even interior necessity, and all determinism. It does not imply the absence of necessity but only the absence of constraint. It is the power of acting in virtue of one's own interior inclination and without undergoing compulsion imposed by any exterior agent.

This kind of freedom admits of all sorts of degrees, from the spontaneity of the electron which turns around the nucleus "freely," that is, without being turned from its path by the interference of a foreign particle, to the spontaneity of the grass in the fields which grows "freely" and of the bird that flies "freely," that is, obeying only the internal necessities of their natures. When freedom of spontaneity crosses the threshold of the realm of spirit, when it is the spontaneity of a spiritual nature, it becomes, properly speaking, freedom of independence. To this extent it does not consist merely in following the inclination of nature, but rather it consists in being or in making oneself actively the sufficient principle of one's own operation; in other words, in possessing, perfecting and expressing oneself as an indivisible whole in the act that one brings about. This is why freedom of independence exists only in beings which also have free will, and presupposes the exercise of free will in order to arrive at its own end.

An independent being is not necessarily an uncaused being; rather, it is a being that is master of itself. If the proper mark of personality consists, as I have just said, in the fact of being independent and of being to oneself a whole, even if only imperfectly, it is clear that personality and freedom of independence are related and inseparable. In the scale of being they increase together; at the summit of being, God is personality in pure act and freedom of independence in pure act. He is so personal that His existence is His very act of knowing and loving; and He is so independent that, while causing all things, He Himself is absolutely without cause, His essence being His very act of existing.

And in each of us, personality and freedom of independence increase together. For man is a being in movement. If he does not improve, he has nothing, and he loses what he had; he must win his being. The entire history of his misery and his greatness is the history of his effort to win, together with his own personality, freedom of independence. He is called to the conquest of freedom.

Two basic truths must be noted here. The first is that the human being, though a person and therefore independent because he is a spirit, is by nature at the lowest degree of personality and independence, because he is a spirit that is one in substance with matter and implacably bound to a bodily condition. The second is that, no matter how miserable, how poor, how enslaved and humiliated he may be, the aspirations of the person remain in him indefectibly; and they tend as such, in the life of each of us as in the life of the human race, toward the conquest of freedom.

The aspirations of personality are of two kinds. On the one

hand, they come from the human person *as human,* or as constituted in such a species; let us say that they are then "connatural"
to man and specifically human. On the other hand, they come from
the human person *so far as he is a person,* that is, so far as he
participates in that transcendental perfection which is personality
and which is realized in God infinitely better than in us; let us say
that they are then "transnatural" and metaphysical.

The connatural aspirations tend to a relative freedom compatible
with conditions here below, and the burden of material nature
inflicts on them from the very beginning a serious defeat, because
no animal is born more destitute and less free than man. The
struggle to win freedom in the order of social life aims at repairing
this defeat.

The transnatural aspirations of the person in us tend to a superhuman freedom, to freedom pure and simple. And to whom does
such a freedom belong by nature if not to Him alone who is freedom of independence itself, subsisting by itself? Man has no right
to the freedom proper to God. When he tends to this freedom with
a transnatural desire, he tends to it in an inefficacious manner and
without even knowing in what it consists. Divine transcendence
thus imposes from the very beginning the admission of a profound
defeat on these metaphysical aspirations of the person in us. However, such a defeat is not irreparable, at least if the victor descends
to the aid of the vanquished. The movement to win freedom in the
order of spiritual life aims precisely at repairing this defeat.

We must not hide from ourselves the fact that the point at which
our reflection has now arrived is a crucial one for the human being.
The least error here costs dearly. At this main point, capital errors,
mortal for human society and the human soul, are mixed with
capital truths to which are bound the life of the soul and that of
society. We must work as hard as possible to distinguish the truths
from the errors. There is a false conquest of freedom which is
illusory and homicidal. There is a true conquest of freedom which
is for man truth and life.

In order to describe both of them briefly, let me say that the
false manner of understanding the conquest of freedom is based on
a philosophy which we can call, in technical language, "univocalist"
and "immanentist." In such a philosophy the notion of independence and freedom admits of neither internal variety nor degrees;

and, on the other hand, God is conceived as a physical agent raised to the infinite. Hence, either He is considered as a *transcendent* being and His *existence* is denied, because a transcendent being would be, as Proudhon, among others, believed, a sort of heavenly Tyrant imposing constraint and violence on everything other than Himself; or His *existence* is affirmed and His *transcendence* is denied—all things are considered, in the manner of Spinoza or Hegel, as modes or phases of His realization. According to this view, there is freedom or autonomy only if no rule or objective measure is received from a being other than oneself. And the human person claims for himself a divine freedom, whether man takes, in atheistic forms of thought and culture, the place of the God he denies, or whether he tries to realize in act, in pantheistic forms, his identity of nature with the God he conceives.

On the contrary, the true manner of understanding the conquest of freedom is based on a philosophy of the analogy of being and a philosophy of divine transcendence. For this philosophy, independence and freedom are realized, on the different levels of being, in ways which are essentially diverse: in God, in an absolute manner, and because, being supereminently all things, He is supreme interiority, of which every existing thing is a participation; in us, in a relative manner, and thanks to the privileges of spirit which, no matter what may be the state of dependency it is subjected to by the nature of things, makes itself independent by its own operation when it interiorizes within itself, by knowledge and love, the law which it obeys. For such a philosophy, divine transcendence does not impose violence and constraint upon creatures, but rather it infuses all of them with goodness and spontaneity and is more intimately present to them than they are to themselves. The autonomy of an intelligent creature does not consist in its receiving no rule or objective measure from a being other than itself. Rather, it consists in its voluntarily conforming itself to such rules and measures, because they are known to be just and true, and because of a love for truth and justice. Such is the properly human freedom to which the person tends as to a connatural perfection; and if he aspires also to a superhuman freedom, this thirst for a transnatural perfection, whose satisfaction is not due to us, will be fully quenched only through his receiving more than he desires, and thanks to a transforming union with Uncreated Nature. God is free, from all eternity; more exactly, He is subsisting Freedom. Man is not born free, except in the basic potencies of his being: he becomes free, by warring upon himself and enduring many hardships. Through the work of the spirit and virtue, by exercising his freedom he wins his freedom, so that, at long last, a freedom better than he expected is *given* him. From the beginning to the end, it is truth which liberates him.

TRUE AND FALSE POLITICAL EMANCIPATION

The first problem of vital importance evoked by the preceding considerations may be called the problem of true and false political emancipation. In fact, the conquest of freedom in the social and political order is the central hope characterizing the historical ideal of the last two centuries, and constituting at the same time this ideal's dynamic élan, its power of truth and its power of illusion. What I call false political emancipation is the philosophy and the social and political practice (and the corresponding emotional orchestration) based on the false manner of understanding the conquest of freedom that I have briefly discussed; of itself it engenders myths which devour the human substance. What I call true political emancipation is the philosophy and the social and political practice (and the corresponding emotional orchestration) based on the true manner of understanding the conquest of freedom; and it is not to a myth that it leads, but to a concrete historical ideal and to a patient labor of forming and educating the human substance.

The misfortune, in the eyes of the philosopher of culture, is the fact that the great democratic movements of modern times, especially those in Europe, have most often sought true political emancipation under the standards of false political emancipation, that is, under the standards of a general philosophy forgetful of Gospel inspiration, from which the democratic élan proceeds and from which it is in reality inseparable, at least as regards the actual movement of life if not the systems of theoreticians. In the obscure work which has taken place in the hearts of men and in their history, a treasury of aspirations, of efforts, of social realizations accomplished sometimes at the price of heroic sacrifices and originally directed to the true conquest of freedom, has been conceptualized in the metaphysics of the false conquest of freedom; and to the extent that this work has been thus preyed upon and deformed by a false philosophy of life, it has been accompanied by errors and destructions which tended to the negation of its own vital principle, and which finally made the democratic ideal seem to many minds an imposture. The totalitarian catastrophe which has unleashed its hell on Europe bears witness to the immense gravity of this historical phenomenon. If the true city of human rights, the true democracy, does not succeed in disengaging itself from the false, and in triumphing at the same time over antidemocratic enslavement, if in the ordeal of fire and blood a radical purification is not accomplished, then Western civilization risks entering upon an endless night. If we are confident that this will not happen, it is because we are confident that the necessary renovations will occur.

In order to try to make some points that will be as brief as possible, let me say that false political emancipation (the false city of human rights) has for its principle the "anthropocentric" conception which Rousseau and Kant had of the autonomy of the person. According to this conception, one is free only if he obeys himself alone, and man is constituted by right of nature in such a state of freedom (which Rousseau regarded as lost by the fact of the corruption inseparable from social life, and which Kant relegated to the noumenal world). In short, we have here a divinization of the individual, of which the logical consequences, in the social and political order, are: 1) a practical atheism in society (for there is no room for two Gods in the world, and, if the individual is in practice God, God is no longer God, except perhaps in a decorative manner and for private use); 2) the theoretical and practical disappearance of the idea of the common good; 3) the theoretical and practical disappearance of the idea of the responsible leader and of the idea of authority, falsely regarded as incompatible with freedom: and this in the political sphere (where the possessors of authority have charge of directing men not towards the private good of another man but towards the common good) as well as in the sphere of labor and of economics (where the technical demands of production oblige men to work, and under extremely different modes, for the private good of other men, at the same time as for their own livelihood). Through an inevitable internal dialectic, the social divinization of the individual, inaugurated

by "bourgeois" liberalism, leads to the social divinization of the
State, and of the anonymous mass incarnate in a Master, who is no
longer a normal ruler but a sort of inhuman monster whose omnipotence is based on myths and lies; and, at the same time, "bourgeois" liberalism gives way to revolutionary totalitarianism.

On the contrary, true political emancipation, or the true city of
human rights, has for its principle a conception of the autonomy
of the person that is in conformity with the nature of things and
therefore "theocentric." According to this notion, obedience, when
consented to for the sake of justice, is not opposed to freedom. It
is, on the contrary, a normal way of attaining to freedom. Man
must gradually win a freedom which, in the social and political
order, consists above all in his becoming, in given historical conditions, as independent as possible of the constraints of material
nature. In short, the human person, so far as he is made for God
and for participation in absolute goods, transcends the earthly society of which he is a member; but, so far as he owes to society
what he is, he is a *part* of society as of a whole that is greater and
better than he is.

Thus the true city of human rights recognizes as God only one
God: God Himself and no created thing. And it understands that
human society, no matter how diverse may be the religious families
which live in common in it, itself implies a religious principle, and
supposes that God is accessible to our reason and that He is the
last end of our existence. It is founded upon the authentic notion
of the common good—which is other than the collection of private
goods, but which demands to flow back upon individual persons,
implies effective respect for their rights, and has as its essential
element their accession to the maximum of development and freedom compatible with given historical conditions. Finally, this city
has an authentic notion of authority.

For the true city of human rights, the possessors of authority in
the political sphere are, in a democratic regime, designated by the
people. They govern the people by virtue of this designation and
under the regulating control of the people (government of the people, by the people), and they exercise authority for the common
good of the people (government for the people). But they really
have the right to command; and they command free persons who
are all called to participate concretely in political life in the great-

est measure possible, and who are not abandoned like atoms but rather are grouped in organic communities, starting with the family, which is the basic natural community.

In the sphere of labor and of economic relations, the true city of human rights demands that the constant development of social justice compensate for the constraints imposed on man by the necessities (in themselves not human but technical) of the work to be done and of the production to be secured. This city knows that to serve the private good of another man and to become to this extent an instrument of him is in itself an affliction for the radical aspirations of personality, but it also knows that this is a condition imposed on men by material nature—a condition over which the progress of conscience and of society must some day triumph here below, though this progress will completely triumph over this condition only in the land of the resurrected. This city demands, too, that by an incessant effort, due both to the perfecting and extension of mechanical equipment and the tension of spiritual energies transforming secular life from within, the conditions of work become less and less enslaving and tend to a state of real emancipation for the human person. At the present stage of historical development, it would seem that for certain categories of workers this result can be obtained to a notable degree—after the crisis into which the world has entered will have led to a recasting of the structures and the spirit of the economic order—not only by the reduction of working hours but also by the accession of the worker to co-ownership and co-management of the enterprise.

But here, as in the political sphere, the establishment of new structures, no matter how important it may be, does not alone suffice. The soul of social life is made of that which superabounds in it of the proper life of persons, of the gift of self which that life implies, and of a free generosity whose source is in the depths of the heart. In short, good will and a relation of respect and love between persons and between the person and the community can alone give to the life of the social body a truly human character. If the person has a chance of being treated as a person in social life, and if the unpleasant works which this life imposes can be made easy and happy and even exalting, it is first of all due to the development of law and legal institutions. But it is also and indispensably due to the development of civic friendship, with the mutual confidence and devotion this implies on the part of those who direct as well as of those who carry out directions. For the true city of human rights, brotherhood is not a privilege of nature which would flow from the natural goodness of man and which the State would only have to proclaim. It is the end of a slow and difficult conquest which demands virtue and sacrifice and a perpetual victory of man over himself. In this sense, we can say that the heroic ideal towards which true political emancipation tends is the establishment of a fraternal city. Thus we see how, in fact, true political emancipation depends on the Christian ferment deposited in the world, and presupposes finally, as its most profound stimulus, evangelical love exalting the things of earthly civilization in their own order.

The properties that I have just sketched were certainly not absent from the democratic movement and hopes of modern times. On the contrary, they characterize what in reality was most fundamental and most vital in them. But this good seed was preyed upon and vitiated by the philosophy of false political emancipation; and the monsters which the errors of this latter engendered through an implacable dialectic, threaten today to smother out the authentic seed. We can thus have some idea of the extent of the purifications and renovations referred to above.

TRUE AND FALSE DEIFICATION OF MAN

There is a true and a false emancipation in the social and political order. In the spiritual order, there is a true and a false deification of man. This is another problem of vital importance— the fundamental and absolutely primary problem posed by the natural instinct which urges man to the conquest of freedom.

I said, at the beginning of this essay, that there are in us, by the very fact that we participate in that transcendental perfection designated by the name personality, transnatural aspirations whose satisfaction is not due to us in justice but which nevertheless torment us and tend to a superhuman freedom, to freedom pure and simple, that is, to a divine freedom. The sages of all times bear witness to these aspirations for the superhuman, to these desires to reach the confines of divinity.

The great spiritual errors also bear witness to these aspirations. They seek the deification of man, but by man's own energies and by the mere development of the powers of his nature. They usually take a pantheistic form, as can be seen in the gnostic currents of former times, in the great monistic systems of metaphysics, and in the quietist forms of mysticism. But it was reserved for modern times to seek the deification of man by doing away with wisdom and by breaking with God. Historically, in my opinion, the two principal sources of this false deification are: 1) the immanentist conception of conscience which, since the Lutheran revolution, has little by little prevailed, and which asks of what is in man, of "my interior freedom," that it alone construct morality for itself, without any indebtedness to law; 2) the idealist conception of knowledge which, since the Cartesian revolution, has little by little prevailed, and which asks of what is in man, of "my self or my spirit," that it alone construct truth for itself, without any indebtedness to things. Hyperspiritualist though they may appear at first sight, these two conceptions, which make knowledge independent of being and conscience independent of law, and which claim for what is in man the kind of independence proper to God, in reality materialize the human soul and plunge it into action *ad extra,* where, seeking its own unique mode of realization, it becomes the slave of time, matter, and the world. In the end, knowledge will be subjugated by a kind of demiurgic imperialism applied to enslave material nature to the lusts of the human being, and conscience will be subjugated by a kind of demonic imperialism directed to its opposing others in order to assert itself, and to its realizing itself by dominating others. Man, become the god of this world, will believe that he will find a divine freedom for himself by being independent of God, and finally by completely denying God. The false deification of man will take the atheistic form which appears in our day in an amazingly barbarous light.

This false deification of man first tried its hand with the disguised atheism of orthodox Kantianism and "bourgeois" liberalism. After the bankruptcy of this atheism, which found religion "good for the people," and after the failure of the false individualistic conquest of freedom and personality, it was inevitable that the false deification of man should take the form of the patent atheism of Marxist Hegelianism which sees in religion "the opium of the people." But it was also inevitable that, taking the form of the negation and derision of man, it should affirm itself better still by the epic of Death and Destruction, and by the depraved paganism of racism, which transforms religion into the idolatry of the "soul of the people"—of people who are misled, who look upon themselves as supermen, and who are public nuisances. With Nazi Racism the radical aspiration of the human person for freedom is not only betrayed, turned aside from its true nature and directed along false roads, it is denied and detested; and the deification of man is no longer sought except in the force and the frenzy of dominating, and in those abject forms of pride whose image the most barbarous idols, with their cruel thirst never satiated, depicted well. By an inevitable repercussion, from the moment that absolute freedom, emancipation pure and simple, divine independence, were sought in the human itself, or, in other words, from the moment that the transnatural aspirations of the person were lowered into the sphere of connatural aspirations (which thus became perverted and were made infinite), the social was to become divinized, the freedom of persons in society was to be banished, the things of Caesar were to absorb monstrously the things of God, and the pagan empire was to make itself adored.

On the contrary, it is towards God, towards the Transcendent Cause of being, that the transnatural aspirations of the human person normally tend, and it is in Him that they urge the soul to seek liberation. Such was, in spite of its imperfections and blemishes, the vital tendency of the great Hellenic wisdom. But it is especially in Hindu spirituality, at least if we reduce its excessive luxuriance, at times venomous, to what is most pure in it, that we find significant examples of states to which these transnatural aspirations can lead through the proper action of man making ascetic use of the powers of his nature and turning this nature back against itself. I think that what, in Christian language, we call "natural" mystical experience and the highest "natural" contemplation then reaches, by way of an entirely intellectual annihilation, the substance of the Self, and, through it and in it, the divine Omnipresence.[2] This is a liberation and a deliverance that are at one and the same time ultimate in the order of what nature is capable of, and not ultimate absolutely or as regards our real destiny and its hidden primordial truth that nature has been made for grace. This conquest of spiritual

---

[2] Cf. my work *Quatre essais sur l'esprit dans sa condition charnelle*, Chapter III.

freedom is thus ambivalent. It is efficacious on its own natural plane, and it can be a true road of deliverance if the soul does not stop with it but rather opens itself to gifts from on high. But it can deceive and mislead if the soul stops with it, or looks upon it as a necessary means, or takes it for a deification.

There is, however, a true deification of man. *Ego dixi: dii estis.* This is called eternal life, and it begins obscurely here on earth. It is as fatal to renounce perfect liberation as it is to try to reach it by wrong ways, that is, by oneself alone. Here the transnatural aspirations are supernaturally fulfilled, and by a gift which surpasses anything we can conceive. What is grace, the theologians ask, if not a formal participation in the Divine Nature, in other words, a deifying life received from God?

The mystery of this is that the supreme freedom and independence of man are won by the supreme spiritual realization of his dependence—of his dependence on a Being who, being Life itself, vivifies, and, being Freedom itself, liberates all that participates in His essence. This kind of dependence is not one of eternal constraint, like that of one physical agent with regard to another physical agent. The more man realizes this dependence, the more he participates in the nature of the Absolute. Men who have become something of God participate in the freedom of Him who cannot be contained by anything. In losing themselves they have won a mysterious and disappropriated personality, which makes them act in virtue of that which they are eternally in the Uncreated Essence. Born of the spirit, they are free like it. To tell the truth, they have won nothing, they have received everything. While they worked and suffered to win freedom, it gave itself to them. The true conquest of supreme and absolute freedom is to be made free, consenting freely to it, by Subsisting Freedom. The true deification of man consists in his opening himself to the gift which the Absolute makes of Himself, and to the descent of divine plenitude into the intelligent creature.

What I am saying is that all this is the work of love. Law protects freedom and educates us to be free. When love follows the path of law, it leads through law to emancipation from all servitude, even the servitude of the law. I have often quoted, and I wish to quote again, the text from the *Summa Contra Gentiles* where St. Thomas comments on St. Paul, which I regard as one of the great texts absolutely fundamental for the spiritual constitution of humanity.

> We must observe [St. Thomas says] that the sons of God are led by the divine Spirit, not as though they were slaves, but as being free. For, since to be free is to be cause of one's own actions, we are said to do freely what we do of ourselves. Now this is what we do willingly: and what we do unwillingly, we do, not freely but under compulsion. This compulsion may be absolute, when the cause is wholly extraneous, and the patient contributes nothing to the action, for instance, when a man is compelled to move by force; or it may be partly voluntary, as when a man is willing to do or suffer that which is less opposed to his will, in order to avoid that which is more opposed thereto. Now, the sanctifying Spirit inclines us to act, in such a way as to make us act willingly, inasmuch as He causes us to be lovers of God. Hence the sons of God are led by the Holy Ghost to act freely and for love, not slavishly and for fear: wherefore the Apostle says (Rom. 8:15): *You have not received the Spirit of bondage again in fear, but you have received the spirit of adoption of sons.*
>
> Now the will is by its essence directed to that which is truly good: so that when, either through passion or through an evil habit or disposition, a man turns away from what is truly good, he acts slavishly, in so far as he is led by something extraneous, *if we consider the natural direction of the will*; but if we consider the act of the will, *as inclined here and now towards an apparent good,* he acts freely when he follows passion or evil habit, but he acts slavishly if, while his will remains the same, he refrains from what he desires through fear of the law which forbids the fulfillment of his desire. Accordingly, when the divine Spirit by love inclines the will to the true good to which it is naturally directed, He removes both the servitude [the heretonomy, as we would say today] whereby a man, the slave of passion and sin, acts against the order of the will, and the servitude whereby a man acts against the inclination of his will, and in obedience to the law, as the slave and not the friend of the law. Wherefore the Apostle says (II Cor. 3:17): *Where the Spirit of the Lord is, there is liberty,* and (Gal. 5:18): *If you are led by the Spirit you are not under the law.*[3]

Great is the distance between the imperfect liberation whereby the highest techniques of natural spirituality oblige nature to satisfy

---

[3] St. Thomas, *Summa Contra Gentiles,* IV, 22.

in some way the transnatural aspirations of the human person, and the perfect freedom whereby the supernatural gift that the Divine Personality makes of itself to created personality far more than fulfills these aspirations. While leaving intact the distinction of natures, love, which at the end of spiritual growth creates this perfect freedom, truly makes man a god by participation. At the same time, far from enclosing itself in an altogether intellectual contemplation which would do away with action, the freedom in question lives on a contemplation which, since it proceeds from love, superabounds in action and penetrates into the most hidden structures of the world. The heroism it implies does not retreat into the sacred; it spills over into the profane and sanctifies it. Detached from perfection in perfection itself, because it thinks of loving more than of being itself without fault, it gradually awakens good will and brotherly love.

To return to the distinction between the socio-temporal and the spiritual, between the things that are Caesar's and the things that are God's, let me say, finally, that, if the false deification of man results, as we have seen, in the confusion of the temporal and the spiritual and in a perverse adoration of the social and of temporal relativities erected into an absolute, the true deification of man, on the contrary, and precisely because it is accomplished by the grace of the Incarnation and draws to itself all that is human, asks of divine things that they descend into the most profound depths of the human. It asks that the social and political order, while remaining essentially distinct from the spiritual, be pervaded and intrinsically superelevated by the sap which flows into souls from the Absolute. In the degree, small as it may be in fact, that things are this way, in that degree the historical march of civilization towards the conquest of *relative freedom*, which answers to the connatural aspirations of human personality, is in accord and in mutual cooperation with the suprahistorical movement of the soul towards the conquest of *absolute freedom*, which answers, though transcending them divinely, to the transnatural aspirations of the person as person.

3 NATURAL LAW*

SHALL WE TRY TO RE-ESTABLISH OUR FAITH IN HUMAN
rights on the basis of a true philosophy? This true philosophy of
the rights of the human person is based upon the true idea of natural law, as looked upon in an ontological perspective and as conveying through the essential structures and requirements of created
nature the wisdom of the Author of Being.

The genuine idea of natural law is a heritage of Greek and Christian thought. It goes back not only to Grotius, who indeed began
deforming it, but before him to Suarez and Francisco de Vitoria;
and further back to St. Thomas Aquinas (he alone grasped the
matter in a wholly consistent doctrine, which unfortunately was
expressed in an insufficiently clarified vocabulary,[1] so that its deepest features were soon overlooked and disregarded); and still further back to St. Augustine and the Church Fathers and St. Paul
(we remember St. Paul's saying: "When the Gentiles who have
not the Law, *do by nature* the things contained in the Law, these,
having not the Law, are a law unto themselves . . .");[2] and even
further back to Cicero, to the Stoics, to the great moralists of antiquity and its great poets, particularly Sophocles. Antigone, who
was aware that in transgressing the human law and being crushed

---

* *Man and the State* (Chicago: University of Chicago Press, 1951),
pp. 84–94.
[1] Especially because the vocabulary of the *Commentary on the Sen-
tences*, as concerns the "primary" and "secondary" precepts of Natural Law, is
at variance with the vocabulary of the *Sum. Theol.* (I–II, 94). Thomas' respect
for the stock phrases of the jurists also causes some trouble, particularly when it
comes to Ulpian.
[2] Rom. 2, 14.

by it she was obeying a better commandment, the *unwritten and unchangeable laws,* is the eternal heroine of natural law: for, as she puts it, they were not, those unwritten laws, born out of today's or yesterday's sweet will, "but they live always and forever, and no man knows from where they have arisen." [3]

THE FIRST ELEMENT (ONTOLOGICAL) IN NATURAL LAW

Since I have not time here to discuss nonsense (we can always find very intelligent philosophers, not to quote Mr. Bertrand Russell, to defend it most brilliantly), I am taking it for granted that we admit that there is a human nature, and that this human nature is the same in all men. I am taking it for granted that we also admit that man is a being gifted with intelligence, and who, as such, acts with an understanding of what he is doing, and therefore with the power to determine for himself the ends which he pursues. On the other hand, possessed of a nature, or an ontologic structure which is a locus of intelligible necessities, man possesses ends which necessarily correspond to his essential constitution and which are the same for all—as all pianos, for instance, whatever their particular type and in whatever spot they may be, have as their end the production of certain attuned sounds. If they do not produce these sounds they must be tuned, or discarded as worthless. But since man is endowed with intelligence and determines his own ends, it is up to him to put himself in tune with the ends necessarily demanded by his nature. This means that there is, by very virtue of human nature, an order or a disposition which human reason can discover and according to which the human will must act in order to attune itself to the essential and necessary ends of the human being. The unwritten law, or natural law, is nothing more than that.

---

[3]
"Nor did I deem
Your ordinance of so much binding force,
As that a mortal man could overbear
The unchangeable unwritten code of Heaven;
This is not of today and yesterday,
But lives forever, having origin
Whence no man knows: whose sanctions I were loath
In Heaven's sight to provoke, fearing the will
Of any man."
(Sophocles *Antigone* ii. 452–60, tr. by George Young)

The example that I just used—taken from the world of human workmanship—was purposely crude and provocative: yet did not Plato himself have recourse to the idea of any work of human art whatever, the idea of the Bed, the idea of the Table, in order to make clear his theory (which I do not share) of eternal Ideas? What I mean is that every being has its own natural law, as well as it has its own essence. Any kind of thing produced by human industry has, like the stringed instrument that I brought up a moment ago, its own natural law, that is, the *normality of its functioning*, the proper way in which, by reason of its specific construction, it demands to be put into action, it "*should*" be used. Confronted with any supposedly unknown gadget, be it a corkscrew or a peg-top or a calculating machine or an atom bomb, children or scientists, in their eagerness to discover how to use it, will not question the existence of that inner typical law.

Any kind of thing existing in nature, a plant, a dog, a horse, has its own natural law, that is, the *normality of its functioning*, the proper way in which, by reason of its specific structure and specific ends, it "*should*" achieve fulness of being either in its growth or in its behavior. Washington Carver, when he was a child and healed sick flowers in his garden, had an obscure knowledge, both by intelligence and congeniality, of that vegetative law of theirs. Horse-breeders have an experiential knowledge, both by intelligence and congeniality, of the natural law of horses, a natural law with respect to which a horse's behavior makes him a *good horse* or a *vicious horse* in the herd. Well, horses do not enjoy free will, their natural law is but a part of the immense network of essential tendencies and regulations involved in the movement of the cosmos, and the individual horse who fails in that equine law only obeys the universal order of nature on which the deficiencies of his individual nature depend. If horses were free, there would be an ethical way of conforming to the specific natural law of horses, but that horsy morality is a dream because horses are not free.

When I said a moment ago that the natural law of all beings existing in nature is the proper way in which, by reason of their specific nature and specific ends, they *should* achieve fulness of being in their behavior, this very word *should* had only a metaphysical meaning (as we say that a good or a normal eye "should" be able to read letters on a blackboard from a given distance).

The same word *should* starts to have a *moral* meaning, that is, to imply moral obligation, when we pass the threshold of the world of free agents. Natural law for man is *moral* law, because man obeys or disobeys it freely, not necessarily, and because human behavior pertains to a particular, privileged order which is irreducible to the general order of the cosmos and tends to a final end superior to the immanent common good of the cosmos.

What I am emphasizing is the first basic element to be recognized in natural law, namely, the *ontological* element; I mean the *normality of functioning* which is grounded on the essence of that being: man. Natural law in general, as we have just seen, is the ideal formula of development of a given being; it might be compared with an algebraical equation according to which a curve develops in space, yet with man the curve has freely to conform to the equation. Let us say, then, that in its ontological aspect, natural law is an *ideal order* relating to human actions, a *divide* between the suitable and the unsuitable, the proper and the improper, which depends on human nature or essence and the unchangeable necessities rooted in it. I do not mean that the proper regulation for each possible human situation is contained in the human essence, as Leibniz believed that every event in the life of Caesar was contained beforehand in the idea of Caesar. Human situations are something existential. Neither they nor their appropriate regulations are contained in the essence of man. I would say that they ask questions of that essence. Any given situation, for instance the situation of Cain with regard to Abel, implies a relation to the essence of man, and the possible murder of the one by the other is incompatible with the general ends and innermost dynamic structure of that rational essence. It is rejected by it. Hence, the prohibition of murder is grounded on or required by the essence of man. The precept *thou shalt do no murder* is a precept of natural law, because a primordial and most general end of human nature is to preserve being—the being of that existent who is a person, and a universe unto himself; and because man, insofar as he is man, has a right to live.

Suppose a completely new case or situation, unheard of in human history; suppose, for instance, that what we now call *genocide* were as new as that very name. In the fashion that I just explained, that possible behavior will face the human essence as incompatible with its general ends and innermost dynamic structure: that is to say, as prohibited by natural law. The condemnation of genocide by the General Assembly of the United Nations [4] has sanctioned the prohibition of the crime in question by natural law—which does not mean that that prohibition was part of the essence of man as I know not what metaphysical feature eternally inscribed in it— nor that it was a notion recognized from the start by the conscience of humanity.

To sum up, let us say that natural law is something both *ontological* and *ideal*. It is something *ideal*, because it is grounded on the human essence and its unchangeable structure and the intelligible necessities it involves. Natural law is something *ontological*, because the human essence is an ontological reality, which moreover does not exist separately, but in every human being, so that by the same token natural law dwells as an ideal order in the very being of all existing men.

In that first consideration, or with regard to the basic *ontological* element it implies, natural law is coextensive with the whole field of natural moral regulations, the whole field of natural morality. Not only the primary and fundamental regulations but the slightest regulations of natural ethics mean conformity to natural law—say, natural obligations or rights of which we perhaps have now no idea, and of which men will become aware in a distant future.

An angel who knew the human essence in his angelic manner and all the possible existential situations of man would know natural law in the infinity of its extension. But we do not. Though the eighteenth-century theoreticians believed they did.

THE SECOND ELEMENT (GNOSEOLOGICAL) IN NATURAL LAW

Thus we arrive at the second basic element to be recognized in natural law, namely natural law *as known*, and thus as measuring in actual fact human practical reason, which is the measure of human acts.

Natural law is not a written law. Men know it with greater or less difficulty, and in different degrees, running the risk of error here

---

[4] December 11, 1948.

as elsewhere. The only practical knowledge all men have naturally and infallibly in common as a self-evident principle, intellectually perceived by virtue of the concepts involved, is that we must do good and avoid evil. This is the preamble and the principle of natural law; it is not the law itself. Natural law is the ensemble of things to do and not to do which follow therefrom in *necessary* fashion. That every sort of error and deviation is possible in the determination of these things merely proves that our sight is weak, our nature coarse, and that innumerable accidents can corrupt our judgment. Montaigne maliciously remarked that, among certain peoples, incest and thievery were considered virtuous acts. Pascal was scandalized by this. All this proves nothing against natural law, any more than a mistake in addition proves anything against arithmetic, or the mistakes of certain primitive peoples, for whom the stars were holes in the tent which covered the world, prove anything against astronomy.

Natural law is an unwritten law. Man's knowledge of it has increased little by little as man's moral conscience has developed. The latter was at first in a twilight state.[5] Anthropologists have taught us within what structures of tribal life and in the midst of what half-awakened magic it was primitively formed. This proves merely that the knowledge men have had of the unwritten law has passed through more diverse forms and stages than certain philosophers or theologians have believed. The knowledge which our own moral conscience has of this law is doubtless still imperfect, and very likely it will continue to develop and to become more refined as long as humanity exists. Only when the Gospel has penetrated to the very depth of human substance will natural law appear in its flower and its perfection.

So the law and the knowledge of the law are two different things. Yet the law has force of law only when it is promulgated. It is only insofar as it is known and expressed in assertions of practical reason that natural law has force of law.

At this point let us stress that human reason does not discover the regulations of natural law in an abstract and theoretical manner, as a series of geometrical theorems. Nay more, it does not discover them through the conceptual exercise of the intellect, or

---

[5] Cf. Raïssa Maritain, *Histoire d'Abraham ou les premiers âges de la conscience morale* (Paris: Desclée de Brouwer, 1947).

by way of rational knowledge. I think that Thomas Aquinas' teaching, here, should be understood in a much deeper and more precise
fashion than is usual. When he says that human reason discovers
the regulations of natural law through the guidance of the *inclinations* of human nature, he means that the very mode or manner in
which human reason knows natural law is not rational knowledge,
but knowledge *through inclination*.[6] That kind of knowledge is not
clear knowledge through concepts and conceptual judgments; it is
obscure, unsystematic, vital knowledge by connaturality or congeniality, in which the intellect, in order to bear judgment, consults
and listens to the inner melody that the vibrating strings of abiding
tendencies make present in the subject.

When one has clearly seen this basic fact, and when, moreover,
one has realized that St. Thomas' views on the matter call for an
historical approach and a philosophical enforcement of the idea of
development that the Middle Ages were not equipped to carry into
effect, then at last one is enabled to get a completely comprehensive
concept of Natural Law. And one understands that the human
knowledge of natural law has been progressively shaped and molded
by the inclinations of human nature, starting from the most basic
ones. Do not expect me to offer an a priori picture of those genuine
inclinations which are rooted in man's being as vitally permeated
with the preconscious life of the mind, and which either developed

---

[6] This is, in my opinion, the real meaning implied by St. Thomas, even
though he did not use the very expression when treating of Natural Law.
Knowledge through inclination is generally understood in all his doctrine on
Natural Law. It alone makes this doctrine perfectly consistent. It alone squares
with such statements as the following ones: "Omnia illa ad quae homo *habet
naturalem inclinationem, ratio naturaliter apprehendit ut bona*, et per consequens
ut opere prosequenda; et contraria eorum, ut mala et vitanda" (I–II, 94, 2); "Ad
legem naturae pertinet omne illud ad quod homo inclinatur secundum natu-
ram. . . . Sed, si loquamur de actibus virtuosis secundum seipsos, prout scilicet
in propriis speciebus considerantur, sic *non* omnes actus virtuosi sunt de lege
naturae. Multa enim secundum virtutem fiunt *ad quae natura non primo inclinat;
sed per rationis inquisitionem ea homines adinvenerunt*, quasi utilia ad bene
vivendum" (I–II, 94, 3). The matter has been somewhat obscured because of the
perpetual comparison that St. Thomas uses in these articles between the speculative
and the practical intellect, and by reason of which he speaks of the *propria principia*
of Natural Law as *"quasi conclusiones principiorum communium"* (I–II, 94, 4).
As a matter of fact, those *propria principia* or specific precepts of Natural Law
are in no way conclusions rationally deduced; they play in the practical realm
a part *similar* to that of conclusions in the speculative realm. (And they appear
as inferred conclusions to the "after-knowledge" of the philosophers who have
to reflect upon and explain the precepts of Natural Law.)

or were released as the movement of mankind went on. They are evinced by the very history of human conscience. Those inclinations *were really genuine* which in the immensity of the human past have guided reason in becoming aware, little by little, of the regulations that have been most definitely and most generally recognized by the human race, starting from the most ancient social communities. For the knowledge of the primordial aspects of natural law was first expressed in social patterns rather than in personal judgments: so that we might say that that knowledge has developed within the double protecting tissue of human inclinations and human society.

With regard to the second basic element, the element of knowledge which natural law implies in order to have force of law, it thus can be said that natural law—that is, natural law *naturally known*, or, more exactly, natural law *the knowledge of which is embodied in the most general and most ancient heritage* of mankind—covers only the field of the ethical regulations of which men have become aware by virtue of knowledge *through.inclination,* and which are *basic principles* in moral life—progressively recognized from the most common principles to the more and more specific ones.

All the previous remarks may help us to understand why, on the one hand, a careful examination of the data of anthropology would show that the fundamental *dynamic schemes* of natural law, if they are understood in their authentic, that is, still undetermined meaning (for instance, to take a man's life is not like taking another animal's life; or, the family group has to comply with some fixed pattern; or, sexual intercourse has to be contained within given limitations; or, we are bound to look at the Invisible; or, we are bound to live together under certain rules and prohibitions), are subject to a much more universal awareness—everywhere and in every age—than would appear to a superficial glance; and why, on the other hand, an immense amount of relativity and variability is to be found in the particular rules, customs, and standards in which, among all peoples of the earth, human reason has expressed its knowledge even of the most basic aspects of natural law: for, as I pointed out above, that spontaneous knowledge does not bear on moral regulations *conceptually* discovered and *rationally* deduced, but on moral regulations known *through inclination,* and, at the start, on general tendential forms or frameworks, I just said on *dynamic schemes* of moral regulations, such as can be obtained by the first, "primitive" achievements of knowledge through inclination. And in such tendential frameworks or dynamic schemes many various, still defective contents may occur—not to speak of the warped, deviated, or perverted inclinations which can mingle with the basic ones.

We may understand at the same time why natural law essentially involves a dynamic development, and why moral conscience, or the knowledge of natural law, has progressed from the age of the cave-man in a double manner: first, as regards the way in which human reason has become aware in a less and less crepuscular, rough, and confused manner, of the primordial regulations of natural law; second, as regards the way in which it has become aware —always by means of knowledge through inclination—of its further, higher regulations. And such knowledge is still progressing, it will progress as long as human history endures. That progress of moral conscience is indeed the most unquestionable instance of progress in humanity.

I have said that natural law is unwritten law: it is unwritten law in the deepest sense of that expression, because our knowledge of it is no work of free conceptualization, but results from a conceptualization *bound* to the essential inclinations of being, of living nature, and of reason, which are at work in man, and because it develops in proportion to the degree of moral experience and self-reflection, and of social experience also, of which man is capable in the various ages of his history. Thus it is that in ancient and mediaeval times attention was paid, in natural law, to the *obligations* of man more than to his *rights*. The proper achievement— a great achievement indeed—of the eighteenth century has been to bring out in full light the *rights* of man as also required by natural law. That discovery was essentially due to a progress in moral and social experience, through which the root *inclinations* of human nature as regards the rights of the human person were set free, and consequently, *knowledge through inclination* with regard to them developed. But, according to a sad law of human knowledge, that great achievement was paid for by the ideological errors, in the theoretical field, that I have stressed at the beginning. Attention even shifted from the obligations of man to his rights only. A genuine and comprehensive view would pay attention *both* to the obligations and the rights involved in the requirements of natural law.

4 HUMAN RIGHTS*

NATURAL LAW AND HUMAN RIGHTS

WE MUST NOW CONSIDER THAT NATURAL LAW AND THE light of moral conscience within us do not prescribe merely things to be done and not to be done. They also recognize rights, in particular rights bound up with the very nature of man. The human person has rights by the very fact that he is a person, a whole who is master of himself and of his acts, and consequently not merely a means, but an end, an end which must be treated as such. The expression, "the dignity of the human person," means nothing if it does not signify that through natural law the human person has the right to be respected and is the subject of rights, is the possessor of rights. Some things are due to man by the very fact that he is man.

The notion of right and the notion of moral obligation are correlative, and each is founded on the freedom proper to spiritual agents. If man is morally bound to the things necessary to fulfill his destiny, this is because he has the right to fulfill his destiny, and if he has the right to fulfill his destiny he has the right to the things necessary for this goal . . .

The true philosophy of the human person's rights is therefore based on the idea of natural law. The same natural law which prescribes our most fundamental duties and in virtue of which all law is binding, is the selfsame law which assigns to us our fundamental rights. Because we are involved in the universal order, in the laws

---

* *Les droits de l'homme et la loi naturelle* (New York: Éditions de la Maison Française, 1942), pp. 84–138.

and regulations of the cosmos and of the immense family of created natures (and ultimately in the order of creative wisdom) and because we have at the same time the privilege of being spirits, we possess rights before other men and before the whole assembly of creatures. In the last analysis, as every creature acts only in virtue of its Principle, which is Pure Act; as every authority worthy of the name, and this means a just authority, binds in conscience only in virtue of the Principle of beings, which is pure Wisdom, so, too, every right possessed by man is possessed only in virtue of the right possessed by God, who is pure Justice, to see the order of His wisdom in beings respected, obeyed and loved by every intelligence.

Quite contrary to this view, another philosophy has tried to base the rights of the human person on the claim that man is not subject to any law except that of his will and his liberty, and that he should "obey only himself," as Jean-Jacques Rousseau said, because any standard or regulation coming from the world of nature, and ultimately from creative wisdom, would destroy at once both his autonomy and his dignity. This philosophy has given no solid base for the rights of the human person, since nothing can be based on illusion. It has compromised and squandered these rights, because it has led men to conceive them as rights properly divine, hence infinite, free of every objective standard, resistant to every limitation imposed on the demands of the ego, and ultimately expressing the absolute independence of the human subject and a so-called absolute right, a right attached to everything in him by the mere fact that it is in him, to unfold himself at the expense of all other beings. Men so instructed have clashed on all sides with the impossible and have thus come to believe in the bankruptcy of the rights of the human person. Some have turned against these rights with an enslaver's fury; others have continued to invoke them, but in their inmost conscience they have suffered in regard to them a temptation to scepticism which is one of the most disturbing symptoms of the present crisis. A kind of intellectual and moral revolution is demanded of us in order to re-establish within a true philosophy our faith in the dignity of man and in his rights, and in order to rediscover the genuine sources of this faith. . . .

Man's right to existence, to personal freedom and to the pursuit of the perfection of moral life, belongs, strictly speaking, to natural law. The right to the private ownership of material goods, a right rooted in natural law,[1] belongs to the Law of Nations, or to the common law of civilization, so far as the right to private appropriation of the means of production supposes the conditions normally required for human work and its management, which latter, moreover, varies with the forms of society and with the state of economic development. The particular modalities of this right are determined by positive law. The freedom of nations to live unburdened by the yoke of want or distress—"freedom from want" —and their freedom to live unburdened by the yoke of fear or ter- ror—"freedom from fear"—as President Roosevelt defined them in his Four Points,[2] correspond to yearnings of the Law of Nations which demand to be fulfilled by positive law and by an economic and political organization of the civilized world. The right of suf- frage, recognized as belonging to each of us in the election of State officials, arises from positive law.

THE RIGHTS OF THE HUMAN PERSON

. . . Aristotle and the wise men of antiquity knew that moral virtues are ordered to a contemplation of truth which sur- passes political inter-communication. It follows that, if humanity were in what theologians call the state of pure nature, a kingdom of spirits akin to that of which Leibniz liked to speak would nor- mally have had its place above political life. We may look upon the spiritual network which, throughout the world, unites artists,

---

[1] See our work *Du régime temporel et de la liberté*, Annex 1 (English translation, *Freedom in the Modern World*, Appendix I) [pp. 45–59, below: Edi- tors]. The right to the private ownership of material goods belongs to the human person as an extension of the person himself, for, enmeshed in matter and without natural protection for his existence and his freedom, the person needs the power to acquire and to possess in order to make up for this protection which nature does not afford him. On the other hand, the use of private property must always be such as to serve the common good in one way or another and to be advan- tageous to all, for it is to Man in the first place, to the human species in general, that material goods are deputed by nature.

[2] "1) Freedom of speech and expression everywhere in the world. 2) Freedom of every person to worship God in his own way everywhere in the world. 3) Freedom from want which, translated into world terms, means eco- nomic understanding which will secure to every nation a healthy peace-time life for its inhabitants everywhere in the world. 4) Freedom from fear which, trans- lated into world terms, means a world-wide reduction of armaments to such a point and in such a thorough fashion that no nation will be in a position to commit an act of physical aggression against any neighbor anywhere."

scientists, poets, true humanists, all those who cherish the works of thought, as the vague outlines of such a natural kingdom of spirits; such a network, we might say, is the rough draught of a single family above national frontiers. It is merely a sketch, of course, and the Leibnizian kingdom of spirits is merely a hypothesis for a possible world, because in reality by the grace of God there has been established above the realm of emperors, kings and parliaments, a better kingdom, the Kingdom of God, the great city of the world to come, of which, in the eyes of Christians, the Church is already the beginning on earth. The fact remains that this kingdom of eternal life corresponds, in virtue of a gift surpassing all the measures of nature, to a natural aspiration of the spirit in us.

That the human person, to the extent that he has a destiny superior to time, naturally transcends the State, is a fact that may be verified in many other ways.

The universe of truths—truths of science, of wisdom and of poetry—towards which intelligence tends of itself, belongs by nature to a realm higher than the political community. State power and the power of social interests may not be exercised on this universe, although such power may and should oppose the propagation, within the social body, of errors which might threaten the fundamental ethics of common life and the principles on which it is founded.[3] The State may, under defined circumstances, require a mathematician to teach mathematics, and a philosopher to teach philosophy: these are functions of the social body. But the State may not oblige a philosopher or a mathematician to adopt a philosophical or a mathematical doctrine, because these depend solely and exclusively on truth.

The secret of the heart and the free act as such, the universe of moral truths, the right of conscience to listen to God and to make its way to Him—none of these things, in either the natural or the supernatural order, may be touched by the State or fall into its clutches. It is true that law binds in conscience, but this is because it is law only if it is just and if promulgated by legitimate authority, and not because the State or the majority would be the rule of conscience. It is true, too, that the State has a moral function and

---

[3] See Yves Simon, "Liberty and Authority," in *Proceedings of the American Catholic Philosophical Association,* 16th annual meeting, 1940, Washington, D.C.

not merely a material one; law has a teaching function and tends
to develop moral virtues. The State has the right to punish me if,
my conscience being blind, I follow my conscience and commit an
act criminal or unlawful in itself. But in the same circumstance
the State has no authority to make me reform the judgment of my
conscience, any more than it possesses power to impose on spirits
its own judgment of good and evil, or to legislate on divine matters,
or to impose any religious faith whatsoever. The State knows this
very well. That is why, whenever it goes beyond its natural limits
in order to penetrate, in the name of totalitarian claims, into the
sanctuary of conscience, it attempts to violate this sanctuary by
monstrous means of psychological poisoning, organized lies and
terror.

. . . The end for which the family exists is to produce and to
bring up human persons and to prepare them to fulfill their total
destiny. And if the State also has an educative function, if education is not outside its sphere, its function is to help the family accomplish its mission, and to complete this mission, not to efface in
the child his vocation as a human person and replace it by that of
a living tool and of material for the State.

In short, the fundamental rights such as the right to existence
and life, the right to personal freedom or to conduct one's life as
master of oneself and of one's acts, responsible for them before
God and the law of the community, the right to pursue perfection
of moral and rational human life,[4] the right to pursue eternal good,
without which pursuit there is no true pursuit of happiness, the
right to bodily integrity, the right to the private ownership of
material goods as a safeguard for the liberties of the person, the
right to marry according to one's choice and to establish a family,
itself assured the liberties proper to it, the right of association, of
respect for the human dignity in each man whether or not he represents an economic value for society—all these rights are rooted
in the vocation of the person, a spiritual and free agent, to the order
of absolute values and to a destiny superior to time.

The French Declaration of the Rights of Man expressed these
rights in the quite rationalist perspective of the Enlightenment and

---

[4] The "pursuit of happiness" consists above all in this: this pursuit here
on earth is not the pursuit of material advantages, but of moral right, of strength
and perfection of soul, with the material and social conditions thereby implied.

the Encyclopedists, and to that extent made them equivocal; the American Declaration of Independence, however marked in it may be the influence of Locke and of "natural religion," kept more closely to the originally Christian character of human rights. . . .

THE RIGHTS OF THE CIVIC PERSON

. . . The celebrated saying of Aristotle that man is a political animal does not mean only that man is naturally made to live in society; it also means that man naturally demands to lead a political life and to participate actively in the life of the political community. It is on this postulate of human nature that political liberties and political rights rest, and in particular the right of suffrage. Perhaps it is easier for men to renounce active participation in political life, and in certain cases it may be that they have lived in a more carefree and happy way as political slaves in the body politic or when they passively handed over to their leaders the whole care of directing the community. But they then gave up a privilege belonging to their nature, one of those privileges which in a sense make life more difficult and which bring with them more or less labor, tension and suffering, but which correspond to human dignity.

A state of civilization in which men as individual persons designate by free choice those who hold authority is in itself a more perfect state. For if it is true that political authority has as essential function to direct free men towards the common good, it is normal that these free men should themselves choose those who have the function of directing them. This is the most elementary form of active participation in political life. . . .

There are other rights of the civic person, in particular those summed up in the three equalities: political equality, assuring to each citizen his status, security and freedoms within the body politic; equality of all before the law, implying an independent judiciary power which assures to each the right of appeal to the law, and the right to be restrained by the law only if he has violated it; equality of opportunity for all citizens in respect to public employment according to their capacity, and free access of all to the various professions, without racial or social discrimination. . . .

THE RIGHTS OF THE WORKING PERSON

Thus we come to a third category of rights, the rights of the social person, and more particularly the rights of the working person. A new age of civilization will have to recognize and define what, generally speaking, are the rights of the human being in his social, economic and cultural functions—producers' rights, consumers' rights, technicians' rights, the rights of those who devote themselves to works of the mind. But the most urgent problems are those that relate to the rights of the human being engaged in the function of labor. . . .

From the old socialistic ideas comes the temptation to grant primacy to the economic set-up, and at the same time the tendency to turn everything over to the authority of the State, administrator of the welfare of all, and to its scientific and bureaucratic machinery: which, like it as we will, moves in the direction of a totalitarianism with a technocratic base. It is not this rationalization of mathematical organization that should inspire the work of reconstruction; rather, it should be a practical and experimental wisdom attentive to human ends and means.

The idea of planned economy should thus be replaced by a new idea based on the progressive adjustment due to the activity and the reciprocal tension of autonomous agencies which, from the bottom up, would bring producers and consumers together, in which case it would be better to say an adjusted rather than a planned economy. Likewise, the notion of collectivization should be replaced by that of associative ownership of the means of production, or of joint ownership of the enterprise . . . substituting, as far as possible, joint ownership for the wage system. . . .

RESUMÉ OF ENUMERATED RIGHTS

Rights of the human person as such. The right to existence. The right to personal liberty or the right to conduct one's own life as master of oneself and of one's acts, responsible for them before God and the law of the community. The right to pursue perfection of rational and moral human life. The right to pursue eternal life in the way conscience has seen as the way marked out by God. The right of the Church and of other religious families to the free exercise of their spiritual activity. The right to follow a religious voca-

tion; the freedom of religious orders and groups. The right to
marry according to one's choice and to establish a family, itself
assured the freedoms proper to it; the right of family society to respect for its constitution, which is based on natural law, not on the
law of the State, a constitution which enlists in a basic way the
morality of the human being. The right to bodily integrity. The
right to ownership. In a word, the right of each human being to be
treated as a person, not as a thing.

Rights of the civic person. The right of every citizen to participate actively in political life, and in particular the right of equal
suffrage for all. The right of the people to establish the constitution of the body politic and to decide for themselves their form of
government. The right of association, limited only by juridically
recognized necessities of the common good, and in particular the
right to form political parties or political schools. The right to free
investigation and discussion (to freedom of expression). Political
equality, and the equal right of every citizen to his security and his
freedoms in the body politic. The equal right of everyone to the
guarantees of an independent judiciary power. Equal opportunity
of admission to public employment and free access to the various
professions.

*Rights of the social person and more particular of the working
person.* The right freely to choose his work. The right freely to
form professional groups or trade-unions. The right of the worker
to be treated socially as an adult. The right of economic groups—
trade-unions and communities of work—and other social groups
to freedom and autonomy. The right to a just wage; and, where an
associative system can be substituted for the wage system, the right
to joint ownership and joint management of the enterprise, and
this "in virtue of work." The right to assistance from the community in case of want and unemployment, in sickness and old age.
The right to have a part, without charge, depending on the possibilities of the community, in the elementary goods, both material
and spiritual, of civilization.

5 PERSON AND PROPERTY*

No attempt is made in the following pages either to deal fully with the problem of property or to propound a new theory of property. On the contrary, our essay refers to the doctrine developed by St. Thomas and his commentators, which is here assumed to be well known.[1] We merely attempt, in brief and schematic form, to draw attention to certain very fundamental principles in this doctrine, to those principles, namely, which have to do with the metaphysics of the human being and human action. In our opinion, these principles control any consideration of the problem of property, and yet they have not always been disengaged with sufficient care.

In the thought of St. Thomas, the theory of property presents three successive stages.

In the first stage he shows [2] that man, considered in his specific nature, has a general right of appropriation over all material goods,

---

* *Du régime temporel et de la liberté* (Paris: Desclée de Brouwer, 1933); pp. 229–255.

[1] The bibliography on the subject is very considerable, but we will refer only to the following: two studies by C. Spicq—*La notion analogique de dominium et le droit de propriété (Revue des sc. phil. et théol.*, 1931, pp. 52–76) and *Comment construire un traité thomiste de la propriété (Bull. thomiste,* July 1931); and the book by A. Horvath, *Eigentumrecht nach dem hl. Thomas von Aquin* (Graz, Moser, 1929), which has recently been the subject of lively controversy (cf. *Bull. thomiste*, January 1932, and July–October 1932). Our point of view, moreover, is somewhat different from that of the classical exponents of the subject. Since moral philosophy, a speculatively practical knowledge, necessarily has its roots in metaphysics, the main object of this essay is to trace some of the roots that underlie the present problem.

[2] *Sum. Theol.*, II–II, 66, 1.

the *vocation* of these being to serve the needs of man. Man's ap-
propriating material things simply realizes in actuality a tendency
inscribed in their very nature. The use (*usus*) which human
freedom makes of them appears then as the joint act of freedom exercising its right and of things fulfilling their natural
destiny.

This is the capital truth which governs the whole discussion. It
discloses that each human person, by the very fact that he belongs
to the human species, ought in one way or another to derive advantage from this common destining of material things to the good
of mankind. Here, in the first stage of the argument, there is as
yet no question of individual appropriation, and it is this very question that seems to present some difficulty.

In the second stage, St. Thomas shows that the appropriation
of external goods should normally take place through individual
ownership. The rights of man over material goods imply in fact
the power to manage, administer and use these goods (*potestas
procurandi et dispensandi*),[3] which power as a rule can be suitably
exercised only by the individual person. In this way alone can
one hope to secure in the ordinary course the care that is required
in the management of goods, the absence of confusion in work,
and the maintenance of public peace. It is thus "natural reason"
which establishes the rule of individual appropriation as the fundamental rule of human possession of material things.[4]

"If a particular piece of land be considered in the absolute,
there is in it no reason why it should belong to one man rather than
to another; but if it be considered from the point of view of con-
venience of cultivation and peaceful use of the land, there is a
certain fitness in its belonging to one man to the exclusion of all
others." [5]

The use (*usus*) of these goods ought nonetheless to be common
and of benefit to all, by virtue of the common destiny of material
goods which has been manifest from the beginning.

"As regards the *use* of external things, a man ought not to possess them as exclusively his own (*ut proprias*), but as common to

---

[3] *Sum. Theol.*, II–II, 66, 2.
[4] *Ibid.*, II–II, 57, 3, ad 3.
[5] *Sum. Theol.*, II–II, 57, 3.

himself and to others (*ut communes*), and thus he should be ready to put them at the disposal of others who are in need." [6]

The third stage of the argument has to do with the particular kinds of ownership. These are subject to evolution in the course of history. Neither legislation nor custom has any power to abolish the principle of the right to private property, for this would involve a violation of natural law; but they may regulate the exercise of this right in different ways, according to the requirements of the common good. [7]

Our remarks here are concerned with the second of these three stages, and therefore with the problem of individual appropriation in general without reference to particular kinds of ownership. Our object is to determine more precisely what it is in human nature on which the general right to own private property is founded; or, in other words, to discover what it is in human nature that calls for the individual appropriation of material goods. This right will thus be universally grounded in a general postulate of human nature, whatever may be the particular *modes* of acquiring property—occupation, succession, contract, etc. According as these vary, the mode of appropriation will itself vary in individual circumstances and different historical conditions, but this is another question. In our view, the postulate we are seeking follows from the activity of man as maker—or as "artist," in the broad sense of the word—an activity which belongs by nature to the human person.

THE PERSON AND THE "FACTIBILE"

1. Practical human activity is divided into "poetic" or "making" activity, which has for its object what the Schoolmen call the *factibile*, a thing to be made or produced; and ethical or moral activity, which has for its object what the Schoolmen call the *agibile*, an act to be done.

2. If we examine thoroughly the principles of Thomist philosophy, it appears that the whole problem of individual appropriation fluctuates between the two branches of an antinomy, between two extreme and apparently contrary affirmations. That which relates, in human nature, to reason as maker, the *factibile*, requires individ-

---

[6] *Ibid.*, II–II, 66, 2.
[7] Cf. *ibid.*, I–II, 95, 2; II *Polit.*, lect. IV.

ual appropriation; that which relates, on the contrary, to morality in the use of terrestrial goods demands that in one way or another such goods be at the service of all. The person as *intellectual maker* is the basis for the right of private property; the person as *moral agent* is bound to the "common use" of goods thus appropriated.

3. Art is defined by the Schoolmen as *recta ratio factibilium*, the straight intellectual determination of works to be made. It is contrasted with prudence, *recta ratio agibilium*.[8] We here use the word "art" not in the strict sense and as opposed to "work" and "play," [9] but in the more general sense of intellectual activity which has to do with the producing of a work or the fashioning of matter, as opposed to moral activity, which has to do with the exercise of free will. We have here the metaphysical root which, in human nature, requires in a general way individual appropriation, and is thus the basis for the right of private property.[10]

Such work may not be "artistic" in the ordinary sense of the word, but it is always artistic in the very broad sense in which we use the word here. It is always the application of human reason to a matter to be fashioned, and it thus relates always to the order of the *factibile* and is accordingly connected with the metaphysical basis of ownership, whether it be the work of a manual laborer or that of a craftsman.

4. We maintain that the activity of art or work is the formal reason for individual appropriation; but only because it presupposes the rationality and personality of the artist or worker. In the case of the bee and the beaver, for instance, there is no activity of art or work in the strict sense, since there is no *reason* in operation; neither is there any individual ownership. The notion of person must enter into a complete theory of property, i.e., the notion of person as the *proper subject* of intellectual making.

---

[8] Cf. *Art et scolastique*, Chapter IV, n. 4 (English translation *Art and Scholasticism*, tr. by J. F. Scanlan. New York: Scribners, 1949, Chapter III, n. 5).

[9] Cf. Etienne Borne, *Travail et esprit chrétien*, Courrier des Iles, No. 1, 1932.

[10] This is a different thing from work viewed as a title to property ("even as the effect follows the cause, so it is just that the fruits of the work should belong to the worker," Leo XIII, *Rerum Novarum*), although the title to property created by work is as an application and a determination, under very variable forms, of this metaphysical principle.

5. In the ontological and immanent order, the person possesses a proprietary right over himself, his nature, and his actions—the person is master of himself and of his acts. In the theological order, the Person of the Word thus possesses His human nature as proper to Him. We have here the metaphysical root principle of individual ownership, but this principle can pass to the ownership of material and external goods only by way of the *factibile*, only by way of the activity of art or work.

It is of the very essence of this activity that it imprint on matter the stamp of the rational person. But, by reason of what the work of art or the work to be done requires for its own proper good, this activity demands of its very nature that man have the maximum of freedom with regard to the matter on which he has to work, that the master of the work have permanent and exclusive disposal of the matter and the means serving the work. This can be realized only through a general system of individual ownership (whatever may be the particular modes, more or less felicitous, in which the system takes shape), even though there may be workers who do not own the means necessary for their work—as is the case with wage-earners—and even though there may be some works which, owing to special circumstances, lie outside the scope of private management, as for instance the public services of the State and undertakings controlled by it.

In the first case, the wage-earner is himself considered as a "member" of another man whom he *serves* and whose practical reason regulates and determines in the first place the work that is to be done. And, so far as he is *a means or instrument of another,* the wage-earner is neither owner nor co-owner of the concern. But his dignity as a *person* fashioning matter, and to this extent master of it, is not abolished. By virtue of this dignity, the individual appropriation radically required by the *factibile* still holds for him, as regards the product of the work, i.e., the profits, for which the fixed wage is a substitute.

In the second case, the work of the government official is grafted on free work and presupposes it. It is in the nature of things that such work should remain exceptional and limited to what directly concerns the common good of the community.

6. By reason of the *factibile*, by reason of the activity of art or

work, the proprietary right of the person over himself is thus extended to the ownership of things. How does this come about? Through those internal qualities which the Schoolmen call *habitus,* i.e., stable dispositions that perfect the subject, especially in the order of operation.

The "artistic" work (using the word "artistic" equivocally) of the bee proceeds from its specific nature, but the artistic or productive work of man proceeds from the personal activity and the habits of each man. The very word *habitus* is significant: one person *has* what the other has not. This is why the work of art or the thing to be made, the *factibile* which proceeds from the *habitus,* requires the personal power of management and use (*potestas procurandi et dispensandi*) of which St. Thomas speaks. It requires that things, the materials and the means of work, be possessed by man in a personal possession, a lasting and permanent possession, one befitting an agent that is intelligent, capable of foresight, and open to the future in his judgments and action. In short, that which is of use in the work of the person needs to be the *thing* of the person, the *thing* of the reason which works, which reason is an individual, and individually perfected, reason.[11]

To this we may add that the man who works and plans his work is also normally the head of a family who makes provision for his children. The work he performs is directed not merely to his own good, but primarily to the good of the community of which he is the head. There is thus a close relationship between personal property and the family viewed as the primordial society, antecedent to the State.[12] To prevent external things from becoming the "things" of the family, and thus from being handed down in various ways to members of the family, is to destroy the material basis of the family. But this truth becomes evident only when we consider the

---

[11] One can understand that, through an illusion proper to it, "machinism" (if one overlooks the wealth of artistic capital that it uses) appears to destroy the right to property, inducing the belief that human life can do without personal *habitus* and operative intellectual virtues, all its necessary work on matter being assured by a world of automatons—as if the manufacture of machines and their control, far from taking the place of art, did not simply shift its ground and carry it (so to speak) to the second degree.

[12] "Immo tanto jus est illud (dominii) validius, quanto persona humana in convictu domestico plura complectitur." Leo XIII, *Rerum Novarum.*

head of the family as "workman" or *artifex*, as an agent who uses his reason in the making of things.

If, on the other hand, civil life implies a mutual communication which takes place through the personal willing of private persons and thus bears witness in social life itself to the freedom of action of persons, and which presupposes the private ownership of things that individual persons can of their own authority exchange by purchase, sale, gift, etc.,[13] —if this is so, I say, then it is because the person is the subject of intellectual making that it is so; it is because the person must impose a rational elaboration on material things.

7. The metaphysical foundation of private property thus relates to the artistic side of human nature. The vocation of human nature to fashion matter according to a rational design requires generally that external things, on which and by which this fashioning is to be exercised, should be possessed as his own by the individual person who is the subject of the operative activity. Here is the metaphysical root of the two fundamental titles to individual ownership, namely, occupation (the first occupier laying hold of a certain good with a view to its later elaboration) and work.

8. This foundation is one based on right and is universal. Because of the disorder peculiar to human things, it rarely happens in fact that the best practical intellect owns goods which correspond to its *habitus*. Herein lies disorder. But a certain disorder is inherent in the very existence of human things; and what we are here seeking is the general foundation of the right of property, so far as it is required once and for all by the human person, and not those particular conditions to which each individual will have to adapt himself in order to be a lawful owner.

9. One may say, however, that a society will be more perfect in proportion as it tends more to have technical competence and effective work go hand in hand with ownership. In fact, when the disorder referred to above passes a certain limit, in particular when supra-individual groups and interests acting irresponsibly and without rational direction impose their disorder on the administration of material goods, and expropriate in reality (in a regime founded

---

[13] *Sum. Theol.*, I–II, 105, 2.

nevertheless on private property) competence and work, then a revolution in the social body becomes inevitable.

10. Finally, the State and just laws may intervene, not to deprive the citizens of their right to own property, but to regulate the exercise of this right and to order it to the common good. They may even intervene to suspend the exercise of this right in certain extreme cases, for example, in the case of those who would refuse to develop the goods they possess (*latifundia*) or who would destroy them rather than develop them.

11. The modes of individual ownership normally correspond to the kinds of work to be done (*factibile*), to the modes of artistic and work activity. It follows that work done on the soil, even if mechanical processes are used, tends of its very nature towards the *family* type of ownership, since this work is typically adapted to the work of a family group, to the art which the head of a family can possess and exercise with the help of the members of the domestic society. This society, of course, can be extended to comprise a greater or lesser number of associated co-workers or wage-earners.

On the contrary, the industrial method of production tends of its very nature towards a *corporate* form of ownership (co-ownership), since this method, especially in large industries, goes beyond the normal sphere of family work (as it is found among farmers or artisans) and is typically adapted to the art and work of a kind of technical community or society, the leaders of which are, as it were, statesmen of the *factibile*. What we have at the present time, as a matter of fact, is a swarm of shareholders, and of technicians and workmen in their service. The salary of the technician and the workman is a substitute (eliminating any share of risk) for what his profit would be as co-owner of the concern and the products of the work. This system has given rise to such serious abuses that the return to a normal administration seems to require that we direct ourselves to a type of industrial ownership in which technicians, workers, and shareholders would all be co-owners of the concern.

USE (*USUS*) AND COMMON USE

12. The thesis of St. Thomas is that the use of things (*usus*) must in some way be common, or, in other words, that it

must somehow benefit all. It is helpful here to recall the technical meaning St. Thomas attaches to the notion of *use* when speaking of *usus activus* in his analysis of human acts.[14]

"The use of any thing implies the application of that thing to some operation: hence the operation itself to which we apply a thing is called its use: thus to ride is the use of a horse and to strike is the use of a stick." Let us remark in passing that, if *equitare* (to ride) is *usus equi* (the use of a horse), *ditari* (to become rich) is not *usus divitiarum* (the use of riches), as the capitalist deviation would have it.

St. Thomas also explains that we bring to the operation the interior powers of the soul, the members of the body, and external things, "sicut baculum ad percutiendum." Here is the *usus* which we have to study. It is an act of the will in its free exercise. We no longer have to do with the order of the *factibile*, with the order of the activity of art or work; it is the order of the *agibile*, i.e., of morality, which now comes into play. Take the example of the stick; there is a technique for the procuring of it and for the wielding of it. But the wielding of the stick, which is an art from the point of view of the *factibile*, is also a moral act from the point of view of *usus*. Thus the administration itself of *my* goods which, in the line of the *factibile*, is a technique personally exercised by me, is also a moral act (*usus*) which, as such, must somehow aim at the good of all—my own good, doubtless, first of all, but my own good only so far as due attention is given to the fact that I am a member of the community.

In Article 2 of the same Question, St. Thomas teaches that *usus* does not belong to irrational animals and that it presupposes free will. In Article 3, he shows that there is no *use* of the last end; we *enjoy* the end, but we *use* means (*useful* things). Finally, in Article 4, he explains how use follows choice. Choice is the last moment of the will in its free relation of affective union with and interior adjustment to the thing willed. But, after choice has been made, there is what we may call another wave of will: it is *usus*, which is the last moment of the will as it tends to *real union*, to the real grasp of the means willed.

13. Use must somehow be common. "As regards use, posses-

---

[14] *Sum. Theol.*, I–II, 16.

sions ought to be rendered in some way common." [15] This law derives in the first place from the prime universal purpose of material goods. The destining of earthly goods not to the individual but to man, to humankind, always holds good and rules all else, since it is original and the very ground of the right to possess material things, before there is any question of the individual ownership of these things.

In the second place (and this is really another aspect of the same consideration) the law that the *usus* of, or benefiting from, terrestrial goods must be common may be derived from the nature of *usus* as such. *Usus* is essentially concerned with means and, with regard to them, it is the last act by which the will directs the faculties to real union and possession; it is the final act of moral freedom in relation to means, i.e., useful things. The act itself is mine: it is personal. But its relation to external goods does not give me in any way a right of ownership over them; rather, it presupposes this right. It would give me this right only if I were personally the end of this useful thing; if this thing were by nature destined for me, which is not the case, since by nature it is destined for man in general; or, if the fact of freely relating a good to myself as end, to my natural love of myself, sufficed to give me a right over this good, which equally is not the case. Furthermore, if we consider exclusively the aspect of the *agibile*, of the position of moral acts in the movement of man towards his last end, there seems to be no reason (since each person is a *whole* vis-à-vis the world) why one person more than another should have the use of the goods of this world.

Thus, from the point of view of *usus*, of the moral use of external goods, it is not individual appropriation which is established, but rather the common destination of goods which must be realized in varying analogical ways. And this ordering of things to the service of all should apply everywhere, and not only in that case where it is, as it were, materially embodied in the gift (which, moreover, I am morally bound to make) [16] of my surplus to the common use.

---

[15] "Unde manifestum est quod multo melius est quod sint propriae possessiones secundum dominium, *sed quod fiant communes aliquo modo quantum ad usum.*" St. Thomas, *Comm. in Polit. Aristotelis,* lib. II, lect. IV. Cf. *Sum. Theol.,* II–II, 32, 5, ad 2; 66, 2.

[16] Cf. *Sum. Theol.,* II–II, 32, 5; 66, 7.

In every human act that has to do with external goods, the two aspects of *factibile* and *agibile*, of making and moral use, appear. Both of them, and therefore individual appropriation and common use, should shine forth in every act which concerns external goods.

Consider that use whereby my will directs my faculties to enjoy a material good, to consume it or to spend it, whether it be a question, for example, of eating some fruit or of spending my salary in the purchase of the *Critique of Pure Reason*. There is use and individual enjoyment of the fruit and of the salary and of the book; and, even in that which concerns the enjoyment itself, the metaphysical root of individual appropriation is found in the claims of the *factibile* (in this case, the maintenance of my bodily and intellectual energies). But where is the echo here of the law which requires that use should be common? It appears in this, namely, that these bodily and intellectual energies must themselves serve the common good. And if my act is governed by reason, not by greed, it is implicitly ordered to the common good, without even my having to think of this latter.

14. Some important consequences can be deduced from the above. We will group them under three remarks:

(1) Every use of goods which is not ruled by reason is an act of *avarice* which deprives others of what is due to them. This is true not only as regards superfluities, but also as regards necessities; in every use of external goods which is governed not by reason but by impassioned egocentrism, I sin not only against God and myself but also against my neighbor. I am never alone in any one of my acts. The poor are always with us, everywhere claiming their right.

(2) The law of "common use" obviously bears on utilization itself and on the *fructus*, the enjoyment of goods. This may be realized in two ways which were foreseen under the Old Law [17] — either the enjoyment of certain goods is actually common or shared amongst all; or the interchange of goods takes place at the will of their owners, through gifts, sales and purchases, loans, rentals, deposits, etc. But the law of "common use" also bears on the *cura*, on the administration of goods.[18] Under a certain aspect, so far as it

---

[17] *Sum. Theol.*, I–II, 105, 2.
[18] *Ibid.*

is a *usus* (and not so far as it is a technique), the administration of goods itself requires their dedication to the common good.

The acquisition and the expenditure or use which I, as a responsible owner, make of my goods (and which in themselves belong to the province of art and technique), must both, by reason of the claims of the moral use which they imply, serve the common good and be of benefit to all.

The law may intervene here, even prior to any consideration of what is superfluous and before any distinction is made between what is necessary and what is superfluous.[19] We are not here concerned with the question whether the owner of goods must give to others of his necessities or of his superfluities. Rather, we are emphasizing the necessity of an *organization*, of a social structure, which would assure a certain measure of enjoyment (*fructus*) for all and also a certain measure of administration (*cura*) on the part of all.

One can see that the claims of moral use (*usus*) may have a repercussion on management and administration, on *cura,* on *procuratio* itself. Thus, even today, we can already cite, in countries where private property is recognized, many instances of industrial undertakings in which the workers share in the management, although they are not yet considered as co-owners of the undertaking but only as wage-earners.[20]

(3) Only now do there arise the questions pertaining to superfluities and the duty of disposing of them for the common good. These questions are concerned more with matters of individual conscience and the confessional than with sociology and legislation. The laws which relate to them (sumptuary laws, income tax laws, etc.) normally only make up for deficiencies in individual virtue. They are therefore inadequate for the proper organization of *usus communis*; whereas, in those matters indicated under our second remark, the law fulfills its primary and proper function.

If we limit ourselves to the consideration of what is necessary and what is superfluous, and if we apply the principle of *usus com-*

---

[19] Cf. St. Thomas, *Comm. in Polit. Aristotelis,* lib. II, lect. IV: "Quomodo autem usus rerum propriarum possit fieri communis, hoc pertinet ad providentiam boni legislatoris."

[20] Consider particularly the experiment carried out at Glenwood by the American Baltimore and Ohio Company (H. Dubreuil, *Standards,* Paris: 1929, pp. 367 ff.; Otto S. Beyer, *Bulletin of the Taylor Society,* February 1926).

munis only in this case, our view of the problem is too narrow and ineffectual.

Let us add that justice here provides only a minimum. The claims of "common use" are much wider; they require friendship as well as justice in the structure of society.

15. When the "common use" of goods fall below a certain limit, a revolution in the social body is inevitable.

The measure of "common use," the manner in which the goods of each fulfill the obligation of benefiting all, follows the measure of individual and social morality. It must therefore be assured by the "just laws and good customs" of which Aristotle and St. Thomas speak.

It would seem that in present-day society disorder has reached an acute stage. Individual ownership has been greatly ridiculed with respect to operative reason, or so far as it is postulated by the needs of work and "artistic" activity (in other words, in the line of the *factibile*). Sharing with all has likewise been greatly diminished with respect to moral reason, or so far as it is postulated by the needs of moral action (in other words, in the line of the *agibile*). The very evident requirements of modern legislation do no more in reality than secure a strict minimum by way of compensation for the absence of a spontaneous "common use."

16. It might be said that, in the same degree in which art is inhuman, so likewise is property. But property, like art, also corresponds to a deep need in human nature. Art, in the most general sense of the term, and property correspond more to the needs of the intellectual side of human nature, to the needs of practical intellect.

"Use," on the contrary, with its obligation to be of benefit to all, corresponds more to the needs of the will and morality. One can understand, therefore, that in reality it is especially moral (humanitarian) arguments which are used against property; whereas it is technical and intellectual (utilitarian) arguments which are used in its favor.

Communism is especially open to criticism on the ethical plane in what relates to the law of "common use," which is badly assured by the State. The spiritual foundation of "common use" is, in the last analysis, personality and love. No social organization, however necessary it may otherwise be with regard to "common use," can take the place of the most human mode of sharing goods, which is the way of friendship. If this way of sharing goods is to prevail in a society, it presupposes that most of the citizens have respect for the soul and the person, it presupposes a social structure built on a spiritual basis.

On the contrary, it is on an especially intellectual ("artistic") plane that Communism is open to criticism in what relates to the *factibile*, to the needs of human activity in its rational fashioning of matter. Individual ownership of material goods is required in virtue of a spiritual foundation, which is the person so far as he is an intellectual subject imposing a form on matter.

In the sphere of purely material (especially industrial) production, Communism can exalt—at least for a time, and by means of tyranny—the operative activity of human reason. But it can do nothing but oppose and weaken this activity in the sphere of its highest civilizing values, in that sphere in which art, as indeed pure speculation, depends most purely on the exigencies of an object to be made or to be contemplated, which object touches the transcendental order.

17. We say that, in the sphere of purely material production and for a time, Communism can exalt operative activity *by means of tyranny* and in no other way. We recall indeed that, according to St. Thomas,[21] the three principal conditions which distinguish good work in a community are care in the administration of goods, absence of confusion in work, and maintenance of the public peace. If these conditions can only be realized under a regime based on the private ownership of material goods, it is according as they are then attained in a manner commensurate with a truly stable and truly human order, as well as with the dignity of the person; it is according as they are then attained in a *natural and free* manner, in such a manner that organization, a work of reason, does not destroy but rather completes the spontaneity of nature and the free play of human activity.

When a regime based on private property becomes depersonalized and passes in actual fact under the sway of inorganic collective forces, the advantages we have cited disappear, as is evident in our day.

---

[21] *Sum. Theol.*, II–II, 66, 2.

On the other hand, wherever the constraints of the collectivity are able to replace in a certain measure a natural and spontaneous order, these same advantages can be realized in a collectivist society, but only in an artificial and tyrannical manner. It is at this price that a communist economy can function and succeed. If the individual is careful about the good administration of goods, it is no longer because he is responsible vis-à-vis the work itself or the thing, which is no longer *his thing*; its success or failure no longer affects or even interests him directly. The reason for his solicitude lies in the fact that he is responsible to the collectivity whose servant he is, and to other men who will punish him if he fails in his duty. If work is done without disorder or confusion in the social body, and if public peace is secured, it is due to the iron discipline imposed on the individual by the collectivity, and on the workers by directors who are alone responsible for the rational regulating of the work to be done.

18. We can understand, then, why Communism is led to postulate a radical change in human nature. It is necessary for it to seek the incentives for work and good work no longer in the proper interests of the person (which interests, by the way, the "bourgeois" world had degraded to the lowest level, for they are not necessarily either selfish or servile or bound up with the desire to accumulate riches endlessly), but rather in a pure mystical devotion to the collectivity and in a heavenly delight in working. Communism leads men to this happy state by flogging (till some better method is devised), by threatening starvation, and by subjecting their imagination to various propaganda myths. Here, in this need to change man in order to make of him a joyously depersonalized slave in the service of the collective work, is doubtless the material basis for the effort which Communism makes to change man by turning him into an atheist; for God is precisely the supreme, and completely dominating, interest of the person.

6 HUMAN EQUALITY*

THE EXPRESSION "EQUALITY OF NATURE," IT SEEMS, HAS the task of consoling us for the wounds incident to social inequalities or of meeting a resentment against these. I shall leave aside these affective connotations and take the expression as purely and simply synonymous with "unity of nature." It appears to me that the problem of the equality or inequality of men is resolved in three principal positions, which vary according as the fundamental fact that all men have the same specific nature is conceived in a thought-reference that is nominalist, idealist or realist. The great classical themes designated by these academic words have to do with concrete attitudes of mind that are of basic practical importance. I shall consider these practical attitudes of mind rather than philosophical theories and schools, in which empiricism and idealism often subtly attenuate each other or are unconsciously mixed with other leading principles. My empiricists are not Bacon, Locke, Bentham or John Stuart Mill, but rather those politicians of the modern world who are inspired by a mediocre Nietzscheanism or Machievellianism or a Rightist Hegelianism or a Rightist positivism. My idealists are not Plato, Descartes, Berkeley or Kant, but rather those politicians of the modern world who are inspired by a popular Rousseauism, a popular philosophy of the Enlightenment or a popular Tolstoyism, or a Leftist Hegelianism or a Leftist positivism. . . .

First, then, I shall examine the pure nominalist or empiricist

---

* *Principes d'une politique humaniste* (New York: Éditions de la Maison Française, 1944), pp. 95–131.

position on human equality, that is to say the philosophy of enslavement. Secondly, the pure idealist position; in other words, the philosophy of egalitarianism. And lastly the realist position, the authentic philosophy of equality. This philosophy does not suppress inequalities, but bases them on equality itself as a more fundamental
reality, and turns them, by virtue of justice, to a new equality
which depends on the use and fruition of the common good.

ANTI-CHRISTIAN ENSLAVEMENT

That men of every color and every condition should all
alike be designated by the name "man" is a radical fact accepted
by everyone. But what is the value of this identity in name? For a
pure empiricist, for one of those thinking beings who, as Plato
said, cling to the trunks of trees and hug rocks, able to compre-
hend only what they see and touch, this identity is a word
only. . . .

Inequalities do exist, they cry out, they cover the whole field of
human reality. Natural or social, they are not only an inevitable
fact of observation; but in general, and with due regard for the
miseries and indignities with which they can be and often are
charged because our species is an ungrateful and unhappy one, they
correspond to the truth of our human condition. As for natural
inequalities, St. Thomas Aquinas goes so far as to say [1] that the
intellectual vigor of one soul differs from that of another, not
merely because the exercise of intelligence depends on dispositions
of the organic and sensitive powers, which are of unequal perfection from person to person, but because the soul—being made to
form with the body a single substance—because such an individual
soul, destined for such a body of better disposition, in itself and
intrinsically has greater intellectual ability than a soul destined for
another body. . . .

When it comes to comparing the characteristics of groups taken
from the bosom of the human species, it is as just to compare the
inhabitant of one suburb with the inhabitant of another as to compare a Parisian with a man of southern France, an Angevin with a
Provençal, a German with a Frenchman, a Nordic with a Mediterranean, a Semite with an Aryan, a Dravidian with an Eskimo.

---

[1] *Sum. Theol.*, I, q. 85, a. 7.

Lion and ass have no common natural capacities which they more or less share. But primitive and civilized man share, in different degrees and in different ways, the virtues common to the human species; and if one shows to better effect the brilliant riches of human intelligence, the other shows to better effect the darker riches of human imagination and human instinct. The animal will always be superior to the vegetable, but the industrial bourgeoisie can replace the feudal nobility at the head of society, and the colored man can become, if historical circumstances favor him, superior to the white man in the civilized virtues.

If, finally, there are in the rule of Providence over man, unequal historical vocations for nations and for great ethnic groups, if there are divine preferences, if the blessing of forefathers have poured on human progeny gifts of unequal splendor and unequal abundance, all these are inequalities in fact and not by right and depend at bottom on divine freedom. They do not break the unity of the human family, but attest in it that diversity which goes with the proper condition of the created and which demands to be perfected in mutual aid and compassion; and they are written into history naturally and spontaneously by the very operation and use of the allotted gifts. To see in them the expression of essential necessities and constitutive laws which the knowledge and power of man are to exploit in order to assure his domination over the universe, is a chimera and presumptuous pride. . . .

The brute empiricism and nominalist pseudo-rationalization I just spoke of are unable to take account of all these truths, so important and vital for the human being. Because the unity of the human race is only a word for them, in practice they erect the natural or social inequalities to which men are exposed into specific differences between groups. . . .

The pseudo-specific categories into which men are thus divided are either social or biological pseudo-essences. The social pseudo-essences often correspond, as was generally the case in antiquity, to the different levels of population which successive conquests have in fact superimposed on a country. In the good old days of the caste, what hindered a Brahmin from killing, in all good conscience, an untouchable whose passing shadow had contaminated him? Or they correspond, thus perverting both the notion and its use, to the privileges of birth normal in a society of aristocratic or feudal type, or to the privileges of wealth normal in a society of a mercantile or "bourgeois" type; or they correspond, thus establishing the notion and its use, to the privileges of a purely cynical "elite" that are normal in a society of a totalitarian type ruled by a Party.

Biological pseudo-essences can be created in men's imaginations through an unconscious process due either to the obscure calculations of the will to power or to the natural ferocity of the defense instinct in an ethnic group. They can also be created in men's imagination when a conscious process duplicates and justifies the unconscious process; then we see a systematic perversion of science placed at the service of political imperialism, and a monstrous flowering of errors arbitrarily torn from the store of biological and ethnological truths and hypotheses. For example, one of the racist theses proclaimed at Nuremberg declared that there is "a greater distance between the lowest forms still called human and our superior races than between the lowest man and the highest monkeys."

In either case, whether it is question of the pseudo-specific categories of the social or of the biological order, the royal race, social or biological, actually concentrates within itself, according to this false logic, all the privileges and all the dignity of the human essence. As indicated in the text just cited, the lower categories are only in part and inchoatively human, midway between beast and man, essentially made to serve the royal race. . . .

The errors we have considered in these pages are those of anti-Christian enslavement.

PSEUDO-CHRISTIAN EGALITARIANISM

. . . For all those who unwittingly think as pure idealists, the unity of human nature is the unity of a subsisting Idea, of a man-in-himself existing outside time, and of whom the individuals in concrete life are shadows without substance; in such a view, this realized abstraction is reality itself. In this purely logical and non-ontological conception of the community of essence among reasoning creatures, the *homo Platonicus* (I use the phrase without any wish to get Plato himself into the debate. . .) absorbs or reabsorbs in himself all the reality of men, the dignity, the greatness and the recognized rights of human nature. And as in him all men are equally himself, the specific equality among them becomes the only reality, it alone has the right to exist, is alone recognized by the mind. The inequalities sworn to by experience are not exactly denied, any more than is the empirical world in the Platonic philosophy; rather they are rebuffed, pushed aside by the mind. . . .

The idealist error on this subject does not consist in thinking there is an essential equality among men. It consists in seeing and affirming only that, in reducing the whole human substance to the abstract species alone, and in taking as practically nothing the reality and value of those individual inequalities inscribed in the world of the singular and historical, which, despite the weight of sorrow or injustice that may be added to them by the sins of men or the vices of institutions, are in themselves as necessary for the development and expansion of human life as diversity of parts for the perfection of a flower or a poem . . .

The first consequence is that . . . all natural privileges, all privileges of mind, natural gifts and acquired virtues must be rigorously levelled. Objects of a special reprobation obviously are the qualities that are incommunicable and not subject to a common measure: no room for the poet or the contemplative in the egalitarian world; culture as such must be put through the mill, and in the corresponding intellectual structures an uneasy irritability arises regarding any possibility of a hierarchy of values among men. . . .

In the abstract, and in its idealistic principle, egalitarianism is like a false replica of Christian truths. Ambivalent in the emotional field as well as in the idea field, it is nourished not only with the vengeful instincts I have mentioned, but also with generous instincts and aspirations truly human; these are in the long run inefficacious, and yet they are like sketches or vestiges of Christian dispositions—either our nature's aspirations for Gospel sentiments or, in fact more often, secularized Gospel sentiments. What makes the great doctrinaires of equality is the passion for justice. It is with the very words of Christianity, if not with its voice, that they proclaim against the apologists of enslavement mankind's equality in nature and the equal rights founded on it. If egalitarianism ends up in the worst forms of slavery, this is a fate contrary to its first intentions. At the start it had or thought it had only one end in view —to affirm and to defend the dignity of man. What gives it its greatest power of seduction is the desire for communion which inhabits the heart of every man and that irresistible attraction exercised by anything telling our hearts—even if meanings are perverted—about the overthrow of the mighty and the exaltation of the humble, about the freeing of the suffering and naked and the calling of all men to the same brotherly feast. . . .

CHRISTIAN EQUALITY

. . . Equality of nature among men consists in their concrete communion in the mystery of the human species. It does not consist in an idea, but is hidden in the heart of the individual and of the concrete, in the roots of each man's substance. Obscure because situated on the very level of substance and of its primordial energies, radical because bound up with the sources of being, human equality reveals itself, as does the nearness of our neighbor, to the man who lives it. . . . If you treat a man as a man, which means if you respect and love the secret he bears within him and the good of which he is capable as an individual person, then to that extent you make effective in yourself his nearness in nature to you and his equality or unity in nature with yourself. It is the natural love of the human being for his kind that reveals and makes living the specific equality among men. . . .

In the experience of misery, in the sorrows of great catastrophes, in humiliations and distress, under the blows of the executioner or the bombs of total war, in concentration camps, in the hovels of starving people in big cities, in common necessity, the doors of solitude fly open and man recognizes man. Also man knows man when the sweetness of a great joy or a great love for a moment makes his eye pure. In helping his fellows or being helped by them, in sharing the same elementary actions and the same elementary feelings, in beholding his neighbor, the humblest gesture shows him, in others and in himself, human nature's common resources and common goodness, a goodness that is primitive, rudimentary, wounded, unconscious and repressed. At one stroke the real equality and community of nature is revealed to him as a most precious good, an unknown marvel, a fundamental stratum of existence, of more worth than all the differences and inequalities grafted onto it. When he returns to his ordinary prosperity, he will forget this discovery.

The instinct of equality is not a secondary instinctive tendency, however profound it be in us, such as pride or envy; it is a primary

instinct, the instinct of communication founded on common part-
nership in the same specific whole. . . . The realist conception of
equality in nature is a heritage of the Judaeo-Christian tradition,
and is a natural presupposition of Christian thought and life. Just
as every being has a natural love for God above everything else,
and indeed without this natural love charity would not perfect but
destroy nature,[2] so man also has a natural love, howsoever en-
feebled by sin, for his kind and for those sharing the same human
essence; and without this natural love the evangelical love for men
of every race and every condition would contradict rather than
superelevate nature. And how would we all be called to love each
other in God, if in the first place we were not all equal in our specific condition and dignity as rational creatures?

Christianity confirms and accentuates the concrete sense of
equality in nature by affirming its historic and genealogical character and by teaching that we have a consanguinity in the strict
sense, since all men are descended from the same original couple
and are brothers in Adam before they are brothers in Jesus Christ.
Heirs of the same sin and the same wounds, but heirs also of the
same original greatness, all created in the image of God and all
called to the same supernatural dignity of adopted sons of God
and to co-inheritance with Christ the Savior, all of us redeemed by
the same vivifying Blood and thus destined to become equal to the
angels in heaven (St. Luke, xx:36), is it possible for any Christian
to look upon man with the demented eyes of racist pride? The unity
of the human race is a foundation stone of Christianity. Pius XII
proclaimed it from the height of his throne when he denounced,
as the number one error among the pernicious errors widespread
today, "the forgetting of that law of human solidarity and charity,
required and imposed as much *by the community of origin and
by the equality of rational nature among all men*, to whatever people they may belong, as by the sacrifice of redemption offered by
Jesus Christ." The Pope recalls for us the teaching of St. Paul on
the subject, and adds, "Marvellous insight, which makes us contemplate the human race in the unity of its origin in God; in the
unity of its nature, similarly composed in all men of a material
body and a spiritual and immortal soul; in the unity of its imme-

---

[2] Thomas Aquinas, *Sum. Theol.*, I, q. 60, a. 5.

diate end and of its mission in the world; in the unity of its dwelling place—the earth, the goods of which all men, by natural right, can utilize to sustain and develop life; in the unity of its supernatural end—God himself, toward whom all should strive; in the unity of the means to attain this end; . . . in the unity of its redemption worked for all men by Christ." [3]

It is because the Christian conception of life is backed by such a concrete, ample and rich certainty of the equality and community in nature among men that it so forcibly insists at the same time on the order and hierarchy which rise and should rise from within this essential community, and on the particular inequalities which they necessarily entail. For in the universe of man as in that of other creatures there can be no concurrence and communication, no life and movement, without differentiation, no differentiation without inequalities.[4]

. . . Inequalities make this unity all the more manifest. Every man is a man by his essence, but no man is man by essence,[5] that is, no man exhausts in himself all the richness of the perfections of which the human species is capable. In this sense all the diversity of perfections and virtues distributed among human generations in space and time is but a varied sharing in the common and inexhaustible potentialities of man.

The Christian name and the truest name for the equality in nature among men is the term "unity of mankind." It helps us to rid the notion of this equality of all erroneous associations and overtones, whether these spring from the geometric imagination or from a passion for levelling. Arithmetical equality between two numbers excludes all inequality, but equality in nature among men or the unity of mankind yearns to flower out in individual inequalities. To affirm equality in nature among men is for egalitarian idealism to want all inequality among them to vanish. To affirm equality in nature among men or the unity of mankind is for Christian realism to wish that the fruitful inequalities by which the multitude of individuals share in the common treasure of humanity be developed. Egalitarian idealism deciphers the word equality on the surface. Christian realism deciphers it in its deeper dimensions. Not only should

---

[3] Encyclical *Summi pontificatus*. Oct. 20, 1939; italics mine.
[4] Thomas Aquinas, *Sum. Theol.*, I, q. 47, a. 2.
[5] Cf. Cajetan, in *Sum. Theol.*, I, 6, 3.

we see equality as something basic on which an infinity of diversities is erected, but equality itself is a living, intensive and qualitative depth. Let us not say that one man is as good as another; that is a nihilistic formula, which gets a true meaning only in deep religious pessimism (*vanitas vanitatum, omnis homo mendax*). Let us say that all men are virtually in one man. The Son of Man, who "knows what is in man," in each man knows all men.

In this way, then, we must affirm both the essential equality which unites men in rational nature and the natural individual inequalities born of that very unity or equality. But by the same token we see that the equality is primary, the inequalities secondary. For, absolutely speaking, community of essence is more important than individual differences, the root more important than the branches. . . .

As regards social life, it is important to say at once that here also, and for the same reasons as indicated above, there are and have to be both equality and inequalities, and that the inequalities —normal, consubstantial with social life, and abounding everywhere—are and ought to be secondary. Equality is primary inasmuch as—taken as equality pure and simple—it is concerned with the fundamental rights and common dignity of the human being, and, taken as equality of proportion, it is concerned with justice. . . .

Social equality itself, so far as it is worthy of the name, also has a value properly and really social. Though founded on unity and equality in nature, it is not one with this, but rather is as it were the expression or expansion of it in the social order. It is first of all equality, recognized and sanctioned by society, in those rights, hard to enumerate and yet real, which we call the fundamental rights of the human person: the right to life, to bodily integrity, to found a family, itself assured the freedoms proper to it, the right to private ownership, the right to tend toward those goods through which the rational creature is perfected, the right to take towards eternal life the road one's conscience sees as mapped out by God. Besides, it is that equality of respect which human dignity demands that social customs show to all by treating them all as men and not as things. Again, it is political equality, the equality of all before the law. . . . Lastly, it is that equal condition as co-heirs of the effort of all, which condition requires that all should as far as possible share "free of charge" in the elementary material and spiritual goods of human existence. . . .

Postulated though it is by nature, social life is a work of reason and virtue, and even when thwarted it implies a movement of progressive conquest of man over nature and himself. Hence, far from being ready-made, social equality itself implies a certain dynamism. Like liberty, it is itself an end to be won, with difficulty and at the cost of a constant tension of the energies of the spirit. . . . It demands not only the practice of distributive justice in the body politic, it demands also, as far as this is possible, the free participation of all in the elementary material and spiritual goods and the redistribution of the common good to persons. It demands progress in social justice; the organic development of legal institutions; the accession, in greater or less degree, of persons as such to political life; a transition to conditions really offering to all an equal opportunity—equal in a proportional sense—to make each one's gifts bear fruit, and permitting an aristocracy born of personal work which turns back to the common good the excellence of its works; a greater and greater sharing by all in the goods of culture and the spirit and in the interior liberty supplied by mastery of oneself and knowledge of the truth.

PART II

Man and Political Society

7 THE BODY POLITIC*

IN CONTRADISTINCTION TO THE *Nation*, BOTH THE *Body Politic* and the *State* pertain to the order of society, even society in its highest or "perfect" form. In our modern age the two terms are used synonymously,[1] and the second tends to supersede the first. Yet if we are to avoid serious misunderstandings, we have to distinguish clearly between the State and the Body Politic. These do not belong to two diverse categories, but they differ from each other as a part differs from the whole. The *Body Politic* or the *Political Society* is the whole. The *State* is a part—the topmost part—of this whole.

Political Society, required by nature and achieved by reason, is the most perfect of temporal societies. It is a concretely and wholly human reality, tending to a concretely and wholly human good—the common good. It is a work of reason, born out of the obscure efforts of reason disengaged from instinct, and implying essentially a rational order; but it is no more Pure Reason than man himself.

---

* *Man and the State* (Chicago: University of Chicago Press, 1951), pp. 9–19.

[1] "The State is a particular portion of mankind viewed as an organized unit." (John W. Burgess, *Political Science and Constitutional Law*. Boston: Ginn & Co., 1896, I, 50.)

A similar confusion between Body Politic and State is usual among jurists. According to Story and Cooley, "a state is a body politic, or society of men, united together for the purpose of promoting their mutual safety and advantage by the joint efforts of their combined strength." (Thomas M. Cooley, *Constitutional Limitations*. Boston: 1868, p. 1; cf. Joseph Story, *Commentaries on the Constitution of the United States*. Boston: 1851, I, p. 142.) The word "state," Story goes on to say (*ibid.*, p. 143), "means the whole people, united into one body politic; and the state, and the people of the state, are equivalent expressions."

The body politic has flesh and blood, instincts, passions, reflexes, unconscious psychological structures and dynamism—all of these subjected, if necessary by legal coercion, to the command of an Idea and rational decisions. Justice is a primary condition for the existence of the body politic, but Friendship is its very life-giving form.[2] It tends toward a really human and freely achieved communion. It lives on the devotion of human persons and their gift of themselves. They are ready to commit their own existence, their possessions and their honor for its sake. The civic sense is made up of this sense of devotion and mutual love as well as of the sense of justice and law.

The entire man—though not by reason of his entire self and of all that he is and has—is part of the political society; and thus all his community activities, as well as his personal activities, are of consequence to the political whole. As we have pointed out, a national community of a higher human degree spontaneously takes shape by virtue of the very existence of the body politic, and in turn becomes part of the substance of the latter. Nothing matters more, in the order of material causality, to the life and preservation of the body politic than the accumulated energy and historical continuity of that national community it has itself caused to exist. This means chiefly a heritage of accepted and unquestionable structures, fixed customs and deep-rooted common feelings which bring into social life itself something of the determined physical data of nature, and of the vital unconscious strength proper to vegetative organisms. It is, further, common inherited experience and the moral and intellectual instincts which constitute a kind of empirical, practical wisdom, much deeper and denser and much nearer the hidden complex dynamism of human life than any artificial construction of reason.

Not only is the national community, as well as all communities of the nation, thus comprised in the superior unity of the body politic, but the body politic also contains in its superior unity the family units, whose essential rights and freedoms are anterior to itself, and a multiplicity of other particular societies which proceed from the free initiative of citizens and should be as autonomous as possible. Such is the element of pluralism inherent in every truly

---

[2] Cf. Gerald B. Phelan, "Justice and Friendship," in the "Maritain Volume" of the *Thomist*. (New York: Sheed & Ward, 1943.)

political society. Family, economic, cultural, educational, religious life matter as much as does political life to the very existence and prosperity of the body politic. Every kind of law, from the spontaneous, unformulated group regulations to customary law and to law in the full sense of the term, contributes to the vital order of political society. Since in political society authority comes from below, through the people, it is normal that the whole dynamism of authority in the body politic should be made up of particular and partial authorities rising in tiers above one another, up to the top authority of the State. Finally, the public welfare and the general order of the law are essential parts of the common good of the body politic, but this common good has far larger and richer, more concretely human implications, for it is by nature the good human life of the multitude and is common to both the *whole* and the *parts,* the persons into whom it flows back and who must benefit from it. The common good is not only the collection of public commodities and services which the organization of common life presupposes: a sound fiscal condition, a strong military force; the body of just laws, good customs, and wise institutions which provides the political society with its structure; the heritage of its great historical remembrances, its symbols and its glories, its living traditions and cultural treasures. The common good also includes the sociological integration of all the civic conscience, political virtues and sense of law and freedom, of all the activity, material prosperity and spiritual riches, of unconsciously operating hereditary wisdom, of moral rectitude, justice, friendship, happiness, virtue and heroism in the individual lives of the members of the body politic. To the extent to which all these things are, in a certain measure, *communicable* and revert to each member, helping him to perfect his life and liberty as a person, they all constitute the good human life of the multitude.[3]

THE STATE

From this enumeration of the features of the body politic, it should be evident that the body politic differs from the State. The State is only that part of the body politic especially concerned with the maintenance of law, the promotion of the common wel-

---

[3] Cf. our book, *The Person and the Common Good* (New York: Scribners, 1947.)

fare and public order, and the administration of public affairs. The State is a part which *specializes* in the interests of the whole.[4] It is not a man or a body of men; it is a set of institutions combined into a topmost machine: this kind of work of art has been built by man and uses human brains and energies and is nothing without man, but it constitutes a superior embodiment of reason, an impersonal, lasting superstructure, the functioning of which may be said to be rational in the second degree, insofar as the reason's activity in it, bound by law and by a system of universal regulations, is more abstract, more sifted out from the contingencies of experience and individuality, more pitiless also, than in our individual lives.

The State is not the supreme incarnation of the Idea, as Hegel believed; the State is not a kind of collective superman; the State is but an agency entitled to use power and coercion, and made up of experts or specialists in public order and welfare, an instrument in the service of man. Putting man at the service of that instrument is political perversion. The human person as an individual is for the body politic and the body politic is for the human person as a person. But man is by no means for the State. The State is for man.

When we say that the State is the superior part in the body politic, this means that it is superior to the other organs or collective parts of this body, but it does not mean that it is superior to the body politic itself. The part as such is inferior to the whole. The State is inferior to the body politic as a whole, and is at the service of the body politic as a whole. Is the State even the *head* of the body politic? Hardly, for in the human being the head is an instrument of such spiritual powers as the intellect and the will, which the whole body has to serve; whereas the functions exercised by the State are for the body politic, and not the body politic for them.

The theory which I have just summarized, and which regards the State as a part or an instrument of the body politic, subordinate to it and endowed with topmost authority not by its own right and for its own sake, but only by virtue and to the extent of the requirements of the common good, can be described as an "instrumentalist" theory, founding the genuinely *political* notion of the State. But

---

[4] Harold Laski described the State as a public service corporation (*A Grammar of Politics*. London: Allen & Unwin, 1935, p. 69).

we are confronted with quite another notion, the *despotic* notion of the State, based on a "substantialist" or "absolutist" theory. According to this theory the State is a subject of right, i.e., a moral person, and consequently a whole; as a result it is either superimposed on the body politic or made to absorb the body politic entirely, and it enjoys supreme power by virtue of its own natural, inalienable right and for its own final sake.

Of course, there is for everything great and powerful an instinctive tendency—and a special temptation—to grow beyond its own limits. Power tends to increase power, the power machine tends ceaselessly to extend itself; the supreme legal and administrative machine tends toward bureaucratic self-sufficiency; it would like to consider itself an end, not a means. Those who specialize in the affairs of the whole have a propensity to take themselves for the whole; the general staffs to take themselves for the whole army, the Church authorities for the whole Church; the State for the whole body politic. By the same token, the State tends to ascribe to itself a peculiar common good—its own self-preservation and growth—distinct both from the public order and welfare which are its immediate end, and from the common good which is its final end. All these misfortunes are but instances of "natural" excess or abuse.

But there has been something much more specific and serious in the development of the *substantialist* or *absolutist* theory of the State. This development can be understood only in the perspective of modern history and as a sequel to the structures and conceptions peculiar to the Medieval Empire, to the absolute monarchy of the French classical age, and the absolute government of the Stuart kings in England. Remarkably enough, the very word *State* only appeared in the course of modern history; the notion of the "State" was implicitly involved in the ancient concept of city (*polis, civitas*) which meant essentially body politic, and still more in the Roman concept of the Empire: it was never explicitly brought out in antiquity. According to a historical pattern unfortunately most recurrent, both the normal development of the State—which was in itself a sound and genuine progress—and the development of the spurious—absolutist—juridical and philosophical conception of the State took place at the same time.

An adequate explanation of that historical process would require a long and thorough analysis. Here I merely suggest that in the Middle Ages the authority of the Emperor, and in early modern times the authority of the absolute King, descended from above on the body politic, upon which it was superimposed. For centuries, political authority was the privilege of a superior "social race" which had a right—a supposedly innate or immediately God-given and inalienable right—to supreme power over, and leadership as well as moral guidance of, the body politic—made up, it was assumed, of people under age who were competent to make requests, remonstrances, or riots, but not to govern themselves. So, in the "baroque age," while the reality of the State and the sense of the State progressively took shape as great juridical achievements, the concept of the State emerged more or less confusedly as the concept of a whole—sometimes identified with the person of the king —which was superimposed on or which enveloped the body politic and enjoyed power from above by virtue of its own natural and inalienable right—that is to say, it possessed Sovereignty. For in the genuine sense of this word—which depends on the historical formation of the concept of sovereignty, prior to jurists' various definitions—sovereignty implies not only actual possession of and right to supreme power, but a right which is *natural and inalienble*, to a supreme power which is supreme *separate from* and *above* its subjects.

At the time of the French Revolution that very concept of the State considered as a whole unto itself was preserved, but it shifted from the King to the Nation, mistakenly identified with the body politic; hence, Nation, Body Politic and State were identified.[5] And the very concept of sovereignty—as a *natural* or *innate* and *inalienable* right to supreme *transcendent* power—was preserved, but shifted from the King to the Nation. At the same time, by virtue of a voluntarist theory of law and political society, which had its acme in eighteenth-century philosophy, the State was made into a person (a so-called moral person) and a subject of right,[6] in such a way

---

[5] This confusion between State, Body Politic, and Law was to become classical. It appeared in a striking manner in the theory of A. Esmein (see his *Éléments de droit constitutionnel*. 6th ed.; Paris: Recueil Sirey, 1914), who insisted that "the State is the juridical personification of the Nation."

[6] The notion of moral or collective personality—in which "personality" has a *proper analogical* value—applies to the *people* as a whole in a genuine manner: because the people as a whole (a *natural whole*) are an ensemble of real

that the attribute of absolute sovereignty, ascribed to the Nation, was inevitably, as a matter of fact, to be claimed and exercised by the State.

Thus it is that in modern times the despotic or absolutist notion of the State was largely accepted among democratic tenets by the theorists of democracy—pending the advent of Hegel, the prophet and theologian of the totalitarian, divinized State. In England, John Austin's theories only tended to tame and civilize somewhat the old Hobbesian Leviathan. This process of acceptance was favored by a symbolical property which genuinely belongs to the State, namely, the fact that, just as we say twenty head of cattle meaning twenty animals, in the same way the topmost part in the body politic naturally *represents* the political whole. Nay more, the notion of the latter is raised to a higher degree of abstraction and symbolization,[7] and the consciousness of the political society is raised to a

---

individual persons and because their unity as a social whole derives from a com mon will to live together which originates in these real individual persons.

Accordingly, the notion of moral or collective personality applies in a genuine manner to the *body politic,* which is the organic whole composed of the people. As a result, both the people and the body politic are *subjects (or holders) of rights*: the people have a right to self-government; there is a mutual relationship of justice between the body politic and its individual members.

But that same notion of moral personality does not apply to the *State* (which is not a whole, but a part or a special agency of the body politic), except in a *merely metaphorical* manner and by virtue of a juridical fiction. The State is not a subject of rights, a *Rechtssubjekt,* as many modern theorists, especially Jellinek, mistakenly put it. (On the opposite side, Léon Duguit clearly realized that the State is not a subject of rights, but he went to the other extreme, and his general theory jeopardized the very notion of right.)

The rights of the people or of the body politic are not and cannot be *transferred* or given over to the State. Furthermore, in so far as the State *represents* the body politic (in the external relations of the latter with the other bodies politic), "the State" is a merely abstract entity which is neither a moral person nor a subject of rights. The rights ascribed to it are no rights of its own; they are the rights of the body politic—which is *ideally* substituted for by that abstract entity, and *really* represented by the men who have been put in charge of public affairs and invested with specific powers.

[7] So it happened that a great theorist like Kelsen could make out of the State a mere juridical abstraction and identify it with Law and the legal order—a concept which uproots the State from its true sphere (that is, the political sphere) and which is all the more ambiguous as the real State (as topmost part and agency of the body politic) will in actual fact avail itself of that fictitious essence, ascribed to it as juridical *ens rationis,* to claim for itself the saintly attributes and "sovereignty" of the Law.

Be it noted, moreover, that the expression "sovereignty of the law" is a merely metaphorical expression, which relates to the rational nature of the law

more completely individualized idea of itself in the idea of the State. In the absolutist notion of the State, that symbol has been made a reality, has been hypostasized. According to this notion the State is a metaphysical monad, a person; it is a whole unto itself, *the* very political whole in its supreme degree of unity and individuality. So it absorbs in itself the body politic from which it emanates, as well as all the individual or particular wills which, according to Jean-Jacques Rousseau, have engendered the General Will in order mystically to die and resurge in its unity. And it enjoys absolute sovereignty as an essential property and right.

That concept of the State, enforced in human history, has forced democracies into intolerable self-contradictions, in their domestic life and above all in international life. For this concept is no part of the authentic tenets of democracy, it does not belong to the real democratic inspiration and philosophy; it belongs to a spurious ideological heritage which has preyed upon democracy like a parasite. During the reign of individualist or "liberal" democracy the State, made into an absolute, displayed a tendency to substitute itself for the people, and so to leave the people estranged from political life to a certain extent; it also was able to launch the wars between nations which disturbed the nineteenth century. Nevertheless, after the Napoleonic era the worst implications of this process of State absolutization were restrained by the democratic philosophy and political practices which then prevailed. It is with the advent of the totalitarian regimes and philosophies that those worst implications were released. The State made into an absolute revealed its true face. Our epoch has had the privilege of contemplating the State totalitarianism of Race with German Nazism, of Nation with Italian Fascism, of Economic Community with Russian Communism.

The point which needs emphasis is this: For democracies today the most urgent endeavor is to develop social justice and improve world economic management, and to defend themselves against totalitarian threats from the outside and totalitarian expansion in

---

and its obligatory moral and juristic quality but has nothing to do with the genuine concept of sovereignty.

The concrete function of the State—its principal function—is to ensure the legal order and the enforcement of the law. But the State is not the law. And the so-called "sovereignty" of the State is in no way the moral and juridical "sovereignty" (that is, the property of binding consciences and being enforceable by coercion) of the Law (the just law).

the world. But the pursuit of these objectives will inevitably involve the risk of having too many functions of social life controlled by the State from above, and we shall be inevitably bound to accept this risk, as long as our notion of the State has not been restated on true and genuine democratic foundations, and as long as the body politic has not renewed its own structures and consciousness, so that the people become more effectively equipped for the exercise of freedom, and the State may be made an actual instrument for the common good of all. Then only will that very topmost agency, which modern civilization has made more and more necessary to the human person in his political, social, moral, even intellectual and scientific progress, cease to be at the same time a threat to the freedoms of the human person as well as of intelligence and science. Then only will the highest functions of the State—to ensure the law and facilitate the free development of the body politic—be restored, and the sense of the State be regained by the citizens. Then only will the State achieve its true dignity, which comes not from power and prestige, but from the exercise of justice.

8 THE PERSON AND THE COMMON GOOD*

THE END OF SOCIETY IS NEITHER THE INDIVIDUAL GOOD nor the collection of the individual goods of each of the persons who constitute it. Such a conception would dissolve society as such to the advantage of its parts, and would amount to either a frankly anarchistic conception, or the old disguised anarchistic conception of individualistic materialism, according to which the whole function of the body politic is to safeguard the liberty of each, thereby giving to the strong freedom to oppress the weak.

The end of society is the good of the community, the good of the social body. But if this good of the social body is not understood to be a common good of *human persons*, just as the social body itself is a whole of human persons, this conception would lead in its turn to other errors of a totalitarian type. The common good of the body politic is neither the mere collection of private goods, nor the good of a whole which, like the species with respect to its individuals or the hive with respect to its bees, draws the parts to itself alone and sacrifices them to itself. It is the good *human* life of the multitude, of a multitude of persons; it is their communion in good living. It is therefore common *to the whole and to the parts*; it flows back to the parts, and the parts must benefit from it. Under pain of being itself denatured, it implies and demands recognition of the fundamental rights of persons, and recognition also of the rights of family society, in which human persons

* *La personne et le bien commun* (Paris: Desclée de Brouwer, 1947), pp. 44–56.

are more primitively engaged than in political society. It includes within itself, as principal value, the highest access possible, i.e., compatible with the good of the whole, of persons to their life as persons and to their freedom of expansion, as well as to the communications of goodness proceeding therefrom. If, as we intend to emphasize later, the common good of the body politic implies an intrinsic subordination to something which transcends it, this is because it requires, by its very essence and within its proper sphere, communication or redistribution to the persons who constitute society. It presupposes these persons and flows back upon them, and, in this sense, is achieved in them. . . .

Let us note in passing that the common good is not only a set of advantages and utilities, but also integrity of life, an end good in itself, or, as the Ancients expressed it, a *bonum honestum*. For, on the one hand, to assure the existence of the multitude is something morally good in itself; on the other hand, the existence, thus assured, must be the just and morally good existence of the community. Only on condition that it is according to justice and moral goodness is the common good what it is, namely the good of a people and a body politic, and not the "good" of a mob of gangsters and murderers. For this reason, perfidy, the scorn of treaties and sworn oaths, political assassination and unjust war, even though they may be *useful* to a government and procure some fleeting advantages for the peoples who make use of them, tend by their nature as political acts—acts involving in some degree the common action—to the destruction of the common good of these peoples.

The common good is something ethically good. Included in it, as essential element, is the maximum possible development, here and now, of human persons, of persons making up a united multitude to the end of forming a people, organized not by force alone but by justice. Historical conditions and the still backward state of the development of humanity make it difficult for social life fully to achieve its end. But the end to which it tends is to procure the common good of the multitude in such a way that each concrete person gains the greatest measure possible, i.e., compatible with the good of the whole, of real independence from the servitudes of nature—an independence assured alike by the economic guarantees of work and ownership, political rights, the moral virtues and the cultivation of the mind.

A twofold observation is pertinent here. First, the common good of civil society implies that the whole man is engaged in this society. Unlike a farmers' cooperative or a scientific association, which requires the commitment of only part of the members' interests, civil society requires the citizens to commit their lives, properties and honor. Second, it is doubtful whether the idea of the "perfect society," to which the idea of the common good of political society is linked, has ever been truly realized within the limits of any particular social group. In any case, its realization has experienced many adventures in the course of history. Contemporary bodies politic are more remote from the ideal type of the "perfect society" than the city-state of Aristotle's day or the body politic in the time of Saurez. The common good in our day has definitely ceased to be just the common good of the nation, and it has not yet succeeded in becoming the common good of the civilized world community. It tends, however, towards the latter. For this reason, it would doubtless be wisest to consider the common good of a state or nation as merely an area, among many similar areas, of the common good of civilized society in its entirety.

We have emphasized the sociability of the person and the properly human nature of the common good. We have seen that this latter is a good according to justice; that it must flow back upon persons; and that it has as its principal value the access of persons to their freedom of expansion.

We have not yet considered what might be termed the typical paradox of social life. Here again we shall find the distinction of the individual and the person. For this paradox results from the fact, already noted, that each of us is in his entirety an individual and in his entirety a person.

A few metaphysical and even theological considerations should help to assure the correct development of the discussion. Let us recall that the idea of person is an analogical idea which is realized fully and absolutely only in its supreme analogue, God, the Pure Act. Let us recall further that, for St. Thomas, the *ratio* or intelligible value of "whole," of "totality," is indissolubly bound to that of person. This is a fundamental thesis of Thomism. The person as such is a whole. "The concept of part is opposed to that of person."[1]

To say, then, that society is a whole composed of persons is to say that society is a whole composed of wholes. Taken in its full sense, this expression leads directly to the society of the Divine Persons (for the idea of society is also an analogical idea). In the Divine Trinity, there is a whole, the divine Essence, which is the common good of the three subsisting Relations. With respect to this whole, the Three who compose the society of the Trinity are by no means parts, since they are perfectly identical with it. They are three Wholes who are the Whole. "Among created things," St. Thomas writes, "*one* is part of *two*, and *two* of *three* (as one man is part of two men, and two men of three). But it is not thus in God. For the Father is as much as the whole Trinity: *quia tantus est Pater, quanta tota Trinitas.*"[2]

We must be aware here of the irremediable deficiency of our language. Since our idea of society originates in and, as far as modes of conceptualization are concerned, is bound to our experience, the only possible way for us to express the fact that persons live in society is to say that they are parts of society or compose society. But can it be said, except quite improperly, that the Divine Persons "are parts of" or "compose" the uncreated society? Here, precisely where we are confronted with the society par excellence, a society of pure persons, our language is irremediably deficient. Let us keep in mind this essential point, which is the proper difficulty of and the key to the precisions to follow, namely that, if the per-

---

[1] In III *Sent.*, d. 5, 3, 2. St. Thomas, in this text, refers to the human composite (*unum per se*) and shows that the separated soul cannot be a person because it is only a part of the human being. To anyone whose knowledge of Thomism is sufficiently deep it is clear that the principle—the *ratio* of part is repugnant to that of personality—is an entirely general principle and is applied analogically depending on the case. Thus, in speaking of the hypostatic union, which takes place *in persona* (*Sum. Theol.*, III, 2, 2.), John of St. Thomas shows that God can be united to human nature only as person, just as He can be united to human intelligence only as *species intelligibilis*, because in both cases He is united to them as term and as whole, not as part (*Cursus Theol.*, De Incarnatione, Disput. IV, a. 1). The same principle must evidently come into play also—though under completely different conditions and following another line of application—when the notion of person is considered with respect to wholes (e.g., the social whole), which are no longer, like the human composite, substantial but have only an accidental unity, and are themselves composed of persons.

[2] *Sum. Theol.*, I, 30, 1, ad 4.

son of himself asks "to be part of" society, or "to be a member of society," this does not at all mean that he asks to be in society in the way in which a part is in a whole, nor does it mean that he asks to be treated in society as a part in a whole. On the contrary, the person, as person, asks to be treated as a whole in society.

To get the right idea of human society, we must consider it as located in the ontological scale between the uncreated exemplar, the super-analogue of the concept of society, namely, the divine society, and that which is not even an analogue, except in an improper and metaphorical sense, of this concept, namely, animal society. Infinitely above the city of men, there is a society of pure Persons, who are at the summit of individuality, but without the shadow of individuation by matter (or even by a form distinct from the act of existence). Each one is in the other, in an infinite communion,[3] and their common good is strictly and absolutely the proper good of each, since it is that which each person is and their very act of existing. Far below the city of men, below even the threshold of all society properly so-called, there is a "society" of material individuals which are not persons, which are so isolated each within itself that they do not tend toward any communion and have no *common* good,[4] but each is totally subservient to the *proper* good of the whole. Human society, located between these two, is a society of persons who are material individuals, who are isolated each within himself, but who nonetheless ask to commune with one another as much as possible here below, before perfectly communing with one another and with God in life eternal. The terrestrial common good of such a society is, on the one hand, superior to the proper good of each member, but it flows back upon each. On the other hand, it sustains in each member that movement by which he strives toward his own eternal good and the transcendent Whole, thus transcending the order in which the common good of the terrestrial city is constituted.

The person as such is a whole, an open and generous whole. In truth, if human society were a society of *pure persons,* the good of

---

[3] *Sum. Theol.,* I, 42, 5.
[4] In the formally social sense. Cf. *La personne et le bien commun,* p. 43, note 1 (English translation *The Person and the Common Good,* p. 39, n. 28).

society and the good of each person would be one and the same good. But man is very far from being a pure person; the human person is the person of a poor material individual, of an animal born more destitute than any other animal. Though the person as such is an independent whole and that which is noblest in all of nature, nonetheless the human person is at the lowest level of personality—naked and miserable, indigent and full of wants. When he enters into society with his kind, therefore, it happens that, by reason of his deficiencies—evidences of his condition as an individual in the species—the human person is present *as part* of a whole which is greater and better than its parts, and of which the common good is worth more than the good of each. Yet it is by reason of personality as such and the perfections which it implies as an independent and open whole, that the human person asks to enter into society. Whence, as previously noted, it belongs essentially to the good of the social whole that it flow back in some fashion upon the person of each member. It is the human *person* who enters into society; as an individual, he enters society as a part whose proper good is inferior to the good of the whole (of the whole constituted of persons). But the good of the whole is what it is, and is therefore superior to the private good, only if it benefits the individual persons, is redistributed to them, and respects their dignity.

On the other hand, because he is ordered to the absolute and called to a destiny above time, or, in other words, because of the highest claims of personality as such, the human person, as a spiritual totality referred to the transcendent Whole, *surpasses* and is superior to all temporal societies. From this point of view, or, if you will, as regards the things *which are not Caesar's,* both society itself and its common good are indirectly subordinated to the perfect fulfillment of the person and his supratemporal aspirations as to an end of another order—an end which transcends them. A single human soul is worth more than the whole universe of material goods. There is nothing higher than the immortal soul, save God. With respect to the eternal destiny of the soul, society exists for each person and is subordinated to him.

We have just stated that the common good is what it is only if it is redistributed to persons. Let us now add a consideration which is derived from the same principles but goes farther, namely, that the common good of political society or of civilization—an essentially human common good, in which the whole man is engaged—does not preserve its true nature unless it respects that which surpasses it, unless it is subordinated, not as a pure means but as an infravalent end, to the order of eternal goods and the supratemporal values to which human life is appendant.

This intrinsic subordination refers above all to the supernatural beatitude to which the human person is directly ordered. It is also and already related—a fact which the philosopher has the duty to reveal—to everything which belongs, even in the natural order, to the realm of the absolute, and thus of itself transcends political society. We have in mind the natural law, the rule of justice, and the requirements of fraternal love; the life of the spirit and all that which, in us, is a natural beginning of contemplation; the immaterial dignity of truth, in all domains and at all levels, however humble they may be, of theoretical knowledge, and the immaterial dignity of beauty, both of which are nobler than the things of common life and never fail, if curbed by these latter, to avenge themselves. In the measure that human society attempts to free itself from this subordination and proclaim itself the supreme good, in the very same measure it perverts its own nature and that of the common good—in the same measure it destroys the common good.

9 PROBLEMS CONCERNING AUTHORITY*

I HAVE TREATED OF AUTHORITY IN DEMOCRACY IN AN-other book.[1] Yet it is necessary to sum up a few considerations of the subject in order to have our concept of the democratic charter sufficiently complete. I am not dissatisfied, moreover, to have this opportunity to make certain positions clearer and more definite—and truer, I hope—than in my previous essays.

Authority and power are two different things. Power is the force by means of which you can oblige others to obey you. Authority is the *right* to direct and command, to be listened to or obeyed by others. Authority requests power. Power without authority is tyranny.

Thus, authority means right. If, in the cosmos, a nature, such as human nature, can be preserved and developed only in a state of culture, and if the state of culture necessarily entails the existence in the social group of a function of commandment and government directed to the common good, then this function is demanded by Natural Law, and implies a *right* to command and govern.

Furthermore, if said function, which in direct democracy is exercised by the "multitude" or the people themselves, can be properly exercised, in larger and more differentiated societies, only on the condition that the people entrust it to certain men who will be henceforth especially concerned with the affairs of the whole, then

---

* *Man and the State* (Chicago: University of Chicago Press, 1951), pp. 126–139.

[1] *Scholasticism and Politics* (New York: Macmillan, 1940), Chapter 4. Corresponding French text in *Principes d'une politique humaniste*, Chapter 2.

those men, once put in charge of the direction of the community, have a *right* (received from and through the people) to be obeyed for the sake of the common good: in other words, the relation of authority among men proceeds from Natural Law. I mean here the relation of authority taken as yet indeterminately, and not in the sense that *some* particular men must command and *some* particular men must obey; but rather in the general sense that there must be people who command and people who obey, the mode of designation of those who shall command being a different matter to be determined subsequently and in accordance with reason.[2]

Finally, since authority means right, it has to be obeyed by force of conscience, that is, in the manner in which free men obey, and for the sake of the common good.[3]

But by the same token there is no authority where there is no justice. Unjust authority is not authority, as an unjust law is not law. At the origin of the democratic sense, there is not the desire to "obey only oneself," as Rousseau put it, but rather the desire to obey only *because it is just.*

Whatever the regime of political life may be, authority, that is, the right to direct and to command, derives from the people, but has its primary source in the Author of nature. Authority derives from the will or *consensus* of the people, and from their basic right to govern themselves, as from a channel through which nature causes a body politic to be and to act.

These two statements, expressed as they are in the most general and still undetermined way, have been a matter of common agreement for a century-old tradition in political philosophy. But they have been understood in quite different and sharply opposed manners.

A first issue, dealing with the relationship between the people

---

[2] Cf. Suarez, *De legibus,* Lib. III, c. 4, n. 5: "Unde potestas regia formaliter ut talis est de jure humano."

[3] For a thorough discussion of the matter see Yves Simon, *Nature and Functions of Authority* (Milwaukee: Marquette University Press, 1940); and *Philosophy of Democratic Government* (Chicago: University of Chicago Press, 1951). Professor Yves Simon has rightly stressed the fact that the basic problem of authority (as a right of the people as a whole) comes prior to the problem of the necessity for having authority entrusted to a distinct governing personnel.

and God, has been: do the people receive from God the right to self-government and authority to rule themselves in a merely *transient and transitory* way, so that when they designate their rulers they act only as an *instrumental cause* [4] through which God alone (as principal agent) invests with authority the man or men designated?

Or do the people receive from God the right to self-government and authority to rule themselves in an *inherent* manner, so that they are possessed of this right and this authority as a "principal agent" (though "secondary" or subordinate with respect to the Primary Cause) which through its own causal power—acting, as everything acts, in virtue of God's universal activation—invests with authority the man or men designated? [5] It is this second alternative which has proved to be the true principle.

And a second issue, dealing with the relationship between the people and their rulers, has been: do the people, when they invest certain men with authority, *divest themselves* of their right to self-government and their authority to rule themselves (whatever the way may be—transient or inherent—in which they have received these rights from God)? So that once the ruler or rulers have been put in charge, the people *lose* their right to self-government and their authority to rule themselves, which have been transferred to the ruler or rulers and are henceforth possessed by them alone?

Or do the people, when they invest certain men with authority, *keep* their right to self-government and their authority to rule themselves, so that they possess these rights, not only *inherently* with respect to the manner in which they receive them from God, but also *permanently* with respect to the manner in which they convey them to their rulers?

In modern history, the age of the absolute kings, as we have seen in discussing Sovereignty,[6] has answered affirmatively the first part

---

[4] Instrumental, not with respect to the choice or designation made, but with respect to the transmission of authority.

[5] Thus, this authority comes from God as Primary Source and Primary Cause, even comes from Him "immediately," in the sense that human nature, naturally demanding what is necessarily implied in social life, immediately proceeds from God. Cf. Josephus Gredt, O.S.B., *Elementa philosophiae Aristotelico-Thomisticae* (St. Louis: Herder, 1946), t. II, n. 1029, 4: "Auctoritas politica immediate est a Deo seu a lege aeterna, quatenus immediate a Deo est humana natura naturaliter ad societatem ordinata."

[6] Cf. *Man and the State*, Chapter 2.

of this alternative, negatively the second. Yet the right answer is *no* to the first part of the alternative, and *yes* to the second. The realization of this basic verity (long ago pointed out by some great Schoolmen) has been an achievement of democratic philosophy. In this connection, whatever the political regime may be, monarchical, aristocratic, or democratic, democratic philosophy appears as the only true political philosophy.

The trouble has been that from the very moment when it gained the upper hand, this philosophy was imperiled by a counterfeit ideology, the ideology of Sovereignty. Instead of getting clear of the concept of Sovereignty (which implies *transcendent* or *separate* supreme power, supreme power *from above*), Rousseau transferred to the people the Sovereignty of the absolute monarch conceived in the most absolute manner; in other terms he made a mythical people—the people as the monadic subject of the indivisible General Will—into a sovereign Person separated from the real people (the multitude) and ruling them from above. As a result, since a figment of the imagination cannot really rule, it is to the State— to the State which, in genuine democratic philosophy, should be supervised and controlled by the people—that, as a matter of fact, Sovereignty, indivisible and irresponsible Sovereignty, was to be transferred. On the other hand, Sovereignty cannot be shared; consequently, the people, or the Sovereign Person, could not invest any official with authority over them; only the people as a whole could make laws, and the men elected by them did not hold any real authority, or right to command. The elected of the people were only passive instruments, not representatives. As a matter of principle, the very concept of "representative of the people" was to be wiped away.

This concept, however, is absolutely essential to genuine democratic philosophy. It is on the notion of representation or vicariousness, by virtue of which the very right of the people to rule themselves is exercised by the officials whom the people have chosen, that all the theory of power in democratic society rests. As I shall emphasize further, the representatives of the people are "sent," missioned or commissioned, by the people to exercise authority because they are made by the people participants, to some given extent, in the very authority of the people, in other words because they are made by the people *images* of and *deputies* for the people.

Those who represent the people are not the image of God. The Pope in the Church, being the vicar of Christ, is the image of Christ. The Prince in political society, being the vicar of the people, is the image of the people. A great deal of confusion occurred in this regard in the age of absolutism, because the authority of the king was often conceived on the pattern of the authority of the Pope, that is to say, as coming down from above, whereas in reality it came up from below. For another reason a great deal of confusion had previously occurred in the Middle Ages: because the solemn anointing or coronation of the king, by sanctioning from the sacred heights of the supernatural order his right to command in the natural order, conveyed to him, as servant or secular arm of the Church, a reflection of the supernatural royal virtues, bounty, justice, and the paternal love of Christ, Head of the Church. From this point of view the Middle Ages might regard the king as the image of Christ.[7] But in the natural order, which is the order of political life, he was not the image of Christ, he was the image of the people. Theologians, especially in the Thomist lineage, were able clearly to make that distinction. But medieval common consciousness remained enmeshed in an ambivalent idea of the Prince.

The civil power bears the impress of majesty. This is not because it represents God. It is because it represents the people, the whole multitude and its common will to live together. And by the same token, since it represents the people, the civil power holds its authority, through the people, from the Primary Cause of Nature and of human society.[8] St. Paul teaches that "there is no authority that is not from God" and that those who bear the sword are "God's ministers" or "functionaries of God," "appointed by God" (let us understand, through the people) "to inflict his wrathful vengeance upon him that doth wrong." [9] Never did he teach that they were the image of God. What essentially constituted, in its own

---

[7] Cf. this passage from Bracton's *De rerum divisione,* quoted by Richard O'Sullivan in his Introduction to *Under God and the Law*: Papers Read to the Thomas More Society of London, Second Series (Oxford: Blackwell, 1949): The king "ought to be under the law since he is God's vicar, as evidently appears after the likeness of Jesus Christ whose representative he is on earth" (*cujus vices gerit in terris*).

[8] And in a sense—a theologian would add—from Christ's universal kingship. But this no more makes him a representative of Christ than an image of God.

[9] Rom. 13, 1–7.

temporal or political order, the majesty of the king is the same as that which constitutes the majesty of the president of a democratic nation, especially when he is invested with such constitutional powers as those in this country. For the president, just as the king, can be a quite ordinary man deprived of any personal prestige; yet look at him when he acts in his capacity of supreme chief of the body politic: millions of citizens, with their collective power, their hopes, their trust, their century-old heritage of suffering and glory, their prospective collective destiny, their collective vocation in mankind's history, are there, in his person, as in a sign which makes them present to our eyes. Here is majesty, here is the essence of his political majesty. Not because he is a Sovereign! since in the political domain there is no such thing as sovereignty. But because he is the image of the people, and the topmost deputy of the people. And behind this majesty, as its first foundation, there is the eternal Law of the primary cause of being, source of the authority which is in the people and in which the vicar of the people participates. And if the man is righteous and faithful to his mission, there is reason to believe that, when the common good of the people is at stake, and when he acts in communion with the people, he may somehow receive, in whatever obscure or even tortuous way, some particular inspiration ("grâce d'état," aid called for by one's vocational duty) from the One who is the Supreme Governor of human history.

The majesty of which I am speaking exists also (in the European parliamentary regimes it exists mainly) in the assemblies composed of the representatives of the people, insofar as they are a collective image of the people and a collective deputy for the people. (They should be conscious of that; when they themselves lose the sense of their inherent majesty, and behave like a throng of irresponsible schoolboys or clan fighters at feud, this is a bad sign for democracy.) And in each one of these representatives separately taken, as deputy for a section of the people, part of that very majesty, broken so to speak into pieces, still really exists.

Thus, in a democratic regime, the fundamental truth, recognized by democratic philosophy, that authority in the rulers derives from the right to rule themselves inherent in the people and permanent in them, is given a particular and particularly appropriate expression in the typical structural law of the body politic. Then authority deriving from the people rises from the base to the summit of the structure of the body politic. Power is exercised by men in whom authority, within certain fixed limits, is brought periodically to reside through the designation of the people, and whose management is controlled by the people: and this very fact is a sign of the continued possession, by the people, of that right to govern themselves, the exercise of which has entitled the men in question to be in command—in political command—of other men, in virtue of the primary Source of all authority. I mean that the supremely just establishment of Uncreated Reason, which gives force of law, or of a just ordinance, to what is necessary for the very existence and common good of nature and society, causes the governing function of those men chosen by the people to be held *by right,* and, by the same token, obedience to them within the limits of their powers to be *required in justice.*

To understand these things correctly, we need, it seems to me, to sharpen the philosophical concepts traditionally used in this matter. In other words, I think that in order to bring to its full significance the political theory of Thomas Aquinas, which has been developed in so valuable a manner by Cajetan,[10] Bellarmine [11] and Suarez [12] in the sixteenth and early seventeenth centuries, we have still to add certain further clarifications, the principle of which is to be found in the very notion of *vicariousness,* as used by St. Thomas himself with respect to the Prince "vicar of the multitude,"[13] and

---

[10] Cf. Cajetan, *Com. on Sum. Theol.,* I–II, 90, 3; *De comparatione auctoritatis papae et concilii* (Romae: Apud Institutum Angelicum, 1936), c. 1, 12; c. 11, 190; c. 24, 359; c. 27, 415; *Apologia ejusdem tractatus* (in the same volume), c. 1, 449–50; c. 8, 533; c. 9, 550, 557–64, 572, 590; c. 16, 801.

[11] Cf. Bellarmine, *Controversiarum de membris Ecclesiae liber tertius, De laicis sive secularibus,* c. 6; *Opera omnia* (Paris: Vives, 1870), III, 10–12. English translation by Kathleen E. Murphy, *De Laicis or the Treatise on Civil Government* (New York: Fordham University Press, 1928).

[12] Cf. Suarez, *Defensio fidei catholicae et apostolicae adversus anglicanae sectae errores,* Lib. III: *De summi pontificis supra temporales reges excellentia, et potestate,* c. 2; *Opera* (Venetiis, 1749), fols. 114 ff.; *De legibus,* Lib. III, c. 4.

[13] "Vicem gerens multitudinis" (*Sum. Theol.* I–II, 90, 3).

elaborated by him in quite another field, namely, the theory of the
sign as "vicar" of the thing signified.[14]

Then two main points of doctrine, to which our preceding remarks have already alluded, would be clearly brought out. The first
relates to the fact that in investing rulers with authority the people
in no way lose possession of their basic right to self-government.
The second relates to the fact that the representatives of the people
are not mere instruments, but rulers invested with real authority,
or right to command.

When I possess a material good, I cannot give it to another without losing by the very fact my possession of it. Conceiving things in
that way has been the trouble with the classical theories of political
power, especially, as we have seen, with the misleading theory of
Sovereignty.[15] But when it is a question of a moral or spiritual quality, such as a right is, I can invest another man with a right of mine
without myself losing possession of it, if this man receives this right
in a vicarious manner—as a vicar of myself. Then he is made into
an image of myself, and it is in this capacity that he participates in
the very same right which is mine by essence. (Similarly, the disciple *as such* participates in the very same science which is in his
teacher, and if he teaches in his turn—I mean in his mere capacity
as a disciple, conveying the science of another—he will teach as a
vicar, or an image of his teacher, and as a deputy for him—and for
all that, his teacher will not have divested himself of any bit of his
own science.) The people are possessed of their right to govern
themselves in an inherent and permanent manner. And the rulers,
because they have been made into the vicars of the people, or into
an image of them, are invested *per participationem*—to the extent
of their powers—with the *very same* right and authority to govern
which exists in the people *per essentiam,* as given them by the
Author of nature and grounded upon His transcendent, uncreated
authority. The people, by designating their representatives, do not

---

[14] Cf. our chapter "Sign and Symbol," in *Ransoming the Time* (New
York: Scribners, 1941).

[15] I am afraid such a concept remains in the background of some
current scholastic views, which would finally reduce the democratic process to a
moment of free choice, by the people, of their masters (just as Rousseau fancied
that the representative system acted, when he condemned it). Cf. Gredt, *op. cit.,*
t. II, nn. 1032, 1033.

lose or give up possession of their own authority to govern themselves and of their right to supreme autonomy.

Now there is a distinction between the possession of a right and the exercise of it. It is the very exercise of the people's right to self-government which causes the rulers chosen by the people to be invested with authority, according to the duration of the office, and to the measure and the degree of their attributions: the very exercise of the right of the people to self-government restricts, therefore, to that extent, not this right itself, but the further exercise of it (in other words, the "power" of the people)—since the right of the people to self-government cannot be exercised in actual fact (except in the smallest groups or in the particular case of popular referendum) without placing certain men in public service, and, by the same token, having them invested with genuine authority. There is no lack of similar examples, where the very exercise of a right (for instance the right to choose one's vocation or state of life) restricts further exercise without causing to end, or lessening in any way, the possession of that right itself.

Thus we come to the second point. The representatives of the people are possessed of authority in a vicarious manner, in their capacity as vicars or image of the people, and deputies for them. But they are a living and active, not a dead image of the people, an image which is a human person, endowed with reason, free will, and responsibility. And they cannot exercise the vicarious authority of which they are possessed if not as human persons and free agents, whose personal conscience is committed in the performance of their mission. So the authority they exercise, which is the very same authority of the people participated in to some given extent and within certain given limits, is a vicarious but a genuine authority, held, like the people's authority, in virtue of the primary Source of all authority;[16] they really hold a right to command and to be

---

[16] The thesis that we propose opposes the so-called *designation* theory insofar as the latter makes the people's right to self-government only transient and transitory, but preserves nevertheless, I think, what there is of truth in this theory. According to our thesis, we must say, strictly speaking, not only that God is the prime source, but that He is the unique and immediate source of authority. For the people do not give those who are chosen or designated by them an authority whose source and origin were, even in a secondary manner, the people themselves. The people make these men participate, to a given extent, in the very authority

obeyed. They are not mere instruments of a mythical general will; they are actual rulers of the people; they have to make their decisions conform to the dictates of their conscience, to the laws of that specific branch of Ethics which is political Ethics, to the judgment of their virtue (if they have any) of political prudence, and to what they see required by the common good—even if by so doing they incur the displeasure of the people.

The fact remains that they are accountable to the people, and that their management has to be supervised and controlled by the people. The fact also remains that, since their authority is but the authority of the people vicariously participated in, they have to rule, not as *separated* from the people (except as regards the existential conditions for exercising authority), but as *united* with the people in their very essence of deputies for them. Here is a difficult question which I should like to try to make clear. I just said that the representatives of the people must be ready to incur the displeasure of the people, if their conscience demands it. Now I am saying that they must carry out their obligations in communion with the people. Are these two statements contradictory? They are not, on the condition that this expression "in communion with the people" be correctly understood.

In what can be called the common psyche of the people there is a huge variety of levels and degrees. At the most superficial level there are the momentary trends of opinions, as transient as the waves on the sea, and subjected to all winds of anxiety, fear, particular passions, or particular interests. At deeper levels, there are the real needs of the multitude. At the deepest level, there is the will to live together, and the obscure consciousness of a common destiny and vocation, and finally the natural trend of the human will, considered in its essence, toward the good. Furthermore—this is a point

---

which is one with the people's right to self-government. Precisely because the people do not divest themselves of this right, and because the authority of the rulers is not a right different from, and superadded to, that of the people, this authority of the rulers is not an authority that the people cause to be. The people do not give a power which they possessed and which they lose. They make somebody participate in an authority they hold. If one says that they confer authority on their rulers, it is only in this sense that they make them participants in the very authority which resides in the people and which has God for its unique and immediate source. God is the immediate foundation of the authority of the rulers, because their authority is but the very authority of the people, immediately received from God, and in which the rulers participate.

which is often neglected—people are ordinarily distracted from their most capital aspirations and interests, as a people, by each one's everyday business and suffering. Under such circumstances, to rule in communion with the people means, on the one hand, educating and awakening the people in the very process of governing them, so as to demand of them, at each progressive step, what they themselves have been made aware of and eager for (I am thinking of a real work of education, grounded on respect for them and trust in them, and in which they are the "principal agent" [17]— just the contrary to selling them ideas through sheer propaganda and advertising techniques). It means, on the other hand, being intent on what is deep and lasting, and most really worthy of man, in the aspirations and psyche of the people. Thus it is that in incurring the disfavor of the people a ruler can still act in communion with the people, in the truest sense of this expression. And if he is a great ruler, he will perhaps convert that disfavor into a renewed and more profound trust. In any case, there is nothing in common between despotically imposing one's own will on the people—as a ruler from above separated from them—and resisting the people, or becoming hated and rejected by them, while being united with them in one's inmost intentions, and heedful of keeping communion with their deepest human will, to which they shut their eyes.

If this question is intricate, it is because no relation is more complex and mysterious than the relation between a man and the multitude for whose common good he is responsible, precisely because the authority he possesses is a vicarious authority, ultimately grounded in God, which he exercises as a free and responsible agent, image of the multitude and deputy for it. If we are looking for the most significant—though too transcendent for our purpose —type of a legislator, let us think of Moses and his relation with the Jewish people. But the rulers of our political societies are not prophets directly commissioned by God, and this makes their case a little more simple.

At this point, it would perhaps be appropriate to use the distinction, which I have emphasized in another essay, between a *law* and a *decree*. "Law and decree belong to two specifically distinct spheres: law, to the sphere of the *structural forms* of authority;

---

[17] Cf. our book, *Education at the Crossroads* (New Haven: Yale University Press, 1943), pp. 29–31.

decree, to the sphere of the *existential exercise* of authority. . . . A law is a general and lasting rule (general, that is to say, which determines in the social body a certain *functional relation;* lasting, that is to say, which is directed to something beyond the present moment or circumstance, and *calculated not to change*). A decree is a particular ordinance, determining a *point of fact* in the framework of the law, and confronted with a given circumstance for a given time." [18] Then I would say that a decree can without too much drawback be promulgated contrary to the trends prevalent at the moment in the people, and forced upon a reluctant public opinion. But a law should normally be laid down (always provided that it be just) in accordance with the common consciousness of the people as expressed in the mores or in collective needs and requests of organic groups of the population, or in spontaneous social and public service regulations in the making. Here could be saved the element of truth in Duguit's theory, unacceptable in itself, of "objective law." Contrary to this theory, the law is and will always remain a work of the reason of those who are in charge of the common good: but this same reason of the Legislator has to give shape to, or to express in a formed "word," an achieved *verbum,* what exists in the common mind in an inchoate, unformulated manner.

---

[18] *Principes d'une politique humaniste,* Annexe to Chapter 2, "Pouvoir législatif et pouvoir exécutif."

10 SOLITUDE AND THE COMMUNITY*

"I HAVE DEEP AFFECTION FOR THE 'LONELY WALKER' IN him; I hate the theorist." This saying of C.-F. Ramuz [1] explains the attraction of Jean-Jacques for many noble souls, and the echo he will always find, even when they hate him, in those who, exempt from his psychopathy, are yet his brothers in lyricism, "sensitive workers" like himself. Why that sympathy? Because of the dreams, tears, transports, sentimental tinsel *à la* Diderot? Nonsense! I am speaking of true lyrics. Because of the wild genius in a true intimate of the woods? Because of the fresh unfolding of a song genuinely springing from the depths of solitude, the purity of a rhythm attuned without artifice to the movements of the soul, a rhythm which is the only thing truly innocent in him? Even that is secondary. The true reason is, as Ramuz again said, that before being an anti-social theorist Rousseau was born non-social, and that he has told incomparably the condition of a soul so made.

Men naturally respect anchorites. They instinctively understand that the solitary life is of itself the most exempt from diminution and the nearest to divine things. Does not the tragic flight of old Tolstoy on the eve of his death come primarily from that instinct? And so many goings forth, so many wanderings! *Quoties inter homines fui, minor homo redii.* In differing degrees, philosophers, poets, or contemplatives, those whose chief work is intellectual,

---

* *Trois réformateurs* (Nouvelle édition. Paris: Librairie Plon, 1930 [1st edition, 1925]), pp. 170–200.
[1] Frédéric Lefèvre, Interview with C.-F. Ramuz (*Une heure avec . . .*, 2e Série, Paris, 1924).

know too well that in man social life is not the heroic life of the spirit, but the realm of mediocrity, and most often of falsehood. There is the burden of the contingent and the sham, from which poets and artists, being less free from the sensible, suffer the most sensitively, but not perhaps the most cruelly. Yet all need to live the social life, so far as the very life of the spirit must emerge from a human life, a rational life in the strict sense of the word.

The solitary life is not human; it is above or below man. "There is for man a double manner of living solitary. Either he so lives because he cannot endure human society, by reason of the brutality of his temperament, *propter animi saevitiam,* and that belongs to beasts. Or else it is because he cleaves wholly to divine things, and that is of the superhuman order. He who has no dealings with others, said Aristotle, is either a beast or a god." [2] Extremes meet! Beast and god, the restless being who is but a fragment of the world, and the perfect being who is a universe unto himself, live an analogous life, whilst man is between the two, at once individual and person. As for Rousseau, paranoiac and genius, poet and madman, he leads at the same time and confuses voluptuously the life of bestiality and the life of intelligence. In this man, forced into solitary life by his physical blemishes, the unadaptability which rebels and complains, apes the unadaptability which dominates, i.e., that of the spirit, *set apart to govern,* as Anaxagoras said of the *nous.* He gives us in his very savagery, in his sickly isolation, a lyrical image, as dazzling as it is deceptive, of the secret demands of the spirit in us.

But let us not forget the theorist. Making his personal misfortune the rule of the species, he will hold the solitary life to be the life natural to the human being. "The breath of man is fatal to his fellow beings; that is no less true strictly than figuratively," he declares.[3] Consequently, the essential inclinations of human nature, and therefore the primordial conditions of moral health, require this blessed state of solitude which he pictures, projecting his own phantoms, as the perpetual flight of animals through the woods, dreamy animals endowed with compassion, mating by chance meetings, and then going on with their innocent wandering. Such is the divine life in his eyes.

---

[2] St. Thomas, *Sum. Theol.,* II–II, 188, 8, ad 5.
[3] *Émile,* Book I.

Thus the decline is immediate. The *supra hominem* has at once turned into the bestial, not without giving it something of a heavenly perfume. The conflict between the social life and the life of the spirit has become a conflict between the social life and savagery—and at the same time a conflict between the social life and human nature. By one stroke it has become an essential opposition, a harsh antinomy, absolutely insoluble.

But what does Christian wisdom say? It knows well that the life of the intellect leads to solitude, and that the more highly spiritual it is, the more apart is its solitude. But it knows also that this life is a superhuman life—relatively so, with respect to the workings of rational speculation; purely and simply so, with respect to the workings of contemplation in charity. That is the supreme end to be reached, the ultimate perfection, the last point of the soul's growth. And for man to arrive at it, his progress must be in a human environment. How would he go to the superhuman without going through the human? "We must consider that the state of a solitary is that of a being who should be self-sufficient; in other words, one who lacks nothing; and that pertains to the definition of one who is perfect. Solitude, therefore, only befits the contemplative who has already come to perfection, either by the divine bounty alone, like John the Baptist, or by the exercise of the virtues. And man could not be exercised in the virtues without the help of the society of his fellow beings—with respect to the intelligence, to be taught; with respect to the heart, that harmful affections be repressed by the example and correction of others. Whence it follows that social life is necessary to the exercise of perfection, and that solitude befits souls already perfect." [4] That is doubtless why, in very early times, people ran to the desert to drag out hermits in order to make them their bishops. Finally, St. Thomas concludes, "the life of solitaries, if it be adopted rightly, is higher than social life; but if it be adopted without previous exercise of that life, it is most perilous, unless, as with the blessed Anthony and Benedict, divine grace supplies what in others is acquired by exercise."

Thus, solitude is the flower of life in community. Thus, social life remains the life natural to man, required by his deepest specific needs. Its conventions and vanities, the tortures and the diminution

---

[4] St. Thomas, *Sum. Theol.*, II–II, 188, 8.

it occasions for the intellectual life, all the "pleasantry" which so struck Pascal, remain accidental defects, which only betray the radical weakness of human nature—the price, sometimes terrible to pay, of an essential advantage. It is social life which leads to the life of the spirit. But by that very ordination, just as the movement of reason is ordered to the simple act of contemplation, so the social life itself is ordered to the solitary life, to the imperfect solitude of the intellectual, to the perfect, at least within, solitude of the saint.[5]

Hence harmony instead of an irreducible antinomy. The conflict is not suppressed (for that you would need to suppress man): it is surmounted. Theoretically it is overcome perfectly; actually it is more or less overcome, according to our own state. The suffering remains, the contradiction vanishes. Where is this seen better than where the harmony of the social and the spiritual is most purely realized, in that state of life specially established for the human conquest of perfection? In the religious state, the very defects of social life work together for the good of the spirit. How is that? By the virtue of obedience, and of a limitless sacrifice. Mistakes of government in superiors, mediocrity in environment, everything that man is capable of and that a calced Carmelite can make a discalced Carmelite suffer, what do these accidents do but hasten the mystical death of a heart vowed to immolation? They throw it deeper into the divine life. So true is it that man has made peace with himself only on the Cross of Jesus.

Not in this way does Jean-Jacques undertake to resolve (for he fears nothing) the opposition which he himself has made absolute and insoluble.

It is a flagrant absurdity, and at the same time an act of cowardly

---

[5] The life of reason as such, a life specifically human and postulating things perceptible by the senses, in itself requires social life; but insofar as the speculative virtues make the activity of reason a participation in the purely mental or spiritual life, in that degree it rises above social life. That is why the philosopher and the artist, because they have an activity which is essentially rational (practical in the one, theoretical in the other), are essentially involved in social life, and yet, by what is most pure and valuable in them, they surpass it and are urged to be free of it. The solitary life thus remains imperfect and virtual in them, they tend towards it, they have a foretaste of it, they snatch what they can of it from the jealousy of nature, it is not their proper climate.

The contemplative alone, leading a life essentially above reason, can perfectly lead the solitary life (yet not without holding on to social and rational life, though as a condition prerequisite to his contemplation, or demanded by holy obligations—*praedicatio ex superabundantia contemplationis*).

deceit, to treat men as if they were perfect; and to treat the perfection which has to be acquired, and from which most of them will remain far removed, as a constituent of nature itself. Yet such is Rousseau's principle, his perpetual postulate. This method of his is an astonishing system of vacuum cleaning, quite typical of his debility, and consists in passing at a leap to the conditions of absolute perfection or of pure act. The geometrician refines the idea of stick or disc in order to define the circle or the straight line. But Rousseau refines the human being of all potentiality, so that he may contemplate the ideal world, alone worthy of his thought, which will allow him piously to condemn the injustice of the existing world. He begins by deliberately placing himself in the unrealizable, so that he may breathe and utter himself as God utters Himself in creation. He dreams, and he tells his dream; and if reality in no way corresponds to it, he cannot help it; it is reality that is wrong. "Only what is not, is beautiful," [6] he delighted to repeat, in a formula which is metaphysically hateful. In 1765, at Strasbourg, a M. Angar procured an introduction to him in order to say to him: "You see, sir, a man who brings up his son according to the principles which he had the happiness to learn from your *Émile*." "So much the worse, sir," he replied, "so much the worse for you and your son!" [7] No, no, he knows better than we—it was his distinct intention—that all his ideology is only a romantic piece of mechanism, an idle dream.

Rousseau begins, then, by assuming that men are humanly perfect. Then solutions come of themselves. And sublime ideas flow. Are you at a loss for the best form of government? It is that designed for the perfect: *"regimen perfectorum, ergo regimen perfectum,"* [8] a heavenly Democracy. Are you looking for a sound method of education? It is the one which requires: 1. princely conditions of wealth and isolation; 2. a single tutor for a single pupil;

---

[6] One of the phrases he most constantly repeated, in speech and writing, is this: "Nothing is beautiful but that which is not." (D'Escherny, *Éloge de J.-J. Rousseau*, at the start of *l'Égalité*, 1796, 1, p. lxxvii.) Pierre-Maurice Masson, *La religion de Rousseau*, II, 260.

[7] Cf. E. Seillière, *Jean-Jacques Rousseau* (Paris: Garnier, 1921), p. 132.

[8] The sophism consists in stating that the perfect government is by definition the government of perfect subjects. On the contrary, government as such is the more perfect the more it succeeds in ordering very imperfect subjects to the common good.

3. an ideal tutor and a pupil good by essence—the hypocritical negative education in which Nature (conveniently faked as needed) alone acts; a method of education in which all is perfect.

As for the social state, it must be built of individuals each of whom is self-sufficient—and who have not, so far, succeeded in uniting without sinking. "The wicked man lives alone." Diderot might hurl this treacherous bolt at him in vain. Jean-Jacques will suffer as an innocent victim, but will hold fast to his axiom: man would be good if he were alone. But if our nature, corrupted by the discovery of civilized life, has to be mended by the help of some more sublime discovery, he, Jean-Jacques, has the secret of the perfect city, built, in his mind, of the perfect, a city which, in the very midst of social life itself, will restore man in a new way to the privileges of the state of solitude.

And at this point there rises before us the rich ideological forest of *The Social Contract*. Let us enumerate here, and try to express in a short formula which will give an idea of their essential spirit, the chief myths which the modern world owes to this famous work.

I. NATURE. In his limpid and subtle Treatise on Law, St. Thomas explains that the term "natural law" can be taken in two quite different senses. A thing can be said to be "of natural law" either because nature inclines towards it (for example, that one should not harm others), or only because nature does not at once assert the contrary disposition. "In this latter sense it might be said that to be naked is *de jure naturali* for man, because it is art, not nature, which provides him with clothes. It is in this sense that we should understand St. Isidore when he says that the state of common possession and of one and the same liberty for all is of natural law; in fact, the distinction of property and submission to a master are not things provided by nature, but introduced by man's reason as useful to human life." [9]

In other words, the word "nature" can be taken in the metaphysical sense of essence involving a certain finality. In this case, that is natural which answers the requirements and propensities of the essence, that to which things are ordered by reason of their specific type and, finally, by the Author of being. And it can be taken in the material sense of an actual primitive state. In this case,

---

[9] *Sum. Theol.*, I–II, 94, 5, ad 3.

that is natural which actually existed before any development due to intelligence.

The weakening of the metaphysical spirit was gradually to obscure the first sense of the word nature. In the radically nominalist and empiricist theory of Hobbes, followed in this regard by Spinoza, the second sense alone remains and, badly stated, leads the philosopher to logical errors. According to Hobbes, the absolute isolation of individuals is "natural"; so is the struggle of every man against all men, which he imagines as the primitive state of humanity. And with the rational mystic's peculiar pessimism, Spinoza declares: "The natural right of each stretches as far as his power. Whoever is deemed to live under the sway of nature alone has absolute right to covet whatever he considers useful, whether he be led to this desire by sound reason or by the violence of the passions. He has the right to seize it in any way, whether by force, by cunning, by entreaty, by whatever means he considers easiest, and consequently to regard as an enemy anyone who would hinder the satisfaction of his desires." [10] Nothing could be clearer.

What does Jean-Jacques do? Because he is of a religious temperament, and also because what good sense he has is solidly traditionalist, he returns to the notion of nature in the first sense of the word, to the notion of a nature ordered to an end by the wisdom of a good God. But because he is powerless to realize this notion intellectually, and to restore to it its metaphysical value and import, he insinuates it into the picture of a certain primitive, and, I may say, pre-cultural state, which exactly corresponds to the second sense of the word nature. He muddles up these two different senses, he locks into a single equivocal pseudo-concept the "nature" of the metaphysicians and the "nature" of the empiricists. Whence the Rousseauist myth of nature, which needs only to be clearly expressed for its absurdity to be seen: Nature is the primitive condition of things, at which they should stop, or which they should restore, in order to comply with their essence. Or again: Nature is the essential need, divinely placed in things, of a certain primitive condition or pre-culture which things are made to realize.

From this myth of nature, the dogma of Natural Goodness will logically arise. All that is necessary is the discovery that nature in

---

[10] *Tractatus theologico-politicus,* cap. XVI.

the sense of the metaphysicians, the immutable essence of things, and particularly the human essence, along with its faculties and specific propensities, is good. The conclusion will follow that the primitive state and the primitive conditions of human life, the state before culture and before the institutions of reason (whether it be pictured as formerly realized in history, or be conceived only as an abstraction), was necessarily good, innocent and happy; and that a state of goodness, a stable condition of innocence and happiness, is due to humanity.

Rousseau's discovery of the dogma of natural goodness dates from the writing of his *Discours,* after the revelation of the Bois de Vincennes and the coat wet with tears. In *The Social Contract,* which he wrote later, but as a sequel to his old Venetian pages, this dogma is not formulated, it is even sometimes contradicted. Yet the myth of nature, which contains the seeds of it, is certainly there. We realize this when we remark that it is the myth of nature that engenders the myth of Liberty, absolutely essential to *The Social Contract.*

II. LIBERTY. "Man is born free." (A savage in the woods.) Otherwise stated, the state of liberty or sovereign independence is the primitive state, and its maintenance or restoration is required by man's essence and the divine order.

Henceforward no kind of submission to a master or rule over a subject is allowable. The condition which, according to theologians, prevailed in the earthly paradise, in which all were of free estate (that is, where none worked in the service of another and for the proper or private good of another, and thus as "something of another," because in the state of innocence there was no servile work), becomes the state demanded by human nature. Nay more! According to St. Thomas, the state of innocence would have involved that kind of rule over free men which consists in guiding them towards the common good, "because man is naturally social, and because the social life is impossible unless someone be in charge to aim at the common good—*multi enim per se intendunt ad multa, unus vero ad unum*—and because, on the other hand, if a man is eminent in justice and knowledge it is in itself normal that he serve the utility of others," [11] that is, that he govern. But Jean-Jacques, on the contrary, would have us say that this very kind of

---

[11] *Sum. Theol.,* I, 96, 4.

governing is precluded by nature. Man is born free, Liberty is an absolute demand of Nature, all subjection of any kind to the authority of any manner of man is contrary to Nature.

III. EQUALITY. An equal condition for all is likewise demanded by Nature. All of us are born equally men, and therefore equally "free," equal as to specific essence and consequently (and this is the tremendous confusion of thought peculiar to egalitarianism) equal as to the existential state whose realization for each individual is required by our essence and the divine order. There are, doubtless, so-called "natural" inequalities between individuals more or less hardy, more or less intelligent. But they are against Nature's desires, and who knows if they do not go back to some remote malformation?

Nature requires that the strictest equality should be realized among men, so that, in every political state which is not directly opposed to Nature and her Author, an absolute social equality should exactly balance natural inequalities.

This myth of Equality is supported by two strange and clumsy sophisms:

1. The confusion of equality with justice—which destroys justice. Justice [12] indeed implies a certain equality, but a geometrical or proportional equality (which treats both sides in proportion to their deserts), and not arithmetical or absolute equality (which treats both sides identically, whatever be their deserts); so that to confound justice with this second species of equality, with equality pure and simple, is just precisely to destroy justice.

2. The confusion—which makes impossible the constitution of any social body—of what concerns recompense to parts with what concerns the constitution of the whole. St. Thomas forcefully explained this against Origen, the metaphysical patriarch of egalitarianism, who claimed that God could not but create all things equal (for before being created they were all equally nothing), and that the diversity of things and the order of the world came from the sin of the creature. He says that in the order of recompense justice should be exercised, and that it demands that equal things should be rendered to equals, because this order necessarily presupposes merit. But in the order of the constitution of things, or of their first institution, these requirements of justice have not to be exercised,

---

[12] We are speaking of distributive justice (*totius ad partes*), the only kind with which we can be concerned here.

because here merits are not necessarily presupposed, but only a work to be brought into existence, a whole to be produced. "The artist places in different parts of the building stones which are by hypothesis all alike, and this without wronging justice: not that he assumes in them some pre-existent diversity, but because he is aiming at the perfection of the whole thing to be built, which could not be if the stones were not placed in the building differently and unequally. Likewise, it is without injustice, and yet without presupposing any diversity of merits, that God from the beginning established in His wisdom different and unequal creatures, that there might be perfection in the universe." [13] And likewise, assuming by hypothesis that all men are equal in worth, it is no injustice that in order to establish the body politic—and otherwise this body could not be—they should be set in different parts of it, and consequently have unequal rights, functions, and conditions.

IV. THE POLITICAL PROBLEM. The myth of Liberty and the myth of Equality led Rousseau to formulate the political problem in a way which is wholly and absurdly utopian. How make a society with individuals all perfectly "free" and "equal"? How, to use Rousseau's own expressions, harmonize men (such as Nature would have them) and laws (such as a social body requires)? How "find a form of association . . . by which each being united with all should yet obey only himself, and still be as free as before"?

It simply amounts to establishing an organic whole without its parts being subordinate to one another. That is absurd; but Jean-Jacques is happy. The more difficult the problem, the more merit he will have for devising the solution. His prophetic mission consists in condemning and anathematizing the existing unjust body politic and in showing men the only conceivable type of just body politic. Suppose it is impossible that this just body politic should exist! Let the unfortunate beings condemned to existence get out of the business as best they can; they can always "throw themselves on the ground and lament that they are men," after the example of Jean-Jacques himself when he despairs of democracy and remembers Caligula.

V. THE SOCIAL CONTRACT. It is the social contract which "gives the solution" of the "fundamental problem" just stated. The social contract is a pact concluded by the deliberate will of sover-

---

[13] *Sum. Theol.*, I, 65, 2, ad 3.

eignly free individuals whom the state of nature formerly held in isolation and who agree to pass into the state of society.

Although it derives from it by a long process of degradation which stretches from Althusius and Grotius to Rousseau, this myth of the Contract is quite different from the *consensus* which the ancients allowed to have been at the origin of human societies, and which was the expression of a natural aspiration. The Rousseauist contract has its first principle in the deliberate will of man, not in nature, and it gives birth to a product of human art, not to a work proceeding from nature; it presupposes that "the individual alone is the work of nature."

It follows from this that the first author of society is not God, the Author of the natural order, but the will of man, and that the birth of civil law is the destruction of natural law. The ancients taught that human law derives from natural law as a specification of what was left indeterminate by the latter. Rousseau teaches that after the pact natural rights no longer exist, and it will henceforth be granted that in the state of society there can be no right but from the agreement of free wills.

But the Rousseauist notion of the contract is not yet complete. It is, indeed, not just any kind of pact; it has a determinate nature, it essentially implies certain terms without which it is nothing and from which Jean-Jacques will deduce his whole system. These terms, if well understood, can all be reduced to a single one: that is, the complete alienation of each associate, with all his rights, to the whole community. What, then, becomes of liberty? And how is the "fundamental problem" solved? Ah! That is just the wonder. "As each gives himself to all, he gives himself to no one"; he is subject to the whole, but he is subject to no man, and that is the essential thing; there is no one above him. Nay more, as soon as the covenant begets the social body, each is so much absorbed in that common "I" which he has willed, that in obeying it he still obeys himself. Thus, the more we obey, not a man—God forbid—but the general will, the freer we are. A happy solution! In the state of nature we existed only as persons, in no way as parts; in the state of society we no longer exist except as parts. It is thus that pure individualism, by the very fact that it misconceives the reality proper to the social bonds added to individuals by the demand of nature, ends inevitably in pure statism as soon as it undertakes to construct a society.

VI. THE GENERAL WILL. This is the finest of Jean-Jacques' myths, the most religiously fabricated. We might call it the myth of political pantheism. The General Will (which must not be confused with the sum of individual wills) is the common "I's" own will, born of the sacrifice each has made of himself and all his rights on the altar of society.

In fact, what we have here is a kind of immanent God mysteriously evoked by the operation of the pact, of whose decrees the majority vote is only a sign, a sacred sign whose validity presupposes certain conditions—particularly, Rousseau teaches, the condition that no partial society shall exist in the whole.

Immanent social God, the common "I" which is more I than myself, in whom I lose myself in order to find myself again, and whom I serve in order to be free—that is a curious specimen of fraudulent mysticism. Note how Jean-Jacques explains that the citizen, subject to a law against which he voted, remains free, and continues to obey only himself: men do not vote, he says, to give their opinion; they vote so that, by the counting of votes, they may ascertain the general will, which each wills above all, since it is by it that he is a citizen and free. "When then the opposite opinion to my own carries the day, that proves nothing but that I was wrong, and that what I thought to be the general will was not so. If my private opinion had carried the day, I should have done differently from what I willed; and then I should not have been free." What does he offer us here but a preposterous transposition of the case of the believer who, when he prays for what he thinks fitting, yet asks and wills above all that God's Will be done? [14] The vote is conceived by him as a species of ritual petition and evocation addressed to the General Will.

VII. LAW. The myth of the General Will is central and dominant in Rousseau's political theory, like the notion of the common good in Aristotle's. The common good, as the end sought, essentially implies direction by an intelligence, and the ancients defined law as an order of reason, an order tending to the common good and promulgated by him who has charge of the community. The General Will, which animates and moves the social body, is imposed on all by its mere existence; it is enough for it to be, and it is mani-

---

[14] In the *Nouvelle Héloïse* (part III, letter 18) he cried to God: "Make all my actions conform to my constant will, which is Yours." The analogy of the formulas is curious.

fested by Numbers. Law will then be defined as the expression of the General Will, and will no longer proceed from reason, but from Numbers.

It was of the essence of law, as the ancients understood it, that it should be just. Modern law has no need to be just, and nevertheless it demands obedience. Law, as the ancients understood it, was promulgated by someone who commands; modern law alone is to command; just as Malebranche's God alone had the power of acting, so this mystical sign enthroned in the heaven of abstractions alone has authority. Below it, on earth, from the point of view of the relations between authority and submission, men are mere dust, homogeneous and absolutely amorphous.

VIII. THE SOVEREIGN PEOPLE. Law exists only so far as it expresses the General Will. But the General Will is the will of the people. "The people, who are subject to the laws, should be author of the laws," for it is thus that they obey only themselves; it is thus that we are at the same time "free and subject to the laws, since they are only the registers of our wills."

Sovereignty, then, resides essentially and absolutely in the people, in the amorphous mass of all individuals taken together; and since the state of society is not natural but artificial, it has its origin not in God but in the free will of the people themselves.[15] Any body politic not built on this foundation is not a body politic governed by laws, a legitimate body politic; it is a product of tyranny, a monster which violates the rights of human nature.

There we have the peculiar myth, the spiritual principle, of modern Democracy, absolutely opposed to Christian law which would have sovereignty derive from God as its first origin and only pass through the people in order to reside in the man or men charged with the care of the common good.

Notice that the question raised here is quite distinct from that of the forms of government. Although in themselves of unequal merit, the three classical forms of government have their place in the Christian system; and in a democratic regime sovereignty will then reside in those chosen by the multitude.[16] And likewise they

---

[15] If Rousseau sometimes repeats classical formulas which make God the source of sovereignty, he does so either illogically, or because he deifies the will of the people.

[16] May it not happen, as an extreme case, that in a very small group (say a Swiss canton) and in very special conditions, the multitude itself would

all three have their place, at least theoretically, in Rousseau's system—and are all three equally vitiated in it. "I call any State that is governed by laws a republic" (that is, any State where the laws are the expression of the General Will and where therefore the people are sovereign), "under whatever form of administration it may be. . . . Every lawful government is" consequently "republican. . . . In order to be legitimate it is not necessary that government be identified with the sovereign, but that it be the minister of the sovereign; then monarchy itself is republican." The prince does not perform acts of sovereignty but of "magistracy"; he is not the author but the minister of the Law, not a scrap of authority resides in him; authority is all in the General Will; there is no man charged with looking after the common good. The General Will suffices for that. In the Rousseauist system, this holds good for the aristocratic or monarchical regime, as well as for the democratic.

In fact, however, in Rousseau himself and in the world which he fathered, there is inextricable confusion between Democracy as myth and universal doctrine of sovereignty, and democracy as a particular form of government. It may be debated whether the democratic form of government is good or bad for a certain people and in certain conditions; but it is indisputable that the myth of Democracy as the sole legitimate sovereign, the spiritual principle of modern egalitarianism, is a gross absurdity.

IX. THE LEGISLATOR. The people always will the good, but they are not always sufficiently informed, often they are even deceived, "and it is only then that they seem to will what is bad." The General Will needs to be enlightened. The immanent God of the republic is a child God who needs to be helped, like the God of the pragmatists. The legislator is the superman who guides the General Will.

He is neither magistrate (for the magistrate administers law already made), nor sovereign (for the sovereign, who is bearer of the law, is the people); in formulating and propounding the law, he is outside and above every human order, in a void. "The legislator is in every respect a man extraordinary in the State. If he should be extraordinary by genius, he is not less so by his work.

---

look after its common good? Historical fact there sets Christian law an interesting problem. In any case, the absurdity lies in turning such a remote possibility into a *de jure* necessity imposed on every form of government.

That work founds the republic; it does not enter into its constitution; it is a peculiar and superior function which has nothing in common with the human order."

This amazingly hackneyed myth is not free of mischief. Let us listen to Rousseau and understand that what he utters is a perfectly logical consequence of his principles, and of the doctrine which will not allow that man is by nature a political animal. "He who dares to undertake to found a nation should feel that he is in a position to change human nature, so to say; to transform each individual, who by himself is a perfect and solitary whole, into part of a greater whole, from which this individual should in some way receive his life and being; to change man's constitution in order to make it stronger. . . . He must, in a word, deprive man of his own powers, to give him powers foreign to him, powers which he cannot exercise without the help of others. The more dead and annihilated these natural powers are, the greater and more lasting are those acquired, the more solid and perfect [sic] too is the foundation; so that if each citizen is nothing and can do nothing except with all the others, and if the power acquired by the whole be equal to or greater than the sum of the natural powers of all the individuals, you can say that the legislation is as perfect as it could possibly be."

Everything in this precious text should be remembered and pondered. But who, then, is this extraordinary and supra-cosmic legislator? We have not far to seek. It is Jean-Jacques himself—Jean-Jacques who, quite meaning to be the perfect Adam who completes by education and political guidance the political work he has fathered, consoles himself for having procreated children for the Foundling Hospital, by becoming Émile's tutor and the lawgiver of the Republic. But it is also the Deputy (*Constituant*), and in general every nation-planner of the revolutionary type, and it is Lenin exactly.

Such, very briefly outlined, are some of the myths of *The Social Contract*. Their "mysticism," which looks reasoned and rational, is no saner than the mysticism of sentiment and passion which we find in *Émile* and the *Nouvelle Héloïse*. It is noteworthy that the former had its chief success in France, where we have tried it to our cost, whilst the second met with extraordinary success in Germany, and there, in another sphere, it did amazing damage.

11 THE DEMOCRATIC CHARTER

A. THE PLURALIST PRINCIPLE IN DEMOCRACY *

A QUALIFIED AGREEMENT

IN AN ARTICLE PUBLISHED UNDER THE TITLE OF *The Dilemma of T. S. Eliot*,[1] Mr. Sidney Hook reaches by means of questionable theoretical arguments a practical solution which for quite different reasons seems to me to be on the right track. Even if we are in agreement—in qualified agreement—on this practical solution, there are important particulars in which we disagree. These I should like to elucidate. Since I have endeavored for many years and in many books to discuss the matters involved, I shall take the liberty of summing up my position here.

1. In the "sacral" era of the Middle Ages a great attempt was made to build the life of the earthly community and civilization on the foundation of the unity of theological faith and religious creed. This attempt succeeded for a certain number of centuries but failed in the course of time, after the Reformation and the Renaissance; and a return to the medieval "sacral"[2] pattern is in no way conceivable. In proportion as the civil community has become more perfectly distinguished from the spiritual realm of the Church—a process which was in itself but a development of the Gospel distinction between the things that are Caesar's and the things that

---

* *The Range of Reason* (New York: Scribners, 1952), pp. 165–171.
[1] *The Nation*, January 20, 1945.
[2] On the notion of "sacral" (or "consecrational") civilization, see *True Humanism*, pp. 137 ff., and *Man and the State*, pp. 157 ff. See also Charles Journet, *L'église du verbe incarné*, Paris: Desclée de Brouwer, 1941, p. 243.

are God's—civil society has come to be based on a common good
and a common task which are of an earthly, "temporal," or "secular" order, and in which citizens belonging to diverse spiritual
groups or "families" equally share. Religious division among men
is in itself a misfortune. But it is a fact that we must recognize,
whether we wish to or not.

2. In modern times an attempt was made to base the life of
civilization and the earthly community on the foundation of mere
reason—reason separated from religion and the Gospel. This attempt fostered immense hopes in the last two centuries, and rapidly faded. Pure reason appeared more incapable than faith of
insuring the spiritual unity of mankind, and the dream of a
"scientific" creed uniting men in peace, and in common convictions
about the aims and basic principles of human life and society, van-
ished in contemporary catastrophes. In proportion as the tragic
events of the last decades have given the lie to the optimistic rationalism of the eighteenth and nineteenth centuries, we have been
confronted with the fact that religion and metaphysics are an essential part of human culture, primary and indispensable incentives
in the very life of society.

3. As concerns, therefore, the revitalized democracy we are
hoping for, the only solution is of the *pluralistic* type. Men belonging to very different philosophical or religious creeds and lineages
could and should cooperate in the common task and for the
common welfare of the earthly community, provided they similarly assent to the charter and basic tenets of a society of free
men.

For a society of free men implies an essential charter and basic
tenets which are at the core of its very existence, and which it has
the duty of defending and promoting. One of the errors of individualist optimism was to believe that in a free society "truth," as to
the foundations of civil life, as well as the decisions and modes of
behavior befitting human dignity and freedom, would automatically
emerge from the conflicts of individual forces and opinions supposedly immune to any irrational trends and disintegrating pres-
sures; the error lay in conceiving of free society as a perfectly *neutral* boxing-ring in which all possible ideas about society and the
bases of social life meet and battle it out, without the Body Politic's
being concerned with the maintenance of any common conditions

and inspiration. Thus democratic society, in its concrete behavior, had no *concept* of itself, and freedom, disarmed and paralyzed, lay exposed to the undertakings of those who hated it, and who tried by all means to foster in men a vicious desire to become free from freedom.[3]

If it is to conquer totalitarian trends and to be true to its own mission, a renewed democracy will have its own concept of man and society, and its own philosophy, its own faith, enabling it to educate people for freedom and to defend itself against those who would use democratic liberties to destroy freedom and human rights. No society can live without a basic common inspiration and a basic common faith.

But the all-important point to be noted here is that this faith and inspiration, this philosophy and the concept of itself which democracy needs—all these do not belong in themselves to the order of religious creed and eternal life but to the temporal or secular order of earthly life, of culture and civilization. Even more, they are matters of *practical* rather than theoretical or dogmatic agreement: I mean that they deal with practical convictions which the human mind can try to justify—rightly or wrongly—from quite different, even conflicting philosophical outlooks; probably because they depend basically on simple, "natural" apperceptions, of which the human heart becomes capable with the progress of moral conscience. Thus it is that men possessing quite different, even opposite, metaphysical or religious outlooks, can converge, not by virtue of any identity of doctrine, but by virtue of an analogical similitude in practical principles, toward the same practical conclusions, and can share in the same practical democratic faith, provided that they similarly revere, perhaps for quite diverse reasons, truth and intelligence, human dignity, freedom, brotherly love, and the absolute value of moral good. As Mr. Hook puts it, "the underlying premises, whether theological, metaphysical, or naturalistic, from which different groups justify their common democratic beliefs and practices must not be subject to integration"—let us say to socially or politically enforced integration. "It is enough, so to speak, that human beings live in accordance with democratic laws" —and, let us add, share in the common—human, earthly, tem-

---

[3] Cf. Augusto J. Duvelli, *Libération de la liberté* (Montreal: L'Arbre, 1944).

poral—democratic faith and inspiration. "It is foolish intolerance to make only one justification of laws legal."

Here, if we want to be thorough in our thought and do not fear words, we should point out that where faith is—divine or human—there are also heretics who threaten the unity of the community, either religious or civil. In the "sacral" society the heretic was the breaker of religious unity. In a lay society of free men the heretic is the breaker of "the common democratic beliefs and practices," the totalitarian, the one who denies freedom—his neighbor's freedom—and the dignity of the human person, and the moral power of law. We do not wish him to be burned, or expelled from the city, or outlawed, or put in a concentration camp. But the democratic community should defend itself against him, by keeping him out of its leadership, through the power of a strong and informed public opinion, and even by handing him over to justice when his activity endangers the security of the state—and over and above all by strengthening everywhere a philosophy of life, intellectual convictions, and constructive work which would make his influence powerless.

On the other hand, a serious task of intellectual re-examination should be undertaken regarding the essentials of democratic philosophy. And it would be especially desirable to develop the understanding of the pluralistic principle and the techniques of pluralistic cooperation. It seems to me that the free traditions and the historical set-up of this country would provide special opportunities for such a development.

POINTS OF DISAGREEMENT

4. Now what about certain statements offered to us by Sidney Hook in connection with the preceding considerations, and which he seems to regard as self-evident? Are we ready to believe that in the type of society which we are discussing, the "world-wide common faith" implied would find in *scientific method* its highest source of authority? That an "intelligent social planning" would be sufficient to insure the "integration" of culture? And that, in the democratic culture of the future—if it has a future—it will be "the teacher dedicated to the scientific spirit," "and not the priest," "who will bear the chief responsibility for nurturing, strengthening, and enriching a common faith"?

Here are the main points on which I should like to express disagreement with Mr. Sidney Hook's views. I am afraid he has been inspired in these passages by that rationalistic bias whose illusory character I pointed out above.

The very expression "common faith" which Mr. Hook uses should make us realize that democratic inspiration cannot find in "scientific method" its highest source of authority. This "faith" is "of a secular not supernatural character"; yet even a secular faith implies the commitment of the whole man and his innermost spiritual energies, and draws its strength, therefore, from beliefs which go far beyond scientific method, being rooted in the depths of each one's individual options and personality. In other words, *the justification of the practical conclusions which make such a "common faith," common to all, is in each one, and in the perspective peculiar to each one, an integral part of this very faith.* As for social planning, even supposedly intelligent, it is hard to imagine a *culture* organized and unified by social planning alone. Planned and plain as it might be, such a cultural paradise would offer, I am afraid, little chance for the creative powers of human personality as well as for the enthusiasm and happiness of the people.

The scientific spirit is of invaluable help for culture insofar as it develops in human minds, in a general way, respect and love for truth and the habits of intellectual accuracy. (This is why, let us observe parenthetically, the scientific spirit of the thirteenth-century Schoolmen played so basic a part in the rise of Western culture.) Yet neither culture nor democracy lives on science alone. Science, especially modern science, deals with the means, especially with the material means, of human life. Wisdom, which deals with the ends, is also—and above all—necessary. And the fact remains that democratic faith—implying as it does faith in justice, in freedom, in brotherly love, in the dignity of the human person, in his rights as well as in his responsibilities, in that power of binding men in conscience which appertains to just laws, in the deep-rooted aspirations which call for the political and social coming of age of the people—cannot be justified, nurtured, strengthened, and enriched without philosophical or religious convictions— "whether theological, metaphysical, or naturalistic"—which deal with the very substance and meaning of human life. Here appears the truth of T. S. Eliot's emphasis on the organic character of culture, as well as the injustice of reproaching him with suggesting proposals which, if enforced, would result in some kind of "ecclesiastical fascism." For we can be sure it is not to the compulsory power of any ecclesiastical agency but rather to the persuasive power of truth that he makes the effort toward the integration of culture appendant. The effort toward integration must not only be brought about on the level of personality and private life; it is essential to culture itself and the life of the community as a whole, on the condition that it tends toward real *cultural* integration, that is, toward an integration which does not depend on legal enforcement but on spiritual and freely accepted inspiration.

As a result, it is but normal that in a democratic culture and society the diverse philosophical or religious schools of thought which in their practical conclusions agree with regard to democratic tenets, and which claim to justify them, come into free competition. Let each school freely and fully assert its belief! But let no one try to impose it by force upon the others! The mutual tension which ensues will enrich rather than harm the common task.

5. As for myself, who believe that the idea of man propounded by the metaphysics of Aristotle and Thomas Aquinas is the rational foundation of democratic philosophy, and that the Gospel inspiration is its true living soul, I am confident that, in the free competition of which I just spoke, the Christian leaven would play an ever-growing part. In any case the responsibility for nurturing, strengthening, and enriching a common democratic faith would belong no less to the priest, dedicated to the preaching of the Gospel, than to the teacher, dedicated to the scientific spirit, if both of them came to a clear awareness of the needs of our times. Moreover, since it is a question of a secular faith dealing with the temporal order, its maintenance and progress in the community depend primarily on lay apostles and genuine political leaders, who are indebted to the scientific teacher for knowledge of the factual conditioning of human life, but much more, certainly, to the priest for knowledge of its meaning, its ends and its ethical standards.

Finally, if I affirm that without genuine and vital reconciliation between democratic inspiration and evangelical inspiration our hopes for the democratic culture of the future will be frustrated, I do not appeal to police force to obtain such reconciliation; I only state what I hold to be true. It would be foolish intolerance to label as intolerance any affirmation of truth which is not watered down with doubt, even if it does not please some of our democratic fellow-citizens. I insist as forcefully as T. S. Eliot that the Christian leaven is necessary to the life and integration of our culture. From the religious point of view, I would wish all men to believe in the integrity of Christian truth. From the social-temporal point of view, I would be satisfied if the Christian energies at work in the community were radiant with the fulness of supernatural faith in a number of men, and retained at least a sufficient degree of moral and rational efficacy in those in whom these energies still exist, but in a more or less incomplete—or secularized—form.

It is true, moreover, that supernatural faith does not provide us with any particular social or political system. In such matters supernatural faith must be complemented by sound practical philosophy, historical information, and social and political experience. Yet supernatural faith, if it is truly lived—in other words, if Christians know "of what spirit they are"—provides them with basic inspiration and vital truths which permeate their social and political systems and work for human dignity, against any kind of totalitarian oppression.

Allow me to add that to consider the religious faith of a poet like T. S. Eliot as "the object of a deliberate will-to-believe enjoying an uneasy triumph over the scruples of intelligence" is perhaps the only way in which an unbeliever can explain to himself such a strange phenomenon, but is, I venture to think, a sure proof of those lofty intellectual scruples and large capacities for explanation fostered by unbelief. It is not more relevant to pretend that the neo-Thomists regard as "disorder" "the spirit of inquiry and innovation"—I don't mean skepticism—and "the advance of liberty of thought and behavior," if this liberty is inspired by a love for what is true and good.

I should like to conclude by saying that I am sincerely pleased in finding myself this once in agreement, even qualified, with Sidney Hook—except for the points to which I have just referred, which are of no little importance. Such an agreement on practical conclusions between philosophers whose basic theoretical outlooks are widely separated is, to my mind, an illustration of the pluralistic cooperation of which I spoke.

B. THE POSSIBILITIES FOR COOPERATION IN A DIVIDED WORLD

Inaugural Address to the Second International Conference
of UNESCO [4]

Preamble

In addressing the Second International Conference of UNESCO,
I should like first to make reference to two remarks made by President Léon Blum on November 1, 1945, when he spoke at the
Conference which established the Organization. At that time Mr.
Léon Blum recalled that, as early as 1944, in San Francisco, the
French delegation had caused a motion to be adopted, the first
clause of which stated that "peace among nations, if it is to be just
and enduring, must be based upon mutual understanding and
knowledge." He added: "What all of us want (not only those of us
here present, but also those whose temporary absence we regret) is
to contribute to international security and peace, as well as to the
welfare of the peoples of the world, as the blue-print of the Conference of ministers states in its first sentence."

Speaking of the French delegation's request to have the head-
quarters of the Preparatory Commission established in Paris, Mr.
Blum also said: "We beg you not to interpret our request as something which France would consider its due because of some intellectual or spiritual prerogative. France's qualifications are more
ancient than those of other nations; they are not more glorious.
If we did have an advantage, it would stem from the fact that
French culture has always tended toward universality, and that
there is in France an age-old tradition of generosity and liberality
with respect to the things of the mind which are in keeping with
the spirit of the future organization. It would also stem from the
fact that in France, all branches or forms of human civilization—
the sciences, general culture, literature, the arts, and technology insofar as it borders upon art—have always developed side by side
and in reciprocal connection."

In my opinion these lines accurately characterize the contribu-

---

[4] United Nations Educational, Scientific and Cultural Organization.
This conference was held in Mexico City, November 6, 1947. See *The Range of
Reason* (New York: Scribners, 1952), pp. 172–184.

tion which the French spirit may be expected to make to the common work of an organization in which all cultures and civilizations must play their part, each being animated by its own particular spirit, whether it springs from the Latin or from the English-speaking world, or from the Eastern or the Far-eastern world, and in which patient experimental inquiry and search after guiding rational principles must complement one another. Mr. Blum's general remarks are also of great value to a philosopher, as I am, whose calling demands that he examine things in their universal aspects, and that he endeavor to bring out from reality the principles of an intelligible synthesis. So I feel encouraged to call to your attention certain general problems which seem to me of crucial importance.

Our Conference meets at a particularly serious moment in the history of the world, a moment when, faced with growing international tension and antagonisms the dangers of which cannot be ignored, vast portions of public opinion risk becoming obsessed by the spectre of catastrophe, and surrendering to the idea of war's inevitability. The anguish of peoples breaks like a mighty surf on every shore. In this world prostrated by post-war grief, and by the leaden mantle of rival economic, political and ideological interests, shall not those who are dedicated to the works of the mind and who feel the responsibility of such a mission give voice to the primitive instinct for preservation, to the immense longing for peace and freedom, to the repudiation of death and misfortune which, despite a strange apparent passivity more closely resembling despair than strength of soul, is stirring within the deepest recesses of men's consciousness? Shall they not proclaim that resignation to disaster is the worst of follies; that fear and fear-engendered reflexes, if one yield to them, attract the very dangers one most apprehends; that the more dramatic the plight of the people becomes, and the more clear-sighted firmness it demands of statesmen, the more vigorously the idea of the inevitability of war must be denounced as a fatal surrender on the part of human intelligence and human dignity? Shall they not, if only for the honor of our race and for the resources of the future, appeal to that conscience of men, which must be awakened and upon which depends the whole outcome of the struggle against collective suicide and for the actual building of peace? I am well aware that such declarations are neither within the province of UNESCO nor of this Conference. At least I may say that the present conjuncture reminds us forcefully that the mission of UNESCO is to contribute effectively—as Mr. Léon Blum said in the speech I have quoted—to international security and peace. I also may say, as Mr. Archibald MacLeish pointed out at the second session of the Executive Council, that UNESCO was not created to look after the theoretical progress of Education, Science and Culture, but to make use of it in the concrete and positive work of peace to be established among peoples.

It is this practical goal of our organization that I wish to emphasize. At the same time, I shall try to analyze its implications.

THREE PROBLEMS

Before coming to UNESCO's specific work, I shall take the liberty of making a few remarks concerning problems which inevitably arise in conjunction with the practical goal just mentioned, and which are of consequence for the personal conscience of each one of us. For it is not through *ideas* alone nor through *facts and figures* alone that the preliminary task which conditions and prepares the work of peace can be brought about both in the world and in human consciousness; it is through an effort of man's spiritual powers to bring to light the basic difficulties, and to reach decisions concerning them; and such an effort can only result from a personal meditation in which each individual commits himself.

The first questions which present themselves to one who meditates seriously on the conditions for a just and enduring peace are obviously those called forth by the idea of a supranational organization of the peoples of the world. Everyone is aware of the obstacles to carrying such an idea into effect; they are even greater today than immediately after victory. At the present time, a truly supranational world organization is beyond the realm of possibility. A philosopher, however, would fail in his duty if he did not add that this very thing which is today impossible, is nevertheless necessary, and that without it the creation of a just and enduring peace cannot be conceived. Hence, it follows that the first obligation incumbent upon the men of today is that they work with all their forces to make possible what is thus necessary.

If you speak to specialists in international law of the ideas set forth by Mr. Emery Reves in his *Anatomy of Peace*, if you tell them that the advent of a state of permanent peace necessarily presupposes the abandonment of the concept of absolute national sovereignty, and demands that relations between nations be regulated no longer by treaties but by law, they will answer that these ideas are not new to them; they have known all this for a long time. What they also know full well is that, in the present structure of the world, as history has formed it, and precisely because it is based on the absolute sovereignty of states, all the paths by which the states and the governments, even if they so desired, could move toward such a transformation, are blocked by insuperable obstacles. What are we to conclude except that this transformation, if it is ever attained, will be attained along other paths? I mean through an impetus arising from human conscience and from the will of the peoples, and so vast and powerful that it will command the assent of states and governments, even of those least disposed to give free rein to spontaneous movements of opinion. If there exists an effort toward creative transformation in support of which men of good will may call upon the peoples of the earth (and even should some irrational currents join in, as usually happens in such cases), it is precisely this effort toward a supranational community founded upon law and directed, within the limits of its well-defined powers, by men whose functions invest them with a citizenship which is itself supranational.

Is the world capable of making such an effort? What crises will still be needed to convince men that it is a necessity? All we can say, without being unduly optimistic, is that a few preliminary signs are to be seen. It is not without significance that under the authority of Dr. Robert M. Hutchins a *Committee* of intellectuals and educators *to Frame a World Constitution* was formed in the United States in 1945, deriving its inspiration from the initiative taken by *The Federalist* at the time of the struggle for the Constitution of the United States of America.[5] It is not without significance (and it is a privilege for me to have the honor of calling it to mind at this time), that one of the paragraphs in the preamble to the Constitution of the Fourth French Republic is drafted in the following terms: "On condition of reciprocity, France consents to those limitations of sovereignty necessary to the organization and defence of peace."

---

[5] Dr. Hutchins, who is now one of the directors of the Ford Foundation, was then President of the University of Chicago. The "Preliminary Draft" for a world constitution was printed in the March, 1948, issue of the monthly *Common Cause* (University of Chicago), edited by Mr. G. A. Borghese.

Now may I be permitted to dwell for a moment on an observation which, however commonplace, commands, I believe, the attention of every one of us, namely, that in human history the spirit's achievement always lags behind matter and factual event. It is all too clear today that the spirit has failed in a certain number of essential tasks which the world expected of it, and whose nonfulfilment may well prove costly. Our intellectual atmosphere will remain poisoned as long as a few crucial problems are not clearly posed, and a solution to them proposed to men, at least as concerns the intrinsic truth of the matter. Among these problems, I shall cite three, each of a very different nature.

The first is the problem of Machiavellianism and *Realpolitik*. The rehabilitation of the post-war world imperiously required that (if not, alas, in the behavior of states, then at least in the consciousness of the peoples, and in common intelligence) it be clearly understood that the maxim according to which politics must not be concerned with moral good and evil is a homicidal error. We had to understand that Machiavellianism, although it may afford immediate success, by its very nature leads to ruin in the long run; that absolute Machiavellianism inevitably devours moderate Machiavellianism, and that the principle and virtue of Machiavellianism, whether absolute or moderate, can only be conquered by the principle and virtue of genuinely political justice, in a spiritual climate fit for the development of some heroic determination.

The second problem concerns the collective moral transgression into which a people may fall, and the collective moral recovery to which they may be bound in conscience. For speculative thought as well as for practical judgment, there is no more difficult, no more perilous problem. But that is no reason for evading it. Ever since we were confronted with the crimes committed against humanity by Nazi Germany, this problem has had us by the throat. It is not good for men to remain in the dark about it.

It is doubtless true that no nation is blameless; in the distant origins of the conflicts which have taken place in the course of history, every nation may have more or less cause for self-accusation. But that is not the point. Nor is it the point that the faults committed by a state and by its leaders entail historical sanctions which the nation must accept, not only as inevitable, but as justified. The true question concerns a people's awareness or lack of awareness of the evil by which they allowed themselves to be contaminated, and of which the members of a community (even those who remained personally immune, even those who fought against that evil) recognize or do not recognize that the community was guilty.

It is not good for a people to humiliate itself before others. But it is not good for a people to settle into stiff-necked pride. There is a way of beating the breast and accepting abjection which destroys the dignity of a nation. But there is also a way of refusing to beat the breast, while deceiving one's conscience and nurturing hatred, which destroys this dignity just as unmercifully. Is there no way out of this dilemma? Is there not a way of acknowledging, with sorrow and strength of soul, the faults of the community to which one belongs, and of desiring at all cost that the community atone for them and free itself of them—a way which, for a people determined to rehabilitate itself morally, is at the same time an evidence and a safeguard of its dignity? After having wished to enslave the world and trusted in a Fuehrer of perdition for the sake of national interest placed above any other consideration, the German people underwent an unprecedented defeat. Today they are suffering grievously, and it is our duty as human beings to have compassion on them in their pain. But the worst tragedy which could befall them would be if such suffering proved vain and failed to awaken an awareness of their responsibilities, and, at the same time, a horror of the evil committed and the will to give worthy service to the human community in a purified moral atmosphere. It is up to the nations to help the German people against despair. It is up to those who are solicitous of the spiritual rehabilitation of the German people, particularly those who, within Germany itself, are in charge of moral and religious interests, also and first of all to tell them the truth, not in order to humiliate them or to overwhelm them, but in order to give them what they have a right to expect in their misfortune, and what is the primary condition of their moral rebirth. At this point it is necessary more than ever to reaffirm the primacy of the spiritual. If, in the depths of the German conscience, repentance and hope—a virile repentance and a righteous hope—are not awakened at one and the same time, then the German problem will continue to be fraught with misery for the German people themselves and for the peace of the world.

The third problem, the urgency of which each one of us realizes, is the problem of the human value and human use of science and technology. The coming of the atomic age has suddenly exposed to the world the terrible countenance of this problem. Man no longer believes that science and technical skills can by themselves ensure the progress and happiness of the race. Rather he is filled with terror at the sight of the destruction and calamities science and technical skills can bring about. Men of science are examining themselves; and it is with profound respect and in a sincere attempt to discern the bearing of the drama involved, that we must consider the anguish of a scientist of genius like Albert Einstein.

It is not enough to draw the attention of the peoples to the world-destroying catastrophes which the discoveries of modern physics may well lead to, if another armed conflict should occur. Fear is not enough to make men wise. And it is not enough to tell them that these same discoveries, if used for purposes of peace, can open unprecedented vistas of prosperity and freedom to the human race. A possibility is not enough to create happiness. What is required of human intelligence is an awareness of the fact that we have entered a crucial age in our history, a period when, under pain of death, the gigantic implements of power obtained by the scientific mastery of matter must be made subject to reason, in overcoming the irrational temptations to which human beings are liable, especially in their collective existence. It is also necessary to understand that there is an inner hierarchy and a vital interconnection among the virtues of the human soul, so that, whereas the province of science deals with the *means*, the realm of *ends* pertains to something which is not science, and is not commensurable with it, and is called wisdom. We can be assured of neither peace, nor liberty, nor dignity in the world of tomorrow so long as, in the structures of civilization and in the consciousness of men (and of the scientists themselves), science and wisdom are not reconciled, and the practical applications of science are not rigorously submitted to right ethical will and to the true ends of human life. There was a time when we expected science to solve or do away with problems of ethics, metaphysics and religion, when we counted on the scientists to constitute one day the spiritual authority which would lead mankind toward the green pastures of necessary progress. Today we have to defend science against those who, after asking of it more than it could give, now accuse it, just as unreasonably, of being bankrupt. And, on the other hand, we see men of science engaged in a serious internal examination, in which is questioned the relationship between their conscience as men and the possible use of their work as scientists. We even see them in danger of being treated by the states as mere industrial ore made particularly valuable by its output in terms of discoveries. Thus, it is the very dignity of science and of the scientist which is at stake; and it is to maintain and preserve this dignity, as well as to direct the applications of science toward the welfare of the world and not toward its destruction, that mankind stands in need of a powerful renewal of the disciplines of wisdom, and of a reintegration of ethical, metaphysical and religious truths into its culture, and of that reconciliation of science and wisdom which I have mentioned above.

CAN INTELLECTUALLY DIVIDED MEN COOPERATE IN PRACTICAL MATTERS?

I have spoken of a few problems which concern all of us because they relate to certain spiritual and cultural conditions dealing with that to which UNESCO aims to contribute, namely the building of peace. My final remarks will bear upon another type of problem, which refers to the proper work of UNESCO and to the kind of agreement in the midst of diversity which is required by that work.

At first glance there is something paradoxical in UNESCO's task: it implies intellectual agreement among men whose conceptions of the world, of culture, of knowledge itself are different or even mutually opposed. In my opinion, it behooves us to face this paradox, which is but an expression of the great distress in which the human spirit finds itself today.

Modern thought has been labeled with *Babelism*, and not without reason. Never indeed have men's minds been so deeply and cruelly divided. As human thought is pigeon-holed into more and more specialized compartments, it becomes more difficult to bring to consciousness the implicit philosophies to which each of us, willy nilly, is committed in actual fact. Doctrines and faiths, spiritual traditions and schools of thought come into conflict without it being possible for the one even to understand the signs which the others use to express themselves. Every man's voice is but noise to his fellow-men. However deep we may dig, there is no longer any common foundation for speculative thought. There is no common language for it.

How then, under these circumstances, is an agreement conceivable among men assembled for the purpose of jointly accomplishing a task dealing with the future of the mind, who come from the four corners of the earth and who belong not only to different cultures and civilizations, but to different spiritual lineages and antagonistic schools of thought? Should an agency like UNESCO throw up the game, give up any assertion of common views and common principles, and be satisfied only in compiling documents, surveys, factual data and statistics? Or should it, on the contrary, endeavor to establish some artificial conformity of minds, and to define some doctrinal common denominator—which would be likely, in the course of discussion, to be reduced to the vanishing point?

I believe that the solution must be sought in another direction; precisely because, as I pointed out at the beginning, UNESCO's goal is a practical one, agreement among its members can be spontaneously achieved, not on common speculative notions, but on common practical notions; not on the affirmation of the same conception of the world, man and knowledge, but on the affirmation of the same set of convictions concerning action. This is doubtless very little; it is the last refuge of intellectual agreement among men. It is, however, enough to undertake a great work, and it would mean a great deal to become aware of this body of common practical convictions.

I should like to note here that the word *ideology* and the word *principle* can be understood in two very different ways. I have just said that the present state of intellectual division among men does not permit agreement on a common *speculative* ideology, nor on common *explanatory* principles. However, when it concerns, on the contrary, the basic *practical* ideology and the basic principles of *action* implicitly recognized today, in a vital if not a formulated manner, by the consciousness of free peoples, this happens to constitute *grosso modo* a sort of common residue, a sort of unwritten common law, at the point of practical convergence of extremely different theoretical ideologies and spiritual traditions. To understand that, it is sufficient to distinguish properly between the rational justifications, inseparable from the spiritual dynamism of a philosophical doctrine or a religious faith, and the practical conclusions which, separately justified for each one, are, for all, analogically common principles of action. I am fully convinced that my way of justifying the belief in the rights of man and the ideal of liberty, equality, fraternity, is the only one which is solidly based on truth. That does not prevent me from agreeing on these practical tenets with those who are convinced that their way of justifying them, entirely different from mine, or even opposed to mine in its theoretical dynamism, is likewise the only one that is based on truth. Assuming they both believe in the democratic charter, a Christian and a rationalist will, nevertheless, give justifications that are incompatible with each other, to which their souls, their minds and their blood are committed, and about these justifications they will fight. And God keep me from saying that it is not important to know which of the two is right! That is essentially important. They remain, however, in agreement on the practical affirmation of the charter, and they can formulate together common principles of action.

Thus, in my opinion, can the paradox I pointed out earlier be solved. The ideological agreement which is necessary between those who work toward making science, culture and education contribute to the establishment of a true peace, is restricted to a certain body of practical points and of principles of action. But within these limits there is, and there must be, an ideological agreement which, for all its merely practical nature, is nonetheless of major importance. In the justification he offers for that body of practical principles, everyone commits himself fully, with all of his philosophical and religious convictions—how could he speak with faith, if not in the light of the speculative convictions which quicken his thought? But he is not entitled to demand that others subscribe to his own justification of the practical principles on which all agree. And the practical principles in question form a sort of charter which is indispensable for any effective common action, and the formulation of which would matter to the good itself and the success of the peace-making work to which their common endeavors are dedicated.

That is why it is fitting to stress the crucial importance—but limited to the merely practical order—of the common ideology to which UNESCO has appealed from the time of its foundation. I am thinking especially of the declaration of principles, in the Preamble drafted at the London Conference, in which it is stated, among other things, "that the great and terrible war which has just ended was made possible by the denial of the democratic ideal of dignity, equality and respect for the human person, and by the will to substitute for that ideal—in making capital out of ignorance and prejudice—the dogma of the inequality of races and of men"; and "that, since the dignity of man requires that culture and education be made available to all in view of fostering justice, freedom and peace, all nations have in this regard sacred obligations to fulfill in a spirit of mutual assistance." That is why I believe that one of the most important tasks undertaken by the United Nations is the new declaration of the rights of man, which UNESCO is helping to draft.[6]

More generally speaking, if it is true not only that the end of UNESCO's task is a practical end, but also that on this practical end depends both the harmony of the minds within the organization and the effectiveness of its action, then is it not obvious that the Organization of the United Nations for Education, Science and Culture can best carry out the difficult work assigned to it, and fulfil the expectations of the peoples, by concentrating primarily on a small number of far-reaching accomplishments? This view has already been supported by the representatives of France on previous occasions.

I should like to add another recommendation: that we should not give to human sciences less interest and favor than to the physical ones. Do we not believe that the knowledge of man and the development of a new humanism are, in the order of science and culture, what matters most for the preparation of a peace lastingly established? Our knowledge of man, moreover, is much more difficult and much less advanced than our knowledge of the physical world; it needs all the more to be helped and encouraged.

---

[6] This new declaration was adopted and proclaimed by the United Nations on Dec. 10, 1948.

In this connection one is surprised to see that up to now, in the budget of UNESCO, not only are the credits set aside for administrative expenses considerably larger than those destined to creative undertakings, but that even within this latter category, the amounts allocated to human sciences—to that science of human relations whose importance President Roosevelt rightly stressed—have been much smaller than those ear-marked for the sciences concerned with material nature.

I should like to add that to make science, culture and education serve the tasks of peace does not mean separating the organization of scientific work from action for peace in such a way that on the one hand we would concentrate on purely theoretical, and supposedly exhaustive, analysis and planning and, on the other hand, we would confine our practical activity for peace to a mere effort to spead UNESCO's ideals by means of the techniques of mass-communication. Our specific task consists rather in organizing the scientific work itself, as well as the cultural and educational work, with a view to the task of peace to be promoted. It is from the very beginning that the organization should aim at that practical goal, so that by serving science itself in its very search for truth, by furthering international cooperation between scholars and scientists, and by urging them to join forces in enlightening common consciousness, we may succeed in interesting the world of science and culture, as well as peoples themselves in the work of peace pursued by UNESCO.

In any case, what I have tried to set forth in the latter part of this address is the practical nature of the goal toward which we are working together, and the necessity that our task be based on practical convictions and practical principles held in common. The goal of UNESCO is to contribute to the peace of the world, to international security and to the lasting welfare of peoples, through the instrumentality of Education, Science, and Culture. We all know that there is no peace without justice. We all know that, in the words of the Preamble I referred to a moment ago, "since wars are born in the minds of men, it is within the minds of men that the defences of peace must be erected." And we all know that if the work of peace is to be prepared in the thought of men and in the consciousness of nations, it is on the condition that minds come to be deeply convinced of principles like the following: Good politics is first and foremost a politics that is just; every people should strive to understand the psychology, the development and traditions, the material and moral needs, the proper dignity and historic calling of the other peoples, because every people should look out not only for its own advantages but for the common good of the assembly of nations; this awakening of mutual understanding and of the sense of the civilized community, though it supposes (given the age-old habits of human history) a sort of spiritual revolution, nevertheless answers requirements of public emergency in a world which, from now on, is one world for life or for death, while it remains disastrously divided as to political passions and interests; to place national interest above everything is a sure means of losing everything; a community of free men is only conceivable if it recognizes that truth is the expression of what *is*, and right the expression of what is *just*, and not of what is most expedient at a given time for the interest of the human group; it is not permissible to take the life of an innocent man because he has become a useless and costly burden to the nation, or because he impedes the successful undertakings of any group whatsoever; the human person is endowed with a dignity which the very good of the community presupposes and must, for its own sake, respect, and is also endowed, whether as a civic, or as a social or working person, with certain fundamental rights and fundamental obligations; the common good comes before private interests; the world of labor has a right to the social transformations required by its coming of age in human history, and the masses have a right to participate in the common treasure of culture and of the spirit; the domain of consciences is inviolable; men of various beliefs and spiritual lineages must recognize each other's rights as fellow-citizens in the civilized community; it is the duty of the state, for the very sake of the common good, to respect religious freedom as well as freedom of research; the basic equality of men makes prejudices of race, class or caste, and racial discrimination, offences against human nature and the dignity of the person as well as a deep-seated threat to peace.

If a state of peace worthy of the name, firm and enduring, is to be established one day among the peoples of the world, this will depend not only upon the economic, political and financial arrangements reached by diplomats and statesmen, nor will it depend solely upon the juridical building up of a truly supranational coordinating organism endowed with efficient means of action; it will depend also upon the deep adherence of men's consciousness to practical principles like those I have recalled. And, to state things as they are, it will depend also upon that *bigger soul* which, according to Bergson, our world, become technically greater, needs, and upon a victorious outpouring of that supreme and free energy which comes to us from on high, and whose name we know— whatever may be our religious denomination or school of thought— to be brotherly love, a name which has been pronounced in such a manner by the Gospels that it has stirred the conscience of man for all time.

C. THE DEMOCRATIC SECULAR FAITH [7]

. . . It seems likely that, if democracy enters its next historical stage with sufficient intelligence and vitality, a renewed democracy will not ignore religion, as the "bourgeois" nineteenth-century society, both individualist and "neutral," did, and that this re- newed, "personalist" democracy will be of a *pluralistic* type.

Thus we would have—supposing that the people have regained their Christian faith, or at least recognized the value and sensible- ness of the Christian conception of freedom, social progress, and the political establishment—on the one hand, a body politic Chris- tianly inspired in its own political life. On the other hand, this per- sonalist body politic would recognize that men belonging to most different philosophical or religious creeds and lineages could and should cooperate in the common task and for the common welfare, provided they similarly assent to the basic tenets of a society of free men. These common tenets, that is the subject matter which requests our attention and which I should like to discuss.

For a society of free men implies basic tenets which are at the core of its very existence. A genuine democracy implies a funda- mental agreement between minds and wills on the bases of life in common; it is aware of itself and of its principles, and it must be capable of defending and promoting its own conception of social and political life; it must bear within itself a common human creed,

---

[7] *Man and the State* (Chicago: University of Chicago Press, 1951), pp. 109–114.

the creed of freedom. The mistake of "bourgeois" liberalism has been to conceive democratic society to be a kind of lists or arena in which all the conceptions of the bases of common life, even those most destructive to freedom and law, meet with no more than the pure and simple indifference of the body politic, while they compete before public opinion in a kind of free market of the mother-ideas, healthy or poisoned, of political life. Nineteenth-century "bourgeois" democracy was *neutral* even with regard to freedom. Just as it had no real *common good*, it had no real *common thought* —no brains of its own, but a neutral, empty skull clad with mirrors: no wonder that before the second world war, in countries that fascist, racist, or communist propaganda was to disturb or to corrupt, it had become a society without any idea of itself and without faith in itself, without any *common faith* which could enable it to resist disintegration.

But the point we are again stressing here is that this faith and inspiration, and the concept of itself which democracy needs—all these do not belong to the order of religious creed and eternal life, but to the temporal or secular order of earthly life, of culture or civilization. The *faith* in question is a *civic or secular* faith, not a religious one. Nor is it that philosophic substitute for religious faith, that adherence forced upon all by reason's demonstrations, which the eighteenth- and nineteenth-century philosophers sought in vain. A genuine democracy cannot impose on its citizens or demand from them, as a condition for their belonging to the city, any philosophic or any religious creed. This conception of the city was possible during the "sacral" period of our civilization, when communion in the Christian faith was a prerequisite for the constitution of the body politic. In our own day it has been able to produce only the inhuman counterfeit, whether hypocritical or violent, offered by the totalitarian States which lay claim to the faith, obedience, love that the religious man owes to his God; it has produced only their effort to impose their creed on the mind of the masses by the power of propaganda, lies, and the police.

What is, then, the object of the *secular faith* that we are discussing? This object is a merely practical one, not a theoretical or dogmatic one. The secular faith in question deals with *practical* tenets which the human mind can try to justify—more or less successfully, that's another affair—from quite different philosophical outlooks, probably because they come primordially from simple "natural" apperceptions, of which the human heart becomes capable with the progress of moral conscience, and which, as a matter of fact, have been awakened by the Gospel leaven fermenting in the obscure depths of human history. As we have said, men possessing quite different, even opposite metaphysical or religious outlooks, can converge, not by virtue of any identity of doctrine, but by virtue of an analogical similitude in practical principles, toward the same practical conclusions, and can share in the same practical secular faith, provided that they similarly revere, perhaps for quite diverse reasons, truth and intelligence, human dignity, freedom, brotherly love, and the absolute value of moral good.

We must, therefore, maintain a sharp and clear distinction between the human and temporal creed which lies at the root of common life and which is but a set of *practical conclusions* or of *practical points of convergence*—on the one hand; and on the other, the *theoretical justifications*, the conceptions of the world and of life, the philosophical or religious creeds which found, or claim to found, these practical conclusions in reason.

The body politic has the right and the duty to promote among its citizens, mainly through education, the human and temporal— and essentially practical—creed on which depend national communion and civil peace. It has no right, as a merely temporal or secular body, enclosed in the sphere where the modern State enjoys its autonomous authority, to impose on the citizens or to demand from them a rule of faith or a conformism of reason, a philosophical or religious creed which would present itself as the only possible justification of the practical charter through which the people's common secular faith expresses itself. The important thing for the body politic is that the democratic sense be in fact kept alive by the adherence of minds, however diverse, to this moral charter. The ways and the justifications by means of which this common adherence is brought about belong to the sphere of inner freedom of mind and conscience.

Certainly, it is supremely important to the common good that the practical assertions which make up the charter in question be true in themselves. But the democratic State does not judge of that truth; it is born out of that truth, as recognized and asserted by the people—by each one of us, to the extent of his abilities.

What would be the content of the moral charter, the code of social and political morality of which I speak and the validity of which is implied by the fundamental compact of a society of free men? Such a charter would deal, for instance, with the following points: rights and liberties of the human person, political rights and liberties, social rights and social liberties, corresponding responsibilities; rights and duties of persons who are part of a family society, and liberties and obligations of the latter toward the body politic; mutual rights and duties of groups and the State; government of the people, by the people, and for the people; functions of authority in a political and social democracy, moral obligation, binding in conscience, in regard to just laws as well as the Constitution which guarantees the people's liberties; exclusion of the resort to political coups (*coups d'état*) in a society that is truly free and ruled by laws whose change and evolution depend on the popular majority; human equality, justice between persons and the body politic, justice between the body politic and persons, civil friendship and an ideal of fraternity, religious freedom, mutual tolerance and mutual respect between various spiritual communities and schools of thought, civic self-devotion and love of the motherland, reverence for its history and heritage, and understanding of the various traditions that combine to create its unity; obligations of each person toward the common good of the body politic and obligations of each nation toward the common good of civilized society, and the necessity of becoming aware of the unity of the world and of the existence of a community of peoples.

It is a fact that in democratic nations, which, like the United States and France, have a hard historic experience of the struggles for freedom, practically everybody would be ready to endorse all the tenets of such a charter. Given that virtue of universality with which the civilization inherited from Christianity is endowed, as Arnold Toynbee has shown in a persuasive manner, we have good reason to hope that in all nations of the world the people—I say the people, whatever their governments may be—would be able to put forward the same endorsement.

I should like to add two remarks which do not deal directly with the issue that I just discussed, but rather with the problems that we shall consider in other chapters.

First: As a matter of fact, the more the body politic—that is, the people—were imbued with Christian convictions and aware of the *religious* faith which inspires it, the more deeply it would adhere to the *secular* faith in the democratic charter; for, as a matter of fact, the latter has taken shape in human history as a result of the Gospel inspiration awakening the "naturally Christian" potentialities of common secular consciousness, even among the diversity of spiritual lineages and schools of thought opposed to each other, and sometimes warped by a vitiated ideology.

Second: To the extent that the body politic—that is, the people—were imbued with Christian convictions, to the same extent, as a matter of fact, the justification of the democratic charter offered by Christian philosophy would be recognized as the truest one—not at all as a result of any interference of the State, but simply as a result of the free adherence which a larger proportion of the people would have given to Christian faith and Christian philosophy in actual fact.

And, of course, no religious pressure would be exercised by the majority. Non-Christian citizens' freedom to found their democratic beliefs on grounds different from those more generally accepted would by no means be jeopardized. What the civil authority and the State would be concerned with is only the common secular faith in the common secular charter.

D. THE POLITICAL HERETICS [8]

The fact must be recognized that the body politic has its own heretics, as the Church has hers. Nay more, St. Paul tells us that there must be heretics [9]—and they are probably still less inevitable in the State than in the Church. Did we not insist that there is a democratic charter, nay, a democratic creed? That there is a democratic secular faith? Well, everywhere where faith is, divine or human, religious or secular, there are also heretics who threaten the unity of the community, either religious or civil. In the sacral society of the Middle Ages the heretic was the breaker of religious unity. In a lay society of free men the heretic is the breaker of the "common democratic beliefs and practices," the one who takes a stand against freedom, or against the basic equality of men, or the

---

[8] *Man and the State* (Chicago: University of Chicago Press, 1951), pp. 114–119.

[9] I Cor. XI: 19.

dignity and rights of the human person, or the moral power of law.

People who remember the lessons of history know that a democratic society should not be an unarmed society, which the enemies of liberty may calmly lead to the slaughterhouse in the name of liberty. Precisely because it is a commonwealth of free men, it must defend itself with particular energy against those who, out of principle, refuse to accept, and who even work to destroy, the foundations of common life in such a regime, the foundations which are freedom and the practical secular faith expressed in the democratic charter.

When the political heretic embarks on *political activity*, he will be met with, and checked by, opposing political activity freely developed by citizens in a body politic sufficiently lively and alive. When he embarks on *illegal activity*, trying to use violence, he will be met with, and checked by, the authority of the State, which, in a society of free men, is exercised against him only in granting him, in a real, not a fake manner, the institutional guarantees of justice and law. There is no problem here. The difficulty begins when it comes to the *speaking and writing activity* of the political heretic.

The question of the freedom of expression [10] is not a simple one.

---

[10] See the important report, *A Free and Responsible Press,* published by the Commission on the Freedom of the Press under the Chairmanship of Robert M. Hutchins (Chicago: University of Chicago Press, 1947).

I would like to recall in this note the various recommendations made by the commission.

I. As concerns government: (1) That the constitutional guaranties of the freedom of the press be recognized as including the radio and motion pictures. (2) That government facilitate new ventures in the communications industry, that it foster the introduction of new techniques, that it maintain competition among large units through the anti-trust laws, but that those laws be sparingly used to break up such units, and that, where concentration is necessary in communications, the government endeavor to see to it that the public gets the benefit of such concentration. (3) As an alternative to the present remedy for libel, legislation by which the injured party might obtain a retraction or a restatement of the facts by the offender or an opportunity to reply. (4) The repeal of legislation prohibiting expressions in favor of revolutionary changes in our institutions where there is no clear and present danger that violence will result from the expressions. (5) That the government, through the media of mass communication, inform the public of the facts with respect to its policies and of the purposes underlying those policies and that, to the extent that private agencies of mass communication are unable or unwilling to supply such media to the government, the government itself may employ media of its own. Also that, where the private agencies of mass communi-

So great is the confusion today that we see common-sense principles, which have been ignored in the past by the worshippers of
a false and deceiving liberty, being now used in a false and deceiving manner in order to destroy true liberty. Those maxims—
dealing with our obligations toward objective truth and with the
rights of the common good—which were branded as an outrage
against human autonomy when the Catholic Church set them forth
to condemn theological liberalism, and which, by opposing un-
bridled, divinely unlimited freedom of expression, were of a nature
to save freedom of expression—the Communist State is now trum-
peting them and perverting them in order simply to annihilate
freedom of expression. It is one of Time's sad revenges. And, for
everybody, an opportunity for melancholy reflections.

In discussing freedom of expression we have to take into account
a variety of aspects. On the one hand, it is not true that every
thought as such, because of the mere fact that it was born in a
human intellect, has the right to be spread about in the body
politic.[11]

---

cation are unable or unwilling to supply information about this country to a
particular foreign country or countries, the government employ mass-communication media of its own to supplement this deficiency.

II. As concerns the press and mass communication media: (1) That the
agencies of mass communication accept the responsibilities of common carriers
of information and discussion. (2) That they assume the responsibility of financ-
ing new, experimental activities in their fields. (3) That the members of the press
engage in vigorous mutual criticism. (4) That the press use every means that can
be devised to increase the competence, independence, and effectiveness of its staff.
(5) That the radio industry take control of its programs and that it treat advertising as it is treated by the best newspapers.

III. As concerns the public: (1) That nonprofit organizations help supply the
variety, quantity, and quality of press service required by the American people.
(2) That academic-professional centers of advanced study, research, and publication in the field of communications be created; and, further, that existing schools
of journalism exploit the total resources of their universities to the end that their
students may obtain the broadest and most liberal training. (3) That a new and
independent agency be established to appraise and report annually upon the performance of the press.

[11] In order to sum up the considerations presented in this section, I
would say:

A. Freedom of expression is a human right, but this right is only a "substantially," not an "absolutely," inalienable right. There are limits to freedom of
expression, which are inevitably demanded both by the common good and by this
very freedom, that would become self-destructive if it were made limitless.

B. The State is entitled to impose limitations on freedom of expression, in
view of particularly serious circumstances. But in actual fact it can do so in a
manner beneficial to a democratic society only in most obvious and externally

On the other hand, not only censorship and police methods, but any direct restriction of freedom of expression, though unavoidable in certain cases of necessity, are the worst way to ensure the rights of the body politic to defend freedom and the common charter and common morality, because any such restriction runs against the very spirit of a democratic society: a democratic society knows that human subjectivity's inner energies, reason, and conscience are the most valuable springs of political life. It also knows that it is no use fighting ideas with *cordons sanitaires* and repressive measures (even totalitarian States know that; consequently they simply kill their heretics, while using psychotechnical means to tame or corrupt ideas themselves).

Moreover we have seen that the common agreement expressed in democratic faith is not of a doctrinal, but merely practical nature. As a result, the criterion for any interference of the State in the field of the expression of thought is also to be practical, not ideological: the more extraneous this criterion is to the very content of thought, the better it will be. It is too much for the State, for instance, to judge whether a work of art is possessed of an intrinsic quality of immorality (then it would condemn Baudelaire or Joyce); it is enough for it to judge whether an author or a publisher plans to make money in selling obscenities. It is too much for the State to judge whether a political theory is heretical with regard to the democratic faith; it is enough for it to judge—always with the institutional guarantees of justice and law—whether a political heretic threatens the democratic charter by the tangible acts he undertakes or by receiving money from a foreign State to subsidize antidemocratic propaganda.

You will answer quite rightly: is not the intellectual corruption of human minds, is not the ruining of primary verities, exceedingly more detrimental to the common good of the body politic than any other work of corruption? Yes, it is. But the fact is that the State is not equipped to deal with matters of intelligence.

---

palpable matters and with regard to those basic ingredients in the common good which are the simplest and the most elementary.

C. When it comes to higher matters, in which freedom of inquiry and the inner values of intelligence and conscience are involved, and with regard to the most vital and spiritual ingredients (which *in themselves* are the most important) in the common good, the factual limitations to be brought to bear on freedom of expression depend on the constructive and regulative institutions, organs, and agencies and the free activities spontaneously developed in the body politic.

Each time the State disregards that basic truth, which depends on its own nature, intelligence is victimized. And since intelligence has always its revenge, it is the body politic which, in one way or another, is finally victimized. Only one society can deal with matters of intelligence—that is the Church, because she is a spiritual society. Yet she, who knows what's what, had in the past some sad experiences in giving an eye to such ideas as the movement of the earth, and she does not use without thoughtful misgivings her spiritual weapons against her own heretics.[12]

Do I mean to imply that even with regard to superior matters the democratic body politic is disarmed? I mean just the contrary. I mean that positive, constructive means are exceedingly more efficacious than mere restriction of freedom of expression. And there are in a living democracy innumerable means of such a nature. Let us consider especially the matter of political heretics: Groups and leagues of citizens could devote themselves to the progress of democratic philosophy, the enlightenment of people with regard to the common charter, and the intellectual struggle against warped political trends. The State itself could have the people informed of the judgments passed upon anti-democratic ideologies by some special body made up of men whose intellectual wisdom and moral integrity would be universally recognized.[13] Still more important, the various organizations, freely starting from the bottom, which in a pluralist society would unite readers and listeners on the one hand, writers and speakers on the other, could develop, as regards the use of the media of mass communication, a ceaseless process of self-regulation, as well as a growing sense of responsibility. Still more important, the body politic, with the sense of community which it normally entails, has at its disposal the spontaneous pressure of the common consciousness and public opinion, which spring from the national ethos when it is firmly established, and which are strong enough to keep political heretics out of leadership. First and foremost it has at its disposal the work of democratic education.

---

[12] The Church, of course, is entitled to bring limitations to bear on freedom of expression in her own spiritual realm, as regards matters of faith and morals and with respect to the common good of the Kingdom of God. The claim to limitless freedom of expression laid by theological liberalism was a direct challenge to that right of the Church.

[13] See also Recommendation I, 5, of the Commission on the Freedom of the Press above, pp. 141–142.

12 PRIMACY OF THE SPIRITUAL*

THE TRUTH IS THAT EUROPE HAS FORGOTTEN EVEN THE subordination of political to spiritual ends. That is its great mistake. Hence comes that general condition oppressive of the spirit and conscience, that practical contempt for the human person and his dignity, the overwhelming burden of which is everywhere more or less obscurely felt. Let us be sorry most of all for nations which, gathered by signal favor around the Pope and with the voice of Christ indefatigably recalling to them the demands of truth, have for centuries been so obstinate as to stop up their ears. *Generatio incredula et perversa, usque quo patiar vos?* [1]

It seems that we are entering an age when, all the hopes founded on rationalism and humanitarian optimism having been frustrated, the great problems of the spiritual order, the war among the angels, will again dominate history and the distress of mankind. This is what the Russian philosopher, Nicholas Berdiaeff, calls a new middle age. It is most striking to consider in this regard the fundamental work being done within the Church. All her aspirations seem in our days strained towards a spiritual restoration of Christendom. . . .

What we have to do is strive with all our will that this spiritual Christendom descend into the temporal and be realized in political Christendom. But can we regard this as at present probable? A

---

* Translated from *Primauté du spirituel* (New and revised edition, Paris: Librairie Plon, n.d. [1st edition, 1927]), pp. 132–165.
[1] Matth. 17, 16.

Christian political order in the world is not constructed artificially, by diplomatic means. It is a fruit produced by the spirit of faith. It presupposes a living and practical faith in a large number of people, a civilization inspired by Christian wisdom, an over-all orientation of political life towards the true goods of the person and of the spirit. We are far from this ideal. Unless God intervenes in a special way, and unless an overwhelming despair brings this unhappy world to a moment of obedience, the kingdoms of the world seem delivered to bloody division for a long time to come.

It is easy to understand that when peoples are so far from genuine order and when the most precarious peace is so difficult to obtain, nations, and especially those whose frontiers are most exposed, should refuse to give up the precaution of force on which their existence depends. Since Catholics in the different countries are as a rule, and as is to be expected, the element most devoted to the principles of natural law, it is also understandable that they should feel from this point of view, as citizens, especially grave obligations, and that they should be the first to watch and safeguard the basic natural goods. To maintain the peace of the country and give it effective protection is the most proximate and most urgent objective of a Christian political prudence.

Nevertheless, this end would not be Christian if it were not related to a more remote and higher end, in such a way that the idea of the good of the human community, founded on justice and charity, and the idea of a lasting peace to be established among nations, exercised over political activity not a mere primacy of honor, but an efficacious guiding influence. Devotion to the country in which we were born and brought up, like devotion to our parents, is a virtue related to justice; we are indebted to our country for innumerable benefits. "After God, it is to his parents and his country that man owes most." [2]

But in the baptized soul, patriotism is not merely an acquired virtue of great nobility. This natural virtue is superelevated and purified by being subordinated to charity and "vivified by the love of God, by the supernatural love of our neighbor and even our enemies." There is an order of charity, that is to say an order of supernatural love of God and neighbor, and within it the love of

---

[2] St. Thomas Aquinas, *Sum. Theol.* II–II, 101, 1 . . .

country has a place.[3] At the same time, charity demands, and not simply as a perfection at which we are to aim, but as an essential necessity imposed by the commandment, that we should indeed love our enemies in general, and yet more that our heart should be ready, if occasion arises, to love them by name and one by one.[4] In this way, supernatural charity reconciles love of country with love of all men, whereas a purely natural benevolence for humanity and a purely natural love of country can only irremediably affront each other.

Without letting itself be infected by humanitarian ideology and without counting on the early abolition of wars—or of war waged against the Church—an integral Christian politics [5] would realize that it is not enough to combat symptoms, to use the means of defence made necessary by the general barbarism of modern peoples: the evil must be fought at the source and men must first habituate themselves to take others' rights and needs into account. Appreciation of problems would then clearly be more sane and equitable, preoccupation with justice would be reconciled with preoccupation with force and would regain its indispensable practical primacy.[6]

And above all, no matter what the urgency of their national duties and no matter what measures of prudence, in their capacity as citi-

---

[3] *Ibid.*, 26, 7 and 8 . . .

[4] "It is by a necessity of charity, *according to the preparation of his soul,* that a man should have his soul ready to love an enemy in the concrete, should the necessity arise." *Ibid.*, 25, 8.

[5] It must be admitted that no great political party up to the present, in France or in Europe or outside Europe, professes integrally Christian principles. ("This was written in 1927 before the emergence of the Christian-inspired parties which were born after the second world war." Jacques Maritain)

[6] In a study on *La politique de Pascal* (1923) we wrote: "A real and not a feigned justice is the 'mystic foundation' of the authority of law as well as of peace in the body politic. . . ." To maintain relations of justice among nations, the Church has always desired the existence of a community of nations (the political organization of Christendom) which, without injuring the rights of the various States or societies capable of self-sufficiency ("perfect societies"), would play a regulatory and pacificatory role among them. "Modern States have arrived at such a degree of interdependence that life in society is almost as necessary for them as for individuals. . . ." (M. Le Fur, *Lettres* 1er mars 1927). But this international temporal organism (of positive law, not of natural law, as some tend to think) is not only incapable of replacing the supranational spiritual unity of the Church of Christ, but it will always run the risk of being more dangerous than beneficent if it does not recognize the principles of Christian law and the real subordination of the temporal to the spiritual.

zens, they may be bound to take in the political sphere, Catholics
have to pursue at the same time, in the spiritual domain, the
restoration of that Christendom of prayer, of knowledge and of
love, if not of public law, mentioned a moment ago: a supranational work to which as Catholics they are summoned by the Holy
Spirit and the Church. . . .

To the methods used by the English in North America and in
India, Protestantism had no opposition to offer. The history of
modern colonization, heroic in its soldiers but dishonored by gold,
carries a heavy load of iniquities, of which the "opium war" . . .
is merely one among many. All of that is in the field of worldly
trafficking, and will be paid for. What I wish to underline is a fact
of the spiritual order. Prejudices about the radical inferiority of the
non-white races, invading the minds of both clergy and laity and
even of many among those consecrated to the apostolate, have too
long caused missionaries to be looked on as apostles not only of
Jesus Christ, but also of a particular human or national culture,
sometimes even as forerunners of colonists and merchants. That
was one of the chief obstacles to the evangelization of the world.
Today the Church is surmounting that obstacle. She is reminding
us that her missionaries must renounce all worldly interest, all concern for national propaganda, know Christ only, and that they are
sent to found churches that will be self-sufficient, complete with
their own clergy. She does not say that all races and all nations
have the same historical vocation and an equal human development; but she does say, and in the most meaningful way, that they
are all called by God, all alike included in His charity, that each
has its legitimate place in the spiritual unity of Christendom. . . .

Orient as well as Occident needs the lessons of a wisdom which
orders all things according to the hierarchies of nature and grace.
Please excuse me for using an earlier study [7] in which I wrote:
"The fact is that the order of reason, no longer kept within the
order of charity, has everywhere disintegrated and is no longer
good for anything. The rationalist evil has caused discord between
nature and the form of reason. It has now become exceedingly
difficult to stay within the bounds of the human. A man must place
his stake either above reason and still for it, or below reason and

---

[7] *Chroniques du roseau d'or,* 1er numéro, 1925.

against it. But only the theological virtues and the supernatural gifts and infused contemplation are above reason. All the so-called suprarational which is not in charity, in the long run serves only animality. Hatred of reason will never be anything but the revolt of genus against specific difference.

". . . Wherever the living faith takes root, there we shall see the adhesion to what is truly above reason, to uncreated Truth and the wisdom of the saints, simultaneously achieve—assuredly not without labor—the restoration of the very order of reason, implied as a condition for supernatural life. And so the Gospel and philosophy, mystic and metaphysician, divine and human go hand in hand."

When we think of Europe, and especially of Mediterranean civilization, all the grandeurs of its vocation and of its past dazzle us. One point, nevertheless, should give us pause. Whatever may be its intrinsic titles, the kind of historic monopoly which that civilization enjoyed in fact, today seems shaken. Here we must understand the significance of the war and the frightful rent it made. The remark of Benedict XV about the suicide of Europe cuts deeper than people think. Europe has killed its past. Let people weep as much as they please over the gods of Hellas and the whole classic past, the vast secular body of Christian lay culture from which every European coming into the world drew some nourishing sap of humanity and which carried him along in life, educated him and bore him up on all sides, seems now as if it were inanimate. In fact, those who received so much from it, today have the feeling that they are no longer receiving anything from it. All the sweetness and beauty, the forms, the values, the very images by which our ancestors lived, which made nature fraternal to them and the universe familiar and which prepared us in them from generation to generation, have all at once become something far off and separate from us: perfectly worthy of admiration and respect, but immobilized in that which is no more. This undoubtedly is the deepest cause of the great disorder suffered by youth today. They are strolling in their own humanity as in a museum, they see their hearts in the show-cases. Too many masterpieces. Is it any wonder that they should want to smash everything? We are exotic to our own selves. Is it any wonder that nothing seems exotic to us and that every human form should indifferently awaken our curiosity, or our ennui?

Souls are stripped bare, and the Church also in a sense is bare. All the wool and silk, all the riches of secular humanity with which the civilization of a chosen part of the world clothed and shielded her, and sometimes oppressed her, are falling in tatters. This clothing is not the Church. It does not matter to her proper life. But the marvellous light which she sheds in the world should not hide from us the fact that the Prince of this world is making the world more and more alien to her. Ah, well, she is not afraid of solitude. If she must, she will live in the desert and make it bloom, and there find new ornaments.

Not that I despair of Europe. This death I just spoke of is not a real death. The deep springs of Europe's life are still there, hidden, not dried up. But I do say that no purely human means, but only the Church and the Faith, can make them gush forth again. Europe will rise again only if she opens her heart to the spirit of Christ. Then only will she be able to resume her mission, which was to serve the world by guiding it, not to rule it for her own profit. Meantime, the Church reminds us that if our culture is Greco-Latin, our religion is not. The Church adopted this culture, but did not subordinate herself to it. . . .

And let it not be thought that she will ever abandon the higher virtues which she herself caused Hellenic and Latin culture to produce. If she made so great a use of this culture, a very simple reason may always be given: like ancient Hebraism in the order of revelation, this culture had received from Providence in the order of reason a privilege it would be senseless to deny; it is the only culture in which human reason nearly succeeded. It was therefore normal that it should furnish the supernatural life of the Church with choice human means. Besides, to achieve this success, the higher influences dispensed by the Church herself were required. Only they enable reason really to reach that universality in the natural order to which it essentially tends, but of which man's weakness leaves it short. It took centuries of Christian elaboration for the intellect finally to attain to the integral universalism which truth requires. St. Thomas Aquinas is the great exponent of this universalism developed in reason under the light of faith, and this is why the Church has such a predilection for his teaching and has made it, in the words of Benedict XV, "her own teaching."

It has been justly said and it will bear repetition: "It is not

Catholicism that is Thomist, it is Thomism that is Catholic, and it is Catholic because it is universal" (H. Woroniecki). The metaphysics and theology of St. Thomas are expressed in a body of symbols in Latin, but this wisdom itself is no more bound to Latinism than to the physics of Aristotle or of Ptolemy. It welcomes all being, because it is absolutely docile to being. . . . Today's demand is that it come forward and occupy the most advanced positions. . . .

Because reason suffers a natural infirmity and has not the divine guarantees of integrity and perfection proper to faith, it may well be that important potentialities of rational wisdom, either philosophical or theological, have been hidden or insufficiently developed in the thought of the West. We have much to learn in this regard from our Slav brothers and from an authentic Christian spirituality which, even if schismatic, still knows how to beget saints. We have something to learn also from non-Christian forms of thought, and, let me say, from all the errors of the world, since they always hold some truth captive . . .

Let us not conceal the fact that an immense and difficult task is imposed on Catholics. To make sure that the universalism of Christ triumphs, it is necessary today to make up for the Christian education which has been lacking to many nations. By adapting Catholicism to them? If adaptation means change, one does not adapt truth, but adapts himself to it. By adapting those peoples to Catholicism? If adaptation means conformity to something alien, there is no need of adaptation to Catholicism, which is nowhere alien. Let us choose a better word and say that much work of preparation is required, such a preparation as will enable these peoples to let the Gospel take root in their own cultures.

This work is possible because in spite of all the accidental differences—exaggerated out of all bounds, it seems, by many philologists and theorists—man and reason are everywhere the same. "What struck me most on my arrival in China," Père Lebbe has told me, "was not the difference, but the likeness." Besides, in every place God has left some marks, some hidden stepping-stones which it is vital to uncover.

This work is terribly difficult because it must respect, in matters where the human subject only too readily confuses everything, both the absolute that is immutable truth, and the relative that is in every contingent mode of cultural development. One law tells us that grace has a natural right over all natures and all nations and that in every country the house of God is man's common birthplace. Another law tells us that every weakness with regard to error is paid for in blood and that we do not lead souls to the light by giving in to darkness.

This work must have universal collaboration. May it please God to awaken intellectual vocations among the converted of every nation! And may they come quickly, before too many ruins and bloody bodies become the guideposts of the earth! . . .

Purely defensive positions, compromises, provisional retreats, partial truths are no longer worth a penny. What we are called to love is a universal expansion of the intellect. The hour has struck. The soul wants to adhere unreservedly to the absolutism of truth and charity. There must appear men free of everything but Christ. Saints—e.g., St. Vincent Ferrer and Blessed Grignon de Montfort —have foretold their coming. They will make no exception of persons, nations, races. Old ways or modern prejudices, the security of the rich, the fate of grammar or of good taste, will occupy them very little. Dividing light from darkness in all things, they will undertake to reconcile human antagonisms in justice and to give man back wholly to God. Love will make them universal by grace as God is universal by nature, and will expand their intelligence to the measure of the divine intentions.

PART III

The Gospel and Human Society

13 CHRISTIAN HUMANISM*

THE SECULARIZATION OF
THE CHRISTIAN IMAGE OF MAN

EVERY GREAT PERIOD OF CIVILIZATION IS DOMINATED BY a certain peculiar idea that man fashions of man. Our behavior depends on this image as much as on our very nature—an image which appears with striking brilliance in the minds of some particularly representative thinkers, and which, more or less unconscious in the human mass, is nonetheless strong enough to mold after its own pattern the social and political formations that are characteristic of a given cultural epoch.

In broad outline, the image of man which reigned over mediaeval Christendom depended upon St. Paul and St. Augustine. This image was to disintegrate from the time of the Renaissance and the Reformation—torn between an utter Christian pessimism which despaired of human nature and an utter Christian optimism which counted on human endeavor more than on divine grace. The image of man which reigned over modern times depended upon Descartes, John Locke, the Enlightenment, and Jean-Jacques Rousseau.

Here we are confronted with the process of secularization of the Christian man which took place from the sixteenth century on. Let's not be deceived by the merely philosophical appearance of such a process. In reality, the man of Cartesian Rationalism was a pure mind conceived after an angelistic pattern. The man of Natural Religion was a Christian gentleman who did not need grace, miracle, or revelation, and was made virtuous and just by his own

---

* *The Range of Reason* (New York: Scribners, 1952), pp. 185–199.

good nature. The man of Jean-Jacques Rousseau was, in a much more profound and significant manner, the very man of St. Paul transferred to the plane of pure nature—innocent as Adam before the fall, longing for a state of divine freedom and bliss, corrupted by social life and civilization as the sons of Adam by original sin. He was to be redeemed and set free, not by Christ, but by the essential goodness of human nature, which must be restored by means of an education without constraint and must reveal itself in the City of Man of coming centuries, in that form of state in which "everyone obeying all, will nevertheless continue to obey only himself."

This process was not at all a merely rational process. It was a process of secularization of something consecrated, elevated above nature by God, called to a divine perfection, and living a divine life in a fragile and wounded vessel—the man of Christianity, the man of the Incarnation. All that meant simply bringing back this man into the realm of man himself ("anthropocentric humanism"), keeping a Christian façade while replacing the Gospel by human Reason or human Goodness, and expecting from Human Nature what had been expected from the virtue of God giving Himself to His creatures. Enormous promises, divine promises were made to man at the dawn of modern times. Science, it was believed, would liberate man and make him master and possessor of all nature. An automatic and necessary progress would lead him to the earthly realm of peace, to that blessed Jerusalem which our hands would build by transforming social and political life, and which would be the Kingdom of Man, and in which we would become the supreme rulers of our own history, and whose radiance has awakened the hope and energy of the great modern revolutionaries.

THE MODERN MAN

If I were to try now to disentangle the ultimate results of this vast process of secularization, I should have to describe the progressive loss, in modern ideology, of all the certitudes, coming either from metaphysical insight or from religious faith, which had given foundation and granted reality to the image of Man in the Christian system. The historical misfortune has been the failure of philosophic Reason which, while taking charge of the old theological heritage in order to appropriate it, found itself unable even to maintain its own metaphysical pretense, its own justification of its secularized Christian man, and was obliged to decline toward a positivist denial of this very justification. Human Reason lost its grasp of Being, and became available only for the mathematical reading of sensory phenomena, and for the building up of corresponding material techniques—a field in which any absolute reality, any absolute truth, and any absolute value is of course forbidden.

Let us therefore say as briefly as possible: As regards man himself, modern man (I mean that man who seemed himself to be modern, and who starts now entering into the past) modern man knew truths—without *the* Truth; he was capable of the relative and changing truths of science, incapable and afraid of any supratemporal truth reached by Reason's metaphysical effort or of the divine Truth given by the Word of God. Modern man claimed human rights and dignity—without God, for his ideology grounded human rights and human dignity on a godlike, infinite autonomy of human will, which any rule or measurement received from Another would offend and destroy. Modern man trusted in peace and fraternity—without Christ, for he did not need a Redeemer, he was to save himself by himself alone, and his love for mankind did not need to be founded in divine charity. Modern man constantly progressed toward good and toward the possession of the earth—without having to face evil on earth, for he did not believe in the existence of evil; evil was only an imperfected stage in evolution, which a further stage was naturally and necessarily to transcend. Modern man enjoyed human life and worshipped human life as having an infinite value—without possessing a soul or knowing the gift of oneself, for the soul was an unscientific concept, inherited from the dreams of primitive man. And if a man does not give his soul to the one he loves, what can he give? He can give money, not himself.

As concerns civilization, modern man had in the "bourgeois" state a social and political life, a life in common, without common good or common work, for the aim of common life consisted only of preserving everyone's freedom to enjoy private ownership, acquire wealth, and seek his own pleasure. Modern man believed in liberty—without the mastery of self or moral responsibility, for free will was incompatible with scientific determinism; and he believed in equality—without justice, for justice, too, was a metaphysical idea that lost any rational foundation and lacked any criterion in our modern biological and sociological outlook. Modern man placed his hope in machinism, in technique, and in mechanical or industrial civilization—without wisdom to dominate them and put them at the service of human good and freedom, for he expected freedom from the development of external techniques themselves, not from any ascetic effort toward the internal possession of self. And how can one who does not possess the standards of human life, which are metaphysical, apply them to our use of the machine? The law of the machine, which is the law of matter, will apply itself to him, and enslave him.

As regards, lastly, the internal dynamism of human life, modern man looked for happiness—without any final end to be aimed at, or any rational pattern to which to adhere; the most natural concept and motive power, that of happiness, was thus warped by the loss of the concept and the sense of purpose or finality (for finality is but one with desirability, and desirability but one with happiness). Happiness became the movement itself toward happiness, a movement at once limitless and increasingly lower, more and more stagnant. And modern man looked for democracy—without any heroic task of justice to be performed and without brotherly love from which to get inspiration. The most significant political improvement of modern times, the concept of, and the devotion to, the rights of the human person and the rights of the people, was thus warped by the same loss of the concept and the sense of purpose or finality, and by the repudiation of the evangelical ferment acting in human history; democracy tended to become an embodiment of the sovereign will of the people in the machinery of a bureaucratic state more and more irresponsible and more and more asleep.

THE CRISIS OF OUR CIVILIZATION

I have spoken just now of the infinite promises made to man at the dawn of modern times. The great undertaking of secularized Christian man has achieved splendid results for everyone but man himself; in what concerns man himself things have turned out badly—and this is not surprising.

The process of secularization of the Christian man concerns above all the idea of man and the philosophy of life which developed in the modern age. In the concrete reality of human history, a process of growth occurred at the same time, great human con-

quests were achieved, owing to the natural movement of civilization and to the primitive impulse, the evangelical one, toward the
democratic ideal. At least the civilization of the nineteenth century remained Christian in its real though forgotten or disregarded
principles, in the secularized remnants involved in its very idea of
man and civilization; in the religious freedom—thwarted as this
may have been at certain moments and in certain countries—that
it willingly or unwillingly preserved; even in the very emphasis on
reason and human grandeur which its freethinkers used as a weapon
against Christianity; and finally in the secularized feeling which inspired, despite a wrong ideology, its social and political improvements, and its great hopes.

But the split had progressively increased between the real behavior of this secularized Christian world and the moral and spiritual
principles which had given it its meaning and its internal consistency, and which it came to ignore. Thus, this world seemed
emptied of its own principles; it tended to become a universe of
words, a nominalistic universe, a dough without leaven. It lived
and endured by habit and by force acquired from the past, not by
its own power; it was pushed forward by a *vis a tergo,* not by an
internal dynamism. It was utilitarian, its supreme rule was utility.
Yet utility which is not a means toward a goal is of no use at all.
It was capitalistic (in the nineteenth-century sense of this word,
which is the genuine and unmitigated sense), and capitalistic civilization enabled the initiatives of the individual to achieve tremendous conquests over material nature. Yet, as Werner Sombart observed, the man of this age was neither "ontologic" nor "erotic";
that is to say, he had lost the sense of Being because he lived in
signs and by signs, and he had lost the sense of Love because he
did not enjoy the life of a person dealing with other persons, but
he underwent the hard labor of enrichment for the sake of enrichment.

Despite the wrong ideology I have just described, and the disfigured image of man which is linked to it, our civilization bears
in its very substance the sacred heritage of human and divine values
which depends on the struggle of our forefathers for freedom, on
Judaeo-Christian tradition, and on classical antiquity, and which
has been sadly weakened in its efficiency but not at all destroyed
in its potential reserves.

The most alarming symptom in the present crisis is that, while engaged in a death struggle for the defense of these values, we have too often lost faith and confidence in the principles on which what we are defending is founded, because we have more often than not forgotten the true and authentic principles and because, at the same time, we feel more or less consciously the weakness of the insubstantial ideology which has preyed upon them like a parasite.

MARXIST AND RACIST DELUSIONS

The great revolutionary movements which reacted against our secularized Christian world were to aggravate the evil and bring it to a peak, for they developed toward a definitive break with Christian values. Here it is a question both of a doctrinal opposition to Christianity and of an existential opposition to the presence and action of Christ at the core of human history.

A first development continued and climaxed the trend of secularized reason, the "anthropocentric humanism," in the direction which it followed from its origin, in the direction of rationalistic hopes, now no longer constituted solely as philosophical ideology but as a lived religion. This development arises from the unfolding of all the consequences of the principle that man alone, and through himself alone, works out his salvation.

The purest case of this tendency is that of Marxism. No matter how strong some of the pessimistic aspects of Marxism may be, it remains attached to this postulate. Marxist materialism remained rationalistic, so much so that for it the movement proper to matter is a *dialectical* movement.

If man alone and through himself alone works out his salvation, then this salvation is purely and exclusively temporal, and must be accomplished without God, and even against God—I mean against whatever in man and the human world bears the likeness of God, that is to say, from the Marxist point of view, the likeness of "alienation" and enslavement; this salvation demands the giving up of personality, and the organization of collective man into one single body whose supreme destiny is to gain dominion over matter and human history. What becomes, then, of the image of man? Man is no longer the creature and image of God, a personality which implies free will and is responsible for an eternal destiny, a being which possesses rights and is called to the conquest of freedom and to a self-achievement consisting of love and charity. He is a particle of the social whole and lives on the collective consciousness of the whole, and his happiness and liberty lie in serving the work of the whole. The whole itself is an economic and industrial whole, its essential and primordial work consists of the industrial domination of nature, for the sake of the very whole which alone presents absolute value, and has nothing above itself. There is here a thirst for communion, but communion is sought in economic activity, in pure productivity, which, being regarded as the paradise and only genuine goal of human endeavor, is but the world of a beheaded reason, no longer cut out for truth, but engulfed in a demiurgic task of fabrication and domination over things. The human person is sacrificed to industry's titanism, which is the god of the merely industrial community.

Rationalistic reason winds up in intoxication with matter. By the same token it enters a process of self-degradation. Thus it is that in the vision of the world offered by Marxist materialism, rationalistic overoptimism comes to coincide, in many respects, with another development, depending upon a quite opposite trend of mind, which may be described as an utter reaction against any kind of rationalism and humanism. The roots of this other development are pessimistic, it corresponds to a process of animalization of the image of man, in which a formless metaphysics avails itself of every misconception of scientific or sociological data to satisfy a hidden resentment against Reason and human dignity. According to this trend of mind the human species is only a branch which sprouted by chance on the genealogical tree of the monkeys; all our systems of ideas and values are only an epiphenomenon of the social evolution of the primitive clan; or an ideological superstructure determined by, and masking the struggle for life of, class interests and imperialistic ambitions. All our seemingly rational and free behavior is only an illusory appearance emerging from the inferno of our unconscious and of instinct. All our seemingly spiritual feelings and activities, poetic creation, human pity and devotion, religious faith, contemplative love, are only the sublimation of sexual libido or an outgrowth of matter. Man is unmasked; the countenance of the beast appears. The human specificity, which rationalism had caused to vanish into pure spirit, now vanishes in animality.

Yet the development of which I am speaking has its real sources in something much more profound, which began to reveal itself from the second half of the last century on: anguish and despair, as exemplified in Dostoevsky's *The Possessed*. A deeper abyss than animality appears in the unmasking of man. Having given up God so as to be self-sufficient, man has lost track of his soul. He looks in vain for himself; he turns the universe upside down trying to find himself; he finds masks and, behind the masks, death.

Then was to be witnessed the spectacle of a tidal wave of irrationality, of hatred of intelligence, the awakening of a tragic opposition between life and spirit. To overcome despair, Nietzsche proclaimed the advent of the superman, of the will to power, the death of truth, the death of God. More terrific voices, the voices of a base multitude whose baseness itself appears as an apocalyptic sign, cry out: We have had enough of lying optimism and illusory morality, enough of freedom and personal dignity and justice and peace and faithfulness and goodness which made us mad with distress. Let us give ground to the infinite promises of evil, and of swarming death, and of blessed enslavement, and of triumphant despair!

The purest case of this tendency was Nazi racism. It was grounded not in an idolatry of reason ending in the hate of every transcendent value, but in a mysticism of instinct and life ending in the hatred of reason. Intelligence for it was of use only to develop techniques of destruction and to pervert the function of language. Its demonic religiosity tried to pervert the very nature of God, to make of God Himself an idol. It invoked God, but as a spirit protector attached to the glory of a people or a state, or as a demon of the race. A god who will end by being identified with an invincible force at work in the blood was set up against the God of Sinai and against the God of Calvary, against the One Whose law rules nature and human conscience, against the Word Which was at the beginning, against the God of Whom it is said that He is Love.

Here, too, man is no longer the creature and image of God; a person animated by a spiritual soul and endowed with free will, and responsible for an eternal destiny, who possesses rights and is called to the conquest of freedom and to a self-achievement consisting of love and charity. And now this disfigured image of man is rooted in a warring pessimism. Man is a particle of the political whole, and lives by the *Volksgeist*. Yet for this collective whole there is even no longer any decoy of happiness and liberty and of universal emancipation, but only power and self-realization through violence. Communion is sought in the glorification of the race and in a common hatred of some enemy, in animal blood, which, separated from the spirit, is no more than a biological inferno. The human person is sacrificed to the demon of the blood, which is the god of the community of blood.

There is nothing but human despair to be expected either from Communism or Racism. On the one hand, Racism, on its irrational and biological basis, rejects all universalism and breaks even the natural unity of the human race, so as to impose the hegemony of a so-called higher racial essence. On the other hand, if it is true that in the dialectic of culture, Communism is the final state of anthropocentric rationalism, it follows that by virtue of the universality inherent in reason—even in reason gone mad—Communism dreams of an all-embracing emancipation and pretends to substitute for the universalism of Christianity its own earthly universalism—the universalism of the good tidings of Deception and Terror, and of the immolation of man to the blind god of History.

THE IDEA OF A NEW CHRISTIAN CIVILIZATION

If the description which I outlined above is accurate, it appears that the only way of regeneration for the human community is a rediscovery of the true image of man and a definite attempt toward a new Christian civilization, a new Christendom. Modern times have sought many good things along wrong tracks. The question now is to seek these good things along right tracks, and to save the human values and achievements aimed at by our forefathers and endangered by the false philosophy of life of the last century, and to have for that purpose the courage and audacity of proposing to ourselves the biggest task of renewal, of internal and external transformation. A coward flees backward, away from new things. The man of courage flees forward, in the midst of new things.

Christians find themselves today, in the order of temporal civilization, facing problems similar to those which their forefathers met in the sixteenth and seventeenth centuries. At that time modern physics and astronomy in the making were at one with the philosophical systems set up against Christian tradition. The defenders of the latter did not know how to make the necessary distinction; they took a stand both against that which was to become modern science and against the philosophical errors which at the outset preyed upon this science as parasites. Three centuries were needed to get away from this misunderstanding, if it be true that a better philosophical outlook has actually caused us to get away from it. It would be disastrous to fall once again into similar errors today in the field of the philosophy of civilization. The true substance of of the nineteenth century's aspirations, as well as the human gains it achieved, must be saved, from its own errors and from the aggression of totalitarian barbarism. A world of genuine humanism and Christian inspiration must be built.

In the eyes of the observer of historical evolution, a new Christian civilization is going to be quite different from mediaeval civilization, though in both cases Christianity is at the root. For the historical climate of the Middle Ages and that of modern times are utterly diverse. Briefly, mediaeval civilization, whose historical ideal was the Holy Empire, constituted a "sacral" Christian civilization, in which temporal things, philosophical and scientific reason, and the reigning powers, were subservient organs or instruments of spiritual things, of religious faith, and of the Church. In the course of the following centuries temporal things gained a position of autonomy, and this was in itself a normal process. The misfortune has been that this process became warped and, instead of being a process of distinction for a better form of union, progressively severed earthly civilization from evangelical inspiration.

A new age of Christendom, if it is to come, will be an age of reconciliation of that which was disjoined, the age of a "secular" Christian civilization, in which temporal things, philosophical and scientific reason, and civil society, will enjoy their autonomy and at the same time recognize the quickening and inspiring role that spiritual things, religious faith, and the Church play from their higher plane. Then a Christian philosophy of life would guide a community vitally, not decoratively Christian, a community of human rights and of the dignity of the human person, in which men belonging to diverse racial stocks and to diverse spiritual lineages would work at a temporal common task which was truly human and progressive.

In the last analysis, I would say that from the end of the Middle Ages—a moment at which the human creature, while awakening to itself, felt itself oppressed and crushed in its loneliness—modern times have longed for a rehabilitation of the human creature. They sought this rehabilitation in a separation from God. It was to be sought in God. The human creature claims the right to be loved: it can be really and efficaciously loved only in God. It must be respected in its very connection with God and because it receives everything—and its very dignity—from Him. After the great disillusionment of "anthropocentric humanism" and the atrocious experience of the anti-humanism of our day, what the world needs is a new humanism, a "theocentric" or integral humanism which would consider man in all his natural grandeur and weakness, in the entirety of his wounded being inhabited by God, in the full reality of nature, sin and sainthood. Such a humanism would recognize all that is irrational in man, in order to tame it to reason, and all that is suprarational, in order to have reason vivified by it and to open man to the descent of the divine into him. Its main work would be to cause the Gospel leaven and inspiration to penetrate the secular structures of life—a work of sanctification of the temporal order.

This "humanism of the Incarnation" would care for the masses, for their right to a temporal condition worthy of man and to spiritual life, and for the movement which carries labor toward the social responsibility of its coming of age. It would tend to substitute for materialistic-individualistic civilization, and for an economic system based on the fecundity of money, not a collectivistic economy but a "Christian-personalistic" democracy. This task is joined to today's crucial effort to preserve freedom from totalitarian aggression, and to a simultaneous work of reconstruction which requires no less vigor. It is also joined to a thorough awakening of the religious conscience. One of the worst diseases of the modern world, as I pointed out in an earlier essay,[1] is its dualism, the dissociation between the things of God and the things of the world. The latter, the things of social, economic, and political life, have been abandoned to their own carnal law, removed from the exigencies of the Gospel. The result is that it has become more and

---

[1] *Scholasticism and Politics* (New York: Macmillan, 1940), Chapter I, p. 22.

more impossible to live with them. At the same time, Christian ethics, not really permeating the social life of people, became in this connection—I do not mean in itself or in the Church, I mean in the world, in the general cultural behavior—a universe of formulas and words; and this universe of formulas and words was in effect made subservient in practical cultural behavior to the real energies of this same temporal world existentially detached from Christ.

In addition, modern civilization, which pays dearly today for the past, seems as if it were pushed by the self-contradiction and blind compulsions suffered by it, toward contrasting forms of misery and intensified materialism. To rise above these blind compulsions we need an awakening of liberty and of its creative forces, of which man does not become capable by the grace of the state or any party pedagogy, but by that love which fixes the center of his life infinitely above the world and temporal history. In particular, the general paganization of our civilization has resulted in man's placing his hope in force alone and in the efficacy of hate, whereas in the eyes of an integral humanism a political ideal of justice and civic friendship, requiring political strength and technical equipment, but inspired by love, is alone able to direct the work of social regeneration.

THE TRUE IMAGE OF MAN

The image of man involved in integral humanism is that of a being made of matter and spirit, whose body may have emerged from the historical evolution of animal forms, but whose immortal soul directly proceeds from divine creation. He is made for truth, capable of knowing God as the Cause of Being, by his reason, and of knowing Him in His intimate life, by the gift of faith. Man's dignity is that of an image of God, his rights derive as well as his duties from natural law, whose requirements express in the creature the eternal plan of creative Wisdom. Wounded by sin and death from the first sin of his race, whose burden weighs upon all of us, he is caused by Christ to become of the race and lineage of God, living by divine life, and called upon to enter by suffering and love into Christ's very work of redemption. Called upon by his nature, on the other hand, to unfold historically his internal potentialities by achieving little by little reason's domination over his own animality and the material universe, his progress on earth is not automatic or merely natural, but accomplished in step with freedom and together with the inner help of God, and constantly thwarted by the power of evil, which is the power of created spirits to inject nothingness into being, and which unceasingly tends to degrade human history, while unceasingly and with greater force the creative energies of reason and love revitalize and raise up this same history.

Our natural love for God and for the human being is fragile; charity alone received from God as a participation in His own life makes man efficaciously love God above everything, and each human person in God. Thus, brotherly love brings to earth, through the heart of man, the fire of eternal life, which is the true peace-maker, and it must vitalize from within that natural virtue of friend-ship, disregarded by so many fools, which is the very soul of social communities. Man's blood is at once of infinite value and must be shed all along mankind's roads "to redeem the blood of man." On the one hand, nothing in the world is more precious than one single human person. On the other hand, man exposes nothing more willingly than his own being to all kinds of danger and waste— and this condition is normal. The meaning of that paradox is that man knows very well that death is not an end, but a beginning. If I think of the perishable life of man, it is something naturally sa-cred, yet many things are still more precious: Man can be required to sacrifice it by devotion to his neighbor or by his duty to his country. Moreover, a single word is more precious than human life if in uttering this word a man braves a tyrant for the sake of truth or liberty. If I think of the imperishable life of man, of that life which makes him "a god by participation" and, beginning here below, will consist in seeing God face to face, nothing in the world is more precious than human life. And the more a man gives him-self, the more he makes this life intense within him. Every self-sacrifice, every gift of oneself involves, be it in the smallest way, a dying for the one we love. The man who knows that "after all, death is only an episode," is ready to give himself with humility, and nothing is more human and more divine than the gift of oneself, for "it is more blessed to give than to receive."

As concerns civilization, the man of Christian humanism knows that political life aims at a common good which is superior to a mere collection of the individual's goods and yet must flow back upon human persons. He knows that the common work must tend above all toward the improvement of human life itself, enabling everyone to exist on earth as a free man and to enjoy the fruits of culture and the spirit. He knows that the authority of those who are in charge of the common good, and who are, in a community of free men, designated by the people and accountable to the people, originates in the Author of Nature and is therefore binding in conscience, and is binding in conscience on condition that it be just.

The man of Christian humanism cherishes freedom as something he must be worthy of; he realizes his essential equality with other men in terms of respect and fellowship, and sees in justice the force of preservation of the political community and the prerequisite which, "bringing unequals to equality," enables civic friendship to spring forth. He is aware both of the tremendous ordeal which the advent of machinism imposes on human history, and of the marvelous power of liberation it offers to man, if the brute instinct of domination does not avail itself of the techniques of machinism, and of science itself, in order to enslave mankind; and if reason and wisdom are strong enough to turn them to the service of truly human aims and apply to them the standards of human life. The man of Christian humanism does not look for a merely industrial civilization, but for a civilization integrally human (industrial as it may be as to its material conditions) and of evangelical inspiration.

THE VERTICAL MOVEMENT AND
THE HORIZONTAL MOVEMENT IN MAN'S LIFE

As regards, finally, the internal dynamism of human life, the man of Christian humanism has an ultimate end, God to be seen and possessed—and he tends toward self-perfection, which is the chief element of that imperfect happiness which is accessible to him in earthly existence. Thus, life has meaning and a direction for him, and he is able to grow up on the way, without turning and wavering and without remaining spiritually a child. This perfection toward which he tends is not perfection of some stoic athleticism wherein a man would make himself impeccable, but rather the perfection of love, of love toward Another Whom he loves more than himself, and Whom he craves above all to join and love even more, even though in the process he carries with him imperfections and weaknesses. In such an evangelical perfection lies perfect freedom, which is to be conquered by ascetic effort but which is finally given by the very One Who is loved, and Who was the first to love us.

But this vertical movement toward divine union and self-perfection is not the only movement involved in the internal dynamism of human life. The second one, the horizontal movement, concerns the evolution of mankind and progressively reveals the substance and creative forces of man in history. The horizontal movement of civilization, when directed toward its authentic temporal aims, helps the vertical movement of souls. And without the movement of souls toward their eternal aim, the movement of civilization would lose the charge of spiritual energy, human pressure, and creative radiance which animates it toward its temporal accomplishment. For the man of Christian humanism history has a meaning and a direction. The progressive integration of humanity is also a progressive emancipation from human servitude and misery as well as from the constraints of material nature. The supreme ideal which the political and social work in mankind has to aim at is thus the inauguration of a brotherly city, which does not imply the hope that all men will someday be perfect on earth and love each other fraternally, but the hope that the existential *state* of human life and the structures of civilization will draw nearer to their perfection, the standard of which is justice and friendship—and what aim, if not perfection, is to be aimed at? This supreme ideal is the very one of a genuine democracy, of the new democracy we are expecting. It requires not only the development of powerful technical equipment and of a firm and rational politico-social organization in human communities, but also a heroic philosophy of life, and the quickening inner ferment of evangelical inspiration. It is in order to advance toward such an ideal that the community must be strong. The inauguration of a common life which responds to the truth of our nature, freedom to be achieved, and friendship to be set up at the core of a civilization vitalized by virtues higher than civic virtues, all these define the historical ideal for which men can be asked to work, fight and die. Against the deceptive myths raised by the powers of illusion, a vaster and greater hope must rise up, a bolder promise must be made to the human race. The truth of

God's image, as it is naturally impressed upon us, freedom, and fraternity are not dead. If our civilization struggles with death, the reason is not that it dares too much, or that it proposes too much to men. It is that it does not dare enough or propose enough to them. It shall revive, a new civilization shall come to life on condition that it hope for, and will, and love truly and heroically truth, freedom, and fraternity.

14 THE MEANING OF CONTEMPORARY ATHEISM*

THE SUBJECT DISCUSSED IN THIS CHAPTER INVOLVES MANY deep and intricate problems. I do not pretend to dogmatize about them; the views that I shall put forward are no more than tentative views, which originate in a desire to look for the hidden spiritual significance which lies within the present agony of the world.

VARIOUS KINDS OF ATHEISM

Let us try, first, to establish in a systematic way the distinction between the diverse forms of atheism. This distinction can be made from either of two points of view: from the point of view of the attitude of the human being who professes himself to be an atheist, or from the point of view of the logical content of various atheistic philosophies.

From the first point of view, or with regard to the manner in which atheism is professed, I have already remarked that there are, in the first place, *practical atheists,* who believe that they believe in God but who in actual fact deny His existence by their deeds and the testimony of their behavior. Then there are *pseudo-atheists,* who believe that they do not believe in God but who in actual fact unconsciously believe in Him, because the God whose existence they deny is not God but something else. Finally there are *absolute atheists,* who really do deny the existence of the very God in Whom the believers believe—God the Creator, Savior and Father, Whose

* The Range of Reason (New York: Scribners, 1952), pp. 103–117.

name is infinitely over and above any name we can utter. Those absolute atheists stand committed to change their entire system of values and to destroy in themselves everything that could possibly suggest the name they have rejected; they have chosen to stake their all against divine Transcendence and any vestige of Transcendence whatsoever.

From the second point of view, that is, with regard to the logical content of various atheistic philosophies, I would divide atheism into negative and positive atheism.

By *negative atheism* I mean a merely negative or destructive process of casting aside the idea of God, which is replaced only by a void. Such a negative atheism can be shallow and empirical, like the atheism of the *libertins* in the eighteenth century—then it digs a hollow in the center of the universe of thought which has taken shape through the centuries around the idea of God, but it does not bother about changing that universe; it is merely concerned with making us live a comfortable life, enjoying the freedom of doing exactly as we please. On the other hand, negative atheism can be lived at a profound and metaphysical level; in which case the hollow it creates at the heart of things extends to and lays waste our whole universe of thought; the freedom it claims for the human Self is absolute independence, a kind of divine independence that this Self, like Dostoevsky's Kirilov, has no better way of affirming than by suicide and voluntary annihilation.

By *positive atheism* I mean an active struggle against everything that reminds us of God—that is to say, antitheism rather than atheism—and at the same time a desperate, I would say heroic, effort to recast and reconstruct the whole human universe of thought and the whole human scale of values in accordance with that state of war against God. Such positive atheism was the tragic, solitary atheism of a Nietzsche; such is today the literary, fashionable atheism of existentialism; such is the revolutionary atheism of dialectical materialism. The latter is of special interest to us, because it has succeeded in getting a considerable number of men to accept whole-heartedly this new kind of faith, and to give themselves to it with unquestionable sincerity.

Now when I speak of contemporary atheism, I have in mind atheism seen under the last aspect I have just mentioned; I consider it the most significant form of atheism, one which spells a new and unheard of historic event because it is an atheism at once *absolute and positive*. Human history has been confronted, for almost a century now, with the stormy bursting forth of an atheism which is both *absolute* (making man actually deny God Himself) and *positive* (antitheism, demanding to be lived in full by man and to change the face of the earth).

THE TWO-FOLD INCONSISTENCY OF CONTEMPORARY ATHEISM

a. *An Act of Faith in Reverse Gear*

After these preliminary signposts I should like to point out that today's absolute-positive atheism involves a dual inconsistency.

How does absolute-positive atheism come to birth in the mind of a man? At this point we are faced with a remarkable fact. A man does not become an absolute atheist as a result of some inquiry into the problem of God carried on by speculative reason. No doubt he takes into account the negative conclusions afforded in this connection by the most radical forms of rationalist or positivist philosophy; he does not neglect, either, the old platitude which will have it that the scientific explanation of the universe purely and simply got clear of the existence of God. But all that is for him a second-hand means of defence, not the prime propelling and determining incentive. Neither those philosophical conclusions nor that nonsensical commonplace does he submit to any critical examination. He takes them for granted. He believes in them. And why? By virtue of an inner act of freedom, in the production of which he commits his whole personality. The starting point of absolute atheism is, in my opinion, a basic act of moral choice, a crucial free determination. If at the moment when he takes stock of himself and decides upon the whole direction of his life, a man confuses the transition from youth to manhood with the refusal not only of childhood's subordinations but of any subordination whatsoever; if he thus considers the rejection of any transcendent law as an act of moral maturity and emancipation; and if he decides to confront good and evil in a totally and absolutely free experience, in which any ultimate end and any rule coming from above are cast aside forever—such a free moral determination, dealing with the pri-

mary values of existence, will mean that this man has entirely ex-
cluded God from his own universe of life and thought. Here is, in
my opinion, the point at which absolute atheism begins in the
depths of a man's spiritual activity.

But what is this I have just been describing if not a kind of act
of faith, an act of faith in reverse gear, whose content is not an adherence to the transcendent God, but, on the contrary, a rejection
of Him?

Thus it is that absolute atheism is positive atheism. This must
be stressed: It is in no way a mere absence of belief in God. It
is rather a refusal of God, a fight against God, a challenge to God.
The absolute atheist is delivered over to an inner dialectic which
obliges him ceaselessly to destroy any resurgence in himself of
what he has buried. In proportion as the dialectic of atheism develops in his mind—each time he is confronted with the natural
notion of and tendency to an ultimate End, or with the natural
notion of and natural interest in absolute values or unconditioned
standards, or with some metaphysical anxiety—he will discover
in himself vestiges of Transcendence which have not yet been abolished. He must get rid of them. God is a perpetual threat to him.
His case is not a case of practical forgetting, but a case of deeper
and deeper commitment to refusal and fight. He is bound to struggle
against God without pause or respite, and to change, to recast
everything in himself and in the world on the base of that antitheism.

Now what does all this mean? Absolute atheism starts in an act
of faith in reverse gear and is a full-blown religious commitment.
Here we have the first internal inconsistency of contemporary atheism: It proclaims that all religion must necessarily vanish away,
and it is itself a religious phenomenon.

b. *An Abortive Protest and Rupture*

The second inconsistency is very like the first one. Absolute atheism starts as a claim of man to become the sole master of
his own destiny, totally freed from any "alienation" and heteronomy, made totally and decisively independent of any ultimate end as
well as of any eternal law imposed upon him by any transcendent
God. According to atheistic theorists, does not the idea of God
originate in an alienation of human nature separated from its true

subject and transmuted into an ideal and sublimated image whose very transcendence and sovereign attributes ensure man's submission to an enslaved state of existence? Is it not by getting rid of that sublimated image and of any transcendence that human nature will achieve the fullness of its own stature and freedom and bring about the final "reconciliation between essence and existence"?

But what is the actual end-all of the philosophy of absolute Immanence which is all one with absolute atheism? Everything which was formerly considered superior to time and participating in some transcendent quality—either ideal value or spiritual reality—is now absorbed in the movement of temporal existence and the all-engulfing ocean of Becoming and of History. Truth and justice, good and evil, faithfulness, all the standards of conscience, henceforth perfectly relativized, become radically contingent: they are but changing shapes of the process of History, just as for Descartes they were but contingent creations of divine Freedom. The truth, at any given moment, is that which conforms with the requirements of History's begettings. As a result, truth changes as time goes on. An act of mine which was meritorious today will be criminal tomorrow. And that is the way my conscience must pass judgment on it. The human intellect and moral conscience have to become heroically tractable.

And what of the Self, the person, the problem of human destiny? A total rejection of Transcendence logically entails a total adherence to Immanence. There is nothing eternal in man; he will die in the totality of his being; there is nothing to be saved in him. But he can give himself, and give himself entirely, to the Whole of which he is a part, to the boundless flux which alone is real and which bears the fate of mankind. By virtue of his decisive moral experience itself, and of that primary moral choice—against any ultimate End—which I have tried to describe and which commits the human personality far more profoundly than individualistic egoism or epicureanism can do, the absolute or positive atheist hands himself over, body and soul, to the ever-changing and all-engulfing Whole —be it the social or the cosmic totality. It is not only that he is satisfied to die in it, as a blade of grass in the loam, and to make it more fertile by dissolving in it. He is also willing to make of his own total being, with all its values and standards and beliefs, an offering given, as I said above, to that great Minotaur that is His-

tory. Duty and virtue mean nothing else to him than a total submission and immolation of himself to the sacred voracity of
Becoming.

Here we are confronted with a new variety of mystical "pure
love"—giving up every hope for personal redemption—a real un-
selfishness, self-denial and self-sacrifice, a total and absolute disinterestedness—but a monstrous one, paid for at a price of the very
Self, and the existence and dignity of the human Person: at the
price of that which, in each one of us, is an end in itself and the
image of God. Christ had said: "He who loses his own soul for
Me, shall find it," [1] because losing one's own soul for God is delivering it over to absolute Truth and Goodness and Love, to the
eternal Law itself which transcends all the contingency and muta-
bility of Becoming. The positive atheist delivers over his own soul
—and not in order to save it—to a worldly demiurge, crazy for
human minds to bend and bow and yield at the event's sweet will.

I am not belittling the spiritual significance of the moral attitude of the absolute atheist. On the contrary, I am emphasizing
the kind of mystical disinterestedness, and the elements of greatness and generosity which are implied in it. But I say that this
moral attitude also involves a basic inconsistency, and that the
whole process is in the end a failure. That rupture with God began
as a claim to total independence and emancipation, as a proud
revolutionary break with everything that submits man to alienation
and heteronomy. It ends up in obeisance and prostrate submission
to the all-powerful movement of History, in a kind of sacred surrender of the human soul to the blind god of History.

THE ATHEIST AND THE SAINT

a. *The Initial Act of Rupture Brought About by the Saint*

The failure I have just mentioned reveals to us a fact
which has, to my mind, a deep significance: I mean the fact that
absolute atheism has a revolutionary power which materially speaking is exceedingly strong, but spiritually speaking is very weak indeed, minute, and deceptive; I mean the fact that its radicalism is
an inevitable self-deluded radicalism, for a genuinely revolutionary

---

[1] Matth. 10, 39.

spirit does not kneel before History, it presumes to make History; I mean the fact that absolute atheism falls short of that uncompromising protest, of that absolute non-compliance the semblance— and the expectation—of which make it seductive for many people.

Thus, we arrive at the point I should like especially to discuss. Which of these two, the Atheist or the Saint, is the more uncompromising and thorough-going, the harder, the more intractable; which has his axe more deeply embedded in the root of the tree? Which brings about the more complete and far-reaching, the cleaner and more radical break?

Let us try to imagine what takes place in the soul of a saint at the crucial moment when he makes his first irrevocable decision. Let us consider St. Francis of Assisi when he threw away his raiment and appeared naked before his bishop, out of love for poverty; or St. Benedict Labre when he decided to become a verminous beggar wandering along the roads. At the root of such an act there was something so deep in the soul that it can hardly be expressed. I would say a simple refusal—not a movement of revolt which is temporary, or of despair, which is passive—rather a simple refusal, a total, stable, supremely active refusal to accept things as they are. Here it is not a question of knowing whether things and nature and the face of this world are good in their essence—to be sure they are good; being is good insofar as it is being; grace perfects nature and does not destroy it—but these truths have nothing to do with the inner act of rupture, of break, that we are now contemplating. This act is concerned with a fact, an existential fact: Things as they are are not tolerable, positively, definitely not tolerable. In actual existence the world is infected with lies and injustice and wickedness and distress and misery; the creation has been so marred by sin that in the nethermost depths of his soul the saint refuses to accept it as it is. Evil—I mean the power of sin, and the universal suffering it entails, the rot of nothingness that gnaws everywhere— evil is such that the only thing at hand which can remedy it, and which inebriates the saint with freedom and exultation and love, is to give up everything, the sweetness of the world, and what is good, and what is better, and what is pleasurable and permissible, in order to be free to be with God; it is to be totally stripped and to give himself totally in order to lay hold of the power of the Cross; it is to die for those he loves. That is a flash of intuition and of will and above the whole order of human morality. Once a human soul has been touched by such a burning wing, it becomes a stranger everywhere. It may fall in love with things, it will never rest in them. To redeem creation the saint wages war on the entire fabric of creation, with the bare weapons of truth and love. This war begins in the most hidden recesses of his own soul and the most secret stirrings of his desire: it will come to an end with the advent of a new earth and new heaven, when all that is powerful in this world will have been humiliated and all that is despised will have been exalted. The saint is alone in treading the winepress, and of the peoples there is no man with him.[2]

And I would say that in that war of which I have just spoken his God has given him the example. For, in calling intellectual creatures to share in His own uncreated life, God uproots them from the very life of which they are possessed as rooted in nature. Jews know that God is a hidden God Who conceals His name and manifests Himself to mankind in prodigies and in the stormy visions of the prophets, in order to renew the face of the earth, and Who has separated for Himself His people from all of the nations of the world. Christians know that God is both so dissatisfied with that lost world which He had made good and which evil has ruined—and at the same time so carried away by love—that He has given His Son and delivered Him over to men, in order to suffer and to die, and in this way redeem the world.

b. *The Great God of Idolaters*

To this true God the saint is entirely given. But there are false gods; even, as I shall shortly say, there is a spurious and distorted image of God that can be called the King or Jove of all false gods, the great god of the idolaters. With regard to *this* god, the saint is a thorough atheist, the most atheistic of men—just because he adores *only* God.

Let us dwell a moment on this point. And let us consider the merely rational, merely philosophical concept of God. This concept is twofold: There is the true God of the philosophers, and there is the false god of the philosophers. The true God of the philoso-

---

[2] Isaiah, 63, 3.

phers is but the true God Himself, the God of the Saints, the God of Abraham, Isaac and Jacob—imperfectly and inchoatively known, known in those attributes only which can be reached by our natural forces. Such a merely rational notion of God is an actual fact open to the supernatural.

But now suppose for yourselves a merely rational notion of God which would know the existence of the Supreme Being, but would disregard at the same time what St. Paul called His glory, deny the abyss of freedom which is meant by His transcendence, and chain Him to the very world He has made. Suppose for yourselves a merely rational—and warped—notion of God which is closed against the supernatural, and makes impossible the mysteries that are hidden in God's love and freedom and incommunicable life. Here we would have the false god of the philosophers, the Jove of all false gods. Imagine a god bound to the order of nature who is no more than a supreme warrant and justification of that order, a god who is responsible for this world without the power of redeeming it, a god whose inflexible will, that no prayer can reach, is pleased with and hallows all the evil as well as all the good of the universe, all the trickery, wickedness and cruelty together with all the generosity which are at play in nature, a god who blesses iniquity and slavery and misery, and who sacrifices man to the cosmos, and makes the tears of the children and the agony of the innocents a stark ingredient of, and a tribute offered without any compensation to, the sacred necessities of eternal cycles or of evolution. Such a god would be the unique supreme Being but made into an idol, the *naturalistic* god of nature, the Jupiter of the world, the great god of the idolaters and of the powerful on their thrones and of the rich in their earthly glory, the god of success which knows no law, and of mere fact set up as law.

I am afraid that such was the God of our modern rationalistic philosophy, the God perhaps of Leibniz and Spinoza, surely the God of Hegel.

Such was also, in quite another mood, not rationalistic, but magical, the God of pagan antiquity, or rather one of the countenances of that double-faced God. For the pagan God was ambiguous; on the one hand, he was the true God of nature and reason, the unknown God of Whom St. Paul spoke to the Athenians; and, on the other hand, he was the false god of naturalism, the self-contradictory god I have just described and who does get on very well with the Prince of this world.

It could be added that among Christian sects, some wild Gnostics, especially the followers of Marcion, who regarded the God of the Old Covenant as an evil world-maker in conflict with the Redeemer, mistook for the Creator the same false god I have been discussing, the same absurd Emperor of the world.

And this brings me to the point I want to drive home. The saint, when he brings about the great act of rupture which I stressed earlier, rejects by the same stroke, breaks and annihilates, with an irresistible violence, this spurious Emperor of the world, this false god of naturalism, this great god of the idolaters, the powerful and the rich, who is an absurd counterfeit of God, but who is also the imaginary focus whence the adoration of the cosmos radiates, and to whom we pay tribute each time we bow down before the world. With regard to this god the saint is a perfect atheist. Well, were not the Jews and the first Christians often called atheists by the pagans at the time of the Roman Empire? There was a hidden meaning in this slander.[3]

c. *The Case of the Absolute Atheist*

But let us turn at present to our modern atheists, our true and actual atheists—what can we say about them? I would suggest that, in the sense I have just emphasized, the absolute atheist is *not atheist enough*. He, too, is indignant against the Jupiter of this world, against the god of the idolaters, the powerful and the rich; he too decides to get rid of him. But instead of hurling against that false god the strength of the true God, and of giving himself to the work of the true God, as the saint does, the atheist, because he rejects the true God, can only struggle against the Jupiter of this world by calling on the strength of the immanent god of History, and by dedicating himself to the work of that immanent god.

It is indeed because he believes in the revolutionary disruptive power of the impetus of History, and because he expects from it the final emancipation of man, that the atheist delivers over his own soul to the blind god of History. Yet he is caught in a trap.

---

[3] St. Justin said: "We are called atheists. And yes, we confess it, we are atheists of those so-called gods." 1st *Apology*, VI, n. 1.

Wait a while, and the blind god of History will appear just as he is—yes, the very same Jupiter of this world, the great god of the idolaters and the powerful on their thrones and the rich in their earthly glory, and of success which knows no law, and of mere fact set up as law. He will reveal himself as this same false god in a new disguise and crowned by new idolaters, and meting out a new brand of power and success. And it is too late for the atheist. As we saw at the beginning, he is possessed by this god. He is on his knees before History. With respect to a god who is not God, he is the most tractable and obedient of the devotees.

And so his break with this world of injustice and oppression was but a shallow and temporary break. More than ever he is subservient to the world. In comparison with the saint, who consummates in his own flesh his initial rupture with the world, and every day dies unto himself, and is blessed with the beatitudes of the poor and the persecuted and all the other friends of God, and who enjoys the perfect freedom of those who are led by the Spirit, the atheist is, it seems to me, a very poor replica of the liberated mind and the heroic insurgent. Nevertheless, as I have tried to point out, it is by an ill-directed longing for inner freedom and for non-acceptance of things as they are that he has been led astray. A somewhat paradoxical, yet, in my opinion, true statement about absolute atheism would be to say that it deprives God and mankind of some potential saints, in bringing to bankruptcy their attempt at heroic freedom, and turning their effort to break with the world into a total and servile subservience to the world. With all his sincerity and devotion, the authentic, absolute atheist is after all only an abortive saint, and, at the same time, a mistaken revolutionist.

THE SAINT AND TEMPORAL HISTORY

a. *A Lost Opportunity*

There is now another paradox, this time in an opposite direction. If we look at the saint, it seems that the inner act through which he achieves his total break with the world and total liberation from the world, making him free from everything but God, will inevitably overflow from the realm of spiritual life onto the realm of temporal life. Thus, if he is not dedicated solely to a contemplative state of existence, he will be led to act as a ferment of

renewal in the structures of the world, as a stimulating and transforming energy in social matters and in the field of the activities of
civilization.

And this is true, of course. As a matter of fact, it is what has been
taking place for centuries. The Fathers of the Church were great
revolutionaries. Thomas Aquinas in the order of culture, St. Vincent de Paul in the social field, were eminent examples of genuine
radicals, whose initiative brought about decisive changes in the
history of civilization. For centuries temporal progress in the world
has been furthered by the saints.

Yet, here is the paradox that I just mentioned—the day when,
in the course of modern history, a particularly inhuman structure
of society, caused by the Industrial Revolution, made the problem
of social justice manifestly crucial; when, at the same time, the
human mind became aware of the *social* as a specific object of
knowledge and activity, and when the first attempts to create
workers' organizations provided the beginnings of a historical force
capable of acting upon social structures—then was it not the moment for the saints to take the lead in the protest of the poor and
in the movement of labor toward its historical coming of age? In
actual fact, except for a few men of faith, like Ozanam in France and
Toniolo in Italy (they are not yet canonized, but some day they
might be), the task, as we know, was not conducted by saints. It
even happened that atheists, instead of saints, took the lead in
social matters, much to the misfortune of all.

Why such a tragic vacancy? It seems difficult not to see in it a
kind of punishment of the Christian world, which for a long period
has more or less failed Christianity in its practical behavior, and
despised the lessons of the saints, and abandoned to their fate, here
below, that great flock which also belongs to Christ, that immense
herd of men whom destitution and unlivable conditions of existence
kept chained to hell on earth. Let us not be mistaken. During the
time of which I am speaking, saints were not lacking on the earth;
there was a considerable flowering of saints in the last century. But
they did not pass beyond the field of spiritual, apostolic or charitable
activities: they did not cross the threshold of temporal, social,
secular activity. And thus the gap was not filled, because in the
historical age which is ours, the indirect repercussion of the inner
renewal of conscience upon the external structures of society is

definitely not enough, although it answers a basic need and has made progressively more possible such social changes as the abolition of slavery. A specifically social activity, an activity which directly aims at improving and recasting the structures of temporal life, is also needed.

Why has this kind of activity been neglected by a great many Christians in the past? Is it on account of their supposed contempt for the world, as people say? Nonsense! The saints break with the world, but they have no contempt for creation; that they leave to apprentices. As for the general run of Christians, one need but look at them—at ourselves—(as François Mauriac reminded us rather bluntly in the second *Semaine des Intellectuels Catholiques*) [4] to be assured that we do not despise the world in the least and that we are "of the earth," as it is said in the new devotional jargon. No; the reason for which activities directly aiming at the structural changes required by social justice have been lacking for so many centuries is quite simple: the means of exercising such activities were non-existent. In the seventeenth century St. Vincent de Paul could found hospitals but he could not found trade unions. It was only after the Industrial Revolution and the way in which it developed that the possibility of directly social activity could enter people's imaginations, and that such a directly social, and not only spiritual or charitable, activity has become a crying need.

Perhaps a concrete example will help to make clear the difference between the two kinds of activity I have mentioned. A poor priest named Cottolengo, who was a saint (though his name is not to be found in the *Encyclopaedia Britannica*) founded in Turin, in the first half of the past century, a hospital that rapidly grew into a sort of huge city of all kinds of infirmity and human misery; hundreds of the poor were fed and cared for every day. But Cottolengo had established the rule that none of the money contributed for the support of his Institute should ever be saved and invested. Money each day received from the Providence of God should be spent each day, for "sufficient unto the day is the evil thereof." [5] There is even a story that one evening, as he saw that his assistants had set aside a certain amount of money for the morrow, Cottolengo threw that

---

[4] See *Foi en Jésus-Christ et monde d'aujourd'hui* (Paris: Éditions de Flore, 1949).

[5] Matth. 6, 34.

money out of the window—which in our modern world is the
height of insanity, and perhaps of sacrilege. This course of action
was in itself perfectly revolutionary, and all the more revolutionary
in that it succeeded (Cottolengo's work has thrived in an astound-
ing manner; it is now one of the most important institutions in
Turin). Yet such a course of action, for all its spiritual significance,
remained of no social consequence. It transcended the social problem. The social problem must be managed and solved in its own
order. For half a century men of good will have realized better and
better that the temporal mission of those who believe in God
is to take over the job. Still, we must not forget that, even in the
simple perspective of the temporal community, Christian social
action is not enough; political action is even less so, however necessary both of them may be. What is required of those who believe
in God is a witness of God; and what the world demands and expects of the Christian is first and foremost to see the love of truth
and brotherly love made genuinely present in and through man's
personal life—to see a gleam of the Gospel shining in the one place
where the crucial tests and crucial proof are to be found, namely, the
obscure context of relations from person to person.

b. *The Christian World Is Neither Christianity Nor the Church*

I have just spoken of the historical deficiencies of the Christian world. Parenthetically, in order to avoid any misunderstanding, I
should like to point out that by the words, "the Christian world,"
I am designating a sociological category, which is involved in the
order and history of temporal civilizations, and is a thing of this
world. The Christian world is neither Christianity nor the Church.
The failures of the Christian world have no power to tarnish the
Church or Christianity.

There has been, moreover, a good deal of confusion on this
score. Neither Christianity nor the Church has a mission to make
men happy, their business is to tell them the truth—not to bring
about justice and freedom in the political society, but to give mankind
salvation and eternal life. No doubt this lays upon them the addi-
tional task of quickening the energies of justice and love in the
depths of temporal existence and thus making that existence more
worthy of man. Yet the successful accomplishment of such a task
depends on the way in which the divine message is received. It is

at this point that we are confronted with the responsibilities of the Christian world, that is, of the social groups of Christian denomination at work in secular history.

It is nonsense to reproach the Christians, as we often see it done today, with not having baptized "the Revolution," and with not having devoted their whole energies to "the Revolution." The messianic myth of "the Revolution" is a secularized perversion of the idea of the advent of God's Kingdom; it is apt to warp the course of human history, and to turn into failures the particular, genuine and genuinely progressive revolutions—the revolutions without a capital R—that are bound to follow one another as long as human history endures. But it is not nonsense to reproach Christians in the world with having failed to bring about at certain given times such needed particular revolutions. It is not nonsense to reproach them, more generally, with being sinners—they know very well that they are—who more or less always betray Christianity. Most important of all, it is certainly not nonsense to reproach the many people in modern times who are paying lip-service to the God in Whom they think they believe, with being in fact practical atheists.

c. *Men Today Need Signs*

If a new age of civilization is to come rather than a new age of barbarism, the deepest requirement of such an age will be the sanctification of secular life, a fecundation of social, temporal existence by spiritual experience, contemplative energies and brotherly love.

I dare say that we have not yet reached that stage. For the moment we are at the lowest point; human history today is in love with fear and absurdity, human reason with despair. The powers of illusion are spreading all over the world, throwing all compasses off direction. The faculty of language has been so dishonored, the meaning of words so thoroughly falsified; so many truths, met with at every corner in press or radio reports, are at each moment so perfectly mixed with so many errors similarly advertised, and trumpeted to the skies, that men are simply losing the sense of truth. They have been lied to so often that they have become addicted, and need their daily dose of lies as a daily tonic. They look as if they believed in all this; but they are beginning to lead a kind of clandestine mental life in which they will believe nothing they are told, but will rely only upon savage experience and elementary instincts. They are surrounded on all sides by spurious marvels and false miracles, which dazzle and blind their minds.

Things being as they are, it seems clear that the wisest reasonings and the most eloquent demonstrations and the best managed organizations are definitely not enough for the men of this time. Men today need *signs*. They need deeds. Above all they need tangible signs to reveal to them the reality of things divine. Yet there is everywhere a considerable shortage of thaumaturges, though they probably are the kind of commodity we need the most.

At this point I should like to bring back to our minds a saying of Pascal. "We always behave," Pascal has said, "as if we were called upon to make the truth triumph, whereas we are called upon only to struggle for it."

It does not rest with us to give men miracles. It is up to us to practice what we believe.

Here it seems well to stress one of the deepest meanings of absolute atheism. In so doing we shall but be brought back to the conclusion previously arrived at.[6] As I put it, absolute atheism is "a translation into crude and inescapable terms, a ruthless counterpart, an avenging mirror of the practical atheism of too many believers who do not actually believe." It is both the fruit and the condemnation of practical atheism, its image reflected in the mirror of divine wrath. If this diagnosis is true, then we must go on to say that it is impossible to get rid of absolute atheism without first getting rid of practical atheism. Furthermore, this has become clear to everyone: that from now onwards a decorative Christianity is not enough, even for our existence in this world. The faith must be an actual faith, practical and living. To believe in God must mean to live in such a manner that life could not possibly be lived if God did not exist. Then the earthly hope in the Gospel can become the quickening force of temporal history.

---

[6] See *The Range of Reason*, pp. 99–100.

15 GOSPEL INSPIRATION AND LAY CONSCIOUSNESS*

I HAVE COMPARED THE SPIRITUAL ESSENCE AND THE authentic principle of democracy to a tree whose sap is healthy and which has been overgrown by parasites. When at the end of the eighteenth century the Rights of Man were proclaimed in America and in France, and the peoples bidden to partake of the ideal of Liberty, Equality and Fraternity, a great challenge of the people, of the plain man, of the spirit of childhood and faith, and at the same time of an ideal of universal generosity, was hurled in the political domain itself at the mighty of this world and their experienced skepticism. The evangelical impulse which thus erupted bore the imprint of a secularized Christianity; rationalist philosophy added to it illusions—which quickly became bloody—and assured mankind that the goodness of nature and reason alone would suffice for the coming of the great promise of justice and peace. But through these illusions the heart of man sensed a sacred truth: that the energies of the Gospel must pass into the temporal life of men; that the good tidings heralded as throwing open heaven and eternal life ask also to transform the life of earthly society in the very midst of its woes and its contradictions; that there are in the Gospel message political and social implications which must at all cost be unfurled in history.

And do you think that peoples born from centuries of Christi-

---

* *Christianisme et démocratie* (New York: Éditions de la Maison Française, 1943), pp. 49–64.

anity would have gone to the trouble of starting revolutions and massacres, would have set out with all their household and the heritage of their labor, if it had not been for the promised and so long-awaited beatitudes? If it is a mirage to believe them within arm's reach, it is not a mirage to set out after them. The Middle Ages sought to erect, through the Holy Empire, a fortress for God on earth. Today the poor and the oppressed are setting out for the society founded on justice and fraternity. To have awakened and then betrayed such a hope is a measure of the failure of the modern world. It would be a worse failure to renounce this hope, and to seek to uproot it from men's hearts. Hard experience has taught us that the kingdom of God is not meant for earthly history, but at the same time we have become aware of this crucial truth that it must be enigmatically prepared in the midst of the pains of earthly history.

Christianity announced to peoples the kingdom of God and the life of the world to come. It has taught them the unity of the human race, the equality of nature in all men, children of the same God and redeemed by the same Christ, the inalienable dignity of work and the dignity of the poor, the primacy of inner values and of good will over external values, the inviolability of conscience, the exact vigilance of God's justice and providence over the great and the small. It has taught them the obligation imposed on those who govern and on those who have possessions to govern in justice, as God's ministers, and to manage the goods entrusted to them for the common good, as God's stewards. It has taught them the submission of all to the law of work and the calling of all to share in the freedom of the sons of God, the sanctity of truth and the power of the spirit, the communion of saints, the divine supremacy of redeeming love and mercy, and the law of brotherly love which reaches out to all, even to those who are our enemies, because all men—no matter what may be the social group, the race, the nation, or the class to which they belong—are members of God's family and adopted brothers of the Son of God. Christianity proclaimed that where love and charity are, there God is; and that it is up to us to make every man our neighbor, by loving him as ourselves and by having compassion for him, that is, by somehow dying unto ourselves for his sake. Christ cursed the rich and the Pharisees. He promised the poor, and those who suffer persecution for the sake of justice, that theirs is the kingdom of heaven, the meek that they shall possess the earth, those who mourn that they shall be comforted, those who hunger and thirst after justice that they shall be satisfied, the merciful that they shall obtain mercy, the pure of heart that they shall see God, the peace-makers that they shall be called sons of God. He declared that everything that is done to the meanest of his brothers is done to him. He gave to his disciples the new commandment: to love one another as he himself loved them.

What, then, are the thoughts and aspirations which the Christian message has by degrees awakened in the depths of the consciousness of peoples, and which moved underground for centuries before becoming manifest? However misunderstood and distorted they may have been in the course of this hidden journey in lay consciousness, what are those truths of Gospel origin with which this consciousness henceforth linked and identified the very idea of civilization?

If we seek to consider them in themselves, disengaging them from any erroneous contexts, we would say that by virtue of the hidden work of Gospel inspiration lay consciousness has understood that human history does not go around in circles, but is set toward a goal and moves in a certain direction. Progress is not automatic and necessary, but threatened and thwarted; it is not due to an advent of pure reason which would invalidate the entire heritage of the past, but rather it is this very heritage which increases the while it groans under the labor of all the human and divine energies in man. Progress does not lead to the recovery of Paradise by a revolution today or tomorrow, it tends to the elevating of the structures of consciousness and the structures of human life to better states, and this all through history up to the advent of the kingdom of God and the land of the resurrected, which is beyond history. Whether or not you believe in this advent, it is toward it that you are moving if you believe in the forward march of humanity. And what at any rate has been gained for lay consciousness, if it does not revert to barbarism, is faith in the forward march of humanity.

Under the often misunderstood but active inspiration of the Gospel, lay consciousness has understood the dignity of the human person and has understood that the person, while being part of the body politic, yet transcends the body politic, because of the inviolable mystery of his spiritual freedom and because of his being called to absolute goods. The body politic's reason for existing is to help him in the acquisition of these goods and of a truly human life. What has been gained for lay consciousness, if it does not revert to barbarism, is faith in the rights of the human person, as a human person, as a civic person, as a person engaged in social and economic life and as a working person; and it is faith in justice as the necessary foundation for communal life, and as the essential property of law, which is not law if it is unjust. Proudhon believed that thirst for justice is the privilege of Revolution, and the object of attentive dread on the part of the Church. The thirst for justice was imprinted in the soul of the Christian ages by the Gospel and the Church; it is from the Gospel and the Church that we learned to obey only if it is just to do so.

Under the inspiration of the Gospel at work in history, lay consciousness has understood the dignity of the people and of the common man. Faithful people, God's little people, kingly people, called to share in the work of Christ; people in the sense of the community of citizens in a country, united under just laws; people in the sense of the community of manual labor and as the stock and resource of humanity in those who toil close to nature—the notion of the people which lay consciousness has gradually formed stems from the meeting and the mingling of all these elements, and it is from the heritage of Christendom that this notion proceeds. The people are not God, the people do not have infallible reason and virtues without flaw, the will of the people or the spirit of the people is not the rule of what is just or unjust. But the people make up the slowly prepared and fashioned body of common humanity, the living patrimony of the common gifts and the common promises made to God's creatures—which are more profound and more essential than all the superadded privileges and social distinctions—and of the equal dignity and equal weakness of all as members of the human race. It is on condition of existing in communion with the people that all efforts bear fruit in temporal history, and that the inspiring leaders which the people need keep both their strength and their legitimacy.

Awakened to a consciousness of himself by the movement of civilization, the man of common humanity knows today that his day has dawned, if only he triumphs over totalitarian corruption and is not devoured by it; and he knows that the idea of a caste, of a class or race hereditarily constituted as master and lord must give way to the notion of a community of free men, equal in rights and in labor, and to the notion of an élite of the mind and of labor which proceeds from the people without cutting itself off from them, and which would truly be the flower and the splendor of their vital energies. What has been gained for lay consciousness, if it does not revert to barbarism, is the sense of men's equality in nature and of the relative equality which justice should establish among them; and the conviction that by means of the functional inequalities demanded by social life, equality should be re-established on a higher level, and should fructify in everyone's possibility of acceding to a life worthy of man, in everyone's assured enjoyment of the elementary goods, both material and spiritual, of such a life, and in the real participation of each one, according to his capabilities and his merits, in the common task and the common heritage of civilization.

By virtue of the hidden work of Gospel inspiration, lay consciousness has understood that the authority of rulers, by the very fact that it emanates from the author of human nature, is addressed to free men who do not belong to a master, and is exercised through the consent of the governed. The dictates of authority are binding in conscience because authority has its source in God; but from the very fact that authority has its source in God and not in man, no man and no special group of men has an inherent right to rule others. The leaders of the people receive the right of authority from the creative and conserving principle of nature through the channels of nature itself, that is, through the consent or will of the people or of the body of the community, through which authority always passes before being vested in the leaders. And it is as vicars or representatives of the multitude that the holders of authority direct the multitude, and it is toward the common good of the multitude that they must direct it. It is contrary to nature for men, members of the same species, all equal before God and before death, to be simple tools of political power—tools of a dictator, the only human person among a flock of organized slaves, or tools of a paternalistic power, the only adult among a regiment of children. Once the man of common humanity has understood that he is born with the right to direct his own life by himself, as a being responsible for his acts before God and the law of the community, how could the people be expected to obey those who govern unless it is because the latter have received from the people themselves the custody of the people's common good? What has been gained for lay consciousness, if it does not revert to barbarism, is the conviction that authority, or the right to exercise power, is held by the rulers of the earthly community only because the common consent is manifested in them, and because they have received their trust from the people; and it is the conviction that the normal state to which human societies ought to tend is a state in which the people will act as mature persons, as persons come of age in political life.

By virtue of the hidden work of Gospel inspiration, lay consciousness has understood that the political realm and the flesh and blood paraphernalia of the things that are Caesar's should nevertheless be subject to God and to justice; it has understood that the entire art of domination and all the crimes which the princes and the heads of nations make use of in order to gain and consolidate their power, can certainly give them power, but inevitably turn out for the people's misfortune. Christianity cast the net of the Gospel upon the Pagan Empire and the Pagan Empire died of it, for there is no quarter given between the Gospel law of the Son of God and the law of the Empire which sets itself up as God. Once man has understood that in the truth of things politics depends on morality because its end is the human good of the community, once he has understood that political life must conform to natural law and, according to the proper conditions of its temporal object, even to the law of the Gospel, he sees at the same moment that to call for justice and law in politics is to call for a great revolution which will substitute for the power politics of masters, men, States or nations, the politics of the common good over which the people themselves must watch as the chief interested parties. A community of free men cannot live if its spiritual base is not, above all, rights. Machiavellianism and the politics of domination, according to which justice and law are a sure means to ruin everything, are the born enemies of a community of free men. What has been gained for lay consciousness, if it does not revert to barbarism, is the condemnation of the politics of domination and of iniquitous and perverse means in the conduct of nations, the deep feeling that justice fosters order and injustice the worst disorder, and the conviction that the cause of the welfare and freedom of the people and the cause of political justice are substantially bound together.

Under the often misunderstood or disfigured but active inspiration of the Gospel, lay consciousness has awakened not only to the dignity of the human person, but also to the aspirations and the élan which are at work in his depths. The human person, in himself a root of independence, but immersed in the constraints which issue from material nature within and outside him, tends to overcome these constraints and to win his freedom of autonomy and expansion. In the very realm of spiritual life the Gospel's message reveals to him that he is called to the perfect freedom of those who have become a single spirit and love with God, but in the realm of temporal life it is the natural aspiration of the person to liberation from misery, servitude, and exploitation of man by man, that the repercussions of the Gospel's message were to stimulate. When a man knows that all are made for beatitude, he no longer fears death; but he cannot become resigned to the oppression and enslavement of his brothers, and he aspires, even for the earthly life of humanity, to a state of emancipation consonant with the dignity of man. What has been gained for lay consciousness, if it does not revert to barbarism, is the sense of freedom, and the conviction that the forward march of human societies is a march toward the conquest of that freedom which is consonant with the vocation of our nature.

Finally, under the inspiration of the Gospel at work in history, lay consciousness has understood that in the misfortunes and suffering of our existence, crushed as it is by the iron làws of biological necessity and by the weight of the pride, injustice and ill will of men, a single principle of liberation, a single principle of hope, a single principle of peace can stir up the mass of servitude and iniquity and triumph over it, because this principle comes down to us from the creative source of the world, from a source stronger than the world: that brotherly love whose law was promulgated by the Gospel to the scandal of the mighty, and which is, as the Christian well knows, God's own charity diffused into the hearts of men. And lay consciousness has understood that in the temporal, social and political order itself, not only is civic friendship, as the ancient philosophers knew, the soul and the constitutive link of the social community (if justice is first of all an essential require-ment, it is as a necessary condition which makes friendship possi-ble), but this very friendship between citizens cannot prevail in actual fact within the social group if a stronger and more universal love, brotherly love, is not instilled into it, and if civic friendship, itself becoming brotherhood, does not overflow the bounds of the social group to extend to the entire human race. Once the heart of man has felt the freshness of that terrible hope, it is troubled for all time. If it fails to recognize its suprahuman origins and exi-gencies, this hope runs the risk of becoming perverted and of changing into violence to impose upon all "brotherhood or death." But woe to us if we scorn this hope itself, and succeed in deliver-ing the human race from the hope of brotherhood. The human race has been exalted by it; it will give it up only at the cost of becoming more savage than before. This hope is holy in itself; it corresponds to the deepest and most ineradicable desires of human nature; it places souls in communion of pain and longing with all the oppressed and the persecuted; it demands heroism; it has a divine power for transforming human history. What has been gained for lay consciousness, if it does not revert to barbarism, is faith in the brotherhood of man, the sense of the social duty of compassion for mankind in the person of the weak and the suffer-ing, the conviction that the political work par excellence is that of rendering common life itself better and more brotherly, and of working to make of the structure of laws, institutions and customs of this common life a dwelling place for brothers.

16 THE MYSTERY OF ISRAEL*

I SHOULD LIKE TO PREFACE THE FOLLOWING REFLECTIONS
with some preliminary remarks.

The essay which forms this chapter was written in France in
1937. At that time, certain racist publications of very low quality
had already dishonored the French press, but the eventuality of
any anti-Jewish legislation in France seemed impossible. (In fact,
the anti-Semitic decrees promulgated later were treason against
the French spirit, imposed by the Vichy government, under German pressure, upon a defeated nation.) At that time the vast majority of French people were nauseated by anti-Semitic trends. It
was possible then to consider the Jewish problem in a purely
philosophical, objective and dispassionate manner. I do not know
whether at the present time I could maintain this manner. I do
not know whether, in the face of the anti-Semitic nightmare
spreading like a mental epidemic even among some groups of democratic people, it is fitting to speak of such questions except to utter
our indignation at the iniquity and spiritual wretchedness now as-
saulting minds and nations.

Yet the publication of these pages, written during a less omi-
nous period, may still be appropriate. We must never despair of
intelligence and the healing power of its dispassionate attempt
toward understanding. . . . I wish to emphasize that the inde-

---

* My study, *A Christian Looks at the Jewish Question* (New York,
Longmans, 1939), on the trials now suffered by Israel in certain countries, contains material which complements from the historical point of view the considerations of a philosophical nature set forth here. (The present pages are from
Ransoming the Time. New York: Scribners, 1941; pp. 141–176—Editors.)

pendence of judgment shown in this essay regarding what is good
and what is bad in the average Jewish behavior and the average
Jewish psychology, supposes and embraces the deepest esteem
and love for the Jewish people; and it must be understood as being
the normal prerequisite for an examination of the problem carried
on "among the mature," as Saint Paul says, and on the plane of
the penetrating, arduous insights given to us by Christian wisdom.
For in reality the point of view from which this essay was written
is neither psychological nor sociological nor ethical, but is primarily
metaphysical and religious. I did not seek to characterize the empirical aspect of events, but rather their hidden and sacred meaning. What I tried to explain has significance only if it is taken in
its total unity. If any one sentence in this essay were taken out of
its context and isolated in order to support or to condemn, as if
it were mine, an opinion which is not mine, such a misfortune
could spring only from a complete misinterpretation.

If these pages are seen by Jewish readers, I hope they will agree
that as a Christian I could only try from a Christian perspective
to understand the history of their people. When this essay was
published in France, there were some who, guided by their prejudice, tried to see latent intentions of proselytism where only a
desire for truth engaged my mind; others took as personal "re-
proaches" what was only a statement of the consequences of the
drama of Calvary regarding the relation of Israel to the world.
They were mistaken. I am perfectly aware that before agreeing
with the statements proposed in my essay, it is necessary to admit,
as a prerequisite, the whole Christian outlook; therefore it would
be inconsistent to hope for any agreement from a reader who does
not place himself in this perspective. I do not intend to try to convince such a reader, but, for the sake of mutual understanding, I
think it would perhaps be interesting for him to know how a Christian philosopher considers this question.

I should like to add that such words as "penalty" or "punishment," which we are obliged to use when we seek to elucidate
human matters from the viewpoint of the divine conduct of history,
must be deprived of any anthropomorphic connotations, and that
they become pitiably inadequate if we fail to do so. In any case,
there is no more absurd abuse than to believe it to be the affair of
poor creatures to foster their pride and injustice by applying to

their neighbors, as if they were the police force of God, "penalties" and "punishments" which concern only the Creator in His intimate dealings of love with those who have been called by Him.

On the other hand, it is to be noted that in this essay the word "Church" is not used in the common sense that it conveys in the unbeliever's language, where it designates only an administrative organization—or the administrative organizations of various denominations—charged with the dispensation of religious matters. This word is used in the strict sense it conveys in the language of Catholic faith and theology. It designates a reality both visible and invisible, both human and divine, the mystical Body of Christ, which is itself a mystery of faith; which bears in itself the blemishes and sins of its weak members, and yet is, in its very essence, life, and inspiration—which it receives, in so far as a living whole, from its divine Head—without any blemish and rust and contamination of the devil; to which all the baptized, gathered together in Catholic faith and discipline, visibly belong, and to the vivifying soul of which all men in good faith and good will, living by divine grace, invisibly belong.

Finally, I should like to point out that the most impressive Christian formulas concerning the spiritual essence of anti-Semitism may be found in a book recently published by a Jewish writer,[1] who seems himself strangely unaware of their profoundly Christian meaning . . .

The simple fact of feeling no sympathy for the Jews or being more sensitive to their faults than to their virtues is not anti-Semitism. Anti-Semitism is fear, scorn and hate of the Jewish race or people, and a desire to subject them to discriminative measures. There are many forms and degrees of anti-Semitism. Not to speak of the demented forms we are facing at present, it can take the form of a supercilious nationalist and aristocratic bias of pride and prejudice; or a plain desire to rid oneself of competitors; or a routine of vanity fair; or even an innocent verbal mania. No one is innocent in reality. In each one the seed is hidden, more or less inert or active, of that spiritual disease which today throughout the world is bursting out into a homicidal, myth-making phobia,

---

[1] Maurice Samuel, *The Great Hatred* (New York: Knopf, 1940).

and the secret soul of which is resentment against the Gospel: "Christophobia."

To undertake the study of the origins and modalities of anti-Semitism, it would be necessary to treat the entire problem of Israel's dispersal. Then there would be the opportunity of pointing out that, despite the economic, political and cultural forms which this problem superficially assumes, it is and remains a mystery of a sacred nature, whose major elements Saint Paul, in a sublime summary, relates in chapters 9, 10 and 11 of his Epistle to the Romans:

"What then shall we say? That the Gentiles who were not seeking after justice have attained to justice, but the justice that is of faith. But Israel, by seeking after the law of justice, is not come unto the law of justice. Why so? Because they sought it not by faith, but as it were of works. For they stumbled at the stumbling-stone. As it is written: *Behold I lay in Zion a stumbling-stone and a rock of scandal. And whosoever believeth in him shall not be confounded. . . .*[2]

"But I say: Hath not Israel known? First, Moses saith: *I will provoke you to jealousy against that which is not a nation: against a foolish nation I will anger you.* But Isaias is bold, and saith: *I was found by them that did not seek me. I appeared openly to them that asked not after me.* But to Israel he saith: *All the day long have I spread my hands to a people that believeth not and contradicteth me. . . .*[3]

"I say then: Did God cast off his people? God forbid. . . .[4]

"I say then: Have they so stumbled, that they should fall? God forbid! But by their lapse salvation is come to the Gentiles, that they may be emulous of them. Now if the misstep of them is the riches of the world and the diminution of them the riches of the Gentiles: how much more the fulness of them? For I say to you, Gentiles: As indeed the Apostle of the Gentiles, I will honour my

---

[2] Rom. 9, 30–33. This is taken from the Douay version of Saint Paul's epistle with a few words modified to make the sense clearer. Cf. the remarkable commentary by Erik Peterson in *Le mystère des Juifs et des Gentils dans l'église* (Paris: Desclée de Brouwer, Les Iles).

[3] Rom. 10, 19–21.

[4] Rom. 11, 1.

ministry. If, by any means, I may provoke to emulation them who are my flesh and may save some of them. For if the dispossession of them hath been the reconciliation of the world, what shall the reintegration of them be, but life from the dead? For if the first fruit be holy, so is the lump also: and if the root be holy, so are the branches. And if some of the branches be broken and thou, being a wild olive, wert ingrafted among them and with them partakest of the root and of the fatness of the olive tree: boast not against the branches. And if thou boast, still it is not thou that bearest the root, but the root thee. Thou wilt say then: branches were broken off that I might be grafted in. Well: because of unbelief they were broken off. Thou standest by faith. Be not highminded, but fear. For if God hath not spared the natural branches, fear lest perhaps also he spare not thee. See then the goodness and the severity of God: towards them indeed that are fallen, the severity; but towards thee, the goodness of God, if thou abide in goodness. Otherwise thou also shalt be cut off. And they also, if they abide not still in unbelief, shall be grafted in; for God is able to graft them in again. For if thou wert cut out of the wild olive tree, which is natural to thee; and, contrary to nature, wert grafted into the good olive tree: how much more shall they that are the natural branches be grafted into their own olive tree?

"For I would not have you ignorant, brethren, of this mystery (lest you should be wise in your own conceits) that blindness in part has happened in Israel, until the fulness of the Gentiles should come in. And so all Israel shall be saved, as it is written: *There shall come out of Zion, he that shall deliver and shall turn away ungodliness from Jacob. And this is to them my covenant*: when I shall take away their sins. As concerning the gospel, indeed they are enemies for your sake: but as touching the election, they are beloved for the sake of the fathers. For the gifts and the calling of God are without repentance. For as you also in times past did not believe God, but now have obtained mercy, through their unbelief: So these also have not believed, for your mercy, that they also may obtain mercy. For God hath concluded all in unbelief, that he may have mercy on all." [5]

The Jews are not a "race" in the biological sense of the word.

---

[5] Rom. 11, 11–32.

Actually, in the present state of the world, there are no pure races among groups of people large enough to have any importance, even among such groups as are, from this viewpoint, the most favored. The Jews do not represent an exception; mixtures of blood and ethnic amalgamations have in the course of history been as important for them as for other groups. In the ethico-historical sense, where the word "race" is above all characterized *by a community of mental and moral patterns, of ancestral experience, of memories and desires,* and where hereditary tendencies, the blood strain and the somatic type play a more or less important part, but only the part of a material foundation—the Jews are a race. As are the Iberians or the Bretons. But they are much more than this.

They are not a "nation" if this word means an historical community of men bound together by a unity of origin or birth (a race or a group of historically associated races, in the ethico-historical sense of "race") and *jointly leading or aspiring to lead a political life.* Yiddish has not the characteristics of a national language.[6] It is the language of misery and dispersal, the slang of the Holy City scattered into pieces among the nations and trampled by them. A small number of Jews (500,000 in 1940), gathered together in Palestine, constitute a nation, and Hebrew is their national language. They are a special and separate group bearing witness that the other Jews (there are about sixteen million in the world) are not a nation.

The Jews of the Palestine homeland are not merely a nation; they are tending to become a state (a complete or "perfect" political whole). But the great mass of Israel obeys a totally different law. It does not tend in any way to set up a temporal society. By reason of a deep vocation and by its very essence, Israel is disinclined—at least, so long as it has not brought to completion its mysterious historic mission—to become a nation, and even more, to become a state. The harsh law of exile, of the Galuth, prevents Israel from aspiring toward a common political life.

If the word "people" means simply a multitude gathered together in a determinate geographical area and populating that region of

---

[6] It might be called a national language in a different sense; in the sense that, like Ladino, it is a criterion of Jewish nationality in several countries. It is well known that Yiddish developed in Southern and Central Germany in the twelfth century.

the earth (*Daseingemeinschaft*), the Jews are not a "people." To the extent that the word "people" is synonymous with "nation," they are not a "people." To the extent that it is synonymous with "race" (in the ethico-historical sense), they are a people, and more than a people; to the extent that it indicates an historical community characterized, not, as is a nation, by the fact (or desire) of leading a political life, but by the fact of being nourished with the same spiritual and moral tradition and of responding to the same vocation, they are a people, the people of peoples, the people of God. They are a consecrated tribe; they are a *house*, the house of Israel. Race, People, Tribe—all these words, if they are to designate the Jews, must be made sacred.

Israel is a mystery. Of the same order as the mystery of the world or the mystery of the Church. Like them, it lies at the heart of the Redemption. A philosophy of history, aware of theology, can attempt to reach some knowledge of this mystery, but the mystery will surpass that knowledge in all directions. Our ideas and our consciousness can be immersed in such things; they cannot circumscribe them.

If Saint Paul is right, we shall have to call the *Jewish problem* a problem *without solution*—that is, until the great reintegration foreseen by the apostle, which will be like a "resurrection from the dead." To wish to find, in the pure, simple, decisive sense of the word, a *solution* of the problem of Israel, is to attempt to stop the movement of history.

What made the rationalist-minded "liberal" position of the nineteenth century intrinsically weak, despite its great historical merit, when it was confronted with this problem, was precisely that it set itself up as a decisive solution.

The solution of a practical problem is the end of tension and conflict, the end of contradiction, peace itself. To assert that there is no solution—in an absolute sense—to the problem of Israel is to insure the existence of struggle. There are two methods for this: an animalistic method, which is one of violence and hate, of war that is open or covert, prudent or furious, a war of the flesh aimed at the extermination, the riddance, or the enslavement of the Jews, a war of the world, of the *animalis homo* against Israel. This is the *anti-Semitic* method. The other is the Christian method. It consists in entering through compassion into the sufferings of the

Messiah and through the intelligence of charity into a spiritual struggle aimed at accomplishing the work of man's deliverance, the struggle of the Church and of the *spiritualis homo* for the salvation of the world and the salvation of Israel. This is the *Catholic*, the Pauline way, which furthermore would have us take part at the temporal level in the constant work of the concrete intelligence which neither definitively resolves nor overcomes antinomies, but at each moment in time discovers whatever is needed to make them bearable and more supple.

. . . It has been said that the tragedy of Israel is the tragedy of mankind; and that is why there is no solution to the Jewish problem. Let us state it more precisely: it is the tragedy of man in his struggle with the world and of the world in its struggle with God. Jacob, lame and dreaming, tireless irritant of the world and scapegoat of the world, indispensable to the world and intolerable to the world—so fares the wandering Jew. The persecution of Israel seems like the sign of the moments of crisis in this tragedy, when the play of human history almost stops at obstacles that the distress and moral weakness of nations cannot surmount, and when for a new start it demands some fresh horror. There is a suprahuman relation between Israel and the world as there is between the Church and the world. It is only by taking into account these three terms that some idea of the mystery of Israel can, even obscurely, be formulated. A kind of inverted analogy with the Church must serve, I believe, as our guide. Through trying to perceive a mystery of suffering by the light of a mystery of grace, we are led to use in an improper meaning ideas and expressions properly belonging to an altogether different object.

Jewish thought itself is aware that Israel is in its own way a *corpus mysticum*.[7] The bond which forms the unity of Israel is not solely the bond of flesh and blood, nor of an ethico-historical society; and yet it is not the bond of the communion of saints, the bond which forms the unity of the Church, through faith in the incarnate God and through the possession of His heritage. (Of course Israel understands the meaning of the communion of saints and longs for it! But if it is true that its Christ came and that Israel

---

[7] Cf. Erich Kahler, *Israël unter den Völkern* (Zürich: Humanitas Verlag).

failed to recognize Him and thus, on that day, failed in its own faith and in its own mission, so straightway it lost the trust of dispensing to souls, through the signs of the Ancient Law, the grace of the Christ to come, while at the same time it repudiated the office of dispensing to souls, through the efficacy of the New Law, the grace of Christ already come; in other words, it repudiated the bond which would have really made the communion of saints its unity within a mystical body.) The bond of Israel remains a sacred and supra-historical bond, but a bond of promise, not of possession; of nostalgia, not of sanctity. For a Christian who re-members that the promises of God are without repentance, Israel continues its sacred mission, but in the night of the world which it preferred to God's night. (There are many Jews who prefer God to the world and many Christians who prefer the world to God. But I am referring to the choice which the religious authority of Israel made when it condemned the Son of Man and rejected the gospel.) Blindfolded, the Synagogue still moves forward in the uni-verse of God's plans. It is itself only gropingly aware of this its path in history.

Kingdom of God in the state of pilgrimage and crucifixion—the Church is in the world and is not of the world; and, however much she suffers from the world, she is free of the world and already delivered.

People of God famished for the Kingdom, and who would not have it—Israel is in the world and is not of the world; but it is attached to the world, subject to the world, in bondage to the world. One day Israel stumbled and was caught in a trap; it stum-bled against God—and in what an encounter, never to be repeated! Israel did not know what it was doing; but its leaders knew that they were making their choice against God. In one of those acts of free will which involve the destiny of a whole community, the priests of Israel, the bad watchers in the vineyard, the slayers of prophets, with excellent reasons of political prudence, chose the world, and to that choice their whole people was henceforth bound —until it changes of its own accord. A crime of clerical misfea-sance, unequalled prototype of all similar crimes . . .

The mystical body of Israel is a Church fallen from a high place. It is not a "counter"-Church, any more than there exists a "counter"-God, or a "counter"-Spouse. It is an unfaithful Church (such is the true meaning of the liturgical phrase, *perfidia Judaica,* which does not at all mean that the Jews are perfidious).[8] The mystical body of Israel is an unfaithful and a repudiated Church (and that is why Moses had figuratively given forth the *libellum repudii*)—repudiated as a Church, not as a people. And ever awaited by the Bridegroom, who has never ceased to love her . . .

A faith which would do violence to the seeming plan of the world in order to give a man today, tangibly, the substance for which he hopes and the accomplishment of the desire which God has planted in him, and hence would have him recapture everything spiritual and temporal—such is the faith of Israel. It is such faith Israel is burning to have, and at the same time doubts it has (for if Israel had it, it would have all justice and plenitude). In modern times this faith has progressively weakened as rationalism has increased. Of such a notion of faith, which seems to me profoundly Jewish, Chestov's philosophy affords us incomparable evidence.

And Jewish charity is also a virtue fallen from a high place. I do not mean in any way that it is a false love. Divine charity can be present in it, as it may be absent from it. Nor is it Lutheran pity, nor Slavic pity. It is an active, and, on occasion, a relentless love of the creature as such; it grapples the creature, torments it, never lets it go, so as to oblige it to become aware of its evil and deliver itself from its evil.

Of earthly hope the Jews have an excess; and of this virtue many Christians have not enough. The basic weakness in the mystical communion of Israel is its failure to understand the Cross, its refusal of the Cross, and therefore its refusal of the transfiguration. The aversion to the Cross is typical of that Judaism of the Exile, which does not mean Christianity's first outline and imperfect beginning, as Judaism is by essence, but which indicates the spiritual pattern which shapes Israel's severance from its Messiah. With all Jews in whom grace dwells, as with all souls of good faith and good will, the work of the Cross is present, but veiled and unperceived, and involuntarily experienced. Despite himself, and in an obscuring mist, the pious Jew, the Jew of the spirit, carries the gentle Cross, and thus betrays Judaism without realizing what he

---

[8] Cf. Erik Peterson, *Perfidia Judaica,* in *Ephemerides Liturgicae,* 1936.

does. The moment he begins to be aware of this mystery of forgiveness and of this putting off of self, he finds himself on the road to
Christianity.

In Jesus alone and in His mystical Body taken as such, the devil
plays no part. He does play his part in Israel, as in the world, but
Israel struggles against him. The drama of Israel is to struggle
against the Prince of this world while yet loving the world and
being attached to the world; and while knowing better than anyone
else the value of the world.

Israel plays a dual part with regard to the history of the world
and the salvation of the world. In what *directly* concerns this salvation, Israel has given the Saviour to the world; and now it remains a witness. It preserves the treasure of the scriptures (it must
not be forgotten that the Church took unto herself for her own
use the labour of the rabbis and the Masoretes for the establishment of the text of scripture, just as she used the work of the philosophers and of Aristotle for her theology); and Israel is itself,
throughout time, a living and indestructible depository of the promise of God.

In what *indirectly* concerns the salvation of the world, Israel is
obedient to a vocation which I think above all deserves emphasis,
and which supplies a key for many enigmas. Whereas the Church
is assigned the task of the supernatural and supratemporal saving
of the world, to Israel is assigned, in the order of temporal history
and its own finalities, the work of the *earthly leavening* of the
world. Israel is here—Israel which is not of the world—at the
deepest core of the world, to irritate it, to exasperate it, to *move*
it. Like some foreign substance, like a living yeast mixed into the
main body, it gives the world no quiet, it prevents the world from
sleeping, it teaches the world to be dissatisfied and restless so long
as it has not God, it stimulates the movement of history.

The passion of Israel is not, like that of the Church, a passion of
co-redemption, completing what is lacking in the sufferings of the
Saviour. This passion is not suffered for the eternal salvation of
souls, but for the stimulation and emancipation of temporal life.
It is the passion of a scapegoat, enmeshed in the earthly destiny
of the world and in the ways of the world mixed with sin, a scapegoat against which the impure sufferings of the world strike back,
when the world seeks vengeance for the misfortunes of its history

upon what activates that history. Israel thus suffers the repercussion of the activation it produces, or which the world feels it is destined to produce . . .

Let us consider once more this strange inter-crossing symmetry which holds our attention. As to Christians, the Church follows her divine vocation, and it is not Christianity, it is Christendom, the Christian world, which has failed (in the temporal order) without being willing to hear the voice of the Church who, while she directs men toward eternal life, also requires them to help the development of life on earth along the lines of the Gospel. For the Jews, it is Israel as a Church, it is Judaism which has failed (in the spiritual order); and it is Israel still as the chosen people, it is "Jewdom" which pursues in history a supernatural (yet ambiguous) vocation.

. . . To recapitulate: Israel's ambivalence and its destiny's ambiguity are most clearly to be seen in the double center of attraction—one illusory, the other real—which divides its existence. To the extent that Israel has quit reality for an illusory image, money (here is one of the most profound themes of Léon Bloy, and certain of Karl Marx's phrases have a similar sound) has for Israel a mystical attraction, for money among the world's most shadowy shadows is the palest and the least real image of the Son of God. Léon Bloy used to say that money is the poor man's blood, the poor man's blood transmuted into a sign. In that sign and through that sign, and the signs of that sign, man serves an inert omnipotence which does everything man wants; he ends up in a kind of cynical theocracy, the ultimate *religious* temptation of whoever refuses the reality of the gift of God.

But to the extent that Israel is ever beloved and ever relies on the promises without repentance, it is God's justice—and God's justice to be made manifest in this life—which is Israel's other center of attraction. It is real this time, not illusory; where others say a wise man, or a saint, the Jew says a "just" man. It is earthly hope and it is poverty—no people know better than the Jewish people how to be poor and know better (however little they love it, however much they dislike it) the generating power of poverty. Here by the waters of Babylon is the sighing for the Jerusalem of

Justice, here is the cry of the prophets, the expectation and the endless desire for the terrible glory of God.

Thus, in such a complexity, in so mad a discord of typical characteristics and inclinations, there will always be reason to exalt Israel, and reason to debase it. Those who want to hate a people never lack pretexts; particularly when that people's vocation is extraordinary and its psychology contrasting. Tactlessness, ostentation, self-esteem, an almost artistic feeling for success and a loud bewailing of suffered injury—many defects are charged to this tenacious people and make some of them irritating. Jews are on the average more intelligent and quicker than Gentiles. They profit thereby; they do not know how to make people forgive them their success. The traffic of the money lender or the merchant, the various non-productive businesses and occupations which, indeed, they are not the only ones to practice, but which have become perforce for them an hereditary habit, and at which they are unbeatable—are not designed to attract the favor of people, themselves as eager for gain but less expert.

When they gather in the high places of culture to worship the idols of the nations Jews become corrupted. And as with other spiritual groups, it is only rarely that the best of them mount the stage of politics and show.

These are pretexts against the Jews; and whenever they would appear to justify hatred or discriminatory measures, such allegations are always unjust. If men could tolerate each other only on condition that no one bear grievance against another, all sections of a country would constantly be at war.

And the Jews have more good qualities than defects. Those who have frequented them enough to have shared in their life know the incomparable quality of Jewish goodness. When a Jew is good, he has a quality and a depth of goodness rarely encountered among people whose natural sharpness has been less matured by suffering. They know of what virtues of humanity, of generosity, of friendship the Jewish soul is capable. Péguy made famous his Jewish friendships. It is among "grasping" Jews that one can meet the most unreasonable examples of that natural propensity for giving, which perhaps comes not so much from the wish to be benefactor as from the utter lack of protective boundaries and defenses against pity. Nothing is more disarmed, more tender than Jewish goodness.

Jews have done more in the world for Knowledge and Wisdom than for commerce and trade. A very high feeling for the purity of the family and for the virtues which follow in its wake has long since characterized Jews. They have the fundamental human virtue of patience in work. They have an innate love for independence and liberty, the abiding flame of the ancient prophetic instinct, the intellectual fire, the quickness of intuition and abstraction, the faculty of passionate dedication and devotion to ideas. If it is true, as Psichari dared to say, that God prefers sin to stupidity, then His liking for the Jews (and for some others) becomes understandable. One is never bored with a Jew. Their nostalgia, their energy, the naïveté of their finesse, their ingenuity, their knowledge of penury are all rare tonics for the mind. I remember with what joy, in a large city of the United States, after lectures and university gatherings, I, who am a *goy*, would go to the home of Jewish friends to refresh myself in the vitality of that tireless pathos and the perpetual motion of ideas which vivified for me long centuries of painful refining of the soul and the intelligence.

But it is above all important to note that the various special causes to which an observer may attribute anti-Semitism, from the feeling of hatred for strangers which is natural—too natural—in any social group, to the social dislocations created by large-scale immigration, and to the various grievances I have already described, serve to hide an even deeper root of hatred. If the world hates the Jews, it is because the world is well aware that they will always be *supernaturally* strangers to it; it is because the world detests their passion for the absolute and the unbearable activation with which this passion stimulates it. It is the vocation of Israel which the world execrates—a hatred which can turn against the race bearing that vocation, or against the various forms of temporal manifestation which outwardly express and mask this vocation. *Odium generis humani.* Hatred by the world—this is their glory, as it is also the glory of those Christians who live by faith. But Christians—by virtue of their Mystical Body—have overcome the world and the Jews have not; that is why for a Jew to become a Christian is a double victory: his people triumphs in him. Woe to the Jew—and to the Christian—who is pleasing to men! And the time is perhaps coming, has already come in certain countries, when the

witnessing of the one and the witnessing of the other being alike
judged intolerable, both will be hated and persecuted together.
And, united in persecution, they will together be brought back to
their sources.

The Jew is lost if he settles down, and by *settling down* I mean
a spiritual phenomenon, like the loss of a stimulating disquiet and
the failure of a vocation. *Assimilation* involves an altogether different problem, in the social and political, not spiritual, order. An
"assimilated" Jew may be one who is not "settled." Assimilation is
not the solution of Israel's problem, any more than is Yiddishism
or Zionism; but assimilation, like autonomy and Zionism, is a partial accommodation, a compromise solution, good and desirable to
the extent that it is possible. Assimilation took place in the past
on a large scale in the Hellenistic and Hispano-Arabic periods. Yet
it carries with it a risk—as does also Zionism (as a state)—the
risk of the Jews becoming settled, becoming *like others* (I mean
spiritually). It is the risk of losing the vocation of the house of
Israel. Their God then strikes them down by the vilest of instruments. Never had there been Jews more assimilated than the German Jews. They were all the more attached to German culture for
its having in part been their achievement. They had become totally
Germans, which did not make them either more discreet or more
humble. They were not only assimilated, but settled down, con-
ciliatory and well reconciled with the Prince of this world. Jews
who become like others become worse than others. (When a Jew
receives Christian grace, he is less than ever like others: he has
found *his* Messiah.) . . .

I have spoken of the extreme stupidity of the anti-Semitic myths,
and I have said that even this stupidity conveys a hidden meaning.
The hatred of the Jews and the hatred of the Christians spring from
the same source, from the same will of the world *which refuses to
be wounded* either with the wounds of Adam, or with the wounds
of the Messiah, or by the spear of Israel for its movement in time,
or by the Cross of Jesus for eternal life. Man is well off as he is;
he needs no grace, no transfiguration; he will be beatified in his
own nature. Here there is no Christian hope in God the Helper,
nor Jewish hope in God on earth. Here is the hope of animal life

and its deep power, in a certain sense sacred, demonic, whenever it takes possession of the human being who believes himself deceived by those who bear tidings of the absolute.

Tellurian racism is anti-Semitic and anti-Christian. Communist atheism is not anti-Semitic; it is sufficient that it be universally against God.[9] In both, the same absolute naturalism, the same detestation of all asceticism and of everything transcendent comes to light . . .

The reflections which make up this chapter have as their object the explanation, in some measure, of the pathos of the position of the Jewish people. Perhaps such reflections help us to understand how, often despite itself, and at times manifesting in various ways a materialized Messianism, which is the darkened aspect of its vocation to the absolute, the Jewish people, ardently, intelligently, actively, give witness, at the very heart of man's history, to the supernatural. Whence the conflicts and tensions which, under all kinds of disguises, cannot help but exist between Israel and the nations.

It is an illusion to believe that this tension can disappear (at least before the fulfilment of the prophecies). . . .

"The history of the Jews," said Léon Bloy, "dams the history of the human race as a dike dams a river, in order to raise its level." [10]

---

[9] The Soviet regime takes pride in its radical opposition to anti-Semitism. Yet on the religious plane, Judaism has suffered as much in Russia as Christianity, and has offered far less resistance to the anti-religious campaign. Cf. *A Christian Looks at the Jewish Question*, pp. 44–46.

[10] Léon Bloy, *Le salut par les Juifs*. Among Catholic contributions to the study of the problem of Israel, I should like to mention the study by Erik Peterson already cited, *Le mystère des Juifs et des Gentils dans l'église;* and the penetrating pages written by Charles Péguy in *Notre jeunesse* and in *Note Conjointe sur M. Descartes*; also Louis Massignon, *Pro Psalmis* (*Revue Juive*, 15 mars, 1925); Jean de Ménasce, *Situation du Sionisme* and *Quand Israël aime Dieu* (*Le roseau d'or*); the Rev. Joseph Bonsirven, *Sur les ruines du temple, Juifs et Chrétiens, les Juifs et Jésus* (I hope that the lectures on Judaism given by the same author at the Institut Catholique of Paris in 1938 may one day be published); O. de Férenzy, *Les Juifs et nous chrétiens;* the article published in *Die Erfüllung* (1937) under the title *Die Kirche Christi und die Judenfrage* and signed by several Catholic writers and teachers (translated in part and published in pamphlet form by National Catholic Welfare Conference, Washington); and the periodicals, *La question d'Israël* (a bulletin published by the Fathers of Our Lady of Zion) and *La juste parole* (Paris). See also Rabbi Jacob Kaplan's work, *Témoignages sur Israël* (Paris; 1935).

This permanent tension appears in two very different manners—one on the spiritual level, the other on the temporal.

On the spiritual level, the drama of love between Israel and its God, which makes Gentiles participate in the economy of salvation, and which is but one element in the universal mystery of salvation, will be resolved only in the reconciliation of the Synagogue and the Church. In the important text quoted at the beginning of this chapter Saint Paul says to the Gentile Christian: "See, then, the goodness and the severity of God, towards them indeed that are fallen, the severity, but towards thee, the goodness of God: if thou abide in goodness, otherwise thou also shalt be cut off." Considering the condition of the world, and the way in which the nations give witness that they *abide in goodness,* one is tempted to wonder whether tomorrow will not see the resolution. In any case nothing requires us to think that the resolution will come at the end of human history, rather than at the beginning of a new age for the Church and the world.

On the temporal level, even if there is no solution in the pure and simple meaning of the word, before the fulfilment of the prophecies—no truly decisive solution for the problem of Israel, there are nevertheless *certain* solutions, partial or provisional, particular answers to the problem whose disentanglement is the duty of political wisdom and which it is the task of various historical periods to attempt.

The Middle Ages tried a "sacral" solution, in accordance with the typical structure of the civilization of that time. This solution, which was based on the presupposition that a sacred penalty, inflicted by God, not by men, weighed on the destinies of Israel, and which gave Jews the status of foreigners in the Christian community, the solution of the ghetto,[11] was hard in itself and often iniquitous and bloody in practice. Yet it proceeded from a high concept, and was in any case better than the bestial materialism of the racist laws initiated in our own day by Germany. It was on

---

[11] The ghetto itself did not become obligatory until the fourteenth and fifteenth centuries. I use this word as the symbol of a certain politico-juridic conception. Concerning this, see P. Browe, S.J., *Die Judengesetzgebung Justinians* (*Analecta Gregoriana*, VIII. Rome: 1935). On the doctrinal controversies and mediaeval *apologiae*, see the important work of A. Lukyn Williams, *Adversus Judaeos* (*A Bird's Eye View of Christian Apologiae until the Renaissance.* Cambridge University Press, 1935).

the religious, not at all on the racial, level. It recognized the privileges of the soul, and the baptized Jews entered as a matter of right into the full fellowship of the Christian community. This mediaeval solution has gone, never to return, like the kind of civilization from whence it sprang.

The emancipation of the Jews, brought about by the French Revolution, is a fact which civilized people, to the extent that they remain such, should consider definitive. If indeed this emancipation was in itself a just and necessary thing (and a thing which corresponded to a Christian aspiration) nevertheless the hopes which the rationalist and bourgeois-optimist way of thinking, forgetful at once of the mystery of Israel and of supra-individual realities, had based upon this emancipation to *extinguish* the Jewish problem, were soon to prove vain.

It looks as if the time into which we are entering is called upon to try another experiment. The régime of which I am thinking and which, far from having been conceived for the particular case of Israel, answers in a general way to the kind of civilization whose historic ideal suits our age, can summarily be described as *pluralist* and *personalist*.[12] In utter contrast to the insane Hitlerian parody of the mediaeval way, shamefully accepted by the unhappy rulers of a crushed France, I think of a pluralism founded on the dignity of man, and which, on the basis of a complete equality in civic rights and of effective respect for the liberties of the person in his individual and social life, would accord to the various spiritual families participating in the fellowship of the temporal community a proper ethico-juridical status for the questions described as mixed (impinging on the spiritual and the temporal). Such a pluralism would represent, along with other advantages, for the nations that might be capable of this kind of civilization, an attempt at the organic ordering of the Jewish question best suited to our moment in history. By means of direct agreements with the Jewish spiritual community—as with the different Christian churches—a community institutionally recognized, such questions as concern this community and the common good of the political whole would be resolved.[13]

---

[12] Cf. *True Humanism*. Chapters IV and V.

[13] It is needless to say that in such a conception which relates to the temporal and socio-political fellowship of various spiritual families in the profane

The pluralism I have outlined concerns the *spiritual families* which live together in the same political community. The same régime of organization of liberties in accordance with an order truly "political," and not "despotic," to use Aristotle's words, could and should extend in the countries which include a diversity of *national minorities,* to those diverse communities living together in the same political community (in the same state). And the horrible oppression suffered in our days by many national minorities seems to demand with a special urgency a solution of this sort. But spiritual family and national community are altogether different things; to a spiritual family one voluntarily gives oneself, to a national community one naturally belongs (although one can renounce it). A pluralist régime of spiritual families is compatible, not only with political fellowship in the State, but with a very complete national *assimilation.* A pluralist régime of national communities or minorities implies by definition the renouncing of *assimilation* (although it is in no way repugnant to political fellowship in the State). As far as the Jews are concerned, it is clear that in the countries where there exists a Jewish national community or minority, an inevitable complication would arise, under a pluralist régime, from the necessary distinction between the Jewish national community and the Jewish spiritual family. A man of non-Jewish nationality can become a convert to Judaism; a man belonging to a Jewish national minority can be a Christian or a freethinker. Jurisdictional tangles of this sort are the price of any organic conception of social life; and moreover, as between the status of the spiritual community and the status of the national community, it is obviously the former which, in the event of a conflict of rights, should be regarded as having greater weight.

As for the Zionist homeland, or the future Jewish State of Palestine, it is to be feared that, even supposing it much larger than it can actually be, it would never suffice to receive all those who will

---

community, it is the *spiritual* not the *racial* which differentiates the statuses in question. In becoming Catholic or Protestant, a Jew would thus quit the juridical status of the Jewish spiritual family: which is not to say that he would quit Israel and its vocation.

Inversely, the Zionist homeland or the eventual Jewish State in Palestine being of a profane kind and based on nationality, not on the Israelite religion, it is logical that it makes room for baptized Jews who shall enjoy the full liberty of their religious life and shall be able to found colonies . . .

flee the lands where anti-Semitic persecution rages. This is not the place to examine the question of Zionism, to which no mind aware of the unfolding of prophecy throughout history could be indifferent. Since it may be called upon to become one day the animating centre for all dispersed Jewry, Zionism seems to me to have an historic importance of the first order. But it does not yet represent deliverance from exile: the return to Palestine is but the prelude to such deliverance. No more than individualist liberalism or than the pluralist regime we have been discussing, can the Zionist State do away with the law of the desert and of the Galuth, which is not consubstantial with the Jewish people—this law *will* come to an end—but is essential to the mystical body and the vocation of Israel in the state of separation.

It is when they obey the spirit of the world, not the spirit of Christianity, that Christians can be anti-Semitic. . . .

Anti-Semitism today is no longer one of the accidental weeds growing in a temporal Christendom intermixed with good and evil, but it is rather a disease of the spirit contaminating Christians.[14]

. . . In truth, we are dealing here with a sort of collective "lapse," or with a substitute for an obscure and unconscious passion of anti-clericalism, or even of resentment against God. For, do what we will—or even do what it will—the people of Israel remains the priestly people. The bad Jew is a kind of bad priest; God will have no one raise his hand against either. And even before recognizing Christ, the true Israelite, in whom there is no

---

[14] Let it not be forgotten that anti-Semitism has been explicitly condemned by the Catholic Church in a document of the Holy Office dated September 5, 1928 (directed against the mistakes of a too zealous "Association of the Friends of Israel"). Racist errors, already denounced in the encyclical *Mit Brennender Sorge,* have been again and expressly condemned in a document (Letter of the Pontifical Sacred Congregation of Seminaries and Universities, April 13, 1938). "Notice that Abraham is called our Patriarch, our ancestor. Anti-Semitism is incompatible with the thought and sublime reality expressed in this text. It is a movement in which Christians can have no part whatsoever . . . Anti-Semitism is unacceptable. Spiritually we are Semites," said Pope Pius XI in September, 1938. The American Hierarchy has also expressed itself on this matter. See article by Emmanuel Chapman, "The Catholic Church and Anti-Semitism," *The Social Frontier,* January 1939.

guile, by virtue of an unbreakable promise, wears the livery of the Messiah.

It is no small thing for a Christian to hate or despise, or to wish to treat in a debasing way, the race whence issued his God and the immaculate Mother of his God. That is why the bitter zeal of anti-Semitism always at the end turns into a bitter zeal against Christianity.

"Suppose [wrote Léon Bloy], that people around you should continually speak of your father and your mother with the greatest scorn and treat them only to insults or outrageous sarcasm, how would you feel? Well, that is exactly what happens to Our Lord Jesus Christ. We forget, or rather we do not wish to know, that our God-made-man is a Jew, in nature the Jew of Jews, the Lion of Judah; that His Mother is a Jewess, the flower of the Jewish race; that the Apostles were Jews, as well as all the Prophets; and finally that our Holy Liturgy is altogether drawn from Jewish books. How, then, can we express the enormity of the outrage and blasphemy which lie in vilifying the Jewish race?

"Anti-Semitism . . . is the most horrible slap in the face suffered in the ever-continuing Passion of Our Lord: it is the most stinging and the most unpardonable because He suffers it on *His Mother's Face*, and at the hands of Christians." [15]

Léon Bloy also said that the "veil," to which Saint Paul refers and which covers the eyes of Israel, is now passing "from the Jews to the Christians." This statement, which is harsh on the Gentiles and on the Christian distorters of Christianity, helps us understand something of the extensive and violent persecution to which the Jews today are victim, and of the spiritual upheaval which has been going on for years among many of them, denoting deep inward changes, particularly in respect to the person of Christ.

The growing solicitude in Israel's heart for the Just Man crucified through the error of the high priests is a symptom of unquestionable importance. Today in America representative Jewish writers like Sholem Asch and Waldo Frank are trying to reinte-

---

[15] Léon Bloy, *Le vieux de la montagne*, 2 janvier 1910.

grate the Gospel into the brotherhood of Israel. While not yet recognizing Jesus as the Messiah, they do recognize Him as the most
pure Jewish figure in human history. They themselves would be disturbed to be considered as leaning toward Christianity. Yet while
remaining closer than ever to Judaism, they believe that the Gospel
transcends the Old Testament and consider it a divine flower issuing from the stem of the patriarchs and the Prophets. Never
forgetful of the conflicts of history and of the harsh treatment
received by their people, the authors of *Salvation* and of *The New
Discovery of America* have long studied and loved mediaeval
Christianity and Catholic spiritual life. They agree with Maurice
Samuel that "christophobia" is the spiritual essence of the demoniacal racism of our pagan world. Many other signs give evidence that
Israel is beginning to open its eyes, whereas the eyes of many self-
styled Christians are blinded, darkened by the exhalations of the
old pagan blood suddenly, ferociously welling up once more among
Gentiles.

17 RELIGION AND CULTURE*

CULTIVATING A FIELD MEANS INCITING NATURE BY SOME human labor to produce fruits which nature left to itself would have been incapable of producing, for what nature left to itself alone produces is "wild" vegetation. Such a figure gives us an idea of what *culture* means in the vocabulary of philosophy—the culture not of an expanse of soil, but of humanity itself. Because man is a spirit animating a body of flesh, his nature in itself is a progressive nature. The labor of reason and the virtues is natural in the sense that it is in conformity with the essential inclinations of human nature; it brings into play the essential springs of human nature. It is not natural in the sense that it is supplied ready-made by nature; it is an addition to what nature produces by itself and by itself alone. Nature, no doubt, can be considered *without* this labor of reason, and as reduced therefore to energies of a sensitive order and mere instincts, or considered *before* this labor of reason, that is to say, in a state, as it were, of embryonic involution and absolute primitiveness.

Culture appears thus to be natural to man in the same sense as the labor of reason and the virtues, of which it is the fruit and earthly fulfilment: it answers a fundamental aspiration of human nature, but it is the work of the spirit and liberty adding their efforts to the effort of nature. Instead of the word "culture," which relates to the rational development of the human being considered in all its generality, I might equally well have used the word "civilization,"

---

* *Religion et Culture* (2 éd. Paris: Desclée de Brouwer, 1946 [1st ed., 1930]), pp. 11–24; 67–75.

which relates to that same development considered in an eminent case—I mean to say in the production of the body politic and civil life, of which civilization is, as it were, the prolongation and enlargement. The body politic and civilization are, at one and the same time, works natural to man and works of reason and virtue.

Many German and Russian philosophers draw a distinction between "civilization" and "culture" and employ the former, conceived in a pejorative sense, to denote a development of social life which is above all material, mechanical and extrinsic (a decrepit and hardened culture). We are free to define the terms we use. In the sense in which I understand it, a civilization is deserving of the name only if it is a culture, a truly human and therefore mainly intellectual, moral and spiritual development (taking the word "spiritual" in its widest acceptation).

Three observations may be related to the foregoing remarks. My first observation is that culture or civilization, presupposing both nature and the work of reason, ought to keep within the line of nature, but can deviate from that line, allow itself to be sponged upon by an artificialism contrary to nature and by perversions of varying degrees of gravity (even in animal "societies" we see communities of ants ruined by a passion for the intoxicating sugar they derive from certain domesticated insects, which devour the eggs of these drug-addicted ants).[1] If the accidental is confused with the essential, it must be admitted with Rousseau, at the sight of such perverted and therefore execrable societies, that culture and civilization of themselves corrupt man.

But as the laws of essences are unavoidable, and as civilization of its very nature derives from reason, it is impossible, and this is my second observation, to execrate civilization without, at the same time, execrating the *form of reason*, the form vitally achieved by reason in human things, and without thereby affirming the primacy of potentiality and the formless, on the pretence that they are more productive.

---

[1] "Many symphilics devour the eggs of ants, others suck their blood, others again lay their eggs in the larvae. Nevertheless, the colony of ants maintains and carefully feeds its guests in order to obtain the liquid for which they have such a marked preference. This liquid is not a food, but a sweet, and the ants sacrifice their young to obtain it, often even to the point of endangering the community." F. Buytendijk, *Psychologie des animaux* (Payot: 1928), p. 161.

My third observation is that, if we do so, we tend to the destruction of man. Unlike the other animals, man has not a solid rock bottom, as it were, of instinctive life, constituting a definite structure of behavior sufficiently determined to make the exercise of life possible. Any erosion or excavation or elimination of rational life in an attempt to discover that solid rock bottom is a deadly error. There will be no end to the excavation, since there is no solid and finished structure, no natural regulation of instinctive life in man. The whole play of the instincts, no matter how numerous and powerful they may be, is open in man, and involves a relative indetermination which finds its normal completion and normal regulation in reason alone. If Freud absurdly calls the child a *polymorphous pervert*, it is because he fails to take account of this indetermination. A general philosophy of a very inferior kind prevents this very remarkable observer (who is also goaded by a violent metaphysical hatred of the form of reason) from distinguishing between potency and act; he substitutes for potentiality a sum of conflicting actualities, for indetermination oriented towards normal actuation (but susceptible of manifold abnormal actuations) an ensemble of opposite actuations, in which what we describe as normal ceases to be normal and becomes merely a particular instance of the abnormal. The truth is that the kind of infinitude proper to spirit gives in man a sort of infinity, a sort of indetermination, to the very life of the senses and instincts, which life is incapable of finding its natural point of fixation—I mean in conformity with the peculiar requirements and destinies of human nature—elsewhere than in reason and the forms which reason produces. Otherwise, it will be fixed awry, as any chance dominating passion determines, and will thus deviate from nature. The truly and fully natural man is not nature's man, the uncultivated soil, but the virtuous man, the human soil cultivated by right reason, man formed by the inner culture of the intellectual and moral virtues. He alone has a consistency, a personality.

If nature were formed in us by itself alone, if it had a countenance of its own, there would be reason to fear that every virtue might be like the false virtues, like the pharisaical virtues, and distort that countenance or cover it with a plaster. But nature acquires a countenance in our case only through the spirit, man acquires his truth only when he is fashioned from within by reason and virtue (I mean right reason, which reigns in our life only when assisted by the supernatural gifts; I mean true virtue, which is entirely deserving of the name only if it is vivified by charity). Genuine sincerity presents a mirror which is clear as crystal to the larvae dwelling in us and contemplates them with courage, in order to give them a human countenance by a work of freedom; it does not refuse to have a countenance. There is no illusion more false than "sincerity" as conceived by André Gide, the resolution of the human being into the vain postulates, discordant and simultaneous, of the formless, of *materia prima*.

I will not continue the parenthesis. Let our conclusion be that culture or civilization is the expansion of the properly human life, including not only whatever material development may be necessary and sufficient to enable us to lead an upright life on this earth, but also and above all moral development, that development of speculative activities and of practical (artistic and ethical) activities which is properly worthy of being called a human development.

It is important in the next place to realize that culture or civilization by its very nature belongs to the *temporal* sphere, in other words, has a specifying object—the terrestrial and perishable good of our life on this earth—belonging of its very nature to the natural order. Doubtless it must be subordinated to eternal life, as an intermediate end to the ultimate end. And such subordination to a higher end gives it an intrinsic superelevation in its own proper order: a Christian civilization has higher standards, a more perfect earthly propriety than a pagan civilization. If we reflect that, in a Christian civilization, charity and the infused moral virtues strengthen the friendship and virtues so vitally necessary for social life, we see that the supreme moral regulations, by virtue of which such a civilization accomplishes its terrestrial task, fall within the province of the supernatural order. Even a Christian civilization, however, a civilization superelevated in its proper order, because it is Christian, by virtues proceeding from above, becomes so superelevated through realizing (better than through the unaided forces of nature) the very postulates of nature. It applies the rules of Christian reason to a subject matter, to activities and goods in the natural order, and the sphere in which it develops is the sphere of natural activities.[2] In itself and by its specific object, it is engaged in time and the vicissitudes of time, is perishable, essentially human. And it incorporates in its own proper substance the goods it receives from the supernatural order, from the virtues of the saints, for example, or from the intercession of the contemplatives; it draws them towards its own end, which still remains, even though superelevated, a certain common good of man on this earth, in his terrestrial life.

Because this human development is not only material, but also and principally moral, it goes without saying that the part played in it by the religious element is consequently a principal part. In truth, the religion which the concept of culture or civilization, *in abstracto*, of itself requires is only natural religion. But human civilizations have in fact received a better, and more onerous, charge. We know that "a *state of pure nature,* one in which God would have abandoned man to the sole resources of the activities of his intellect and will, has never existed. From the very beginning God willed to make known to men things surpassing the requirements of any nature that ever was or ever could be created. He revealed to them the depths of His divine life, the secret of His eternity. And to guide their footsteps to such heights, to prepare them, on this earth already, for the vision of such splendors, He spread over the world, like a cloth, grace capable of divinizing our knowledge and our love. God makes such divine advances to all men at all times; for He is the light 'which enlighteneth every man.' [3] He wills that all men 'be saved and come to the knowledge of the truth.' [4] His advances are accepted or rejected." [5]

This is the reason why none of the religions recorded in history is the simple natural religion contemplated in the abstract by philosophers. Doubtless there are to be found in such religions many features which answer to the natural religious aspirations of the human being, but all in fact derive from a higher source, all retain some vestige of the primordial revelations and ordinations. All of them, with the exception of the religion of Christ, have declined

---

[2] For the distinction and relation of the natural moral virtues and the infused moral virtues, see my work *Science et sagesse,* pp. 346–356 (English translation, *Science and Wisdom,* pp. 210–216).

[3] John 1, 9.

[4] 1 Tim. 2, 4.

[5] Charles Journet, *Vie intellectuelle,* March 1929, p. 439.

from the supernatural order, and they have all more or less deviated from the natural-order.

And these religions, let it be observed, by the very fact of becoming naturalized, of shrinking to the dimensions of fallen nature, became particularized to some definite culture hostile to other cultures, became differentiated like languages and social groups. The piety of pagan antiquity admirably perceived the vital need the body politic has of religion; its great misfortune was that it absorbed religion into civilization, into a particular local civilization, by confusing the body politic and religion, by deifying the body politic, or—it comes to the same thing—by nationalizing the gods, who were turned into the first citizens in the body politic. In this *sociological* collapse of religion is doubtless to be found the deepest cause or, at all events, the most significant characteristic of polytheism, which was nevertheless powerless to efface completely the fundamental "henotheist" feeling. The marvel of Israel, a supernatural marvel forcibly imposed on rebellious necks, is that the God of Israel is also the one, transcendent, ineffable God, the God of Heaven and earth, of the whole earth. Exclusivism and universality, observed Père Clérissac—"the Decalogue appeals not to a local conscience but to the conscience of all mankind; and the Jerusalem of Messianic times is the vision of a country which is chiefly spiritual, the country of souls. The Prophets speak and strive with the sole object of securing the predominance of the Kingdom of God which is in men's hearts in the first place and embraces all nations." [6]

Everywhere else in the ancient world nationalism sponged upon and corrupted religion; it absorbed religion in culture, made it an element of a civilization, of a culture. I mean to say that the ancient world, while riveting social life to, and occasionally crushing it under religion, while honoring religion with a terrifying power of veneration, while enslaving man to the gods, nevertheless enfeoffed religion to civilization. It did so not in the least after the manner of the modern profane world, which makes religion the mere servant of civilization considered as something superior, but on the contrary by making religion the governing principle of the body politic, yet individuated by the body politic, living with the same

---

[6] *Le mystère de l'église*, 3 éd., Saint Maximin, 1952, p. 22.

unique and indistinct life, ruling like a despot over the body politic, but inconceivable without it, bound substantially to it, enclosed within it, defined and circumscribed by it and, finally, in an absolutely metaphysical sense, existing *for* it, as the soul of a plant exists for the plant. The *caritas humani generis* appears but as a wan, sublime and ineffective prefiguration of authentic charity, a mere philosopher's ideal, a sigh heaved by reason, alien, if not hostile, to religion.

The true religion, however, is supernatural, come down from Heaven with Him Who is the Author of grace and truth. It is not of man or of the world, or of *a* civilization or *a* culture, or of civilization or culture: it is of God. It transcends every civilization and every culture. It is the supreme animating and beneficent principle of all civilizations and cultures, while in itself independent of them all, free, universal, strictly universal, catholic . . .

There are two functions to be considered in an instrument, its own proper causality and its instrumental causality. In the case of the temporal, the very subtle relation between these two functions imposes a varying measure upon the endless intertwinings of gains and losses. In the temporal's own proper order, so far as the temporal is of worth in itself the while it is ordered to still higher ends, that is, so far as it has its own proper goods to safeguard, its proper function, and what really counts, is victory or defeat. Here we ought—yet without ever exalting it above the law of God—terribly to wish for victory. But so far as the temporal acts precisely as the instrument of the spiritual, so far as it serves the proper order of the spiritual, what really counts is not victory in the battle, but the way in which the battle is fought and the weapons employed. Weapons of light! Of truth, loyalty, justice, innocence! Let our weapons be unsullied! We shall be beaten—that goes without saying—and historians and politicians are right in warning us of this. But it is impossible to be beaten; when the stake is not biological but spiritual, defeat or victory with unsullied weapons is always a victory.

It is not enough to understand that the things of time must be, on the double ground just mentioned, the means of the eternal—not a temporal means imposing on the eternal, to make it succeed here on earth, the law of the flesh and of sin, for that would be an outrageous prevarication, but a temporal means itself subject to the supreme law of the spirit. It must also be understood that there is an order and hierarchy of these temporal means, I mean of temporal means good in themselves, legitimate and normal. There is the labor of the soldier and the labor of the farmer, the labor of the politician, the poet, the philosopher; there are the works of us ordinary Christians, and the works of the saints; there are the works of saints charged with a temporal duty of State, as was St. Louis, or with a temporal mission, as was Joan of Arc, and the works of saints free of any such responsibility.

Well, then, the richer such temporal works and means are in matter, the more they have their own proper demands and their own proper conditions, the more unwieldy they are. The more also, in accordance with the law just mentioned, is a certain measure of temporal success regularly demanded by them. "Whosoever loses his soul for my sake," our Lord said, "shall find it." He did not say, "Whosoever loses his kingdom shall save it." St. Louis was an excellent administrator of his kingdom; he increased its power and prosperity. Controlled by the strong hand of the eternal decrees, the Roman soldier was bound to subject the world to his arms and thus to prepare unconsciously the arena in which the Church would fight her first battles. More profoundly still, what a weight of glory for the temporal was the history of the patriarchs and the long carnal preparation for the Incarnation! A work of time, but of eternal importance, in the least mesh of which God Himself was interested, the model of the natural sanctity, if I may say so, of every successful and well-made work.

We may describe as *rich temporal means* those which, engaged thus in the density of matter, of their nature demand a certain measure of tangible success. By this very fact the Gospel law of the reversal of values and immolation, which is the supreme law of the spiritual, affects them only imperfectly; it is the shadow of the Cross which passes over them. Such means are the proper means of the world; the spirit, as it were, ravishes them, they do not belong to it; in truth, and in fact, ever since the sin of Adam, they fall within the dominion of the Prince of this world. Our duty is to wrest them from him by the virtue of the blood of Christ. It would be absurd to despise or reject them, they are necessary, they

are part of the natural stuff of human life. Religion must consent
to receive their assistance. But it is proper for the health of the
world that the hierarchy of means, and their due relative proportions, be safeguarded.

There are other temporal means, and these are the proper means
of the spirit. They are *humble temporal means* (*"moyens temporels
pauvres"*). The Cross is in them. The less burdened they are by
matter, the more destitute, the less visible—the more efficacious
they are. This is because they are pure means for the virtue of the
spirit. They are the proper means of wisdom, for wisdom is not
dumb; it cries in the market-place, it is its peculiarity so to cry, and
hence it must have means of making itself heard. The mistake is to
think that the best means for wisdom will be the most powerful
means, the most voluminous.

The pure essence of the spiritual is to be found in wholly immanent activity, in contemplation, whose peculiar efficacy in touching
the heart of God disturbs no single atom on earth. The closer one
gets to the pure essence of the spiritual, the more do temporal
means employed in its service diminish. And that is the condition
of their efficacy. Too tenuous to be stopped by any obstacle, they
pierce where the most powerful equipment is powerless to pierce.
Propter suam munditiam. Because of their purity they traverse the
world from end to end. Not being ordered to tangible success, involving in their essence no internal need of temporal success, they
participate, for the spiritual results to be secured, in the efficacy of
the spirit.

When Rembrandt painted, when Mozart and Satie composed
their works, when St. Thomas wrote his *Summa* and Dante his
Divina Commedia, when the author of the *Imitation* wrote his book
and St. Paul his epistles, when Plato and Aristotle spoke to their
disciples, when Homer sang, when David sang, when the prophets
prophesied—these were all humble temporal means.

Finally, let us consider the spiritual man *par excellence.* What
were the temporal means of Wisdom incarnate? He preached in
villages. He wrote no books—to have done so would have been
a means of action too heavily weighted with matter. He founded no
newspapers or reviews. His sole weapon was the poverty of preaching. He prepared no speeches or lectures—He simply opened his
lips and the clamor of wisdom, the freshness of Heaven, passed

over men's hearts. What liberty! If He had willed to convert the world by the great means of power, by *rich temporal means,* by the methods of big business, what could have been easier? Did not somebody offer Him all the kingdoms of the earth? *Haec omnia tibi dabo.* What an opportunity for an apostolate! The like will never be had again. He refused it.

The world is perishing of dead weight. It will recover its youth only through the poverty of the spirit. To wish to save the things of the spirit by trying to seek out first of all, in order to serve it, the most powerful means in the order of matter, is an illusion which is all too common. You might as well tie the wings of a dove to a steam-hammer. In the last resort, it is the great modern Minotaur itself, all the gear and strategy of big financial business, which would be entrusted with the task of saving souls; banks would be founded and world-wide trust companies organized for the worldly success of the Gospel, with founders' shares. It would be hypocrisy to deny that the apostolate itself and every spiritual undertaking need money, as a man needs food. Much money is required for missions, schools and charitable enterprises. But money can be used as a humble temporal means (it is then spent in order to procure things) or as a rich temporal means (it is then used to set up machinery for acquiring more money). With the divine freedom of sanctity, a Blessed Cottolengo testifies to the modern world to what an extent money, even if it abounds, can yet remain a means of poverty. What makes the modern world such a terrible tempter is that it puts forward, it so greatly vulgarizes, rich temporal means, means which are heavy and crushing; it uses them with such ostentation and such power as to induce the belief that they are the principal means. In truth, they are the principal means for matter, but not for the spirit.

When David resolved to face Goliath, he first tried on the armor of King Saul. It was too heavy for him; he preferred a humble weapon. David was the spirit. Poor Saul, a pitiable figure of temporal power royally equipped to serve the divine order and fight the Devil! And when David became king, he in his turn sinned. David, however, repented. And Jesus, "when he knew that they would come to take him by force and make him king, fled again into the mountain himself alone." [7]

---

[7] John 6, 15.

PART IV

The New Socio-Temporal Order

18 NEED OF A NEW HUMANISM*

I AM WELL AWARE THAT FOR SOME PEOPLE AN AUTHEN-
tic humanism can by definition only be an anti-religious humanism.
My idea is quite the contrary, as will be evident in the following
chapters. For the moment I would simply make two statements
of fact on this subject.

In the first place, it is quite true that since the dawn of the
Renaissance the Western world has passed progressively from a
regime of Christian sacral heroism to a humanistic regime. But
Western humanism has religious and transcendent sources without
which it is incomprehensible to itself: I call "transcendent" all
forms of thought, however diverse they may otherwise be, which
find as principle of the world a spirit superior to man, which find
in man a spirit whose destiny goes beyond time, and which find at
the center of moral life a natural or supernatural piety. The sources
of Western humanism are classical sources and Christian sources;
and it is not only in the bosom of mediaeval times, it is also in one
of the least questionable parts of the heritage we have from pagan
antiquity, the part evoked by the names of Homer, Sophocles,
Socrates and Virgil, "the Father of the West," that the qualities
which I have just mentioned appear. On the other hand, by the very
fact that it was a regime of a unity of flesh and of spirit, a regime
of incarnate spirituality, mediaeval Christendom embodied in its
sacral forms a virtual and implicit humanism. In the twelfth and

---

* *Humanisme intégral* (new ed. Paris: Fernand Aubier, 1947 [1st ed.
1936]), pp. 12–15, 36–42.

thirteenth centuries, this humanism was to "appear" and to manifest itself—with the radiance of a beauty that was unstable and as if in a hurry to exist, for soon the discord between the mediaeval style of culture and the style of classical humanism (to say nothing of the diverse disfigurations which Christianity itself was to suffer, chief among which were Puritanism and Jansenism) was to mask and to keep hidden for a time the fundamental agreement between Christianity and humanism seen in their essences.

In those mediaeval times a communion, in one and the same living faith, of the human person with other real and concrete persons and with the God whom they loved and with the whole of creation, made man, amidst plenty of troubles, fruitful in heroism and in activities of knowing and in works of beauty; and in the purest hearts a great love, exalting nature in man above itself, extended even to things the sense of fraternal piety. Then a St. Francis understood that, before being exploited by our industry for our use, material nature demands in some way to be itself familiarized by our love: I mean that in loving things and the being in them, man should draw them to the human rather than make the human submit to their measure.

On the other hand, and this is my second point, if we consider Western humanism in those of its contemporary forms which appear to be most emancipated from every metaphysics of transcendence, it is easy to see that, if there still remains in them some common conception of human dignity, of liberty and of disinterested values, this is a heritage of ideas and sentiments once Christian but today little loved. I fully appreciate, of course, that "liberal-bourgeois" humanism is now no more than barren wheat and a starchy bread. Against this materialized spirituality, the active materialism of atheism and paganism has the game in its hands. But cut off from their natural roots and transplanted into a climate of violence, disaffected Christian energies, in fact and existentially, whatever the theories behind them, do in part move men's hearts and rouse men to action. Is it not a sign of the confusion of ideas reaching throughout the world today, to see these formerly Christian energies helping to exalt precisely the propaganda of cultural conceptions opposed head-on to Christianity? It is high time for Christians to bring things back to truth, reintegrating in the fullness of their original source those hopes for justice and those nostalgias for communion on which the world's sorrow feeds and which are themselves misdirected; thus awaking a cultural and temporal force of Christian inspiration able to act on history and to be a support to men.

For this Christians must have a sound social philosophy and a sound philosophy of modern history. Thus they would work to substitute for the inhuman regime in agony before our eyes a new form of civilization which would be characterized by an *integral humanism*, and which would represent for them a new Christendom, no longer a sacral, but a secular or lay one, on the lines we have endeavored to make clear in the studies brought together in this volume.

We see this new humanism, which has no standards in common with "bourgeois" humanism and which is all the more human because it does not worship man, but really and effectively respects human dignity and does justice to the integral demands of the person, as orientated towards a socio-temporal realization of the Gospel's concern for human things (which ought not to exist merely in the spiritual order, but to be made incarnate) and towards the ideal of a fraternal community. It is not to the dynamism or the imperialism of race or class or nation that this humanism asks men to sacrifice themselves, it is to a better life for their brothers and to the concrete good of the community of human persons; it is to the humble truth of brotherly love to be realized— at the cost of an always difficult effort and of a relative poverty [1]— in the social order and the structures of common life. In this way such a humanism can make man grow in communion, and if so, it cannot be less than an heroic humanism. . . .

As regards man, we may remark that in the beginnings of the modern age, with Descartes first and then with Rousseau and Kant, rationalism had raised up a proud and splendid image of the *personality* of man, inviolable, jealous of his immanence and his autonomy and, last of all, good in essence. It was in the very name of the rights and autonomy of this personality that the rationalist

---

[1] I regard as quite necessary what in our time we call an *economy of abundance*; but without mentioning the serious problems posed by the progress of science and of technology, so far as this progress lessens the need of manual labor and creates risks of unemployment, we must hold that this abundance, while it will be distributed to all, will mean for each a relative poverty in which sufficiency will be assured but in which luxury will be difficult.

polemic had condemned any intervention from the outside into this perfect and sacred universe, whether such intervention would come from Revelation and Grace, from a tradition of human wisdom, from the authority of a law of which man is not the author, or from a Sovereign Good which solicits his will, or finally from an objective reality which would measure and rule his intelligence.

Yet in little more than a century this proud anthropocentric personality has fallen, has quickly crumbled to dust, caught in the dispersion of its material elements.

In this process a first significant moment is noted in biology, in the triumph of the Darwinian ideas of man's simian origin. According to this view, man is regarded not only as coming from a long evolution of animal species—that, after all, is a secondary, purely historical question—but as issuing from this biological evolution *without metaphysical discontinuity,* without, at a given moment, with the arrival of the human being, anything absolutely new appearing in the series, namely, spiritual subsistence, implying that at each generation of a human being an individual soul is created by the Author of all things and cast into existence for an eternal destiny.

Supported by revealed dogma, the Christian idea of man and of the human person has not been shaken by Darwinism. But the rationalist idea of the human person has received a mortal blow.

The second blow, the knockout, if I may so speak, was in the psychological domain, and it was Freud who gave it (I do not speak of Freud's methods of psychological investigation, which include discoveries of genius, but of his metaphysics). The Christian knows that the heart of man, as Pascal said, is hollow and full of rottenness, but that does not prevent him from recognizing man's spiritual grandeur and dignity. But for rationalist and naturalistic thought, what has man become in our day? The center of gravity in the human being has sunk so low that, properly speaking, we no longer have any personality but only the fatal movement of polymorphous larvae in the subterranean world of instinct and desire—*Acheronta movebo,* Freud himself says; and all the well-regulated dignity of our personal conscience appears as a deceitful mask. In short, man is only the place of intersection and conflict for a radically sexual libido and an instinct for death. This mystery of sorrowing life and divine life, bearing the imprint of the Creator's face, becomes an enigma despondent over the complications of death. Man, who at first had been looked upon as both an heroic and quasi-divine figure and a purely natural being, thus falls, following the law of all paganism, into an unnatural mockery of his own nature, which he scourges all the more cruelly the more of complacency and sentimental pity he nourishes for it. He is sacked and pillaged, he becomes a monster, a monster dear to himself.

After all the dissociations and dualisms in the age of anthropocentric humanism—the separation and opposition of nature and grace, of faith and reason, of love and knowledge, as also of love and the senses in affective life—we are now witnessing a dispersion, a final decomposition. This does not prevent man from claiming sovereignty more than ever. But this claim is no longer made for the individual person, for he no longer knows where to find himself, he sees himself only as torn apart from society and fragmentized. Individual man is ripe for abdication—what a rebirth if he refuses to abdicate and at the point where he refuses! He is ripe to abdicate in favor of collective man, in favor of that great historic image of humanity which for Hegel, who gave us the theology of it, consisted in the State with its perfect juridic structure, and which for Marx will consist in Communist society with its immanent dynamism.

Let us look at things now from the point of view of culture. From this point of view, what has been the dialectic of anthropocentric humanism?

Three aspects or moments inseparably bound together may be distinguished in what we may call the dialectic of modern culture. These three moments are in continuity in spite of strong secondary oppositions; they have followed one another in time, but they also co-exist, mixed one with another in varying degrees. We have attempted to characterize them elsewhere.[2]

In the first moment (sixteenth and seventeenth centuries), when civilization was prodigal of its fairest fruits, forgetful of the roots whence the sap comes, man thought civilization should inaugurate solely by the power of reason a human order, still conceived according to the Christian pattern inherited from preceding ages, a pattern which became forced and began to be corrupted. We may

---

[2] *Religion et culture* and *Du régime temporel et de la liberté.*

call this the *classical* moment of our culture, the moment of Christian naturalism.

In the second moment (eighteenth and nineteenth centuries) man saw that a culture which separates itself from supreme supernatural standards is bound to take sides against them. The demand then was for culture to free man from the superstition of revealed religion and to open up to his natural goodness the perspectives of a perfect security to be attained through the spirit of riches accumulating the goods of the earth. This is the moment of rationalist optimism, the *bourgeois* moment of our culture. Even now we are scarcely out of it.

A third moment (twentieth century) is the moment of the materialistic overthrow of values, the *revolutionary* moment when man, placing his last end decisively in himself and no longer able to endure the machine of this world, engages in a war of desperation to make a wholly new humanity rise out of a radical atheism.

Let us take a closer look at the character of these three moments.

The first moment is a reversal in the order of ends. Instead of orientating its proper good, which is an earthly good, towards eternal life, culture seeks its supreme end in itself. And the end it seeks is the domination of man over matter. God becomes the guarantor of this domination.

The second moment is like a demiurgic imperialism in relation to the forces of matter. Here culture fails to understand that the effort to perfect man's nature by a process itself conformed to the profound demands of this nature, that is to say by an interior perfection of wisdom both in knowing and in living, should always be its principal effort. Instead, culture puts before all else the aim to be lord of exterior nature and to reign over it by means of technological procedures, an aim good in itself, but raised to first place and expected to create, thanks to physico-mathematical science, a material world where man will find, following Descartes' promises, a perfect felicity. God becomes an idea.

The third moment consists in a progressive driving back of the human by matter. In order to rule over nature and yet take no account of the basic laws of his own nature, man, in his knowing and his living, is in reality forced to submit himself more and more to technological and inhuman necessities, and to energies of the material order which he makes use of and which invade the human world itself. God dies; materialized man thinks he can be man or superman only if God is not God.

Whatever may be the gain from other points of view, the conditions of life for the human being thus become more and more inhuman. Let things continue in this way and it seems that earth will no longer be habitable, to use a phrase of the venerable Aristotle, except by beasts or gods.

Let us consider now the dialectic of anthropocentric humanism relative to God or to the idea man has of God. We may remark that this idea, so far as it ceases to be supported and purified by Revelation, itself follows the fate of culture. We said that in the first moment of the humanist dialectic, God becomes the guarantor of the domination of man over matter. This is the Cartesian God. Divine transcendence is then maintained, but it is taken in a human sense—univocally—by a geometric reason incapable of rising to analogical understanding. This transcendence thereby begins to be in danger.

At the opposite pole from rationalism, Jansenius already was affirming the inscrutable transcendence of the divine majesty, but only in the sense that this majesty confounded reason and smashed it to pieces. Reason could know the divine majesty only by sacrificing itself. Why is that so? Because the reason of theologians in the classic age had lost the sense of analogy and had become a geometrical reason, the enemy of mystery, like the reason of the philosopher in the same age. Let reason recognize mystery and annihilate itself, or let it refuse to annihilate itself but deny mystery.

In Descartes' case, God is the guarantor of science and of geometric reason, and the idea of God is the clearest of all ideas. And yet the divine infinite is declared to be absolutely inscrutable; we are blind to it; and so a germ of agnosticism is already present in Cartesian rationalism. God acts by a pure plenitude of efficiency, without ordering things to an end; and just as His despotic liberty could make square circles and mountains without valleys, so it rules good and evil by an act of pleasure.

In spite of his polemics against anthropomorphism, Malebranche will represent the glory of God (the most mysterious of all concepts, a concept related to the depths of uncreated love) as the glory of a monarch or of an artist glorified by his works and causing his own perfection to be admired in them. Leibniz, too, will want the perfection of the divine artisan to be judged by the perfection of His work (in-which case the work also should be divine), and he will undertake to justify God by showing that the ways of Providence agree with the reason of philosophers.

We have said that in the second moment of the humanist dialectic, God becomes an idea. This is the God of the great idealist metaphysicians. Divine transcendence is now rejected, and a philosophy of immanence takes its place. In Hegel, God will appear as the ideal limit of the development of the world and of humanity.

Finally, in the third moment of the humanist dialectic, Nietzsche will feel it his terrible mission to announce the death of God. How could God still live in a world from which His image, that is to say the free and spiritual personality of man, is in the act of being effaced? The most proudly representative form of this moment of anthropocentric humanism is contemporary atheism.

Come to the end of an historic, secularistic evolution, we find ourselves face to face with two pure positions: *pure atheism,* and *pure Christianity.*

19 SACRAL AND LAY CIVILIZATION*

THE END OF POLITICAL SOCIETY IS NOT TO LEAD THE
human person to his spiritual perfection and to his full freedom of
autonomy, that is to say to sanctity, to a state of freedom which is
properly divine because it is the very life of God living then in man.
Nevertheless, political society is essentially destined, by reason of
the earthly end itself which specifies it, to the development of those
environmental conditions which will so raise men in general to a
level of material, intellectual and moral life in accord with the good
and peace of the whole, that each person will be positively aided
in the progressive conquest of his full life as a person and of his
spiritual freedom. . . .

The paradoxical necessity of a being lured by nothingness, to
progress to the superhuman, causes man to have no static equilibrium, but only an equilibrium of tension and movement. It is
also the reason why political life, which should tend to raise as
high as possible, relative to given conditions, the level of existence
of the multitude, must also tend to a certain heroism and must ask
much of man in order to give him much.

It follows that the condition of life of members in the temporal
city should not be confounded with either an earthly beatitude or
with a felicity of ease and repose. But it certainly does not follow
that temporal civilization is nothing more than a mere means to
eternal life and has not in itself the dignity of an end (infravalent),

_____

* _Humanisme intégral_ (New edition. Paris: Fernand Aubier, 1947), pp.
141–159.

nor, on the pretext that the present life is a vale of tears, that the Christian should resign himself to injustice or to the servile condition and misery of his brothers.

The Christian is in fact never resigned. His conception of the body politic has within it the aim to adjust the vale of tears so as to secure for the assembled multitude a relative though real earthly happiness, a good and livable structure of existence for the whole, a state of justice, of friendship and of prosperity making possible for each person the fulfilment of his destiny. He asks that the earthly city be ordered so as effectively to recognize the right of its members to existence, to work and to the growth of their life as persons. And his condemnation of modern civilization is really more serious and better based than is the Socialist or Communist condemnation, because it is not only the earthly happiness of the community, it is also the life of the soul, the spiritual destiny of the person that is menaced by this civilization.

ANALOGOUS NATURE OF THIS CONCEPTION

This conception of the earthly city was that of mediaeval Christendom. But mediaeval Christendom was only one of its possible realizations.

In other words, it is not in a *univocal* manner that such a conception can be realized at different epochs of the world's history, but in an *analogous* manner. Here we see the primary importance of the idea of analogy for a sane philosophy of culture. . . .

In our opinion, the philosophy of culture must avoid two opposed errors, one of which brings all things together as if univocal, while the other separates all things as if equivocal. A philosophy of *equivocity* will imagine that with a change in time historical conditions become so different that they depend on supreme principles which are themselves heterogeneous: as though truth and right, the supreme rules of human action, were mutable. A philosophy of *univocity* would lead us to believe that these supreme rules and principles always apply in the same way, and that in particular the way in which Christian principles are proportioned to the conditions of each age and are realized in time should not vary at all.

The true solution is found in the philosophy of *analogy*. The principles do not change, nor the supreme practical rules of human life. But they are applied in ways essentially diverse, ways answering to the same concept only according to a similitude of proportion. And this supposes that one has not merely an empirical and, we might say, a blind notion, but a truly rational and philosophical notion of the diverse phases of history. A simple empirical ascertainment of factual circumstances could give rise only to a certain opportunism in the application of principles, and leave us poles apart from wisdom. An historical climate or sky is not determined in this way. It can only be done by making rational judgments of values, and discerning the form and significance of the intelligible constellations dominating the diverse phases of human history.

MEDIAEVAL CHRISTENDOM AND
A NEW CHRISTENDOM

Hence, the particular problem which we wish to treat now and which can be formulated in the following way: Should a new Christendom, in the conditions of the historic age we are entering, while incarnating the same analogical principles, be conceived according to a type essentially (specifically) distinct from that of the mediaeval world? To this question we reply in the affirmative. We think that a new age of the world will allow the principles of any vitally Christian civilization to be realized in terms of a new concrete *analogue.*

In fact, not only do we recognize the radical irreversibility of historical movement, as against pagan conceptions of eternal recurrence, but we further believe that this movement is the stage of a human and divine drama of which visible events are only signs; we believe that humanity, borne on by this irresistible movement, passes underneath various historical constellations, typically different constellations that create for the principles of culture specifically different conditions of realization; and we believe that the moral physiognomy of these historical constellations is far more profoundly different than is ordinarily believed. For what reasons in general is this so?

First, in virtue of a law dominating the temporal as such, and concerned, if it may be so expressed, with the junction of Man and Time. This law is that a fully lived experience cannot be begun again. By the simple fact that man has lived, and lived to its depths, a certain form of life, has experienced to their depths the good and evil which the pursuit of a certain historic ideal has brought to pass in his flesh, those things are ended; it is impossible to return to them, it is a law of the temporal as such, of history. Only things of the suprahistorical and supratemporal order, the things of eternal life, escape this law. The Church does not die, but civilizations do.

"Suffering passes," Léon Bloy used to say, "to have suffered does not pass." All the past which man has suffered remains; it has its place, but it has it as something past, already lived, defunct: it is not possible for man to live it again, to suffer it again. Do we not say, in the grand manner, "he has lived," meaning "he is dead"? So it is with mediaeval civilization, it has borne its fruit.

Second, it is impossible—it would be contrary to the mental make-up of humanity, since every great experience, even one accomplished in error, is orientated by the attraction of a certain good, however badly this is sought, and consequently unearths new areas and new riches to be exploited—it is impossible to conceive that the sufferings and experiences of the modern world have been useless. This world, we have said, has sought the rehabilitation of the creature; and if it has sought it by wrong roads, still we ought to recognize and to save the truth which was there hidden and captive.

Finally, if it is true, and a Christian cannot fail to think it true, that God governs history, that, whatever the obstacles, He pursues in history certain designs and that thus in time and through time a divine work and divine preparations are achieved, it would be to go against God Himself and to wrestle with the supreme government of history to claim to immobilize in a past form, in a univocal form, the ideal of a culture worthy to be the end of our action.

TWO PRELIMINARY REMARKS

We shall attempt to characterize at the outset the historic ideal of mediaeval Christendom, and then, in relation to the points of comparison thus determined, try to characterize what we have called *the prospective image* of a new Christendom.

Regarding this prospective image or this historic ideal of a new Christendom, we make two preliminary remarks.

The first is that it goes without saying—apart from the more specific indications which we will give in a later chapter—that it refers to a concrete, particular future, to the future of our time, but it does not greatly matter whether this future be at hand or far off. As distinguished from the ideals for immediate application invoked by the practitioner of politics or of revolution, ours is a universe of possibilities seen by the philosopher on the level of a (practical) knowledge still speculative in its mode. . . .

Our second remark is that, viewing things, not with Marxist Hegelianism or with historical materialism—those who criticize these, often accept their way of posing the problem—but with a Christian philosophy of culture, we shall envisage from another angle than do most socialist or anti-socialist theorists the same socio-temporal matter. . . .

The Idea of the Holy Empire or the Christian Sacral Conception of the Temporal

In a very general way, we may remark that the historical ideal of the Middle Ages was controlled by two dominants: on the one hand, the idea or myth (in the sense given this word by George Sorel) of force in the service of God; on the other, this concrete fact that temporal civilization itself was in some manner a function of the sacred, and imperiously demanded unity of religion.

To sum up in a word, let us say that the historical ideal of the Middle Ages could be expressed in the idea of the Holy Empire. We do not refer here to the Holy Empire as historical fact; strictly speaking, we may say that this fact never truly existed. The idea of the *sacrum imperium* was preceded by an event: the empire of Charlemagne, the aims of which, it seems, were not exempt from caesaro-papism; and the idea, arising after this event, was capable of only precarious, partial and contradictory realizations. It was hindered and thwarted on the one hand by the actual opposition between Pope and Emperor, "those two halves of God," as Victor Hugo said, and on the other by the opposition between the Empire and the French monarchy, which never did admit that it was dependent in temporalities on a higher authority.

Nor do we speak of the Holy Empire as a theocratic utopia (a question covered in other chapters).

We speak of the Holy Empire as a concrete historic ideal or historic myth, that is to say as the lyrical image which orientated and upheld a civilization. Taken in this sense, it must be said that the Middle Ages lived on the ideal of the Holy Empire (and died of it). If we understand this myth in a sufficiently broad manner, in all its representative and symbolic value, it dominates ideally all mediaeval temporal forms and even the conflicts, the contradictory realizations which kept the *sacrum imperium* from truly existing as a fact.

It is by this title of concrete historic ideal that the Holy Empire still impregnates our imaginations, and on this point we need to submit our more or less unconscious images to a drastic revision. In countries of Latin culture, this ideal exercises a secret influence (under various cultural aspects, for example those of the conflicts between clericalism and anti-clericalism) on the conceptions which certain Catholics, and perhaps still more their opponents, have of a Christian restoration. In countries of Germanic culture, the image of the Holy Empire survives in its properly imperial form. . . .

The concrete historic ideal of the Middle Ages, the myth or symbol of the Holy Empire, corresponds to what may be called a *Christian sacral conception of the temporal.* Let us try to disengage the typical features of this conception, features organically bound to each other. In our view, five points above all are characteristic and typical of it.

We notice in the first place the tendency to an organic unity qualitatively maximal. This unity does not exclude either diversity or pluralism, since without them it would not be organic; and its demand is to center the unity of the temporal city as high as possible in the life of the person, in other words to found it on spiritual unity.

This movement toward unity is evident at the heart of each of the political unities which composed Christendom. A typical instance of it is the work accomplished by the French monarchy and people, or by the people and kings of Castile. And when this impulse toward national unity ceased to be kept balanced by the more spiritual impulse, of a religious origin, toward the unity of Christendom, when at the decline of the Middle Ages it swept everything before it, then it passed into absolutism and into a type of unity more mechanical than organic, in which the political really had primacy over the spiritual.

Again, is anything more evidently characteristic of the Middle Ages than the effort toward this organic unity in the order of civilization itself and the community of Christian peoples? The effort was to unify the world in temporal matters under the Emperor as in spiritual matters the Church is one under the Pope. Without question this historic ideal failed in its highest ambitions, mainly due to the pride and cupidity of princes. Nevertheless, in as precarious a fashion as you wish, though in a fashion that today seems mighty enviable to us, there was a Christendom then, a Christian temporal community in which national quarrels were quarrels within a family and did not shatter the unity of culture. There was a Christian Europe.

Whether it is a question of each Christian nation or of Christendom in its higher unity, the temporal unity aimed at by the Middle Ages was a *maximal* unity, a unity of the most exacting and the most completely monarchical sort. The center of its formation and consistency was set very high in the life of the person, above the temporal, in that spiritual order itself to which the temporal order and the temporal common good are subordinated; its source was thus in men's hearts, and the unity of national or imperial political structures only manifested this primordial unity.

But this temporal unity of Christian Europe had not merely religious unity as its source.

It included (as was indispensable when it was a question of a maximal temporal unity) a powerful unity—a unity that was quite general, and compatible with extremely sharp divisions and particular rivalries—of a certain common basis of thought and of doctrinal principles. In the diversity of philosophical schools, human intelligence had a common tongue. It included a really remarkable and tremendously vigorous effort aiming at—what was not reached—a high and perfect unity of the intellectual structure and the political structure. Such was the grand and sublime, too grand and sublime, conception of the popes at the most vigorous time of the Middle Ages. In order to form a Christian world, a Christian Europe according to a type of perfect unity, in order to form, in other words, that figurative but so powerful and energetic refraction of God's kingdom in the socio-temporal realm of which we have already spoken, the popes knew it was necessary to have, and they wanted, a high doctrinal, theological and philosophical, unity, a unity of wisdom of minds under the light of faith. From this point of view the center of Christendom, a supranational scientific center, was the University of Paris.

They also knew that it was necessary to have, and they wanted, a high degree of political unity among the different peoples, an imperial unity over and above the various kingdoms, as the unity of wisdom is over and above the various sorts of sciences. The supranational political center of Christendom was the Roman Germanic emperor.

Effective Predominance of the Ministerial Role of the Temporal

So high a unity was conceivable only because it was a unity of sacral type. To say that the center of its formation was very high in the human person is to say that the chief thing in the temporal order was its subordination to the spiritual order. This brings us to the second typical trait of the mediaeval historical ideal, namely, the predominance of the *ministerial role of the temporal* in relation to the spiritual.

The scholastics, as is well known, distinguish between the *infravalent end*—e.g., the professional activity of the philosopher or the artisan, which has a proper value as end though it is subordinated to a higher end such as a morally good life—and the *means,* which as such exists only for the sake of the end and is specified by the end, as reasoning, for example, is for the sake of, and is specified by, knowledge. Again, they distinguish in the line of efficient causality between the *secondary principal cause*—for example, the vegetative energies of the plant—which, though inferior to a higher cause—such as solar energy—nevertheless produces an effect proportioned to its specific degree of being; and the *instrumental cause*—such as the brush in the hands of the artist—which, exercising its proper causality only so far as a higher agent makes use of it for this agent's own end, produces an effect higher than its specific degree of being.

Granting these notions, we must remark that in mediaeval civilization the things that are Caesar's, though clearly distinguished from the things that are God's, had in great measure a ministerial function in regard to them. To that extent, they were instrumental causes in regard to the sacred. Their own end had the rank of means, a simple means in regard to eternal life.

Need we give examples? Need we recall the notion and role of the secular arm, or the name "exterior bishop" often given to kings, or cite typical occurrences such as the Crusades?

There is no question of theocratic order here; the proper finalities of the temporal were quite clearly recognized, as also the proper domain of civil society. But, accidental as it may have remained in itself and as judged relatively to the political order, the observed ministerial function of the political in relation to the spiritual order was often exercised in a normal and quite typical way.

The Use of Temporal Means for Spiritual Ends

The third typical mark of the mediaeval historical ideal, correlative to this ministerial function of political life, is the use made of means proper to the temporal and political order (visible and external means in which social constraint takes a big part, constraint of opinion, coercion, etc.), the use of the institutional setup of the State, for the spiritual good of men and for the spiritual unity of the social body itself—for that spiritual unity by reason of which the heretic was not only a heretic, but indeed a man who attacked the socio-temporal community at its living sources.

I have no mind to condemn this regime in principle. In a sense, an earthly city capable of the death sentence for the crime of heresy showed a greater care for the good of souls and a higher idea of the nobility of the human community, thus centered on truth, than a city which only knows how to mete out punishment for crimes against the body. Nevertheless, it was precisely here that human nature was inevitably to introduce the worst abuses, and these became more and more intolerable (in fact, the situation was monstrous) when after the ruin of mediaeval Christendom the State, ceasing to act as instrument of a legitimate spiritual authority superior to it, arrogated to itself and in its own name the right to act in matters spiritual. The absolutism of a Henry VIII and of a Philip II, Gallicanism, Josephism, the enlightened despotism of the eighteenth century, and Jacobinism form in this regard a highly significant series which is continued by the totalitarian States of our day.

Diversity of "Social Races"

The fourth trait of the mediaeval historical ideal I find in the fact that a certain disparity as of essence between leader and

led, I mean a certain essential disparity of hereditary social categories, or to use the amplifications of meaning of which the word
"race" is susceptible, a diversity of *social races*, was then recognized at the base of the hierarchy of social functions and the relations of authority, whether it was a question of political authority
in the body politic or of other kinds of authority which occur in the
social and economic life of the country. We may say that in the
Middle Ages temporal authority was primarily conceived according
to the type of paternal authority found in the conceptions, themselves sacral, of the family—conceptions of which we have an example in the Roman notion of the *paterfamilias*, a notion which
Christian faith was able to sublimate by allying it with the notion
of God's universal fatherhood.

I used the phrase "disparity as of essence," though father and
children are evidently of the same kind and of the same race! Yet
the child as such is in a position of natural inferiority to his father
who seems to him as of a higher essence, and this situation is
further confirmed where, according to the conception held of the
family, the father exercises his authority as a sacred function, invested, we may say, with the personality of God.

The consecration of a king makes him father of the people, and
confirms in the order of grace his natural authority as head of the
body politic by witnessing that he governs the temporal in the
name of the Sovereign King. The whole political thought of the
Middle Ages blazed up with its last splendor in Joan of Arc when
Joan put such energy and such obstinacy into her demand for the
king's consecration, and when she persuaded Charles VII to give
up his "holy kingdom" to Christ, then solemnly returned it to him
in Christ's name, so that he should hold it "in commendam." When
the king has received the unction of consecration he is vicar not
only of his people, but also of God (in the age of monarchical
absolutism he was God's vicar, but no longer the people's).

For the Middle Ages the community of work was an extension
of domestic society. Workers were parts and organs of this community, and the guild was like a family at second remove, a family
of workers which brought together masters and workers in such a
way that, although there undoubtedly were rich and poor, and
mountains of misery, yet the existence of a class reduced to the
level of tools or of marketable work, of a proletariat in the strict

sense, was then inconceivable. Rigorous hierarchies were at the base of the relations of authority in this family or quasi-family organization and in the feudal economic system.

Such a heterogeneity in the social structure was, however, compensated for in the Middle Ages (and precisely by reason of this family conception of authority) by an organic suppleness and a familiarity (sometimes brutal, but anything is better than indifference and contempt) in the relations of authority, and by a spontaneous and progressive springing up—more lived than conscious, yet real and efficacious—of freedoms and popular immunities. If the sketch we draw were not designedly reduced to a mere schematic line, it would be a propos to insist here on popular movements and on their economic and social importance.

Let us add in parenthesis that, like the first and the third traits pointed out by us—the movement toward organic unity, and the use of temporal means for spiritual ends—this fourth trait gave way in the age immediately following the Middle Ages, I mean under the *ancien régime*, to its opposite, not by defect, but by excess and by petrification.

If we want a representative example of the mediaeval conception of authority, we find it in the religious order which, founded before the Middle Ages properly speaking, was one of the most typical agents of its culture and, we may say, is the key to it. In the Benedictine Order and the Benedictine conception of authority, a father, the abbot, the *paterfamilias* was invested with an evangelical and sacred character, and the other monks were as children, his children.

The Common Work: to Build Up an Empire for Christ

The fifth mark of the mediaeval historical ideal has to do with the common end for which the body politic labors. It is the establishment of a social and juridical structure dedicated to the service of the Redeemer, by the power of baptized man and a baptized political life.

As we said earlier, with childhood's absolute ambition and simple courage Christendom then built an immense fortress on the summit of which God reigned. Without ignoring the temporal order, its limits, its miseries, and the conflicts proper to it, without falling into a theocratic utopia, believing humanity attempted to build up a figurative and symbolic image, as it were, of God's kingdom.

THE HISTORICAL CLIMATE OF MODERN CIVILIZATION *

The modern age is not a sacral, but a secular age. The order of terrestrial civilization and of temporal society has gained complete differentiation and full autonomy,[1] which is something normal in itself, required by the Gospel's very distinction between God's and Caesar's domains. But that normal process was accompanied—and spoiled—by a most aggressive and stupid process of insulation from, and finally rejection of, God and the Gospel in the sphere of social and political life. The fruit of this we can contemplate today in the theocratic atheism of the Communist State.

Well, those Christians who are turned toward the future and who hope—be it a long range hope—for a new Christendom, a new Christianly inspired civilization, know that "the world has done with neutrality. Willingly or unwillingly, States will be obliged to make a choice for or against the Gospel. They will be shaped either by the totalitarian spirit or by the Christian spirit." [2] They know that a new Christianly inspired civilization, if and when it evolves in history, will by no means be a return to the Middle Ages, but a typically different attempt to make the leaven of the Gospel quicken the depths of temporal existence. They feel that such a new age will aim at rehabilitating man in God and through God, not apart from God, and will be an age of sanctification of secular life. But along what lines can this be imagined? This means that the Christians of whom I am speaking have to establish and develop a sound philosophy of modern history, as well as to separate from the genuine growth of time, from the genuine progress of human consciousness and civilization, the deadly errors which have preyed upon them, and the tares which are also growing among the wheat and which foster the wickedness of the time. In order to conceive our own concrete historical image of what is to be hoped

---

* The rest of this chapter is from *Man and the State* (Chicago: University of Chicago Press, 1951), pp. 159–162.
[1] I mean, in its own sphere and domain. See supra (*Man and the State*), pp. 152–153.
[2] Cf. our book, *The Rights of Man and Natural Law* (New York: Scribners, 1943), p. 23.

for in our age, we have to determine and take into account, as an existential frame of reference, the basic typical features which characterize the essential structure of our age, in other words, the *historical climate* or the *historical constellation* by which the existence and activity of the human community is conditioned today.

As I just put it, the historical climate of modern civilization, in contradistinction to mediaeval civilization, is characterized by the fact that it is a "lay" or "secular," not a "sacral" civilization. On the one hand, the dominant dynamic idea is not the idea of strength or fortitude at the service of justice, but rather that of the conquest of freedom and the realization of human dignity. On the other hand, the root requirement for a sound mutual cooperation between the Church and the body politic is not the unity of a religio-political body, as the *respublica Christiana* of the Middle Ages was, but the very unity of the human person, simultaneously a member of the body politic and of the Church, if he freely adheres to her. The unity of religion is not a prerequisite for political unity, and men subscribing to diverse religious or non-religious creeds have to share in and work for the same political or temporal common good. Whereas "mediaeval man," as Father Courtney Murray puts it,[3] "entered the State (what State there was) to become a 'citizen,' through the Church and his membership in the Church, modern man is a citizen with full civic rights whether he is a member of the Church or not."

Hence, many consequences derive. First, the political power is not the secular arm [4] of the spiritual power, the body politic is autonomous and independent within its own sphere. Second, the equality of all members of the body politic has been recognized as

---

[3] John Courtney Murray, *Governmental Repression of Heresy*, reprinted from the *Proceedings of the Catholic Theological Society of America*, 1949, p. 57.

[4] On the question of the "secular arm" see *ibid.*, pp. 62 ff.; Journet, *L'église du verbe incarné*, pp. 249, 317–326. Be it noted in passing that the stock phrase "recourse to the secular arm," that is, to civil law, to enforce, in certain circumstances dealing with the public order and the temporal domain, a canonic regulation concerning the members of the Church, means something quite different from the concept of the political power as being the secular arm or instrument of the Church. In a pluralistic society it is but normal that the particular regulations of an autonomous body may be sanctioned by civil law, from the civil society's own viewpoint, when the interests of the common good are concerned.

a basic tenet. Third, the importance of the inner forces at work in
the human person, in contradistinction to the external forces of
coercion; the freedom of individual conscience with regard to the
State; the axiom—always taught by the Catholic Church, but disregarded as a rule by the princes and kings of old—that faith cannot be imposed by constraint [5]—all these assertions have become,
more explicitly than before, crucial assets to civilization, and are
to be especially emphasized if we are to escape the worst dangers
of perversion of the social body and of state totalitarianism. Fourth,
a reasoned-out awareness has developed, at least in those parts of
the civilized world where love for freedom is still treasured—and
is growing all the keener as freedom is more threatened—with
regard to the fact that nothing more imperils both the common
good of the earthly city and the supratemporal interests of truth
in human minds than a weakening and breaking down of the internal springs of conscience. Common consciousness has also become aware of the fact that freedom of inquiry, even at the risk
of error, is the normal condition for men to gain access to truth, so
that freedom to search for God in their own way, for those who
have been brought up in ignorance or semi-ignorance of Him, is
the normal condition in which to listen to the message of the Gospel
and the teachings of the Church, when grace will illumine their
hearts.[6]

Given such an existential frame of reference, what can be the
ways of applying and realizing, in our historical age, the supreme
principles that govern the relationship between Church and
State? Let us say that in a new Christianly inspired civilization, as
far as we are able to see it,[7] those principles would in general be
applied less in terms of the social power than in terms of the vivifying inspiration of the Church. The very modality of her action upon
the body politic has been spiritualized, the emphasis having shifted
from power and legal constraints (which the Church exercises, now
as ever, in her own spiritual sphere over her own subjects, but
not over the State) to moral influence and authority; in other

---

[5] See Journet, *L'église du verbe incarné*, pp. 261–264.
[6] Cf. infra (*Man and the State*), pp. 181–182 (and nn. 33 and 34).
[7] On the notion, and possible advent, of a "Chrétienté profane" (lay
or secular Christendom, in contradistinction to the sacral Christendom of the
Middle Ages) see Journet, *L'église du verbe incarné*, pp. 243–252.

words, to a fashion or "style," in the external relations of the Church, more appropriate to the Church herself, and more detached from the modalities that had inevitably been introduced by the Christian Empire of Constantine. Thus, the superior dignity of the Church is to find its ways of realization in the full exercise of her *superior strength of all-pervading inspiration.*

20 THE ROOTS OF SOVIET ATHEISM*

"RELIGIOUS" SIGNIFICANCE OF COMMUNISM

I SHALL DWELL AT SOME LENGTH ON THE PROBLEMS CONcerned with atheism as an historical force, and shall consider it in its expressly atheistic form, of which recent history gives us a typical example in Russian Communism (not that the pseudo-religious, or even the pseudo-Christian forms of atheism are less perfidious, as a study of racist doctrines would readily show). We shall first inquire what the deeper reasons for contemporary Russian atheism are; then we shall examine the philosophical problem posed by this atheism; lastly, we shall inquire what its cultural significance is.

The question is sometimes asked why the Communist social solutions, concerned with the organization of work and of the temporal community, cannot be separated from atheism, which is a religious and metaphysical position.

The reply, we believe, is that, taken in its spirit and its principles, Communism as it exists, above all the Communism of the Soviet republics, is a complete system of doctrine and of life pretending to reveal to man the meaning of his existence, answering all the fundamental questions posed by life, and manifesting an unparalleled power of totalitarian envelopment. It is a religion, and a most imperious religion, certain that it is called to replace all

* *Humanisme intégral* (New edition. Paris: Fernand Aubier, 1947), pp. 43–61.

other religions, an atheistic religion for which dialectical materialism is dogma and of which Communism as a regime of life is the
ethical and social expression. Thus atheism is not demanded as a
necessary consequence of the social system—that would be incomprehensible; on the contrary, it is presupposed as the principle of
this system. It is the starting point.[1] And that is why Communist
thought holds so ardently to it, as to the principle which stabilizes
its practical conclusions and without which these would lose their
necessity and their value.[2]

How is this atheism of principle constituted, and what is its logical tie-in with a particular social conception? This is what we wish
to examine. A difficulty arises, however, and one which would
seem of its nature to bar our inquiry at the outset: if one takes a
merely psychological point of view and considers the actual (1935–
1936) state of mind among Communists, particularly in France,
one gets the impression that if many of them have received with
satisfaction the new directives of the Party as to collaboration with
believers, it is precisely because, contrary to what we have just
advanced, Communism has in their eyes no metaphysical or religious significance, but only the significance of a socio-economic
ethics, or even only the significance of a technique for changing
the economic regime—and belief in this significance appears to be
the only faith they have. If then they can henceforth attract to this
faith some "separated brethren" whom the discipline of their party
had formerly obliged them to avoid on a priori grounds—because
they were Christians—it is natural that they would feel some joy
and exaltation over it, for in this they have a promise of apostolic
expansion and a release of the natural desire for human communication and fraternizing.

. . . It would seem that they do not disengage, in order to bring
fully to light, the philosophical problems underlying their revolu-

---

[1] Historically, atheism is also the starting point for the thought of
Marx himself. Marx was an atheist before he was a Communist . . .

[2] On the Communist side the objection has been raised (by Georges
Sadoul in *Commune*, Dec. 1935) that no doubt Marxism is "entirely and totally
atheistic," but that atheism is a consequence in it and not a starting point. The
consequence of what? Of the recognition of the fact that "the class war" exists.
It is not easy to see how one passes from the recognition of the fact that a class
war exists to the conclusion that God does not exist . . .

tionary faith, problems which this faith assumes to be solved. The fact is that their atheistic position has become so total and unconditional, so detached from the conditions of its own origins, that henceforth they take it to go on its own, like a truth known *per se* or a datum of experience. They are established on the ground of atheism as if it were the only ground on which anyone could build and as if a philosophical journey were not needed in order to reach that ground. In a word, neither in atheism nor in the materialistic conception of the world do they see any problem, and that is why they are unaware of the metaphysical process logically implied by these positions.

This itself confirms the assertion that faith in the Communist revolution really presupposes a whole universe of faith and of religion, in the midst of which the revolution takes place. But this universe is so natural to them that they do not bother to notice it. Besides, this religion and this faith do not appear to them as a religion because the religion and faith are atheistic, nor as a faith, because the religion and faith are seen as an expression of science. Thus, they do not sense that Communism is a religion for them, and yet that is what it really is. The perfect religious prays so well that he does not know that he prays. Communism is so profoundly and substantially a religion, an earthly one, that the Communist does not know it is a religion.

That this religion, though naturally intolerant as is any strongly dogmatic religion (to make a strongly dogmatic religion tolerant, supernatural charity is needed), should now call to a common temporal action the believers of other religions whose ultimate end is in heaven, and should contemplate the hypothesis that it would really recognize their freedoms in the temporal city, this is a paradoxical psychological fact to be taken account of, a fact which, considered in itself and whatever be the tactical reasons for it and the political Machiavellianism provoking it, certainly has a human significance. A precarious one, however, we may believe; the precariousness of these good dispositions is in fact all the greater as it is a question of a religion entirely and exclusively directed to earthly ends, and as the least diversion or opposition in regard to the "general line," defined in relation to these ends, hurts it at once and awakens in its believers the sense of the sacred. It is in the logic of things that some day or other a religious hatred and vindictiveness will be aroused, in particular, against the faithful of other religions, and, more generally, against every political non-conformist.

These questions of concrete psychology are not our concern. It is from the point of view of the content of doctrines, taken in itself and its intimate structure, that we claim that Communism comes, as from a first principle, from atheistic and anti-religious thought. We have to understand the roots and the development of this atheism and of this opposition to religion.

But still further precision is important. Some of the elements of Communism are Christian. St. Thomas More expressed some communist ideas. In its early phases Communism was not always atheistic. The idea itself of communion, which gives Communism its spiritual power and which it means to realize in the socio-temporal life (and in fact it ought to be realized there, but not exclusively there, nor by ruining the life in which it is realized in the most perfect way and in line with the highest aspirations of the human person), the idea itself of communion is of Christian origin. And it is alienated Christian virtues, the "virtues gone mad" of which G. K. Chesterton spoke, it is the spirit of faith and of sacrifice, it is the religious energies of the soul which Communism endeavors to drain off for its own uses, and these it needs in order to subsist.

RESENTMENT AGAINST THE CHRISTIAN WORLD

But it is perfectly typical of Communist thought, as it was formed in the second half of the nineteenth century and as it exists today, that it has used these energies of Christian origin in an atheist ideology whose intellectual structure is turned against Christian beliefs. Why is this so? It is, we believe, because at the origin of Communism, and above all due to the fault of a Christian world unfaithful to its principles, there lies a profound resentment against the Christian world, and not only against the Christian world, but (here is the tragedy) against Christianity itself, which transcends the Christian world and should not be confused with it, and against every notion related, however remotely, to what we may call the natural Platonism of the human mind. Let me add—since otherwise I am not a Platonist at all—that the Platonism in question amounts to something Plato was able to infer about the essence of man: if I speak here of a Platonism natural to our mind, it is only so far as our mind is naturally drawn to admit eternal truths and transcendent values.

I just said that the Christian world is other than Christianity. It is essential to get this distinction clearly. "Christianity," like "the Church," is a word that has a religious and spiritual meaning; it stands for a faith and a supernatural life.[3] On the contrary, "the Christian world" means something of time and of earth, and relates not to the order of religion itself, but to the order of civilization and nature. It is a particular body of cultural, political and economic formations characteristic of a given age in history, and the typical spirit of this body is mainly due to the social elements which play the directive and predominant role in it: the clergy and nobility in the Middle Ages, the aristocracy and royalty under the *ancien régime*, the bourgeoisie in modern times. When the philosopher of culture raises the question of the Christian world, he is not posing the problem of the truth of Christianity, but rather that of the temporal responsibilities of Christians.

Well, then, the Christian world has a temporal task, an earthly task to fulfil; an earthly task, because a civilization, as civilization, is directly ordered to an end specifically temporal; a Christian earthly task, because this civilization is by hypothesis a Christian civilization, the world in question having received the light of the Gospel. The temporal task of the Christian world is to work on earth for a socio-temporal realization of the Gospel truths. For if the Gospel is concerned first of all with the things of eternal life and infinitely transcends any and all sociology and philosophy, nevertheless it gives us sovereign rules for the conduct of our lives, and traces for us a very precise ethical code to which any Christian civilization, so far as it is worthy of the name, should try to conform socio-temporal reality, with due respect to varying histori-

---

[3] The word *Church* means "the Mystical Body of Christ," at once visible in its social pattern, and divine in its soul, whose proper life belongs to the supernatural order. The "temporal Christian world" may introduce, certainly not into the heart of the Church, but into the more or less extended parts of its human structure, impurities which come from the spirit of the world: intoxication with magnificence and *virtù* at the time of the Renaissance, the "bourgeois" spirit in the nineteenth century. Then, because the "Gates of Hell" cannot prevail against her, purifications come. Saints had been clamoring in vain for three centuries for the reform of the Church before the great Lutheran tempest arrived.

cal conditions. A socio-temporal realization of the Gospel truths—how ridiculous the expression appears when we take a look at the temporal structures of modern centuries, in particular of the nineteenth century!

Meditating on these things, we have good reason to say that the Christian world of modern times has failed in the duty of which we just spoke. In general it has shut up truth and the divine life within a limited part of its existence, within the things of worship and religious practice, and, at least in the case of the best men and women, within the things of the interior life. Matters of social and economic and political life it has abandoned to their own carnal law, withdrawn from Christ's light. . . .

Hence the resentment of which we spoke, resentment against those who have not made real the truth which they bore, resentment which reacts against this truth itself.

FIRST SUBSTITUTIONAL STEP:
REHABILITATION OF MATERIAL CAUSALITY

What has occurred as a consequence is a process of *substitution*. This has been effected by Marxism above all, and several stages of it are evident.

In the first place, the proper task of Marxism as a philosophy of resentment has been, as one has put it, to denounce "the lie of exalted ideas." It claims to pronounce a death sentence on idealism, both as a metaphysical doctrine—which leaves us few regrets; and as—quite another thing—a simple affirmation of the value of the immaterial in general. In short, Marxism is an *absolute realist immanentism*, and this vast ideological proliferation of resentment and indignation would have been impossible without Hegel.

In a sense, Marx appears to be the most consistent of the Hegelians. For if "all that is rational is real," and if historical reality, which means temporal existence, entirely and absolutely absorbs, because it is identical with, the whole "ideal" order, which used to be thought supratemporal and was later confused with the logical being of reason and its characteristic movement, then the subversion to which Marx, following up Feuerbach, subjected Hegelian dialectic is justified. And just as philosophy should become practical, not in the Aristotelian sense, but in the sense that speculative philosophy should give way to thought wholly involved in *praxis*, to thought which in its very essence would be an activity transformative of the world,[4] so the dialectical movement should for the future be wholly absorbed in matter, that is to say in historical reality separated from any transcendent element and considered above all in its primordial concrete substructures.

It is quite clear that the materialism of Marx is no ordinary materialism, neither that of the French materialists of the eighteenth century nor mechanistic materialism. But for the metaphysician, its wholly Hegelian quality and its confusion with pure immanentism only make it more real and more profound. To try to understand it we may . . . use the Aristotelian distinction between formal causality and material causality. The foolish idealist or "angelic" non-acknowledgment of material causality was to lead by reaction to an equally strong defence of material causality, justified in its origin though equally untenable in its results, since these two kinds of causality must go together as a principle of explanation. In Aristotelian language we may say that Marxism comes from a sort of revengeful perception of the importance of material causality; that is, in a very general way, of the part played by material factors in the course of nature and of history. This material causality gets the primacy, and, by making dialectic integral with itself, becomes the matrix of all activity.

What does material causality represent in the historical and social order? The process of human activities of the economic order. An Aristotelian will not contest that the economic order really plays a role of essential importance. But Marx gives it the principal role and makes it the radically determining factor.

MARX SAW THE ESSENTIAL IMPORTANCE OF MATERIAL CAUSALITY, BUT MADE IT PURELY AND SIMPLY PRIMARY

I know quite well that there is reason to revise the current interpretation of historical materialism, according to which interpretation everything else, all ideology, the spiritual life, religious

---

[4] "The question of knowing whether human thought can reach objective truth is not a theoretic question, but a practical one. It is in *praxis* that man should demonstrate truth, that is, the reality, precision and power of his thought . . . Hitherto, philosophers have only given different interpretations of the world; what counts is to transform it . . ." Marx, *Second* and *Eleventh Theses on Feuerbach.*

beliefs, philosophy, art, etc., is but an epiphenomenon of economics. This is the interpretation of popular Marxism, and it is far from negligible, for it is now the opinion of many people and has become an historical force. But Marx himself saw more deeply into things, and just as we may speak of a first "spiritual" impulse in him (his indignation at the conditions imposed on man oppressed by things born of himself and his work, and himself made a thing), so we must say that in spite of certain formulas he always believed in a reciprocal action between economic and other factors; [5] economics taken alone was not in his view the one and only source of history.

Nevertheless, on deeper reflection and with more careful study it appears that his rejection of the metaphysical primacy of act over potency, of form over matter, and the consequent rejection of the proper autonomy of spiritual energies—it appears that this double rejection, which is the metaphysical characteristic of materialism, is inevitably tied up, as we suggested earlier, with Marx's radical realist immanentism.[6]

On the one hand, Marx had a profound intuition—an intuition we believe to be the great flash of truth running through his work— of the conditions of heteronomy and estrangement engendered in the "capitalist" world of slave-labor, and of the dehumanization with which the owners and the proletariat are thereby simultaneously stricken. But he immediately conceptualized this intuition in an anthropocentric monist metaphysics,[7] in which work is hypostasized into the very essence of man, and in which, by recovering his essence through the transformation of society, man is called to take on the attributes which the religious "illusion" would confer on God. . . . If then the economic servitude and the inhuman

---

[5] "Marx and myself must bear responsibility for the fact that young people sometimes attach more than due weight to the economic side. Faced with adversaries we had to underline the essential principle denied by them, and thus we did not always find time, place or occasion to do justice to the other factors which share in the reciprocal action." (From Engels' letter dated Sept. 21, 1890.)

[6] Hegel's immanentism is already, as such, a virtual materialism, and only his idealism prevents it from unveiling itself.

[7] See Paul Vignaux's study, "Retour à Marx" (*Politique*, Nov. 1935). The proper task of a Christian critique of Marx would be to strip this intuition of the philosophical errors in terms of which Marx conceptualizes it. Such a task is all the more imposed on truth; and no matter what personal feelings Marx has. against Christianity, this intuition itself is pregnant with Judeo-Christian values.

condition of the proletariat are to cease, it is not in the name of the human person—whose fundamental dignity is in reality spiritual, and has, as regards economic conditions, such imperious demands only because it is in the last analysis bound up with transcendent goods and rights; it is in the name of collective man, in order that in his collective life and in the free discharge of his collective work he may find an absolute deliverance (strictly speaking, *aseitas*), . . . and in a word deify within himself the titanism of human nature.

On the other hand, if the economic factor taken alone is not for Marx the one and only source of history, it still remains that, since the essential dynamism from which the evolution proceeds is that of the economic contradictions and social antagonisms engendered by the production system, it is the economic factor which plays the significant and primarily determining [8] role with regard to the various superstructures in reciprocal action with it . . . And how could it be otherwise, once there is eliminated, together with all transcendence in general, the transcendence of the proper object which gives them their stability? [9] These superstructures thus lose their proper autonomy. In order to exist in history and in order to act in it, they are not only conditioned by the economic and the social, but from these they have their primary determination, and it is from them they get their meaning, their real significance for human life.

It is quite true that economic conditions, like all conditions generally of the material order, are important in the career of spiritual activities among men, that they have a constant tendency to enfeoff them, and that in the history of culture they make one body with them. From this point of view, the cynicism of Marx, like that of

---

[8] I say "primarily determining," not, of course, with respect to the intrinsic content of the superstructures—unlike Freud, Marx was not preoccupied with furnishing explanations of the content of art or of religion (by a natural and inevitable bent, more or less orthodox Marxists were to show themselves less discreet)—but with respect to their existence and their historical energy and their real significance for human life. As regards religion, Marx assumed besides that Feuerbach's criticism was decisive, as is clear in *Das Capital*. . . .

[9] In religion, metaphysics and the fine arts this transcendence is obvious, and even in the case of science it exists, too, so far as even in science in the modern sense of the word we still find that ordination of the mind to intelligibles whose necessity, according to the part of Platonism saved by Aristotle, is as such above time.

Freud, has brought many truths to light . . . But it is nonsense to take material conditioning, no matter how real it may be, as the prime determining reason—were it only as regards its historical existence—of a spiritual activity, and as that which above everything else discloses significance for human life.[10]

Of course, it is necessary to take into account Marx's polemical position, which of itself involves a provocative overstatement. In his ardent polemic against idealism, Marx doubtless called materialism what would often have been better called realism, but this does not matter much as regards the doctrinal characteristics we have pointed out; the really important thing is that the problem itself of a possible distinction between realism and materialism did not for a moment come to Marx's mind. Since his whole philosophy is essentially polemical, polemical overstatement is not an accident in it.

The fact remains that, taken not in isolation, but with all the superstructures which, while acting on it, are first determined by it, economics—I mean that tissue of human relations and energies which constitute for Marx, and with good reason, the misunderstood reality of the economic process—was made by him into the determining cause of history. "The materialistic conception of history, according to which the conditions and forms of production determine the formation and evolution of human societies, is the basic element in the doctrine of Karl Marx." [11] What distinguishes Marxism is not simply that it teaches that economics is preponderant—other schools have committed and are now committing this same error—but that it makes all the forms of life, with all their values and all their efficacy, dependent on—they are not denied, but subordinated to—this human material absolute in dialectic movement. To use Aristotle's language again, let us say that material causality thus becomes the purely and simply primary causality.

---

[10] "This mode of production (Capitalism) is essentially cosmopolitan, as is Christianity. The result is that Christianity is the special religion of capital." Such a statement is a remarkable instance of the possibilities of nonsense contained within historical materialism. See Henri de Man, *L'idée socialiste* (Paris: Grasset, 1935), p. 126.

[11] Auguste Cornu, *Karl Marx, de l'hégélianisme au matérialisme historique* (Paris: Alcan, 1934), Introduction.

SECOND AND THIRD SUBSTITUTIONAL STEPS:
THE DYNAMISM OF MATTER AND
THE REDEMPTIVE MISSION OF THE PROLETARIAT

In the second place, it is from this material causality Marxism expects salvation and the realization, as it were, of the kingdom of God. With the dynamism of the Hegelian dialectic thrust back into matter, its proponents would think that the economic process—not automatically, but with all the energies which it engenders and which react on it, and especially with the energies of the revolutionary mind—must lead to the rule of reason, to the elimination of man's enslavement to irrational forces, to man's victory over necessity, to his mastery of his history. At the end of this development, social man will be absolute master of history and of the universe. The convergence of the messianism of Marx, which is at once Jewish and Hegelian, with Russian messianism is in this regard singularly significant.

Finally the third step: through what mediator will this redemption take place? Through the proletariat. The theory of class war seemed to Marx like a revelation because, in his view, it essentially implies this messianism. Not only are the proletariat's hands unstained by the original sin of the exploitation of man by man, but precisely because it is stripped of everything and occupies the lowest place in history, it is the bearer of human liberation, it is the messianic victim whose triumph will be the definitive victory over all that oppresses humanity, and as a resurrection from the dead. Berdiaeff likes to stress the presence of this eschatological element in the thought of revolutionary Communism: in the very womb of history will take place a total and definitive deliverance which will cut time in two. The leap will be made, from the kingdom of necessity to the kingdom of freedom.

The substitutional process of which we spoke is thus complete in three stages. Anything which would have reference to a Christian value, or even, in the sense we have indicated, to any token of the Platonism natural to our minds, is henceforth replaced.

God is absolutely rejected on principle and in virtue of an absolute metaphysical dogmatism, not in the name of the human person, as was the case in rationalist or deist humanism, but along with the person as a spiritual being made in the image of God. This is done in the name of the historical dynamism of the social collectivity, in the name of collective or collectivized man, in whom and through whom human nature is to find its fulfilment. And at the same stroke and as a necessary consequence, a social conception is imposed which—no matter how multiform and varied may be its integration of the individual with the group—can be nothing but a monism of collective humanity. This gives Communism the value, not of a relative economic solution, but of an absolute historical exigency, necessary with a metaphysical necessity. And by reason of this exigency man, fully raised to social and political life, collective man, who is man restored to truth and in whom freedom finally comes to flower, is to integrate in an absolute way the individual man-person, up to now a transient moment of the dialectic and even yet subject to heteronomous forces.

In this way the social themes of Communism appear as the conclusion of an initial atheism posed on principle, or of a humanism essentially conceived as an atheistic humanism. This Marxist humanism should be regarded as the perfect fruit of Hegelian immanentism, once the reversed Hegelian dialectic has passed from the ideal to the real, that is to say, to social and historical man. In the last analysis it consists in claiming for man, once he is freed by the abolition of private property, that sovereign independence in the mastery of nature and the government of history which, formerly, in the times of "alienated" consciousness, religion attributed to God.

21 CONCRETE HISTORICAL IDEAL OF A NEW CHRISTENDOM*

AT THE OUTSET IT IS PROPER TO DELIMIT OUR SUBJECT and make precise our aim. We are to consider the concrete historical ideal of a new Christendom. What do we understand by "concrete historical ideal"? It is a prospective image standing for the particular type, the specific type of civilization to which a certain historical age tends.[1]

When a Thomas More, a Fénelon, a Saint-Simon or a Fourier works out a utopia, he works out a construct, an *ens rationis*, isolated from existence at any particular time and from any particular historical climate, and expressing an absolute *maximum* of social and political perfection; and this construct has an architecture whose imaginary detail is pushed as far as possible, since what is in question is a fictitious paragon proposed to the mind in place of reality.

On the contrary, what we call a concrete historical ideal is not an *ens rationis*, but an ideal essence that is realizable—with more or less difficulty, more or less imperfection, but that is another matter, and realizable not as something made, but as something on the way to being made—an essence capable of existing and calling for existence in a given historical situation, and as a result corre-

* *Humanisme intégral* (New ed. Paris: Fernand Aubier, 1947), pp. 134–135; 168–169.
[1] On this question see *Du régime temporel et de la liberté*, pp. 120–131.

sponding to a *relative* maximum of social and political perfection, a maximum relative to that historical situation; and precisely because this essence implies a real relating to concrete existence, it merely presents a framework and a rough draught which may later be determinative of a future reality.

In thus opposing a concrete historical ideal to a utopia, we still are appreciative of the historical role played by utopias and especially of the importance which the so-called utopian phase of Socialism has had for its subsequent development. We feel, nevertheless, that the notion of concrete historical ideal and a just use of the notion would enable a Christian philosophy of culture to prepare future historical realizations, by dispensing it from the need to pass through a utopian phase or to have recourse to any utopia. . . .

We think that the historical ideal of a new Christendom, of a new Christian temporal order, though founded on the same principles, analogically applied, as the order of mediaeval Christendom, would entail a Christian "lay" conception and not a Christian "sacral" conception of the temporal.

Its characteristic features would thus be at once opposed to those of the liberalism and inhumanism of the anthropocentric age and the reverse of the features we have remarked in the mediaeval historical ideal of the *sacrum imperium*; they would answer to what we might call an integral or theocentric humanism henceforth freed for its own work. The supernatural idea and guiding star of this new humanism—not that it claims to bring this star down to earth as if it were something of this world and could be the basis here below for men's common life, but that it would be refracted in the earthly and sinful sphere of the socio-temporal and orient this latter from on high—the supernatural idea of this humanism would no longer be that of God's holy empire over all things, but the idea of the holy freedom of the creature whom grace unites to God. The freedom of liberalism, in the anthropocentric and materialistic sense which prevailed in the nineteenth century, was only the caricature and sometimes the mockery of this freedom.

22 POSITIVE CONSTRUCTION*

PLURALIST STRUCTURE OF THE BODY POLITIC [1]

THE FIRST CHARACTERISTIC OF A NEW CHRISTENDOM would be that in place of the predominance of the movement toward unity, so typical, it seems to us, of the Middle Ages—after it there came, together with a progressive spiritual dispersion, a more and more mechanical and quantitative idea of political unity —there would be a return to an organic structure implying a certain pluralism, much more developed than that of the Middle Ages.[2]

In the Middle Ages this pluralism was manifested chiefly by the multiplicity, sometimes by the overlapping, of jurisdictions, and by the diversities of customary law. Today, we believe, it is proper to conceive it in another fashion. We have in mind not merely the just degree of administrative and political autonomy which should belong to regional units, without, of course, sacrificing to region or to nationality higher political ideas and values: it is evident that problems concerning national minorities call of themselves for a pluralist solution. We have in mind above all an organic heterogeneity in the very structure of civil society, whether it is a question, for example, of certain economic structures or of certain juridical and institutional structures.

---

* *Humanisme intégral* (Paris: Fernand Aubier, 1947), pp. 169–173; 181–212.

[1] The word *cité* has no equivalent in English; in *Man and the State*, Maritain uses "body politic" for the ideas covered by it here. Ed. Cf. above, "The Body Politic," pp. 73–81.

[2] See *Du régime temporel et de la liberté*, pp. 71–86; translation, *Freedom in the Modern World*, pp. 60 ff.

As opposed to the various totalitarian conceptions of political society in vogue today, the conception here is of a pluralist body politic bringing together in its organic unity a diversity of social groupings and structures, each of them embodying positive liberties. "It is an injustice, a grave evil and a disturbance of right order for a larger and higher organization to arrogate to itself functions which can be performed efficiently by smaller and lower bodies." [3] Civil society is made up not only of individuals, but of particular societies formed by them, and a pluralist body politic would allow to these societies the greatest autonomy possible and would diversify its own internal structure in keeping with what is typically required by their nature.[4]

ECONOMIC PLURALISM

Thus, so it appears to us, in a society consonant with the concrete historic ideal with which we are dealing, and if we take into account the conditions created by economic evolution and modern technology, the status of industrial economy, which the machine inevitably takes beyond the limits of family economy, and the status of agricultural economy, a type much more closely linked to family economy, would be fundamentally different. In an industrial economy the very interests of the person demand some collectivization of ownership. In the "capitalistic" regime, is not an industrial enterprise a hive made up, on the one hand, of salaried workers and, on the other, of corporation capital—a society not of men but of money and paper, of symbols of wealth, a society whose soul is the desire to produce more titles of possession? The more the enterprise is perfected by machinery, the rationalization of labor and ways of mobilizing finance, the stronger becomes this tendency to collectivization. In place of the capitalistic regime, let us suppose a future regime whose spirit and economic structure would be in line with the personalist and communal conception of social life: the status of the industrial economy would not suppress this collectivization but would organize it on quite other lines and this time for the benefit of the human person. We shall return to this point in a moment.

On the other hand, the status of rural economy—the rural econ-

---

[3] Pius XI, encycl. *Quadragesimo Anno.*
[4] Cf. *Man and the State,* 19–23.—Ed.

omy is, in any case, more fundamental than industrial economy, and indeed the economy whose good should be the first assured in a normal society—would tend toward a renewal and a vivification of family economy and family ownership, under modern forms and with the use of the facilities of mechanization and cooperation. Cooperative services, no matter how much developed, and a trade-union organization, no matter what new forms it might take, would have to respect this fundamental direction. On this point I shall repeat the saying of a peasant as told by Proudhon: "When I turn my furrows it seems to me that I am a king." The basic relation between property and the work of the person, and between property and the affective tone of the person—this is evident here with an original simplicity that the industrial economy, once it has passed under the law of the machine, cannot know.

JURIDICAL PLURALISM

But it is in the field of the relations between the spiritual and the temporal that the pluralist principle which we believe to be characteristic of a new Christendom would have its most meaningful application. The first, central and concrete fact which imposes itself as characteristic of modern civilizations, as opposed to mediaeval civilization, is that the selfsame civilization, the selfsame temporal regime of men admits into its bosom religious diversity. In mediaeval times, unbelievers were outside the walls of the Christian body politic. In the body politic of modern times, believers and unbelievers intermingle. Today, of course, the totalitarian body politic seeks anew to impose a single rule of faith on all, in the name, nevertheless, of the State and the temporal power; but this solution is unacceptable to a Christian. A Christian body politic in the conditions of modern times can only be a Christian body politic within whose walls unbelievers and believers live together and share in the same temporal common good.

This is to say that, short of limiting ourselves to simple empirical expedients, we must invoke the pluralist principle of which we just now spoke and apply it to the institutional structure of the body politic.

In matters in which civil law is most typically related to a conception of the world and of life, legislation would then grant a different juridical status to the various spiritual stocks within the same body politic. For a sane philosophy it is evident that the only morality is the true morality. But for the legislator who must aim at the common good and the peace of such and such a given people, is it not necessary to take into account the existential conditions of this people and the condition of the moral ideal, the more or less defective, yet a de facto existing ideal, of the various spiritual stocks or lineages which make up this people, and consequently must he not use the principle of the lesser evil?

There is a way of understanding this pluralist solution which would fall into the error of theological liberalism; perhaps we have an instance of this in Hindu legislation. Then one would think that human opinions of whatever kind have a right to be taught and propagated, and that, as a result, the body politic is bound to recognize as the proper juridical status of each spiritual stock the law worked out by that stock in conformity with its own principles. That is not the way I understand this solution. To me this solution means that, in order to avoid greater evils (that is, the ruin of society's peace and the petrification or the disintegration of consciences), the body politic could and should tolerate within it—to tolerate is not to approve—ways of worship more or less removed from the true one: the practices of unbelievers are to be tolerated, St. Thomas taught; [5] ways of worship and also ways of conceiving the meaning of life and modes of behavior; in consequence, the solution means that the various spiritual groups living within the body politic should be granted a particular juridical status. The legislative power of the commonwealth itself in its political wisdom would adapt this juridical status, on the one hand, to the condition of the groups and, on the other, to the general line of legislation leading toward the virtuous life, and to the prescriptions of moral law, to the full realization of which it should endeavor to direct as far as possible this diversity of forms.[6]

Thus it is toward the perfection of natural law and Christian law that the pluriform juridic structure of the body politic would be orientated, even at those stages of it which would be the most imperfect and the farthest removed from the Christian ethical ideal.

---

[5] *Sum. Theol.* II–II, 10, 11.
[6] Cf. *Man and the State*, pp. 167–171, including n. 24 and n. 25—Ed.

The body politic would be directed toward a positive pole that would be integrally Christian, and its different structures would deviate more or less from this pole, according to a measure determined by political wisdom.

In this way the body politic would be vitally Christian, and the non-Christian spiritual stocks within it would enjoy a just liberty.

The phrase "la cité chrétienne" must be rightly understood. In the absolute sense of the words, the true Christian city is the Church and not any temporal city whatsoever. Just here, however, we are speaking of the temporal city.

Like philosophy, the political order has its own proper specification. But like philosophy, it can receive influences from Christianity and thus be under Christian existential conditions. Moreover, just as there is, so we hold, a practical philosophy, an "ethics adequately considered" which is subalternated to theology and which for this reason has in its very specification a Christian impregnation,[7] so the political order, by the fact that it is intrinsically subordinated to ethics, can have and should have, the while it remains in its own order, a Christian impregnation in its properly political specification. A Christian body politic is a body politic intrinsically vivified and impregnated by Christianity. . . .

THE AUTONOMY OF THE TEMPORAL

The second characteristic feature of the temporal regime which we envisage has to do with what we may call a Christian conception of the secular or lay body politic. This would be an affirmation of the autonomy of the temporal as an *intermediate or infravalent* end, in line with the teachings of Leo XIII which say that the authority of the State is supreme in its own order. In a preceding chapter we noted the distinction between the intermediate end and the means, and that between the secondary principal cause and the instrumental cause. We also remarked that in mediaeval Christendom the temporal actually often had the simple role of means, a simple ministerial or instrumental function in relation to the spiritual.

In virtue of a process of differentiation normal in itself, though

---

[7] See my work *Science et sagesse,* pp. 288–345; English translation *Science and Wisdom,* pp. 174–209.

vitiated by the most erroneous ideologies,[8] the secular or temporal order has in the course of modern times been established, as regards the spiritual or sacred order, in such a relation of autonomy that in fact it excludes instrumentality. In short, it has come of age.

Here is a real historical gain which a new Christendom should preserve. Certainly this does not mean that the primacy of the spiritual would be ignored. The temporal order would be subordinate to the spiritual, no longer, of course, as an instrumental agent, as was so often the case in the Middle Ages, but as a *less elevated principal agent*; and above all, the earthly common good would no longer be taken as a mere means in relation to eternal life, but as what it essentially is in this regard, namely, as an *intermediary or infravalent end*. A real and effective subordination—that is the contrast with modern Gallican and "liberal" conceptions; but a subordination which no longer takes a purely ministerial form— this is the contrast with the mediaeval conception.

In this way we disengage and make precise the notion of a *vitally Christian lay body politic* or a *Christianly constituted secular body politic*. This means a body politic in which the secular and temporal have their full role and dignity as end and as principal agent, though not as ultimate end nor as the most elevated principal agent. This is the only sense in which the Christian can take the words "secular body politic." Taken in any other way the words have only a tautological sense, the lay character of the body politic then meaning that the body politic is not the Church; or the words are false, the lay character of the body politic then meaning the body politic is either neutral or anti-religious, i.e., at the service of purely material ends or of forces opposed to religion. . . .

THE FREEDOM OF PERSONS

Along with this insistence on the autonomy of the temporal order, the third characteristic feature of a conceivable new Christendom would be an insistence on the extra-territoriality of the person so far as temporal and political means are concerned.

We encounter here the second central fact, a fact of the ideo-

---

[8] A process begun in the Middle Ages. See Georges de Lagarde, *La naissance de l'esprit laïque au déclin du moyen âge* (I, Bilan du xiiie siècle; II, Marsile de Padoue), éd. Béatrice, 1934.

logical order, by which the modern age is opposed to the Middle
Ages. For the idea of strength or fortitude in the service of God is
substituted the idea of the conquest or realization of freedom.

But of what freedom above all is it a question for a Christian
civilization? Not of freedom in the individualist-liberalist conception; that is, not the individual's mere freedom of choice, which is
but the beginning or root of freedom; and not of freedom in the
imperialist or dictatorial conception, that is, the freedom which
would consist in the grandeur and power of the State. Rather the
question primarily regards the freedom of autonomy [9] of persons,
a freedom that is one with their spiritual perfection.

Thus, while the center of unification of the temporal and political
order is lowered, as we saw, at the same stroke the dignity and the
spiritual freedom of the person emerge still higher above that order.

A complete change in perspective and "style" thereby occurs in
temporal organization. The Christian knows that the State has
duties to God and that it should collaborate with the Church. But
how this collaboration is achieved can vary typically with historical
conditions: formerly it was mainly by way of temporal power itself
and legal constraints; in the future it may chiefly be, even in
politico-religious matters themselves, by way of moral influence.
St. Albert the Great and St. Thomas [10] explain by the diversity of
states or ages of the Church the fact that in the time of the apostles
and martyrs it was not proper for the Church to use coercion, but
that afterwards it was proper. That in yet another age it is again
not proper for her to use coercion is explicable in the same way.

It is necessary that Christ be made known, and to make him
known is the proper mission of the Church, not of the State. Yet
whether it be of a sacral or of a lay and secular type, a Christian
body politic knows that it should aid the Church in the free accomplishment of this mission. . . .

In the case of a civilization of a lay or secular type, it is by
pursuing its own (infravalent) end and in its capacity as (subordinate) principal agent that the Christian temporal city acquits

---

[9] We use the expression "freedom of autonomy" in a sense at once
Aristotelian and Pauline, and not at all Kantian. See our work *Du régime temporel
et de la liberté;* English translation, *Freedom in the Modern World.*

[10] St. Thomas in his Prologue to the Apocalypse, and in his Commentary on St. Luke; St. Albert in Quodlibet XII (c. 1268), a.19, ad 2.

itself of this duty towards the Church. It is by integrating, in line with the pluralist idea described here, Christian activities in the temporal work itself—for example, by giving to Christian teaching its just place in educational life, or by asking religious institutions of mercy to carry a just share of works of social assistance—and in that way itself receiving, as autonomous agent in free accord with an agent of a higher order, the aid of the Church, that the temporal city will help the latter to carry out its own mission. The mode of activity most proper to the eternal city, namely, spiritual and moral activity,[11] then becomes the dominant mode in the collaboration of the two powers. . . .

FREEDOM OF EXPRESSION

It is interesting to observe that in his youth Marx began by fighting for freedom of the press. . . .

When, in the time of Gregory XVI and of Pius IX, Rome condemned the claim to make freedom of the press and freedom of expression of thought ends in themselves and unlimited rights, it was only recalling a basic necessity of human government. These freedoms are good and answer to radical needs in human nature: they have to be regulated, as does everything that is not of the order of Deity itself. The dictatorial or totalitarian way of regulating them—by annihilation—seems detestable to us; the pluralist way—by justice and a progressive self-regulation—seems good to us, and is as strong as it is just. Let us suggest that in virtue of an institutional status various groups of publicists and writers, assembled in an autonomous body, would have a progressive control over the duties of their profession. Then we would see whether, through the natural severity with which the potter judges the work of the potter, they would not be able to exercise an efficacious control; it would rather be to protect the individual from his associates that the supreme judicial organs of the State would have to interfere.

Even so, the most happy solution is yet another. That the police judge a work of art gives little satisfaction to our sense for the hierarchy of values, but that another artist judge it and decide its fate scarcely suits this sense any better. All exterior regulation is useless unless its aim is to develop in the person the sense of his own

---

[11] See *Du régime temporel et de la liberté*, p. 78.

creative responsibility and the sense of communion. To feel responsible for one's brothers does not lessen freedom, though it puts on it a heavier load.

LAW AND THE PLURALIST BODY POLITIC

The pluralist body politic of which we are speaking, though much less concentrated than the mediaeval body politic, is much more concentrated than the "liberalistic" one. It is a body politic with authority. The function of law is to constrain the *protervi,* the perverse and the hardened, to a behavior of which they are not of themselves capable, and also to educate men so that in the end they may cease to be under the law—since they themselves will voluntarily and freely do what the law enjoins, a condition reached only by the wise. Law will regain in this pluralist body politic its moral function, its function as pedagogue of freedom, which it has almost totally lost under Liberalism. No doubt those supreme values with reference to which it regulates the scale of its prescriptions and sanctions will no longer be the sacral values to which the common good of the mediaeval city was appendant, and yet they will still be something sacred: not the sacred material privileges of a class, nor the sacred prestige of a nation, nor the sacred production of a state modelled on the beehive, but something truly and already by nature sacred, the vocation of the human person to a spiritual fulfilment and to the conquest of true freedom, and the reserves of moral integrity required for this. . . .

THE PERSON AND THE ECONOMIC COMMUNITY

In today's civilization, everything is referred to a measure which is not human, but external to man: primarily to laws belonging to material production, to the technological domination of nature and to the utilization of all the forces of the world for the fecundity of money. In a truly humanist culture, it is to man and his measure that the things of the world would be referred.[12] The vocation of man is great enough, his needs and desires are suffi-

---

[12] In line with this principle, on which he rightly insists, Max Hermant has very usefully brought to light, in a report to *l'Union pour la vérité* (June 22, 1935), what he calls the law of "the optimum greatness" and that of "the greatest speed." See also the work by Georges Cazin, *La sagesse du chef d'entreprise* (Paris: Desclée de Brouwer).

ciently capable of growth, that we may rest assured that such a measure would not imply a renunciation of greatness.

Greatness demands both abundance and poverty; nothing great is done without a certain abundance, nothing great without a certain poverty. Can a man understand life at all if he does not begin by understanding that always it is poverty which superabounds in greatness? It is the tragic law of man's sin, not of his nature, that makes the poverty of some create the abundance of others: the poverty of misery and enslavement, the abundance of covetousness and pride. This is the law of sin which we must not accept, but fight. What would be in conformity with nature, and what we should demand in the social order of new forms of civilization, is that the poverty of each—neither penury nor misery, but sufficiency and freedom, renunciation of the spirit of riches, the gaiety of the lilies of the field—is that a certain individual poverty create a common abundance, superabundance, riches, and glory for all. . . .

The crucial problem at this point is that of knowing how to subordinate technology, the machine and industry to man. Grandnephews of Descartes, the last heirs of rationalism and anthropocentric humanism, the Communists believe in an easy answer. On the one hand, they grant that the new civilization must be, like the capitalistic one, and more so if possible, an industrial civilization. On the other hand, they hold that science, understood in the rationalist sense of the word, science as distinguished from wisdom,[13] should be sufficient, through a perfect planning, to put industry at the service of man. Yet despite themselves they have inevitably ended up by making man the slave of industry and technology. A science of the non-human, the science of the production of things, if it becomes the rule of life, can only impose inhuman rules. The supreme work of the social body, if it is not ordered to the higher values of the person, cannot fail to exact for itself all that man is and to put in, along with God and with man himself, a jealous claim for man. "For God is indeed the highest interest of the person, an interest that absolutely cannot be subordinated to any other."[14]

The truth is that it does not belong to science to regulate our

---

[13] See *Science et sagesse*, ch. 1; English translation, *Science and Wisdom*.
[14] *Du régime temporel et de la liberté*, p. 255; English translation, *Freedom in the Modern World*, p. 214.

lives, but to wisdom; the supreme work of civilization is not in the order of transitive activity, but of immanent activity: really to make the machine, industry and technology serve man necessitates making them the servants of an ethics of the person, of love and of freedom. It would be a serious error to repudiate the machine, industry and technology, things good in themselves and, far from having to be repudiated, to be used for an economy of abundance. But it is the very illusion of rationalism not to see that we must choose between the idea of an essentially industrial civilization and the idea of an essentially human one, for which industry is really only an instrument and is therefore subjected to laws that are not its own.

The notion of planning—a notion present from the moment it is recognized that the economy has to be organized and rationalized —now gets a new meaning. This organization and rationalization must be the work of a political and economic wisdom which above everything else is a science of freedom, proceeding according to the dynamism of means to ends and in continuity with the nature of the human being; it must not be a so-called universal mathematical prevision.[15] Such a political and economic wisdom would aim to regulate industry, not according to industry's own laws alone, but according to laws to which these are subordinated; in the first place, it would aim always to regulate the movement of production according to the real needs and capacities of consumption. . . . If we adopt a Christian philosophy of man, of work and the ownership of material goods, the way in which the most important economic problems are posed takes, we may say, a new direction. . . .

THE UNITY OF SOCIAL RACE

Let us proceed to the fourth characteristic of our new Christendom. A certain parity of essence between the leader and the led, I mean an essential parity in the common condition of men bound to labor, will really be at the foundation of all relations of authority and the hierarchy of temporal functions, whether it is a

---

[15] In his work, *La sagesse du chef d'entreprise*, Georges Cazin has shown that even within the limits of a particular enterprise, wisdom should take the lead over mathematical technique. See also Lucien Laine, *Une communauté économique, le tapis*, 1934.

question of political authority or any other kind of social authority.

This conception of authority, we may suggest, is typified, not in the Benedictine rule, but in the Dominican rule, in the Order of Preachers, which is at the threshold of modern times as the Benedictine Order is at the threshold of the Middle Ages: a society of brothers where one of them is chosen as ruler by the others.

In the political order (which form of regime this takes is quite another question), the organs of government are then regarded by the Christian as having in God, as does any legitimate power, the source of their authority, yet as not taking on, even by participation, a sacred character. Once the organs are designated, authority resides in them, but in virtue of a certain *consensus,* of a free and vital determination made by the people, whose personification and vicar they are: *vices gerens multitudinis,* as St. Thomas puts it. This consent itself must be understood in various senses. It can be formulated or unformulated. In the system of hereditary monarchy, it is once for all given for an indeterminate future, both as to the form of the regime and the eventual holders of power. In the democratic system, it is once for all given for an indeterminate future as regards the form of the regime, but it is periodically renewable as regards the holders of power. In any case, nevertheless, where a purely secular and "homogeneous" conception of temporal authority prevails, the head is simply a companion who has the right to command others.

As for the economic order, fellowship in work is not resolvable, in this new Christendom of which I am speaking, into domestic society, as it was in the Middle Ages, nor into the confrontation of two classes alien to each other, as in the age of "bourgeois" liberalism. Rather, it will constitute . . . a specific institutional form corresponding to the natural association of *collaborators* in one work.

There are two sides to the picture. Because the order necessary for political life is more difficult to achieve in a commonwealth where authority runs its risks within one and the same "social race" than in a commonwealth where authority descends from a superior "social race," the burden of social life will be heavier, and discipline will be stricter.

A PERSONALIST DEMOCRACY

This brings us once more to an opposition to both the false liberal conception of modern times and the sacral ideal of the Middle Ages. Take the word "democracy" as the progeny of Jean-Jacques Rousseau understood it, and our plan for civilization would surely be opposed to that kind of democracy, for it is not through an abstract freedom, impersonal freedom, but through concrete and positive freedoms incarnated in social institutions and in social bodies that the interior freedom of the person demands to be expressed on the external and social plane. On the other hand, one of the essential values included in the very ambiguous word "democracy" is saved in our plan. I have in mind a meaning of this word that is rather affective and moral, having reference to the dignity of the person, a dignity of which the people themselves have become conscious, not, of course, as possessing or truly meriting that dignity, but at least as being called to it. This popular civic awareness consequently excludes the heterogeneous, even if good, domination of one social category over the mass of the people considered as minors, and it implies even on the level of social life respect for the human person in the individuals who make up this mass.

I have just said that the people have become conscious in modern times of this dignity of the person, not as truly meriting or truly possessing it, but as laying claim to it. And yet it is most often under symbolic and figurative and at times very deceptive forms that modern democracies in fact profess respect for the person in each individual in the mass of the people. This is precisely the drama which the Communist revolution claims to bring to a denouement, and which Christianity alone, and this socially lived, could truly bring to a denouement by making real what to date is only symbol and figure. This is why it is only in a new Christendom, one that is yet to come, that this ethical and affective value of the word democracy, answering to what we may call popular civic consciousness, could really be saved. Besides, if the present division into classes [16] must then be overcome, this society, having neither

---

[16] I understand this word in its strict and most exact sense, as Briefs for example determines it in his studies of the industrial proletariat; "class" implies a permanent and hereditary condition; the proletariat being without property and forced to trade hard labor for a salary which is not high enough to let him

bourgeoisie nor proletariat, will not be a society without internal structure and without organic differentiations or inequalities. But the hierarchy of functions and advantages will no longer be tied to hereditary categories fixed as of old by blood, which in principle was not an unhealthy solution, or as today by money, which is an unhealthy solution. It is to a genuine aristocracy of work—in the whole amplitude and qualitative diversity of this word [17]—that a vitally Christian temporal regime will then teach (which will still be difficult) respect for the human person in the individual and in the people.

THE BODY POLITIC AND BROTHERLY LOVE

We come to the fifth and last characteristic. As for the common aim of the body politic, let us say . . . that for a Christian civilization which can no longer be naive, the common aim in our time would not appear as a divine work to be brought about on earth by man, but rather as a human work to be brought about on earth by the passing of something divine, namely, love, into human means and into human work itself.

Thus for such a civilization the dynamic principle of common life and common work would not be the mediaeval idea of God's empire to be built on earth, and still less would it be the myth of Class or Race, Nation or State.

Let us say that it would be the idea, though according to the Gospel and not on the Stoic or the Kantian plan, of the human person's dignity and his spiritual vocation, and of the fraternal love which is his due. The work of the body politic would be to realize a common life on earth, a temporal regime truly in conformity with that dignity, that vocation and that love. We are far enough away from such a goal to be sure that there will be work to do! The task is arduous, paradoxical and heroic. There is no such thing as a lukewarm humanism.

A conception of this sort would be utopian if the fraternal love just mentioned were regarded as the sole bond and basis of the

---

accumulate anything, it is inevitable that, outside of exceptional cases, his condition should be transmitted generation after generation to his descendants. See Goetz Briefs, *The Proletariat, a challenge to Western civilization* (New York: McGraw-Hill, 1937), Chapter 4.

[17] See *Du régime temporel et de la liberté*, pp. 68–70.

temporal community. I am well aware that a certain material and, in a sense, a biological weight of community of interests and passions, and of social animality, so to speak, is indispensable in common life. And I have sufficiently stressed in preceding sections the organic character which in this regard a new Christendom will of necessity show. I am also aware that if it has not as base a conception of human nature at once pessimistic and exacting, so as to make the most important appear as the most difficult and the best among political tasks appear as requiring the greatest pains, an ideal of brotherly love would be the worst of illusions. Such an ideal is not easy to realize in religious communities, where man is vowed to strive for perfection; and of course it is much less easy in the order of lay and temporal life, a humbler order, it is true, and one nearer to the elementary realities of life, and yet much less solicitous about virtue.

It is absurd to expect the body politic to make all men, taken as individuals, good and fraternal to one another. Yet we may and should demand, which is quite another thing, that it have social structures, institutions and laws which are good and inspired by the spirit of fraternal love, and that it the more powerfully orientate the energies of social life toward such a friendship because this friendship, natural as it may fundamentally be, is extremely difficult for the sons of Adam. Thus, to begin with, this friendship or fraternal love is, if one chooses to use the word, like a primordial "myth" giving direction to common life, it is an heroic idea to be realized, a typical end to be pursued, the animating theme of a common enthusiasm, bringing into action the profound energies of the people. In this way, fraternal love appears as an essential dynamic principle in our new Christendom. It is because this Christendom would be truly orientated in its entirety toward a socio-temporal realization of Gospel truths that it would properly apply itself to a Christian lay common task.

Previously, I underlined a characteristic paradox in the political life of human beings: on the one hand, human persons, as parts of the political community, are subordinate to it and to the common work to be done; on the other hand, the human person, in the highest values of his life as a person, is superior to this common work and gives finality to it. We see now the solution of this antinomy.

It is not enough to say that justice demands a certain redistribution of the common good, common to the whole and to the parts, to each person. We must say that since the temporal common good is a common good of human persons, then each one, by subordinating himself to the common task, subordinates himself to the fulfilment of the personal life of others, of other persons. But this solution has a practical and existential value only in a body politic where the true nature of the common task is recognized, and along with it, as Aristotle divined, the value and political importance of fraternal love. It would be a great misfortune if the failure of the vain optimistic "fraternity" inscribed on the banners of the French "bourgeois" revolution made us forget such a truth. There is no more fundamentally anti-political frame of mind than the distrust entertained by the enemies of the Gospel for the idea of fraternal love, whether by great indignant souls like Proudhon and Nietzsche, or by cynics, like so many adorers of what they call order.

A problem is posed here which we must briefly examine. It is the question of the collaboration and participation of non-Christians in the life of a Christianly established temporal society, of a vitally Christian lay body politic which, as we said earlier, can include unbelievers and believers.

To try to establish a common doctrinal minimum among them, to serve as a base for common action, is, as we have also pointed out, to engage in fiction. Each engages himself and should engage his whole self, should give his maximum. The task is not to look for a common theoretic minimum; all alike are called to work out a common practical task. And with this the solution begins to dawn.

This common practical work, we just said, is not a Christian sacral, but a Christian lay work. Taken in the fulness and perfection of the truths it implies, it engages the whole of Christianity, indeed the whole of Christian dogma and ethics: it is only through the mystery of the redeeming Incarnation that the Christian perceives the dignity of the human person, and what that person costs. The idea he has of it stretches out as if infinitely and attains its absolutely full meaning only in Christ.

But by the very fact that it is lay and not sacral, this common work does not exact as starting point that every man profess all Christian truths. On the contrary, it allows among its characteristic features a pluralism which makes possible the *convivium* of Christians and non-Christians in the same body politic. Hence, if from the very fact that it is a Christian work it proceeds on the hypothesis that those who will take the initiative in it are Christians, with a full and total grasp of the end to be attained, it nevertheless asks all of good will to cooperate, all those who grasp in a more or less partial and defective way, perhaps an extremely defective way, the truths which the Gospel knows in their fulness, and who are thus enabled to give themselves in a practical way to this common work, and perhaps without being the least generous or the least devoted. In this case the Gospel text applies with all its force: "He who is not against you is with you" (Mark, 9, 39).

Such then, in our view, is the concrete historic ideal which we ought to have of a new Christendom; such, we believe, is the way in which Christianity can save in order to transmit to the future, while it purifies them of the mortal errors in which they are enveloped, the truths towards which the modern age has been struggling in the cultural order. If we have made ourselves understood, it is obvious that as we see it, this purification is wholly different from a simple empiric arrangement or from what I may call a patchwork. Modern civilization is a worn-out garment. One cannot sew new pieces on it. It requires a total and, I may say, substantial recasting, a transvaluation of cultural principles. What is needed is a vital primacy:

    of quality over quantity,
    of work over money,
    of the human over the technological,
    of wisdom over science,
    of the common service of human persons over the individual covetousness of unlimited enrichment, and
    of the common service of human persons over the State's covetousness of unlimited power.

THE RELATIONSHIP BETWEEN CHURCH AND STATE [18]

. . . The things that are Caesar's are not only distinct from the things that are God's; but they must cooperate with them.

---

[18] The rest of this chapter is from *Man and the State* (Chicago: University of Chicago Press, 1951), pp. 171–179 (with a few additions made by the author for the French and British editions).

What, then, in the particular type of Christian political society which I am discussing, would be the appropriate means through which the principle of the *necessary cooperation* between the Church and the body politic would apply?

The question, it seems to me, has three implications: the first, which concerns both the body politic and the State, deals with the most general and indirect form of mutual assistance between them and the Church; the second, which concerns especially the State or the civil authority, deals with the public acknowledgment of God; the third, which concerns in one case especially the State, in another case especially the body politic, deals with the specific forms of mutual help between the Church and the political society.

THE MOST GENERAL AND INDIRECT FORM OF COOPERATION

As regards the first point (the most general and indirect form of mutual assistance), I would say with Father John Courtney Murray, in the remarkable study he has written on the matter, that "the major assistance, aid and favor" that the body politic and the State "owe to the Church (one might better say, to the human person with respect to his eternal destiny)" consists in the entire fulfilment of their own duties with respect to their own ends, in their own attention to Natural Law, and in the full accomplishment of their political duty of creating "those conditions in society—political, social, economic, cultural—which will favor the ends of human personality, the peaceful enjoyment of all its rights, the unobstructed performance of all its duties, the full development of all its powers. There is here a material task, the promotion of prosperity, the equitable distribution of the material things that are the support of human dignity. There is also a moral task, the effective guarantee of the juridical order. This organization of society according to the demands of justice" is "the first, most proper and necessary contribution" of the body politic and the State to the spiritual interests of the Church—"an indirect contribution, but one apart from which the end of the Church is impossible, or too difficult, of attainment." [19]

---

[19] John Courtney Murray, *Governmental Repression of Heresy*, reprinted from the *Proceedings of the Catholic Theological Society of America* (1949), p. 48. "Nothing is clearer than the Pope's insistence that the conscientious

THE PUBLIC ACKNOWLEDGMENT OF
THE EXISTENCE OF GOD

As concerns the second point (the public acknowledgment of the existence of God), let it be observed that a political society really and vitally Christian would be conscious of the doctrine and morality which enlighten for it—that is, for the majority of the people—the tenets of the democratic charter, and which guide it in putting those tenets into force. It would be conscious of the faith that inspired it, and it would express this faith publicly. Obviously, indeed, for any given people such public expression of common faith would by preference assume the forms of that Christian confession to which the history and traditions of this people were most vitally linked. But the other religious confessions institutionally recognized would also take part in this public expression—just as it happens now in this country—and they would also be represented in the councils of the nation, in order that they might defend their own rights and liberties and help in the common task. As for the citizens who were unbelievers, they would have only to realize that the body politic as a whole was just as free with regard to the public expression of its own faith as they, as individuals, were free with regard to the private expression of their own non-religious convictions.

THE SPECIFIC FORMS OF
MUTUAL COOPERATION

With respect to the third point—the specific forms of mutual help between the body politic and the Church—I should like first to make clear some preliminary remarks. It is obvious that it is the spiritual mission of the Church which is to be helped, not the political power or the temporal advantages to which certain of her members might lay claim in her name. In the stage of development and self-awareness which modern societies have reached, a social or political discrimination in favor of the Church, or the

---

exercise by the State of its direct power over temporal life is the essential exercise of its indirect power and duty to favor and assist the ends of the Church . . . The spiritual problem of our times is in fact centered in the temporal order. And the modern 'welfare-state,' simply by serving human welfare, would serve the Church better than Justinian or Charlemagne ever did" (*ibid.,* p. 49).

granting of juridical privileges to her ministers or to her faithful, would be precisely of a nature to jeopardize, rather than to help, this spiritual mission.

I just spoke of the ministers of the Church. Regarding their particular position, it is appropriate to enter into some more detailed elucidations, even at the price of a rather extensive digression.

The exemption from military obligations granted to the clergy in many countries is not a social privilege. To be exempted from having to shed blood is for a man a high moral privilege, but it is at the same time, from the temporal and terrestrial point of view—because in the modern regime of "a nation in arms" it involves an exception to a common rule and to common dangers—a socially humiliating condition (not to speak of the resentment it may sometimes engender) imposed on men consecrated to God by the recognition of their essentially peaceful mission to the human community.

On the other hand, a distinction must be made between *simple adjustment of law and custom* to various functions or states of life which matter to the common good of the social body, and *juridical privilege* favoring a particular category with certain temporal advantages by virtue of an infraction of the principle of the equality of all before the law. The rights enumerated in the Code of Canon Law, in the chapter *de privilegiis clericorum,* through which the Church sanctions from her own point of view certain requirements of the priestly condition, should be recognized by a civil society of a pluralistic type as pertaining to the first case: adjustment of law and custom to various functions or states of life.

Instances of the same case are obviously to be found in certain advantages sometimes granted to the clergy, which it would never occur to the Church, for her own part, and at her own level as an autonomous society, to inscribe in her Code, and which she does not regard as rights required by the priestly condition. Thus it is that in certain countries, the United States for instance, the railroad companies offer clergymen reduced fares. Similar advantages might conceivably be granted to persons exercizing other functions, the medical function for instance. The fact remains that in any case the use of such advantages supposes in those who profit by them a general behavior that is modest enough to prevent these minor inequalities from seeming offensive, or even scandalous, as the equestrian array of Benedictine abbots did in the thirteenth century

(St. Thomas Aquinas rode a donkey, as was suitable for a member of a mendicant Order).

Let us note, finally, in order to avoid any misinterpretation, that, from the point of view of what is usually called the "thesis," and on the condition that one be aware of the real bearing of words, there is no opposition between all that is said in this chapter and the fact of considering a privileged juridical situation for the Catholic Church the ideal situation to be sought, by virtue of the rights she possesses as a messenger of divine truth. For, given the factual circumstances created by the advent of modern societies and democratic regimes, the conditions of realization (what is called the "hypothesis") for such an ideal situation suppose a people in whom division in religious matters has disappeared, and in whom the Catholic faith is accepted by all. Then the Catholic Church would obviously be alone in enjoying in actual fact the rights and liberties granted *de jure* to the various religious bodies institutionally recognized in a Christian society of the type we are describing; consequently the ideal envisaged in the thesis would be fulfilled in a situation which was actually privileged, but which implied neither temporal advantages granted to a category of citizens as opposed to the others, nor any departure from the principle of the equality of all before the law, nor, with greater reason, any pressure exercized by the State in matters of conscience, nor any instrumental role played by the State as secular arm of the Church. And, to tell the truth, the ideal situation in question would correspond to the rights of the Church—the first of which is to convey divine truth—as well as to the dearest aspirations of the Christian heart, first and foremost through that which it presupposes, namely the general disappearance of religious division in the world, and the general adherence to the true faith.

But let us leave this digression, and return to our purpose. The care that the State must take not to encroach upon matters of religion does not imply that as soon as it comes to the moral and religious realm the State should stand aloof and be reduced to sheer impotency. The State has no authority to impose any faith whatsoever upon, or expel any faith whatsoever from, the inner domain of conscience. But the State, as we have seen in a preceding chapter, has to foster in its own way general morality, by the exercise of justice and the enforcement of law, and by supervising the development of sound conditions and means in the body politic for good human life, both material and rational. And as to religious matters, the State has to deal with them on a certain level, which is the level of civil peace and welfare, and from its own point of view, which is the point of view of the temporal common good; for instance, as we just said, the civil power has, as representing the people, to request the prayers of the religious communities historically rooted in the life of the people. And it is but normal that in applying the laws concerned with the exercise of the right of association, it should grant institutional recognition to those religious communities—as well as to all associations, religious or secular, educational, scientific, or devoted to social service, whose activity is of major importance for the common welfare—in contradistinction to other religious groups or secular associations which enjoy freedom but not institutional recognition. Moreover, assuming the formation of some religious sect aimed at the destruction of the bases of common life, say, prescribing collective suicide or racial annihilation, it would be up to the State to dissolve such a religious sect, as well as any other association either criminal or destructive of national security. All this deals with the administration of justice, and implies the equality of rights of all citizens, whatever their race, their social standing, or their religious denomination may be.

It should be pointed out in this connection, first, that the subjects of rights are not abstract entities like "truth" or "error," but human persons, individually or collectively taken; second, that the equality of rights of all citizens is the basic tenet of modern democratic societies. Therefore the very fact (on which I have so often laid stress in this book) that the temporal society, now become secular or strictly temporal, unites in its common task and common good, men belonging to different religious lineages, has as its consequence that the principle of equality of rights is to be applied—not to "doctrines" or "creeds," this would have no meaning—but to the *citizens* who belong in these different religious lineages, which the body politic, from its own point of view, regards as parts of its own common moral heritage. Is it not, as I have previously remarked, through the citizens who are members of the Church that the Church, who is above the body politic, enters the sphere of the body politic and of its temporal common good? As a result it is from the point of view of the rights of the citizens who compose the body politic that the State will define its own positions with regard to the juridical status of the Church within the temporal sphere and in relation to the temporal common good.

Thus, the Christian political society which I am discussing—supposing that the faith to which the majority of the people belonged were the Catholic faith—would know perfectly well that the Church herself was no part of it, but above it. And in this connection it would recognize the juridical personality of the Church as well as her spiritual authority in ruling her members in her spiritual realm, and it would deal with her as a perfect and perfectly independent society, with which it would conclude agreements and with the supreme authority of which it would maintain diplomatic relations. Yet, for all that, this Christian political society would have to hold that, in its own temporal sphere, and with regard to the rights they possess, Christian citizens (with the collective activities they and their multifarious institutions freely display in the national community) are no more legally privileged than any other citizens.

In other terms, this Christian political society would realize that there is only one temporal common good, that of the body politic, as there is only one supernatural common good, that of the Kingdom of God, which is supra-political. Once the political society had been fully differentiated in its secular type, to insert into the body politic a particular or partial common good, the temporal common good of the faithful of one religion (even though it be the true religion), and claiming for them, accordingly, a privileged juridical position in the body politic, would be inserting into the latter a divisive principle and, to that extent, interfering with the temporal common good.[20]

After these preliminary remarks, I come to the point under discussion, namely, the specific forms of mutual help between the Church and the political society.

As I have often had occasion to observe, man is a member both of the body politic and, if he adheres to the Church,

---

[20] Cf. our book, *The Rights of Man and Natural Law*, pp. 26–27. See also Heinrich Rommen, "Church and State," *Review of Politics*, July 1950.

of that supra-temporal society which is the Church. He would be cut in two if his temporal membership were cut off from his spiritual membership. They must be in actual contact and connection. And an actual contact and connection, if it is not a contact and connection of mutual antagonism, is a contact and connection of mutual help. Moreover, the common good itself of the temporal society implies that human persons are indirectly assisted by the latter in their movement toward supra-temporal achievement, which is an essential part of the pursuit of happiness. Finally (not to speak even of the fact, defined by theology, that human nature in its existential condition needs divine grace in order to achieve its highest human ends, social as well as individual), the Christian political society which we are discussing would be aware of the fact that Christian truths and incentives and the inspiration of the Gospel, awakening common consciousness and passing into the sphere of temporal existence, are the very soul, inner strength, and spiritual stronghold of democracy. Just as democracy must, under penalty of disintegration, foster and defend the democratic charter; so a Christian democracy, that is, a democracy fully aware of its own sources, must, under penalty of disintegration, keep alive in itself the Christian sense of human dignity and human equality, of justice and freedom. For the political society really and vitally Christian which we are contemplating, the suppression of any actual contact and connection, that is, of any mutual help, between the Church and the body politic would simply spell suicide.

What are, then, the specific forms of mutual assistance to which I am alluding?

The most basic of them is the recognition and guarantee by the State of the full freedom of the Church. For the fact of insuring the freedom of somebody is surely an actual, though negative, form of cooperation with him and assistance to him. It has been an illusion of modern times to believe that mutual freedom means mutual ignorance. Can I be ignorant of the one whose freedom I insure? The theory of mutual ignorance between State and Church is self-deluding: either it veers in actual fact (as was the case in France in the nineteenth century) to having the State encroach upon spiritual matters and oppose the Church in order to define and enforce in its own way a so-called freedom of the Church; or it veers in actual fact to having the State know the Church (without confessing it) in order really to insure, somehow or other, the freedom of the Church.

To insure to the Church her full liberty and the free exercise of her spiritual mission is fundamentally required by the God-given rights of the Church as well as by the basic rights of the human person. But it is also required by the common good of the body politic. For it is the condition for that spreading of the leaven of the Gospel throughout the whole social body which the temporal common good needs in its own sphere. The State acts simply in its own way, as providing the common good of the body politic, in guaranteeing the full freedom of the Church in her spiritual mission. And, as we have seen, it can insure that guarantee—in our historical age it insures it in the best way—without granting any juridical privilege to the citizens who are members of the Church.

Finally, there is a second specific form of mutual assistance which is also required. I mean not only a negative assistance, as is the assurance of freedom, but a positive one. This time I am not speaking of the State, but of the body politic with its free agencies and institutions. In the Christian political society which we are discussing this positive form of assistance would in no way infringe upon the basic rule of equal laws and equal rights for all citizens. The State would not assist the Church by granting her favored juridical treatment, and by seeking to gain her adherence through temporal advantages paid for at the price of her liberty. It is rather by *asking the assistance* of the Church for its own temporal common good that the body politic would assist her in her spiritual mission. For the concept of help is not a one-way concept; help is a two-way traffic. And after all, is it not more normal to have what is superior, or of greater worth in itself, aiding what is of lesser dignity, than to have what is terrestrial aiding what is spiritual? For the latter, moreover, to give more help is equivalent to being better assisted in its proper task.

Thus the body politic, its free agencies and institutions, using their own freedom of existential activity within the framework of laws, would ask more of the Church. They would ask, on the basis of freedom and equality of rights for all citizens, her cooperation in the field of all the activities which aim at enlightening human minds and life. They would positively facilitate the religious, social, and educational work by means of which she—as well as the other spiritual or cultural groups whose helpfulness for the common good would be recognized by them—freely cooperates in the common welfare. By removing obstacles and opening doors, the body politic, its free agencies and institutions, would positively facilitate the effort of the apostles of the Gospel to go to the masses and share their life, to assist the social and moral work of the nation, to provide people with leisure worthy of human dignity, and to develop within them the sense of liberty and fraternity.[21]

Such would be, as I see it, the positive cooperation between the body politic and the Church. And because of the fecundity of truth, we may have confidence that among all the religious or cultural institutions thus freely cooperating with the body politic, the Church which holds in trust the true faith—in contradistinction to religious creeds whose message is more or less faltering, and with greater reason to more or less erroneous human philosophies— would, as a matter of fact, turn to better account the opportunities offered to all by freedom.

---

[21] Cf. our books, *Humanisme intégral*, pp. 184–185 (*True Humanism*, pp. 172–173), and *The Rights of Man and Natural Law*, pp. 28–29.

23 THE END OF MACHIAVELLIANISM*

MACHIAVELLI'S MACHIAVELLIANISM

MY PURPOSE IS TO DISCUSS MACHIAVELLIANISM. REGARDing Machiavelli himself, some preliminary observations seem necessary. Innumerable studies, some of them very good, have been dedicated to Machiavelli. Jean Bodin, in the sixteenth century, criticized *The Prince* in a profound and wise manner. Later on Frederick the Great of Prussia was to write a refutation of Machiavelli in order to exercise his own hypocrisy in a hyper-Machiavellian fashion, and to shelter cynicism in virtue. During the nineteenth century, the leaders of the conservative "bourgeoisie," for instance the French political writer Charles Benoist, were thoroughly, naïvely and stupidly fascinated by the clever Florentine.

As regards modern scholarship, I should like to note that the best historical commentary on Machiavelli has been written by an American scholar, Professor Allan H. Gilbert.[1] As regards more popular presentations, a remarkable edition of *The Prince* and *The Discourses* has been issued by the Modern Library.

---

* *The Range of Reason* (New York: Scribners, 1952), pp. 134–164.

[1] *Machiavelli's Prince and its Forerunners, The Prince as a Typical Book De Regimine Principum,* by Allan H. Gilbert (Durham: Duke University Press, 1938). I think that Professor Gilbert is right in locating *The Prince* in the series of the classical treatises *De Regimine Principum.* Yet *The Prince* marks the end of this series, not only because of the political changes in society, but because its inspiration utterly reverses and corrupts the mediaeval notion of government. It is a typical book *De Regimine Principum,* but which typically puts the series of these books to death.

Mr. Max Lerner, in the stimulating, yet somewhat ambiguous Introduction he wrote for this edition of *The Prince* and *The Discourses*, rightly observes that Machiavelli was expressing the actual ethos of his time, and that as "power Politics existed before Machiavelli was ever heard of, it will exist long after his name is only a faint memory." This is perfectly obvious. But what matters in this connection is just that Machiavelli *lifted into consciousness* this ethos of his time and this common practice of the power politicians of all times. Here we are confronted with the fundamental importance of the phenomenon of *prise de conscience*, and with the risks of perversion which this phenomenon involves.

Before Machiavelli, princes and conquerors did not hesitate to apply on many occasions bad faith, perfidy, falsehood, cruelty, assassination, every kind of crime of which the flesh and blood man is capable, to the attainment of power and success and to the satisfaction of their greed and ambition. But in so doing they felt guilty, they had a bad conscience—to the extent that they had a conscience. Therefore, a specific kind of unconscious and unhappy hypocrisy—that is, the shame of appearing to oneself such as one is—a certain amount of self-restraint, and that deep and deeply human uneasiness which we experience in doing what we do not want to do and what is forbidden by a law that we know to be true, prevented the crimes in question from becoming a rule, and provided governed peoples with a limping accommodation between good and evil which, in broad outline, made their oppressed lives, after all, livable.

After Machiavelli, not only the princes and conquerors of the *cinquecento*, but the great leaders and makers of modern states and modern history, in employing injustice for establishing order, and every kind of useful evil for satisfying their will to power, will have a clear conscience and feel that they accomplish their duty as political heads. Suppose they are not merely skeptical in moral matters, and have some religious and ethical convictions in connection with man's personal behavior, then they will be obliged, in connection with the field of politics, to put aside these convictions, or to place them in a parenthesis; they will stoically immolate their personal morality on the altar of the political good. What was a simple matter of fact, with all the weaknesses and inconsistencies pertaining, even in the evil, to accidental and contingent things, has become, after Machiavelli, a matter of right, with all the firmness and steadiness proper to necessary things. A plain disregard of good and evil has been considered the rule, not of human morality—Machiavelli never pretended to be a moral philosopher—but of human politics.

For not only do we owe to Machiavelli our having become aware and conscious of the immorality displayed, in fact, by the mass of political men, but by the same stroke he taught us that this very immorality is the very law of politics. Here is that Machiavellian perversion of politics which was linked, in fact, with the Machiavellian *prise de conscience* of average political behavior in mankind. The historic responsibility of Machiavelli consists in having *accepted*, recognized, indorsed as normal the fact of political immorality, and in having stated that good politics, politics conformable to its true nature and to its genuine aims, is by essence nonmoral politics.

Machiavelli belongs to that series of minds, and some of them more profound than his, which all through modern times have endeavored to unmask the human being. To have been the first in this lineage is the greatness of this narrow thinker eager to serve the Medici as well as the popular party in Florence, and disappointed on both counts. Yet in unmasking the human being he maimed its very flesh, and wounded its eyes. To have thoroughly rejected ethics, metaphysics and theology from the realm of political knowledge and political prudence is his very own achievement, and it is also the most violent mutilation suffered by the human practical intellect and the organism of practical wisdom.

BECAUSE MEN ARE BAD

Radical pessimism regarding human nature is the basis of Machiavelli's thought. After having stated that "a prudent ruler ought not to keep faith when by so doing it would be against his interest, and when the reasons which made him bind himself no longer exist," he writes: "If men were all good, this precept would not be a good one; but *as they are bad*, and would not observe their faith with you, so you are not bound to keep faith with them." Machiavelli knows that they are bad. He does not know that this badness is not radical, that this leprosy cannot destroy man's original grandeur, that human nature remains good in its very essence and its root-tendencies, and that such a basic goodness joined to a swarming multiplication of particular evils is the very mystery and the very motive power of struggle and progression in mankind. Just as his horizon is merely terrestrial, just as his crude empiricism cancels for him the indirect ordainment of political life toward the life of souls and immortality, so his concept of man is merely animal, and his crude empiricism cancels for him the image of God in man—a cancellation which is the metaphysical root of every power politics and every political totalitarianism. As to their common and more frequent behavior, Machiavelli thinks, men are beasts, guided by covetousness and fear. But the prince is a man, that is, an animal of prey endowed with intelligence and calculation. In order to govern men, that is, to enjoy power, the prince must be taught by Chiron the centaur, and learn to become both a lion and a fox. Fear, animal fear, and animal prudence translated into human art and awareness, are accordingly the supreme rulers of the political realm.

Yet the pessimism of Machiavelli is extremely removed from any heroical pessimism. To the evil that he sees everywhere, or believes he sees everywhere, he gives his consent. He consents, he aspires to become a clearsighted composite of fox and lion. "For how we live," he says, "is so far removed from how we ought to live, that he who abandons what is done for what ought to be done, will rather learn to bring about his own ruin than his preservation." Therefore we have to abandon what *ought to be done* for *what is done,* and it is necessary for the prince, he also says, "to learn how not to be good, and to use this knowledge and not use it, according to the necessity of the case." And this is perfectly logical if the end of ends is only present success. Yet such an abandonment, such a resignation would be logical also, not only for political life, but for the entire field of human life. Descartes, in the provisory rules of morality which he gave himself in the *Discours de la Méthode,* made up his mind to imitate the actual customs and doings of his fellow-men, instead of practicing what they say we ought to do. He did not perceive that this was a good precept of immorality; for, as a matter of fact, men live more often by senses than by reason. It is easy to observe with Mr. Max Lerner that many Church princes, like the secular princes, and above all that Alexander VI whom Machiavelli gives often as an example, were among the prin-

cipal followers of Machiavelli's precepts. But never has any cate-
chism taught that we must imitate the Church princes in our conduct—it is Christ that religion teaches us to imitate. The first step
to be taken by everyone who wishes to act morally is to decide not
to act according to the general customs and doings of his fellow-
men. This is a precept of the Gospel: "Do not ye after their works;
for they say, and do not." [2]

A CIVILIZED CYNICISM AND A PESSIMISM COMFORTED BY AN OVERSIMPLIFIED IDEA OF MORALITY

The practical result of Machiavelli's teachings has been,
for the modern conscience, a profound split, an incurable division
between politics and morality, and consequently an illusory but
deadly antinomy between what people call *idealism* (wrongly confused with ethics) and what people call *realism* (wrongly confused
with politics). Hence, as Mr. Max Lerner puts it, "the polar conflict between the ethical and the ruthlessly realistic." I shall come
back to this point. For the present I wish to note two kinds of
complications which arise in this connection in the case of Machiavelli himself.

The first complication comes from the fact that Machiavelli, like
many great pessimists, had a somewhat rough and elementary idea
of moral science, plainly disregarding its realist, experiential, and
existential character, and lifting up to heaven, or rather up to the
clouds, an altogether naïve morality which obviously cannot be
practiced by the sad yet really living and laboring inhabitants of
this earth. The man of ethics appears to him as a feeble-minded
and disarmed victim, occasionally noxious, of the beautiful rules of
some Platonic and separate world of perfection. On the other hand,
and because such a morality is essentially a self-satisfying show
of pure and lofty shapes—that is, a dreamed-up compensation for
our muddy state—Machiavelli constantly slips from the idea of
well-doing to the idea of what men admire as well-doing, from
moral virtue to appearing and apparent moral virtue; his virtue is
a virtue of opinion, self-satisfaction and glory. Accordingly, what
he calls vice and evil, and considers to be contrary to virtue and

---

[2] Matth. 23, 3.

morality, may sometimes be only the authentically moral behavior of a just man engaged in the complexities of human life and of true ethics: for instance, justice itself may call for relentless energy —which is neither vengeance nor cruelty—against wicked and false-hearted enemies. Or the toleration of some existing evil—if there is no furthering of or cooperating with the same—may be required for avoiding a greater evil or for slowing down and progressively reducing this very evil. Or even dissimulation is not always bad faith or knavery. It would not be moral, but foolish, to open up one's heart and inner thoughts to every dull or mischievous fellow. Stupidity is never moral, it is a vice. No doubt it is difficult to mark exactly the limits between cunning and lying, and even some great Saints of the Old Testament—I am thinking of Abraham—did not take great care of this distinction—this was a consequence of what may be called the twilight status of moral conscience in the dawn-ages of mankind.[3] Yet a certain amount of cunning, if it is intended to deceive evil-disposed persons, must not be considered fox's wiles, but intellect's legitimate weapon. Oriental peoples know that very well, and even evangelic candor has to use the prudence of the serpent, as well as the simplicity of the dove (the dove tames the serpent, but the lion does not tame the fox). The question is to use such cunning without the smallest bit of falsehood or imposture; this is exactly the affair of intelligence; and the use of lying, namely, the large-scale industrialization of lying, of which the great dictatorships of our age have offered us the spectacle, appears from this point of view, not only as moral baseness, but also as vulgarity of mind and thorough degradation of intelligence.

The second complication arises from the fact that Machiavelli was a cynic operating on the given moral basis of civilized tradition, and his cruel work of exposure took for granted the coherence and density of this deep-rooted tradition. Clear-sighted and intelligent as he was, he was perfectly aware of that fact; that is why he would pale at the sight of modern Machiavellianism. This commentator of Titus Livius was instructed by Latin tradition; he was a partaker as well as a squanderer of humanist learning, an inheritor as well as an opponent of the manifold treasure of knowledge

---

[3] Cf. Raissa Maritain, *Histoire d'Abraham ou les premiers âges de la conscience morale* (Paris: Desclée de Brouwer, 1947).

prepared by Christian centuries, and degenerating in his day. Machiavelli never negates the values of morality, he knows them and recognizes them as they have been established by ancient wisdom, he occasionally praises virtuous leaders (that is, those whose virtues were made successful by circumstances). He knows that cruelty and faithlessness are shameful, he never calls evil good or good evil. He simply denies to moral values—and this is largely sufficient to corrupt politics—any application in the political field. He teaches his prince to be cruel and faithless, according to the case, that is, to be evil according to the case, and when he writes that the prince must learn how not to be good, he is perfectly aware that not to be good is to be bad. Hence his difference from many of his disciples, and the special savor, the special power of intellectual stimulation of his cynicism. But hence also his special sophistry, and the mantle of civilized intelligence with which he unintentionally covered and veiled for a time the deepest meaning, the wild meaning, of his message.

A MERELY ARTISTIC CONCEPT OF POLITICS

Finally, the "grammar of power" and the recipes of success written by Machiavelli are the work of a pure artist, and of a pure artist of that Italian Renaissance where the great heritage of the antique and Christian mind, falling in jeopardy, blossomed into the most beautiful, delightful and poisonous flowers. What makes the study of Machiavelli extremely instructive for a philosopher is the fact that nowhere is it possible to find a more purely artistic conception of politics.[4] And here is his chief philosophical fault, if it is true that politics belongs to the field of the "praktikon" (to do), not of the "poietikon" (to make), and is by essence a branch—the principal branch, according to Aristotle—of ethics. Politics is distinct from individual ethics as one branch from another branch on the same tree. It is a special and specific part of ethics, and it carries within itself an enormous amount of art and technique, for the role played by the physical elements to be known and utilized, the forces and resistances to be calculated, the role played by the *making*, or by the work to perform success-

---

[4] ". . . In these things lie the true originality of Machiavelli; all may be summed up in his conviction that government is an independent art in an imperfect world." Allan H. Gilbert, *op. cit.,* p. 285.

fully, the role played by the molding intelligence and imagination is much greater in political than in individual or even familial ethics. But all this amount of art and technique is organically, vitally and intrinsically subordinated to the ethical energies which constitute politics, that is to say, art is there in no manner autonomous; art is there embodied in, and encompassed with, and lifted up by ethics, as the physico-chemical activities in our body are integrated in our living substance and superelevated by our vital energies. When these merely physico-chemical activities are liberated and become autonomous, there is no longer a living organism, but a corpse. Thus, merely artistic politics, liberated from ethics, that is, from the practical knowledge of man, from the science of human acts, from truly human finalities and truly human doings, is a corpse of political wisdom and political prudence.

Indeed, Machiavelli's very own genius has been to disentangle as perfectly as possible all the content of art carried along by politics from the ethical substance thereof. His position, therefore, is that of a separate artistic spirit contemplating from without the vast matter of human affairs, with all the ethical cargo, all the intercrossings of good and evil they involve. His purpose is to teach his disciple how to conquer and maintain power in handling this matter as a sculptor handles clay or marble. Ethics is here present, but in the matter to be shaped and dominated. We understand from this point of view how both *The Prince* and *The Discourses* are rich in true observations and sometimes in true precepts, but perceived and stated in a false light and in a reversed or perverted perspective. For Machiavelli makes use of good as well as evil, and is ready to succeed with virtue as well as with vice. That specific concept of *virtù*, that is, of brilliant, well-balanced and skilled strength, which was at the core of the morality of his time, as an aesthetic and artistic transposition of the Aristotelian concept of virtue, is always present in his work.[5] He knows that no political

---

[5] According to a very just remark by Friedrich Meinecke, the two concepts of *fortune* and *necessity* complete the trilogy of the leading ideas of Machiavelli: *Virtù, fortuna, necessità*. Cf. Friedrich Meinecke, *Die Idee der Staaträson* (München and Berlin: 1924), Chapter I.

Some authors magnify the divergences between *The Prince* and *The Discourses*. In my opinion these divergences, which are real, relate above all to the literary genus of the two works and remain quite secondary. *The Discourses on the first ten Books of Titus Livius* owed it to their own rhetorical and academic mood as

achievement is lasting if the prince has not the friendship of the people, but it is not the good of the people, it is only the power of the prince which matters to him in this truth perversely taught. *The Discourses* eloquently emphasize the fundamental importance of religion in the state, but the truth or falsity of any religion whatsoever is here perfectly immaterial, even religion is offered as the best means of cheating the people, and what Machiavelli teaches is "the use of a national religion for state purposes," by virtue of "its power as a myth in unifying the masses and cementing their morale." [6] This is a perversion of religion which is surely worse and more atheistic than crude atheism—and the devastating effects of which the world has been able to see and enjoy in the totalitarian plagues of our day.

Here we are confronted with the paradox and the internal principle of instability of Machiavelli's Machiavellianism. It essentially supposes the complete eradication of moral values in the brain of the political artist as such, yet at the same time it also supposes the actual existence and actual vitality of moral values and moral beliefs in all others, in all the human matter that the prince is to handle and dominate. But it is impossible that the use of a supramoral, that is, a thoroughly immoral art of politics should not produce a progressive lowering and degeneration of moral values and moral beliefs in the common human life, a progressive disintegration of the inherited stock of stable structures and customs linked with these beliefs, and finally a progressive corruption of the ethical and social matter itself with which this supramoral politics deals. Thus, such an art wears away and destroys its very matter, and, by the same token, will degenerate itself. Hence Machiavelli could only have rare authentic disciples; during the classical centuries of Henry VIII and Elizabeth, Mazarin and Richelieu, Frederick, Catherine of Russia and Talleyrand, the latter was perhaps the only perfect pupil of Machiavelli; finally Machiavelli's teachings, which imply an essentially rational and well-measured, that is, an artistic use of evil, were to give place to that use of every kind of seemingly

---

well as to Roman antiquity to emphasize the republican spirit and some classical aspects of political virtue. In reality neither this virtue (in the sense of the Ancients) nor this spirit ever mattered to Machiavelli, and his own personal inspiration, his quite amoral art of using *virtù* to master fortune by means of occasion and necessity are as recognizable in *The Discourses* as in *The Prince*.

   [6] Max Lerner, Introduction, p. xxxvii.

useful evil by great irrational and demonic forces and by an intelligence no longer artistic but vulgar and brutal and wild, and to that immersion of the rulers as well as of the ruled in a rotted ethics, calling good evil and evil good, which constitute the common Machiavellianism of today.

MACHIAVELLIANISM AND THE PHILOSOPHY OF THE COMMON GOOD

But so much for Machiavelli. It is this common Machiavellianism that I wish now to consider. In so doing, I should like briefly to touch the three following points: first, the notion of common good and the factual successes of Machiavellianism; second, the crucial conflict which here constitutes the main problem, and the resolution thereof; third, the roots and the more subtle implications of this resolution, which concern the specific structure of politics in its relationship with morality.

For Machiavelli the end of politics is power's conquest and maintenance—which is a work of art to be performed. On the contrary, according to the nature of things, the end of politics is the common good of a united people, which end is essentially something concretely human, therefore something ethical. This common good consists of the good life—that is, a life conformable to the essential exigencies and the essential dignity of human nature, a life both morally straight and happy—of the social whole as such, of the gathered multitude, in such a way that the increasing treasure and heritage of communicable good things involved in this good life of the whole be in some way spilled over and redistributed to each individual part of the community. This common good is at once material, intellectual and moral, and principally moral, as man himself is; it is a common good of human persons.[7] Therefore, it is not only something useful, an ensemble of advantages and profits, it is essentially something good in itself—what the Ancients termed *bonum honestum*. Justice and civic friendship are its cement. Bad faith, perfidy, lying, cruelty, assassination, and all other procedures of this kind which may occasionally appear *useful* to the power of the ruling clique or to the prosperity of the state, are in themselves —insofar as they are political deeds, that is, deeds involving in

---

[7] See our little book, *The Person and the Common Good* (1947).

some degree the common conduct—injurious to the common good
and tend by themselves toward its corruption. Finally, because
good life on earth is not the absolute ultimate end of man, and
because the human person has a destiny superior to time, political
common good involves an intrinsic though indirect reference to the
absolutely ultimate end of the human members of society, which is
eternal life, in such a way that the political community should
temporally, and from below, help each human person in his human
task of conquering his final freedom and fulfilling his destiny.

Such is the basic political concept which Machiavellianism broke
down and destroyed. If the aim of politics is the common good,
peace—a constructive peace struggling through time toward man's
emancipation from any form of enslavement—is the health of the
state; and the organs of justice, above all of distributive justice, are
the chief power in the state. If the aim of politics is power, war is
the health of the state, as Machiavelli put it, and military strength
is the chief power in the state. If the aim of politics is the common
good, the ruler, having to take care of the temporal end of a community of human persons, and having to avoid in this task any lack
of clear-sightedness and any slip of will, must learn to be, as St.
Thomas taught, a man good in every respect, *bonus vir simpliciter*.
If the aim of politics is power, the ruler must learn not to be good,
as Machiavelli said.

The great rulers of modern times have well understood and
conscientiously learned this lesson. Lord Acton was right in stating
that "the authentic interpreter of Machiavelli is the whole of later
history." We have to distinguish, however, two kinds of common
Machiavellianism. There was a kind of more-or-less attenuated,
dignified, conservative Machiavellianism, using injustice within
"reasonable" limits, if I may so put it; in the minds of its followers,
what is called *Realpolitik* was obfuscated and more or less paralyzed, either by a personal pattern of moral scruples and moral
rules, which they owed to the common heritage of our civilization,
or by traditions of diplomatic good form and respectability, or
even, in certain instances, by lack of imagination, of boldness, and
of inclination to take risks. If I try to characterize more precisely
these moderate Machiavellianists, I should say that they preserved
in some way, or believed they preserved, regarding the *end* of

politics, the concept of common good—they were unfaithful to their master in this regard; and that they frankly used Machiavellianism regarding the *means* of procuring this common good. Such an unnatural split and disproportion between means and ends was, moreover, inevitably to lead to a perversion of the idea of common good itself, which became more and more a set of material advantages and profits for the state, or territorial conquests, or prestige and glory. The greatest representative of moderate Machiavellianism was, in my opinion, Richelieu. Bismarck was a transition from this first form of Machiavellianism to the second one.

This second form of Machiavellianism is absolute Machiavellianism. It was intellectually prepared, during the nineteenth century, by the Positivist trend of mind, which considered politics to be, not a mere art, but a mere natural science, like astronomy or chemistry, and a mere application of so-called "scientific laws" to the struggle for life of human societies—a concept much less intelligent and still more inhuman than that of Machiavelli himself. Absolute Machiavellianism was also and principally prepared by the Romanticist German philosophy of Fichte and Hegel. It is well known that the author of the *Address to the German Nation* wrote a *Character of Machiavelli*. As to the Hegelian cult of the state, it is a metaphysical sublimation of Machiavelli's principles. Now the turn has been completed, ethics itself has been swallowed up into the political denial of ethics, power and success have become supreme moral criteria, "the course of world history stands apart from virtue, blame and justice," as Hegel put it, and at the same time "human history," he also said, "is God's judgement." Machiavellianism is no longer politics, it is metaphysics, it is a religion, a prophetic and mystical enthusiasm.

It sufficed for such an enthusiasm to enter into some desperados who were empty, as it were, of the usual characters of rational personality, but open to the great collective forces of instinct, resentment and tellurian inspiration; it sufficed for such leaders to give a full practical significance to the old infernal discovery of the endless reserves of evil when thoroughly accepted and utilized, and of the seemingly infinite power of that which negates, of the dissolving forces and of the corruption of human consciences—in order for absolute Machiavellianism to arise in the world, and in order for the unmasking Centaur to be unmasked in its turn.[8] Here we are confronted with that impetuous, irrational, revolutionary, wild, and demoniacal Machiavellianism, for which *boundless* injustice, *boundless* violence, *boundless* lying and immorality, are normal political means, and which draws from this very boundlessness of evil an abominable strength. And we may experience what kind of common good a power which knows perfectly how not to be good, and whose hypocrisy is a conscious and happy, ostentatious and gloriously promulgated hypocrisy, and whose cruelty wants to destroy souls as well as bodies, and whose lying is a thorough perversion of the very function of language—what kind of common good such a power is able to bring to mankind. Absolute Machiavellianism causes politics to be the art of bringing about the misfortune of men.

That's how it is. But absolute Machiavellianism *succeeds,* does it not? At least it has succeeded for many years. How could it not succeed, when everything has been sacrificed to the aim of success? Here is the ordeal and the scandal of contemporary conscience. Moreover it would be astonishing if a timid and limited Machiavellianism were not overcome and thrown away by a boundless and cynical Machiavellianism, stopping at nothing. If there is an answer to the deadly question which we are asked by the Sphinx of history, it can only lie in a thorough reversal of a century-old political thought. In the meantime, the peoples which stand against absolute Machiavellianism will be able to stop its triumphs and to overcome its standard-bearers only in risking in this struggle their blood and their wealth and their dearest treasures of peaceful civilization, and in threatening this Machiavellianism with its own material weapons, material techniques and gigantic means of destruction. But will they be obliged, in order to conquer it and to maintain themselves, to adopt not only its material weapons, but also its own spirit and philosophy? Will they yield to the temptation of losing for the sake of life their very reason for living and existing?

---

[8] "Hitler told me he had read and reread *The Prince* of the Great Florentine. To his mind, this book is indispensable to every political man. For a long time it did not leave Hitler's side. The reading of these unequalled pages, he said, was like a cleansing of the mind. It had disencumbered him from plenty of false ideas and prejudices. It is only after having read *The Prince* that Hitler understood what politics truly is." Hermann Rauschning, *Hitler m'a dit.* (*The Voice of Destruction,* 1940.)

THE GREAT PROBLEM

Here we arrive at the crucial conflict.

Confronted with any temptation of Machiavellianism, that is, of gaining success and power by means of evil, moral conscience answers and cannot keep from answering, just as when it is tempted by any profitable fault: It is never allowed to do evil for any good whatsoever. And Christian conscience in this case is strengthened by the very word of the Gospel. When the devil tempted Jesus by showing Him all the kingdoms of the world, and the glory of them, and telling Him: "All these things, will I give thee, if thou wilt fall down and worship me."—"Get thee hence, Satan," Jesus answered. "For it is written, Thou shalt worship the Lord thy God, and Him only shalt thou serve."

Such is the answer that the human Person, looking up to his own destiny as a person, to his immortal soul, his ultimate end and ever-lasting life, to his God, gives to Politics when Politics offers him the kingdom of the world at the price of his soul. This answer, and the personage to whom it was given, show us the root significance of Politics making itself absolutely autonomous, and claiming to be man's absolutely ultimate end. It shows us the transcendent meaning of the Pagan Empire, and of any paganized Empire, and of any self-styled Holy Empire if its Caesar—be he a Christian Emperor or a Socialist Dictator, or any kind of Grand Inquisitor in the sense of Dostoevsky's famous legend—wills to settle and manage on earth the final kingdom of God or the final kingdom of Man, which they see as the same final kingdom. "Get thee hence, Satan," answers Christ. State and politics, when truly separated from ethics, are the realm of those demoniacal principalities of which St. Paul spoke; the Pagan Empire is the Empire of Man making himself God: the diametrical opposite of the kingdom of Redemptive Incarnation.

Yet the answer we are considering does not solve our conflict; on the contrary, it increases this conflict, it widens the tear to the infinite, it clamps down on the Machiavellian temptation without appeasing the anguish and scandal of our intellect. For it is an answer given by Personal Ethics to a question asked by Political Ethics; its transcends the question, as the Person, with regard to his eternal destiny, transcends the state; it cuts short the question, it does not resolve it. Obviously no assertion of the individual Ethics of the Person, absolutely true, absolutely decisive as it may be, can constitute a sufficiently adequate and relevant answer to a problem stated by the Ethics of the Body Politic. Exactly because it is a transcendent answer, it is not a proper one. Machiavellianism succeeds, does it not? Absolute Machiavellianism triumphs on earth, as our eyes have seen for years. Is Morality willing, is Christianity willing, is God willing that, of necessity, all our freedoms be conquered, our civilization destroyed, the very hope annihilated of seeing a little justice and brotherly amity raise our earthly life—are they willing that, of necessity, our lives be enslaved, our temples and institutions broken down, our brethren persecuted and crushed, our children corrupted, our very souls and intelligences delivered over to perversion by the great imperial standard-bearers of Machiavellianism—because of the very fact that we adhere to justice and refuse the devil, while they dare to use injustice and evil and accede to the devil up to the end?

It is the true goal of the *Person* which is eternal, not that of the *Body Politic*. If a man suffers martyrdom and enters paradise, his own soul enjoys bliss; but suppose all the citizens of a state satellite to some Nero suffer martyrdom and enter paradise, it is not the soul of this state which will enjoy bliss; moreover, this state no longer exists. The Body Politic has no immortal soul, nor has a nation, unless perhaps as concerns a merely spiritual survival of its common moral heritage in the memory of men or in the virtues of the immortal souls which animated its members long ago, at the time when it existed. During the Second World War it was grim nonsense to console Frenchmen by asking them to accept destruction or enslavement of their country while speaking to them of la France éternelle. The soul of a nation is not immortal. The direct and specifying end, the common good of a nation is something temporal and terrestrial, something which can and should be superelevated by Gospel virtues in its own order, but whose own order is natural, not supernatural, and belongs to the realm of time. Therefore, the very existence, temporal and terrestrial, the very improvement, temporal and terrestrial, the very prosperity of a nation, and that amount of happiness and glory which arises from the crises themselves and from the ordeals of history, really and essentially pertain to the common good of this nation.

No doubt—to imagine a thoroughly extreme example—a nation or a state could and should accept destruction, as did the legion of Mauritius, if its citizens were summoned to choose between martyrdom and apostasy; but such a case would not be a political case, it would be a case of sacrifice of political life itself to divine life, and a witnessing, in some way miraculous, of the superiority of the order of grace over the order of nature. But in political life itself, in the order of nature, in the framework of the temporal laws of human existence, is it not impossible that the first of the normal means of providing the common good of a body politic, that is, justice and political morality, should lead to the ruin and disaster of this body politic? Is it not impossible that the first of the means of corrupting the common good of a body politic, that is, injustice and political treachery, should lead to the triumph and prosperity of this body politic?

Yes, this is impossible.

Yet Machiavellianism succeeds in political history? Evil succeeds?

What is, then, the answer?

MACHIAVELLIANISM DOES NOT SUCCEED

The answer is that evil *does not* succeed. In reality Machiavellianism does not succeed. To destroy is not to succeed. Machiavellianism succeeds in bringing about the misfortune of men, which is the exact opposite of any genuinely political end. More or less bad Machiavellianists have succeeded for centuries against other more or less bad Machiavellianists: this is mere exchange of counterfeit coin. Absolute Machiavellianism succeeds against moderate or weak Machiavellianism: this also is normal. But if absolute Machiavellianism were to succeed absolutely and definitely in the world, this would simply mean that political life would have disappeared from the face of the earth, giving place to an entanglement and commixture of the life of animals and slaves, and of the life of saints.

But in saying that evil and injustice do not succeed in politics, I mean a more profound philosophical truth. The endless reserves of evil, the seemingly infinite power of evil of which I spoke a moment ago, are only, in reality, the power of corruption—the squandering and dissipation of the substance and energy of Being and of Good.

Such a power destroys itself by destroying that good which is its subject. The inner dialectic of the successes of evil condemn them not to be lasting. The true philosophical answer consists, therefore, in taking into account the dimension of time, the duration proper to the historical turns of nations and states, which considerably exceeds the duration of a man's life. According to this *political duration,* to the duration required by political reality to mature and fructify, I do not say that a just politics will, even in a distant future, always actually succeed, nor that Machiavellianism will, even in a distant future, always actually fail. For with nations and states and civilizations we are in the order of nature, where mortality is natural and where life and death depend on physical as well as moral causes. I say that justice works through its own causality toward welfare and success in the future, as a healthy sap works toward the perfect fruit, and that Machiavellianism works through its own causality for ruin and bankruptcy, as poison in the sap works for the illness and death of the tree.

Now, what is the illusion proper to Machiavellianism? It is the illusion of *immediate success.* The duration of the life of a man, or rather the duration of the activity of the prince, of the political man, circumscribes the maximum length of time required by what I call *immediate success,* for immediate success is a success that our eyes may see. And what we are speaking of, what Machiavelli is speaking of, in saying that evil and injustice succeed in politics, is in reality *immediate success,* as I have defined it. Yet immediate success is success for a man, it is not success for a state or a nation; it may be—it is, in the case of Machiavellian successes considered as to their inner causal law—a disaster according to the duration proper to state-vicissitudes and nation-vicissitudes. It is with regard to immediate success that evil and injustice enjoy a seemingly infinite power, a power which can be met and overcome only by a heroic tension of antagonistic powers. But the more dreadful in intensity such a power of evil appears, the weaker in historic duration are the internal improvements, and the vigor of life, which have been gained by a state using this power.[9]

---

[9] Three years after these pages were written (they were first drafted in 1941, for a symposium on "The Place of Ethics in Social Science" held at the University of Chicago) the world contemplated the inglorious fall of Mr. Benito

As I have already put it in another study,[10] the good in which the state's justice bears fruit, the misfortune in which the state's in-justice bears fruit, have nothing to do with immediate and visible results; historic *duration* must be taken into account; the temporal good in which the state's justice bears fruit, the temporal evil in which its iniquity bears fruit, may be and are in fact quite different from the immediate results which the human mind might have ex-pected and which the human eyes contemplate. It is as easy to dis-entangle these remote causations as to tell at a river's mouth which waters come from which glaciers and which tributaries. The achievements of the great Machiavellianists seem durable to us, because our scale of duration-measurements is an exceedingly small one, with regard to the time proper to nations and human com-munities. We do not understand the fair play of God, Who gives those who have freely chosen injustice the time to exhaust the benefits of it and the fulness of its energies. When disaster comes to these victors, the eyes of the righteous who cried against them to God will have long putrefied under the earth, and men will not know the distant source of the catastrophe.

Thus it is true that politics being something intrinsically moral, the first political condition of good politics is that it be just. And it is true at the same time that justice and virtue do not, as a rule, lead us to success in this world. But the antinomy is solved, because, on the one hand, success in politics is not material power nor material wealth nor world-domination, but the achievement of the common good, with the conditions of material prosperity which it involves. And because, on the other hand, these very conditions of material prosperity, terrible as the ordeals may be which the requirements of justice impose on a people, are not and cannot be put in jeopardy or destroyed by the use of justice itself, if historical duration is taken into account and if the specific effect of this use of justice is considered in itself, apart from the effect of the factors at play.

I do not mean that God recompenses the just peoples by the

Mussolini. The triumphs of this wretched disciple of absolute Machiavellianism (he wrote a Preface to an edition of *The Prince*) lasted twenty years.

Hitlerist Machiavellianism had a similar fate. Sooner or later Communist Machiavellianism will have a similar fate.

[10] *Humanisme intégral*, pp. 229–230 (English translation, *True Human-ism*, pp. 219–220).

blessings of military triumphs, territorial aggrandizements, accumu-
lation of wealth, or infinite profit in business; such values are but
secondary, sometimes even injurious to the political common good.
Moreover, if it is true that the political life of peoples may be permeated in its own order by Christian influences, it may be that a
Christian nation has to undergo in a measure the very law of
evangelic trials, and to pay for a certain abundance of spiritual or
cultural improvements at the price of certain weaknesses and in-
firmities in worldly values; such was the case of Italy in the Middle
Ages and the Renaissance; never did Italy know a more splendid
civilization than in those times when the power of the Popes
brought her, as Machiavelli takes pleasure in pointing out, weakness and pain regarding her political unity. Nor do I mean that a
body politic using political justice is by this fact alone protected
against ruin or destruction. What I mean is that in such a misfortune the very cause of ruin or destruction is never the use of
justice. What I mean is that the very order of nature and of natural
laws in moral matters, which is the natural justice of God, makes
justice and political righteousness work towards bearing fruit, in the
long run, as regards their own law of action, in the form of improvement in the true common good and the real values of civilization. Such was the case for the policy of St. Louis, although he was
beaten in all his crusading enterprises. Political injustices, on the
other hand, political treacheries, political greed, selfishness or
cowardice, exploitation of the poor and the weak, intoxication with
power or glory or self-interest—or that kind of political cleverness
which consists, as a professor in international politics told me
candidly some years ago, in using flattery and leniency toward our
enemy, because he is an enemy, and therefore is to be feared, and
in forsaking our friend, because he is a friend, and therefore is not
to be feared—or that kind of political firmness which consists in
denouncing some predatory state which is attacking a weak nation,
and in selling weapons and supplies to the same aggressor, because
business must keep going—all this is always dearly paid for in the
end. Wars, even just wars which must be waged against iniquitous
aggressors, are often the payment thus exacted from a civilization.[11]

---

[11] What Sir Norman Angell said in Boston in April, 1941, is true for
all contemporary democracies. "If we applied," he said with great force, "ten

Then war must be waged with unshaken resolution. But victory will be fruitful only on the condition of casting away the wrongdoings of the past, and of decidedly converting oneself toward justice and political righteousness.

The more I think of these things, the more I am convinced that the observations I proposed a moment ago on the dimension of time are the core of the question. To be lasting is an essential characteristic of the common good. A forester who would seek immediate visible success in planting plenty of big old trees in his forest, instead of preparing young saplings, would use a foolish forest policy. Machiavelli's prince is a bad political man, he perverts politics, because his chief aim is his own personal power and the satisfaction of his own personal ambition. But, in a much more profound and radical sense, the ruler who sacrifices everything to the desire of his own eyes to see the triumph of his policy is a bad ruler and perverts policies, even if he lacks personal ambition and loves his country disinterestedly, because he measures the time of maturation of the political good according to the short years of his own personal time of activity.

As regards the great representatives of contemporary Machiavellianism—either Fascist and Nazi (they have been dealt with) or Communist (they are still threatening the world)—nothing is more instructive in this connection than the ferocious impatience of their general policy. They apply the law of war, which requires a series of immediate striking successes, but which is a supreme and abnormal crisis in the life of human societies, to the very development of the normal life of the state. In so doing, they appear, not

---

years ago resolutely the policy of aiding the victim of aggression to defend himself, we should not now be at war at all.

"It is a simple truth to say that because we in Britain were deaf to the cries rising from the homes of China smashed by the invader we now have to witness the ruthless destruction by invaders of ancient English shrines.

"Because we would not listen to the cries of Chinese children massacred by the invader, we have now, overnight, to listen to the cries of English children, victims of that same invader's ally.

"Because we were indifferent when Italian submarines sank the ships of republican Spain, we must now listen to the cries of children from the torpedoed refugee ship going down in the tempest 600 miles from land."

But the remote responsibilities thus alluded to by Sir Norman Angell go back much further than ten years. Western civilization is now paying a bill prepared by the faults of all modern history.

as Empire-builders, but as mere squanderers of the heritage of their nations.

Yet a fructification which will come into existence in a distant future but which we do not see, is for us as immaterial as a fructification which would never exist on earth. To act with justice, without picking any fruit of justice, but only fruits of bitterness and sorrow and defeat, is difficult for a man. It is still more difficult for a man of politics, even for a just and wise one, who works at an earthly work that is the most arduous and the highest among temporal works—the common good of the multitude—and whose failures are the failures of an entire people and of a dear country. He must live on hope. Is it possible to live on hope without living on faith? Is it possible to rely on the unseen without relying on faith?

I do not believe that in politics men can escape the temptation of Machiavellianism, if they do not believe that there exists a supreme government of the universe, which is, properly speaking, divine, for God—the head of the cosmos—is also the head of this particular order which is that of ethics. Nor is escape from this temptation possible if they do not entrust the providence of God with the care of all that supraempirical, dark and mysterious disentanglement of the fructification of good and evil which no human eye can perceive —thus closing their eyes, by faith, as regards the factual achievements in the distant future, while they open their eyes and display, by knowledge and prudence, more watchfulness than any fox or lion, as regards the preparations of these achievements and the seeds to be right now put into the earth.

A merely natural political morality is not enough to provide us with the means of putting its own rules into practice. Moral conscience does not suffice, if it is not at the same time religious conscience. What is able to face Machiavellianism, moderate Machiavellianism and absolute Machiavellianism, is not a just politics appealing only to the natural forces of man, it is Christian politics. For, in the existential context of the life of mankind, politics, because it belongs by its very essence to the ethical realm, demands consequently to be helped and strengthened, in order not to deviate and in order to attain a sufficiently perfect point of maturity, by everything man receives, in his social life itself, from religious belief and from the word of God working within him. This is what the authors of the Declaration of Independence and of the Constitution of this country understood and expressed in a form adapted to the philosophy of their time, and what makes their accomplishment so outstanding to the mind of everyone who believes Christianity to be efficacious not only for heaven but also for earth.

Christian politics is neither theocratic nor clerical, nor yet a politics of pseudo-evangelical weakness and non-resistance to evil, but a genuinely political politics, ever aware that it is situated in the order of nature and must put into practice natural virtues; that it must be armed with real and concrete justice, with force, perspicacity and prudence; a politics which would hold the sword that is the attribute of the state, but which would also realize that peace is the work not only of justice but of love, and that love is also an essential part of political virtue. For it is never excess of love that fools political men, but without love and generosity there is regularly blindness and miscalculation. Such a politics would be mindful of the eternal destiny of man and of the truths of the Gospel, knowing in its proper order—in a measure adapted to its temporal ends —something of the spirit, and of love, and of forgiveness.

THE SPECIFIC STRUCTURE OF POLITICAL ETHICS

We arrive now at the third consideration I indicated at the beginning, in which I should like to make clearer certain particular points concerning the relationship between Politics and Morality.

As I have previously pointed out, political reality, though principally moral, is by essence both moral and physical, as man himself, but in a different manner from man, because it does not have any substantial immortal soul. Societies are like ever-growing organisms, immense and long-living trees, or coral-flowers, which would lead at the same time a moral and human life. And in the order to which they belong, which is that of Time and Becoming, death is natural; human communities, nations, states and civilizations naturally die, and die for all time, as would these morally-living coral-flowers of which I just spoke. Their birth, growth and decay, their health, their diseases, their death, depend on basic physical conditions, in which the specific qualities of moral behavior are intermingled and play an essential part, but which are more primitive than these qualities. Similarly, imprudence or intemperance may hasten the death of a man, self-control may defer this death, yet in any case this man will die.

Justice and moral virtues do not prevent the natural laws of senescence of human societies. They do not prevent physical catastrophes from destroying them. In what sense are they the chief forces of the preservation and duration of societies? In the sense that they compose the very soul of society, its internal and spiritual force of life. Such a force does not secure immortality to the society, no more than my immortal soul protects me from death. Such a force is not an immortal entelechy, because it is not substantial; yet, insofar as it is spiritual, it is by itself indestructible. Corrupt this force, and an internal principle of death is introduced into the core of the society. Maintain and improve this force, and the internal principle of life is strengthened in the society. Suppose a human community is hammered, crushed, overwhelmed by some natural calamity or some powerful enemy; as long as it still exists—if it preserves within itself justice and civic friendship and faith, there is within it actual hope of resurging, there is a force within it which tends by itself to make it live and get the upper hand and avail itself of disaster, because no hammer can destroy this immaterial force. If a human community loses these virtues, its internal principle of life is invaded by death.

What therefore must be said is that justice and righteousness *tend by themselves* to the preservation of states, and to that real *success* at long range of which I spoke a moment ago. And that injustice and evil *tend by themselves* to the destruction of states, and to that real *failure* at long range of which I also spoke.

Such is the law of fructification of human actions which is inscribed in the nature of things and which is but the natural justice of God in human history.

But if the normal fruit of success and prosperity called for by political justice and wisdom does not come into actual existence because the tree is too old or because some storm has broken its branches; or if the normal fruit of failure and destruction, called for by political wickedness and madness, does not come into actual existence because the physical conditions in the sap or in the environment have counterbalanced the internal principle of death —such an accident does not suppress that regularity inherent in the law which I emphasized in the previous part of this essay, and only bears witness to the fact that nations and civilizations are naturally mortal. As I previously observed, justice may sometimes, even in a distant future, not actually succeed in preserving a state from ruin and destruction. But justice tends by itself to this preservation; and it is not by virtue of justice, it is by virtue of physical conditions counterbalancing from without the very effects of justice that misfortune will then occur. Machiavellianism and political perversion may sometimes, even in a distant future, not actually break, they may triumph decisively over weak and innocent peoples. But they tend by themselves to self-destruction; and it is not by virtue of Machiavellianism and political perversion, it is by virtue of other conditions counterbalancing from without the very effects of these, that success will then occur.

If a weak state is surrounded and threatened by Machiavellian enemies, it must desperately increase its physical power, but also its moral virtues. Suppose it delivers its own soul to Machiavellianism —then it only adds a principle of death to its already existing weaknesses. If a civilization grown old and naturally bound to die, as the Roman Empire was at the time of St. Augustine, if a political state artificially and violently built up, and naturally bound to fail, as was the German Reich of Bismarck and Wilhelm, wished nonetheless to escape either death or failure by letting loose evil and perversion, then it would only poison centuries and prepare for itself a historical hell worse than death.

It seems not irrelevant to add the two following observations. First: innumerable are, in the history of mankind, the cases where the strong have triumphed over the weak; yet this was not always a triumph of strength over right, for most often right's sanctity was as immaterial to the conquered weak as it was to the conquering strong. Greece was conquered by Rome (and was to conquer intellectually Roman civilization). At that time Greece had lost its political soul.

Second: as to the lasting or seemingly lasting triumphs of political injustice over innocent people, they also are not rare, at least at first glance. They concern most often, however, the enslavement, sometimes the destruction, of populations or human groups not yet arrived at a truly political status by nations enjoying this very status—of such a fact the most striking instance is to be found in the history of modern colonization. But it seems that in proportion as peoples arrive at a truly political status, and really constitute a *civitas,* a political house and community, in this proportion the immaterial internal force which abides in them and is made up of long-lived justice and love and moral energies, and of deep-rooted memories, and of a specific spiritual heritage, becomes a more and more *formed* and cohesive soul; and in this very proportion this soul takes precedence over the merely physical conditions of existence and tends to render such peoples unconquerable. If they are conquered and oppressed, they remain alive and keep on struggling under oppression. Then an instinct of prophecy develops among them, as in Poland at the time of Mickiewicz, and their hopes naturally lift up toward the supernatural example of any historical duration in the midst of oppression, the example of the house of Israel, whose internal immaterial force and principle of communion is of a supra-political and supra-temporal order.

JUSTICE AND NATURE IN HUMAN HISTORY

Yet a final question arises now, which is of a rather metaphysical nature. I have said that the natural laws, according to which political justice fructifies by itself into the good and the preservation of a given human community, evil and political injustice into its destruction, are to be identified with the natural justice of God in human history. But is not an essential *tendency* only connoted here? Did I not emphasize the fact that even at long range such normal fructifications may fail, that the fruit of evil for the unjust state, the fruit of good for the just one, may be marred, because of the physical factors and particularly because of the physical laws of senescence and death which interfere here with the moral factors? If this is the case, where is the natural justice of God? Justice does not deal with tendencies, essential as they may be, whose factual result may fail to appear, it deals with sanctions which never fail.

The question we are confronting here transcends the field of moral philosophy and historical experience, and deals with the knowledge we are able to stammer of the divine government of created things. The first answer which comes to the mind of a Christian metaphysician consists in affirming a priori that the natural fructifications of good and evil never fail, the fruit of justice and the fruit of injustice are never marred—which seems self-evi-. dent, since the justice of God cannot be deceived. Because states and nations have no immortal destiny, not only must the sanctions deserved by their deeds reach men within time and upon the earth, but they must do so in an absolutely infallible manner.

In considering the problem more carefully, I believe, however, that this answer results from a kind of undue reverberation of considerations pertaining to theology upon metaphysical matters, which causes things which belong to time and history to be endowed with that absolute firmness which is proper to things relating to eternity.

It is perfectly true that God's justice cannot fail as regards the immortal destiny of each human person, which is accomplished in fact, according to Christianity's teachings, in the supernatural order. Yet it would be too hasty a procedure simply to conceive the divine justice which rules the historical fate of human societies, according to the pattern of that divine justice which rules the suprahistorical destiny of the human person. In these two cases justice applies to its subject-matter in an analogical fashion. The suprahistorical justice cannot fail, because it reaches moral agents—human persons—who attain their final state above time. But the historical justice, dealing with human societies, reaches moral agents who do not attain any final state. There is no final sanction for them, sanctions are spread out for them all along time and intermingled at each moment with their continuing and changing activity; often the fruit of ancient injustice starts up into existence at the very moment when a revival of justice occurs in a given society. Moreover, and by the same token, it appears that these sanctions *in the making* do not enjoy that absolute necessity which is linked with the immutability of some ultimate, eternal accomplishment. What seemed to us, a moment ago, to be self-evident, is not self-evident. It is possible that in the case of human societies the natural fructifications of good and evil are sometimes marred. The sanctions deserved by the deeds of nations and states must reach men within time and upon the earth, yet it is not necessary that they do so in a manner absolutely infallible and always realized.

Consider the civilization of the peoples which lived on legendary Atlantis. The good and bad political deeds of these peoples tended by themselves to bear fruit and to engender their natural sanctions. Yes, but when Atlantis was engulfed by the ocean, all these fruits to come were cancelled from being as well as the peoples and the civilization from which they were to spring forth. The natural justice of God, as regards human societies, that is, moral agents immersed in time, may fail just as nature may fail in its physical fructifications: because this natural historical justice of God is nothing else than nature itself in its not physical, but moral fructifications. God's justice is at work in time and history, it reigns only in heaven and in hell. The concept of perfect and infallible retribution for human deeds, with its absolute adamantine strength, is a religious concept relating to the eternal destiny of human Persons; it is not the ethico-philosophical concept which has to be shaped relating to the destiny of human communities in time and history.

Such is the answer which appears to me the true answer to the question we are considering. But we must immediately add that these failures of historical justice are to occur in the fewest number of cases, just as do the failures of nature in the physical order, because they are accidents, in which the very laws of essences do not reach their own effect. I do not ignore the fact that there is in nature an immense squandering of seeds in order that a few may have the chance of springing up, and still fewer the chance of bearing fruit. But even if the failures of natural historical justice were *abnormities as regards individual accomplishment*, as frequent as the failures of so many wasted seeds, the truth that I am pointing out throughout this chapter would nonetheless remain unshaken, namely, that justice tends by itself toward the welfare and survival of the community, injustice toward its damage and dissolution, and that any long-range success of Machiavellianism is never due to Machiavellianism itself, but to other historical factors at play. Yet the abnormities which really occur *ut in paucioribus* in physical nature are *abnormities as regards specific accomplishment*—as in the production of something deviating from the very essence of the species, the production of "freaks." And it is with such physical abnormities as regards specific accomplishment that the failures of the natural fructification of good and evil, the failures in the accomplishment of the specific laws of moral essences, must rather be compared. We must therefore emphasize more strongly than ever the fact—which I have already stressed in a previous section—that the sanctions of historical justice fail much more rarely than our short-sighted experience might induce us to believe.

Here a new observation seems to me particularly noticeable. These sanctions, which have been deserved by the deeds of the social or political whole, must not necessarily reverberate on this political whole as such, on the nation itself in its existence and power, they may concern the common cultural condition of men considered apart from the actual framework of this whole, yet in some kind of solidarity with the latter—because the political whole is not a substantial or personal subject, but a community of human persons, and a community related to other communities through vital exchanges. Thus, during the life of a nation the fruit of its just or of its perverted deeds may appear only either in some particular improvement or in some particular plague of part or all of its internal strata. Still more, when a state, a nation, a civilization dies, it is normal that the fructifications of good and evil which its deeds had prepared pass over—in the cultural order and as regards such or such a feature of the common social or cultural status—to its remnants, to the scattered human elements which had been contained in its unity and to their descendants, or to the human communities which are its successors and inheritors.

Then a state or a civilization dissolves, but its good or bad works continue to bear fruit, not strictly political (for the word political connotes the common life of a given self-sufficient society) yet political in a broader and still genuine sense, which relates to the cultural life and to the common cultural heritage of mankind. For there exists a genuine temporal community of mankind—a deep intersolidarity, from generation to generation, linking together the peoples of the earth—a common heritage and a common fate, which do not concern the building of a particular *civil society*, but of *civilization*, not the prince, but culture, not the perfect *civitas* in the Aristotelian sense, but that kind of *civitas*, in the Augustinian sense, which is imperfect and incomplete, made up of a fluid network of human communications, and more existential than formally organized, but all the more real and living and basically important. To ignore this non-political *civitas humani generis* is to break up the basis of political reality, to fail in the very roots of political philosophy, as well as to disregard the progressive trend which naturally tends toward a more organic and unified international structure of peoples.

Thus another fundamental consideration must be added to that of *historic duration*, which I previously emphasized, namely, the consideration of the *human extension*, down through generations, of the fructifications of political deeds. Then we see in a complete manner the law which binds Machiavellianism to failure, as a rule and as regards the essential tendencies inscribed in nature. If, even at long range, political justice and political injustice do not ever fructify into the political success or disaster of the state itself which has practiced them, they may still produce their fruit according to the laws of human solidarity. By the same stroke we perceive Machiavellianism's mischievousness, weakness and absurdity in their full implications. It is not only for particular states that it prepares misfortune and scourges—first the victims of Machiavellian states, then the Machiavellian states themselves—it is also for the human race in general. It burdens mankind with an ever-growing burden of evil, unhappiness and disaster. By its own weight and its own internal law it brings about failure, not only with reference to given nations, but with reference to our common kind, with reference to the root community of nations. Like every other sort of selfishness, this divinized selfishness is essentially blind.

HYPERMORALISM AND MACHIAVELLIANISM

To sum up all that I have stated, I would say:

First: It suffices to be just in order to gain eternal life; this does not suffice in order to gain battles or immediate political successes.

Second: In order to gain battles or immediate political successes, it is not necessary to be just—it may occasionally be more advantageous to be unjust.

Third: It is necessary, although it is not sufficient, to be just, in order to secure and further the political common good, and the lasting welfare of earthly communities.

The considerations I have developed in this chapter are founded on the basic fact that Politics is a branch of Ethics but a branch specifically distinct from the other branches of the same generic stock. One decisive sign of this specificity of Political Ethics in contradistinction to Personal Ethics is that earthly communities are mortal as regards their very being and belong entirely to time. Another sign is that political virtues tend to a relatively ultimate end which is the earthly common good, and are only indirectly related to the absolutely ultimate end of man. Hence, the authentic moral character, and at the same time the genuinely realist quality of many features of Political Ethics. Many rules of political life, which the pessimists of Machiavellianism usurp to the benefit of immorality, are in reality ethically grounded—say, for instance, the political toleration of certain evils and the recognition of the *fait accompli* (the so-called "statute of limitations") which permits the retention of long ago ill-gotten gains because new human ties and vital relationships have infused them with new-born rights. In the last analysis, Political Ethics is able to absorb and digest all the elements of truth contained in Machiavelli, I mean to say, to the extent that power and immediate success are actually part of politics— but a subordinate, not the principal, part.

May I repeat that a certain hypermoralism, causing Political Ethics to be something impracticable and merely ideal, is as contrary to this very Ethics as Machiavellianism is, and finally plays the game of Machiavellianism, as conscientious objectors play the game of the conquerors. Purity of means consists in not using means morally bad in themselves; it does not consist in refusing pharisaically any exterior contact with the mud of human life, and it does not consist in waiting for a morally aseptic world before consenting to work in the world, nor does it consist in waiting, before saving one's neighbor who is drowning, to become a saint, so as to escape any risk of false pride in such a generous act.

If this were the time to present a complete analysis of the particular causes of lasting success and welfare in politics, I should add two observations here. First: while political justice—which is destroyed both by the dismissal of Ethics, that is, by Machiavellianism, and by its senseless exaltation, that is, by Hypermoralism—is the prime *spiritual* condition of lasting success and welfare for a nation as well as for a civilization, the prime *material* condition of this lasting success and welfare is, on the one hand, that heritage of accepted and unquestionable structures, fixed customs and deep-rooted common feelings which bring into social life itself something of the determined physical data of nature,[12] and of the vital unconscious strength proper to vegetative organisms; and, on the other hand, that common inherited experience and that set of moral and intellectual instincts which constitute a kind of empirical practical

---

[12] Cf. "The Political Ideas of Pascal," in *Ransoming the Time* (1941).

wisdom, much deeper and denser and much nearer the hidden complex dynamism of human life than any artificial construction of reason. And both this somewhat physical heritage and this inherited practical wisdom are intrinsically and essentially bound to, and dependent upon, moral and religious beliefs. As regards Political Ethics and political common good, the preservation of these common structures of life and of this common moral dynamism is more fundamental than any particular action of the prince, however serious and decisive this may be in itself. And the workings of such a vast, deep-seated physico-moral energy are more basic and more important to the life of human societies than particular political good or bad calculations; they are for states the prime cause of historic success and welfare. The Roman Empire did not succeed by virtue of the stains, injustices and cruelties which tainted its policy, but by virtue of this internal physico-moral strength.

Now—and this is my second observation—what is in itself, even in the order of material causality, primarily and basically destructive of lasting historic success and welfare for a nation as well as for a civilization, is that which is destructive of the common stock and heritage I just described, that is, Machiavellianism, on the one hand, and Hypermoralism on the other. Both destroy, like gnawing worms, the inner social and ethical living substance upon which depends any lasting success and welfare of the commonwealth, as they also destroy that political justice which constitutes the moral righteousness, the basic moral virtue and the spiritual strength of human societies.

Thus the split, the deadly division created between Ethics and Politics both by Machiavellianists and by Hypermoralists is overcome, because Politics is essentially ethical, and because Ethics is essentially realistic, not in the sense of any *Realpolitik*, but in the sense of the full human reality of the common good.

I am aware that if this antinomy which has been the scourge of modern history, is to be practically, not only theoretically, overcome, it will be only on condition that a kind of revolution take place in our conscience. Machiavelli has made us conscious of what is in fact the average behavior of politics in mankind. In this he was right. There is, here, a natural slope that the man who endeavors to overcome dissociation, the man of unity will have to climb up again. But slopes are made to be climbed. As Bergson pointed out, a genuine democracy, by the very fact that it proceeds from an evangelic motive power, works against the grain of nature and therefore needs some heroic inspiration.

With whatever deficiencies human weakness may encumber the practical issue, the fact remains, in any case, that such an effort must be made, and that the knowledge of what is true in these matters is of first and foremost importance. To keep Machiavelli's awareness, with reference to the factual conduct of most of the princes, and to know that this conduct is bad politics, and to clear our conscience of Machiavelli's rules, precepts and philosophy—in this consists the very end of Machiavellianism.

Here I emphasize anew what I pointed out at the beginning of this chapter. Machiavellianism does not consist of this unhappy lot of particular evil and unjust political deeds which are taking place in fact by virtue of human weakness or wickedness. Machiavellianism is a philosophy of politics, stating that by rights good politics is supramoral or immoral politics and by essence must make use of evil. What I have discussed is this political philosophy. There will be no end to the occurrence of misdeeds and mistakes as long as humanity endures. To Machiavellianism there can and must be an end.

ABSOLUTE MACHIAVELLIANISM AND MODERATE MACHIAVELLIANISM

Let us conclude. Machiavellianism is an illusion, because it rests upon the power of evil, and because, from the metaphysical point of view, evil as such has no power as a cause of being; from the practical point of view, evil has no power as a cause of any lasting achievement. As to moral entities like peoples, states, and nations, which do not have any supratemporal destiny, it is within time that their deeds are sanctioned; it is upon earth that the entire charge of failure and nothingness, with which is charged every evil action committed by the whole or by its heads, will normally be exhausted. This is a natural, a somewhat physical law in the moral order (though it is thwarted in some cases by the interference of the manifold other factors at play in human history). As a rule Machiavellianism and political injustice, if they gain immediate success, lead states and nations to misfortune or catastrophe in the long run; in cases where they seem to succeed even in the long run, this

is not by virtue of evil and political injustice, but by virtue of some
inner principle of misfortune already binding their victim to submission, even if the latter did not have to face such iniquitous enemies.
Either the victims of power politics are primitive tribes which had
been in a state of non-existence as to political life and therefore as
to political justice, and their unjustly-suffered misfortune, which
cries out against heaven and makes God's justice more implacable
with regard to the personal destiny of their executioners, does not
reverberate upon the unjustly conquering state unless in the form
of some hidden and insidious, not openly political, self-poisoning
process. Or else the victims of power politics are states and nations
which were already condemned to death or enslavement by the
natural laws of senescence of human societies or by their own internal corruption. And here also the very effect of the injustice
which has been used against them is to introduce a hidden principle
of self-destruction into the inner substance of their conquerors.

When the victims of power politics are mature and vital people,
who keep struggling against oppression, they can be subjugated for
a time, but the very order of nature promises that a day will come
when they will reassert themselves over the oppressor's ruins.

In truth, the dialectic of injustice is unconquerable. Machiavellianism devours itself. Common Machiavellianism has devoured and
annihilated Machiavelli's Machiavellianism; absolute Machiavellianism devours and annihilates moderate Machiavellianism. Weak or
attenuated Machiavellianism is inevitably destined to be vanquished
by absolute and virulent Machiavellianism.

If some day absolute Machiavellianism triumphs over mankind,
this will only be because all kinds of accepted iniquity, moral weakness and consent to evil, operating within a degenerating civilization, will previously have corrupted it, and prepared ready-made
slaves for the lawless man. But if absolute Machiavellianism is ever
to be crushed, and I hope it will be, it will only be because what
remains of Christian civilization will have been able to oppose it
with the principle of political justice integrally recognized.

In his introduction to Machiavelli, Mr. Max Lerner emphasizes
the dilemma with which democracies are now confronted. This
dilemma seems to me perfectly clear: either to perish by continuing
to accept, more or less willingly, the principle of Machiavellianism,
or to regenerate by consciously and decidedly rejecting this prin-

ciple. For what we call democracy or the commonwealth of free men is by definition a political regime of men the spiritual basis of which is uniquely and exclusively law and right. Such a regime is by essence opposed to Machiavellianism and incompatible with it. Totalitarianism lives by Machiavellianism; freedom dies by it. The only Machiavellianism of which any democracy as such is capable is attenuated and weak Machiavellianism. Facing absolute Machiavellianism, either the democratic states, inheritors of the *Ancien Régime* and of its old Machiavellian policy, will keep on using weak Machiavellianism, and they will be destroyed from without, or they will decide to have recourse to absolute Machiavellianism, which is only possible with totalitarian rule and totalitarian spirit; and thus they will destroy themselves from within. They will survive and take the upper hand only on condition that they break with Machiavellianism in any of the forms in which it may appear.

24 THE REINTEGRATION OF THE MASSES*

To WHAT DO OUR MANY CONSIDERATIONS LEAD IF NOT TO the conclusion that the coming of a new Christendom depends, above everything else, on the interior and full realization of a Christian lay vocation in a certain number of hearts? This future also depends in fact on whether a great Christian renaissance will take place not only among the intellectuals, but in general throughout the popular masses.

With these remarks we come to another complementary point. The idea of a Christian renovation of temporal existence forces us to abandon the anthropocentric humanistic age, and especially the "capitalistic" and "bourgeois" epoch, in order to bring ourselves into a new world. If this is so, such a renovation has internal dimensions of incomparably greater height and breadth and depth than any other revolution; it is linked to a vast historical process of *integration* and *reintegration*.

The fact is that in the nineteenth century the working class for the most part turned away from Christianity. We have already [1] said a word about the causes of this fact and the responsibilities of the Christian world. Those remarks concerned the past. Here we have to deal with a second problem, concerning the future: the reintegration of the working class and of the masses. Let us try to indicate its main features as the problem confronts the Christian.

---

* *Humanisme intégral* (Paris: Fernand Aubier, 1947), pp. 232–244.
[1] See Chapter 3 of *Humanisme intégral*; also, *Freedom in the Modern World*.

One of the most instructive chapters in a Christian philosophy of history would deal with what we may call the interlacing of masks and roles. Not only are roles of evil often played by masks or figures of justice, but roles of justice are often played (and spoiled) by masks of evil. Not only is bad and useless historical work done by those who carry the standards of truth, but some good and useful work is done (and spoiled) by adversaries of the standards of truth. This occurs because the whole truth is too heavy for human weakness, a weakness which, except in the saints, needs the abatement provided by error. Historical processes which were in themselves normal and providential and which naturally demanded development in a Christian direction, were in the course of modern history, and through the fault of both Christians and their adversaries, thus forestalled, masked and warped by anti-Christian forces.

In the intellectual order, since the sixteenth century, rationalism and the most erroneous philosophies have at once activated and deformed, by a sort of parasitism or symbiosis, something as normal and good in itself as the admirable growth of the experimental sciences of nature. Likewise, in the social order, the growth of Socialism during the last century—itself automatically called forth by the excesses of capitalism, yet constituting a new and typical reaction to evils which circulated for centuries in the underground of history, and articulating in a sonorous voice the immense anonymous cry of the poor—this growth of Socialism has activated, masked and deformed certain historical gains that in themselves were normal and good.

In each of these instances, the historical phenomenon in question was bound up with that tendency towards the rehabilitation of the creature which we have pointed out as characteristic of the modern age. In the case of Socialism, then, of what acquisition and historical gain do we primarily speak? We do not speak primarily of the demand for and the conquest of better material living conditions, of an amelioration, as people put it, of the condition of the working classes.

No, no matter how just this demand and this conquest may be, of themselves they concern only a particular economic matter, and are so little typical of Socialism that one can find them in reformist or paternalist conceptions, and that, if we suppose them possible under the present regime, they would rather lead to a kind of "bourgeois-ing" of the proletariat.

On the contrary, it is rather because of the misery and the social non-existence in which it has been kept throughout what we may call the golden age of "liberal" individualism and capitalism, that the proletariat has been able, wearing the colors of systems that were illusory, and especially when they pretended to be scientific, to realize the gain of which we are speaking. While affecting the order of earthly and temporal civilization, this gain is in the spiritual order, and this is what makes it important. It is a certain growth in self-awareness, the growth in self-awareness of an offended and humiliated human dignity, and the growth in awareness of an historical mission. Marxism was constructed to activate and distort this growth in awareness. And I say that it is impossible to attach too much importance to this phenonemon of *prise de conscience*, for all the great advances in the modern age, in art, in science, in philosophy, in poetry, in the spiritual life itself, seem to belong principally to this order of growth in self-awareness.

In the socialist vocabulary this growth in self-awareness has been given a name: it is the coming of the proletariat to "class-conscious-ness."

Two errors appear in the Socialist or Communist notion of "class-consciousness." One is an error of a "liberal" and "bour-geois" origin—Proudhon thereby remained *petit-bourgeois,* and Marx did, too; this error makes the liberation of the working class a final episode in the struggle of liberty against Christianity and the Church, seen as forces of enslavement and obscurantism. The other error is revolutionary and eschatological in origin; [2] it is the Marxist notion of class warfare and of the messianic role devolving on the proletariat.

But, disengaged from these errors and considered in itself, this growth in self-awareness appears as a considerable historical gain. It means the rise towards liberty and personality—these taken both in their interior reality and in their social expression—of a community of persons, the community at once nearest to the material bases of human life and the most sacrificed, the community of

---

[2] See our Preface to the French translation of Goetz Brief's *Le prolé-tariat industriel. . . .*

manual labor, the community of the human persons engaged in this labor.

Naturally, I am speaking here of a fact typical for this community as such, and not necessarily for each individual in it. We may believe with Aristotle that there will always be men who are constitutionally unfit to work otherwise than in the service of another man or a group of men and as in some sense "organs" of the latter. The fact remains that the collective consciousness of which we are speaking demands for the working community (whose most typical expression today is the proletariat) a kind of social coming of age and a condition concretely free.

In short, the historical gain of which we speak is the growth in awareness of the dignity of work and of the worker's dignity, of the dignity of the human person in the workman as such. It is to this that the leaders among the workers, awakened to social realities, hold most of all. To maintain the sense of this dignity and the rights tied up with it, these men are ready to face all kinds of evil and also to sacrifice themselves to the most murderous ideologies.

It is the tragedy of our times that a primarily spiritual gain such as this should seem to be bound up with an atheistic system such as Marxism. . . .

In our view the inevitable option is this: either the popular masses will become more and more attached to materialism and to the metaphysical errors which for almost a century have fed parasitically on their movement of historical advance, and in that case the movement will develop in forms ultimately deceptive; or it is out of the principles which Christianity holds in trust and maintains among us that their philosophy of the world and of life will be born. If the latter occurs, it is through the formation of a theocentric humanism whose universal value can reconcile, even in the temporal and cultural sphere, men of all conditions, that their will for social restoration will come to its fruition. Through the formation of such a humanism they will achieve the freedom of grown-up persons, the freedom and personality not of a class absorbing man in order to crush another class, but of man communicating to the class his proper human dignity, for the common inauguration of a society from which will have disappeared, I certainly do not say all differentiation and all hierarchy, but our present division into classes.

We need not insist on the proportions of the historical reorientation implied in such an hypothesis. On the one hand, powerful centers of spiritual and religious rebirth must be formed among the masses. On the other hand, Christians will have to free themselves from many more-or-less unconscious sociological prejudices. Christian thought will have to integrate truths discerned or surmised in the effort for social emancipation carried out during the whole of modern times, and yet purify them from the anti-Christian errors in the midst of which they were born. Social and political action inspired by this thought will have to be developed on a vast scale.

25 CONFESSION OF FAITH*

As a child I was brought up in "liberal Protestant-ism." Later on I became acquainted with the different phases of secularistic thought. The scientist and phenomenist philosophy of my teachers at the Sorbonne at last made me despair of reason. At one time I thought I might be able to find complete certitude in the sciences, and Félix Le Dantec thought that my fiancée and I would become followers of his biological materialism. The best thing I owe to my studies at that time is that they let me meet, in the School of Sciences, the woman who since then has always, happily for me, been at my side in a perfect and blessed communion. Bergson was the first to answer our deep desire for metaphysical truth—he liberated in us the sense of the absolute.

Before being captured by St. Thomas Aquinas, I underwent some great influences, those of Charles Péguy, Bergson, and Léon Bloy. A year after we met Bloy, my wife and I were baptized Catholics, and we chose him as our godfather.

It was after my conversion to Catholicism that I came to know St. Thomas. I had voyaged passionately among all the doctrines of modern philosophers and had found in them nothing but deception and grandiose uncertainty. What I now experienced was like an illumination of reason. My vocation as philosopher became perfectly clear to me. *Woe to me if I do not thomisticize,* I wrote in one of my first books. And through thirty years of work and battles I have kept to this same path, with the feeling of sympathizing all the more profoundly with the researches, the discoveries and the

---

* *Confession de foi* (New York: Éditions de la Maison Française, 1941).

agonies of modern thought, the more I tried to penetrate them with
the light which comes to us from a wisdom worked out through the
centuries, a wisdom resistant to the fluctuations of time.

In order to advance in this path we are obliged constantly to
bring together singularly distant extremes, for no solution of our
problems is found ready-made in the heritage of the ancients. We
are also obliged to make a difficult sifting of the pure substance of
truths which many a modern rejects in his loathing of the trashy
opinions of the past, from all the dross, the prejudices, the out-of-
date images and arbitrary constructions which many a traditionalist
confuses with what is really worthy of being venerated by intelligence.

I have spoken of the different experiences through which I
passed, because they gave me the occasion to try personally the
state of mind of the idealist freethinker, of the inexperienced convert, and of the Christian who becomes aware, in proportion as his
faith takes root, of the purifications to which that faith must be
subjected. I was also able to obtain some experimental idea of what
the anti-religious camp and the straddlers' camp are worth. Neither
of them is worth very much. And the worst disgrace of the second
camp is that it runs the risk of compromising along with itself the
innocent and persecuted Church, the Mystical Body of Christ,
whose essential life, *sine macula sine ruga,* is in the Truth and in
the saints, and which travels towards its fulness through the weaknesses of its own and the ferocity of the world. In my view, God
educates us through our deceptions and mistakes, in order to make
us understand at last that we ought to believe only in Him and not
in men—which readily brings one to marvel at all the good which
is in men despite everything and at all the good they do in spite of
themselves.

I have decidedly come to the conclusion that in practice there
are only two ways to know the depths of things, or, if one wishes,
two "wisdoms," each of them a kind of folly, though in opposite
manners. One is the way of sinners, who in order to drain things to
the dregs embrace the nothingness of which all things are made and
thereby have a full experience of this world, in the evil of the world
more than in its good. The other way is the way of the saints, who
adhere to subsisting Goodness, maker of all things, and receive in

love a full experience of God and of creation, and who stand surety
for all the world by their suffering and compassion. Well, it is
normal to hope that the disciples of vain wisdom, if they are not
hardened by pride and if they are loyal to their own experience,
will finally be saved "through fire" by the lovers of true wisdom.
And if they should live to be converted, they will perhaps be
harsher than others in censuring any of their brothers still in darkness, so that, after having long tasted the delights of the world, they
will taste for a moment the delights of their virtues and will continue vain till the last day, till they enter eternity.

This is not the place to give an exposition of theses in speculative
philosophy. I will only say that I consider Thomistic philosophy to
be a living and present philosophy, with all the greater power to
make conquests in new fields of discovery just because its principles are so firm and so organically bound together. Confronted
with the succession of scientific hypotheses, some minds are surprised that anyone could find inspiration today in metaphysical
principles acknowledged by Aristotle and Thomas Aquinas and
rooted in the oldest intellectual heritage of the race. My reply is
that the telephone and the radio do not prevent man from still
having two arms, two legs and two lungs, or from falling in love
and seeking happiness as did his faraway ancestors. Besides, truth
recognizes no chronological criteria, and the art of the philosopher
is not to be confused with the art of the great dressmakers.
On a deeper level, we must explain that progress in the sciences
of phenomena, where the "problem" aspect is so characteristic,
takes place chiefly by *substitution* of one theory for another which
saved less well the known facts and phenomena; but in metaphysics
and philosophy, where the "mystery" aspect is predominant,
progress takes place chiefly by *deeper penetration*. Besides, the
different philosophical systems, however ill founded they may be,
constitute in some way, in their totality, a virtual and fluent philosophy, overlapping contrary formulations and unfriendly doctrines
and carried along by the elements of truth they all contain. If,
therefore, there exists among men a doctrinal organism entirely
supported by true principles, it will incorporate—more or less
tardily, due to the laziness of its defenders—it will progressively

realize within itself this virtual philosophy, and this will thereby, and in a proportionate degree, take on form and organic arrangement. Such is my idea of progress in philosophy.

If I say next that the metaphysics which I hold to be founded on truth may be described as a critical realism and as a philosophy of intelligence and of being, or still more precisely as a philosophy of the *act of existing* regarded as the act and perfection of all perfections, these formulas, of course, will be of interest only to specialists. A brief reflection on the historical significance of modern philosophy will no doubt be more appropriate.

In the Middle Ages, philosophy was in fact ordinarily treated as an instrument in the service of theology. Culturally, it was not in the state required by its nature. The coming of a philosophical or lay wisdom which had completed its own formation for itself and according to its own finalities was therefore a response to an historical necessity. But unfortunately this work was brought about under the aegis of division and of a sectarian rationalism; Descartes *separated* philosophy from any higher wisdom, from anything in man which comes from above man. I am convinced that what the world and civilization have lacked in the intellectual order for three centuries has been a philosophy which would develop its autonomous exigencies in a Christian climate, a wisdom of reason not closed but open to the wisdom of grace. Today reason must battle an irrational deification of elemental and instinctive forces that threatens to ruin all civilization. In this struggle, reason's task is one of integration; understanding that intelligence is not the enemy of mystery, but lives on it, reason must come to terms with the irrational world of affectivity and instinct, as well as with the world of the will, of freedom and of love, and the suprarational world of grace and of divine life.

The dynamic harmony of the degrees of knowledge will at the same time become manifest. From this point of view, the problem proper to the age we are entering will be, it seems, to reconcile *science* and *wisdom*. The sciences themselves seem to invite intelligence to this work. We see them stripping themselves of the remains of materialistic and mechanistic metaphysics which for a time hid their true features. They call for a philosophy of nature, and the wonderful progress in contemporary physics restores to the scientist the sense of the mystery stammered by the atom and by the universe. A critique of knowledge formed in a genuinely realist and metaphysical spirit has a chance henceforth to be heard when it affirms the existence of structures of knowledge specifically and hierarchically distinct—distinct, but not separated—and shows that they correspond to original types of explanation which cannot be substituted one for another.

The Greeks recognized the great truth that contemplation is in itself superior to action. But they at once transformed this truth into a great error: they believed that the human race exists for a few intellectuals. As they saw it, there was a category of specialists, the philosophers, who lived a superhuman life, and the properly human life, namely, civil or political life, existed to serve them. To serve civil or political life, in turn, there was the subhuman life of labor, which in final analysis was the life of the slave. The lofty truth of the superiority of the contemplative life was thus bound to a contempt for labor and to the evil of slavery.

Christianity transfigured all this. It taught men that love is of more value than intelligence. It transformed the notion of contemplation, which henceforth does not stop in the intellect, but only in the love of God, the contemplated object. It restored to action its human significance as a service to our neighbor, and rehabilitated work by disclosing in it a value of natural redemption, as it were, and even a natural prefiguration of the communications of charity. It called to the contemplation of the saints and to perfection, not a few specialists or privileged persons, but all men, who are all bound proportionately by the law of work. Man is at once "homo faber" and "homo sapiens," and he is "homo faber" before truly and actually being "homo sapiens" and in order to become the latter. In this way Christianity saved, but by transforming and delivering from the error which tainted it, the Greek idea of the superiority of the contemplative life.

The saints' contemplation completes and consummates a natural aspiration to contemplation consubstantial to man, of which the sages of India and Greece especially give testimony. It is through love that the knowledge of divine things becomes experimental and fruitful. And precisely because this knowledge is the work of love in act, it also passes into action by virtue of the very generosity and abundance of love, which is gift of self. Then action proceeds from the superabundance of contemplation, and that is why, far from suppressing action or being opposed to it, contemplation vivifies it. It is in this sense, which relates to the essential generosity of the contemplation of love, that we must recognize with Bergson, in the superabundance and excess of the giving of self shown by the Christian mystics, the sign of their success in reaching the heroic summit of human life.

The pursuit of the highest contemplation and the pursuit of the highest freedom are two aspects of the same pursuit. In the order of spiritual life, man aspires to a perfect and absolute freedom, and therefore to a superhuman condition; sages of all times give evidence of this. The function of law is a function of protection and education of freedom, the function of a pedagogue. At the conclusion of this tutelage the perfect spiritual man is freed from every servitude, even, St. Paul says, from the servitude of the law, because he does spontaneously what is of the law and is simply one spirit and one love with the Creator.

To my way of thinking, the pursuit of freedom is also at the base of the social and political problem. But in the order of temporal life, it is not a divine freedom which is the object of our desires, but rather a freedom proportionate to the human condition and to the natural possibilities of our earthly existence. It is important not to deceive ourselves on the nature of the good thus pursued. It is not simply the preservation of each one's *freedom of choice,* nor the social community's *freedom of power.* The good in question is the *freedom of expansion* of human persons making up a people and participating in its good. Political society has as an end to develop conditions of life in common which, while assuring first of all the good and peace of the whole, will positively aid each person in the progressive conquest of this freedom of expansion, a freedom which consists above all in the flowering of moral and rational life.

Thus justice and friendship are the very foundations of society's life; and it is to truly human goods that society ought to subordinate all material goods, technical progress and the implements of power which also make up part of society's common good.

I believe that historical conditions and the yet backward state of human development make it difficult for social life fully to reach its end, and that in regard to the possibilities and demands which the Gospel brings to us in the socio-temporal order, we are still in a prehistoric age. As we see today in the psychoses of the masses which adore Stalin or Hitler, or dream of exterminating certain groups that they judge to be diabolical, in particular the Jews, doubtless because they are the people of God, human collectivities bear such a burden of willingly diseased animality that it will still require many centuries for the life of personality to be able truly to take on among the masses the fulness to which it aspires. But it still remains that the end towards which social life of itself tends is to procure the common good of the multitude in such a way that the concrete person, not merely in a privileged class but in the entire mass, may truly reach that measure of independence which belongs to civilized life and which is assured alike by the economic guarantees of work and property, by political rights, civic virtues and the cultivation of the mind.

These ideas are tied up with wider views which seem to me most properly designated by the expression *integral humanism,* and which involve a whole philosophy of modern history. Such a humanism, considering man in the integral wholeness of his natural and supernatural being and setting no a priori limits to the descent of the divine into man, may also be called a humanism of the Incarnation.

In the socio-temporal order it does not ask men to sacrifice themselves to the imperialism of race, of class or of nation. It asks them to sacrifice themselves to a better life for their brothers and to the concrete good of the community of human persons. That is why it cannot be less than an heroic humanism.

It has often been remarked that "bourgeois" liberalism, which tries to base everything on the individual taken as a little god and on his good pleasure, on an absolute freedom of ownership, of business and the pleasures of life, ends up fatally in statism. The rule of numbers produces the omnipotence of the State, of a ruminant or plutocratic State. Communism may be regarded as a reaction against this individualism. It claims to be orientated towards the absolute emancipation of man, who would thus become the god of history, but in reality this emancipation, supposing it were accomplished, would then be that of collective man, not that of the human person. Society as economic community would enslave the whole life of the person, because the essential work of civil society would be made to consist in economic functions, instead of subordinating this work to the freedom of expansion of persons: what the Communists propose as the emancipation of collective man would be the enslavement of human persons.

What of the anti-communist and anti-individualistic reactions of a totalitarian or dictatorial type? It is not in the name of the social community and the freedom of collective man, it is in the name of the sovereign dignity of the State, a state of the carnivorous type, or in the name of the spirit of a people, in the name of race or of blood, that they would annex man in his entirety to a social whole where the person of the ruler is the only one, properly speaking, to enjoy the privileges of personality. This is why totalitarian states, needing for themselves the total devotion of the person and having no sense of or respect for the person, inevitably seek a principle of human exaltation in myths of external grandeur and in the never-ending struggle for power and prestige. By its nature this tends to war and the self-destruction of the civilized community. If there are people in the Church—and they are fewer and fewer—who count on dictatorships of this kind to promote the religion of Christ and Christian civilization, they forget that the totalitarian phenomenon is an aberrant religious phenomenon in which an earthly mysticism devours every other mysticism whatever it may be, and will tolerate none besides itself.

Confronted with "bourgeois" liberalism, communism and totalitarian statism, what we need, I do not cease to say, is a new solution, one that is at the same time personalist and communal, one that sees human society as an organization of freedoms. We are thus brought to a conception of democracy, the community of free men, very different from that of Jean-Jacques Rousseau. We may call it *pluralist*, because it requires that the body politic guarantee the organic freedoms of the different spiritual families and different social bodies assembled within it, beginning with the basic natural community, the society of the family. The drama of modern democracies is that, under the appearance of an error—the deification of a fictitious individual entirely closed up in himself—they have without knowing it pursued a good thing: the expansion of the real person open to higher realities and to the common service of justice and friendship.

Personalist democracy holds that each is called, by virtue of the common dignity of human nature, to participate actively in political life, and that those who hold authority—which is a vital function in society and a real right to direct people—should be freely designated by the people. This is why personalist democracy sees in universal suffrage the first practical token by which a democratic society becomes aware of itself and which it may not in any case renounce. It has no better or more meaningful motto than the republican motto, understood as indicating, not an established condition in which man has only to be installed, but an end to be reached, a difficult and lofty goal to which man must tend by force of courage, justice and virtue. For freedom must be conquered, by the progressive elimination of the several forms of servitude, and it is not enough to proclaim equality of the fundamental rights of human persons, whatever one's race, one's religion, one's condition. This equality ought to pass in a real way into custom and into social structures and ought to yield fruit in a larger and larger participation by all in the common good of civilization. Finally, fraternity in the body politic requires that the loftiest and most generous of virtues, the love to which the Gospel has called our ungrateful species, pass into the very order of political life. A personalist democracy is not really conceivable without the super-elevations which nature and temporal civilizations receive, each in its own order, from the energies of the Christian leaven.

I am convinced that the coming of such a democracy, which presupposes that class antagonism has been overcome, demands that, by a genuine renewal of life and of justice, we truly go beyond "capitalism" and beyond socialism, each of which is vitiated by a materialistic conception of life. Nothing is more opposed to personalist democracy than fascist totalitarianism—whether social-nationalist or national-socialist; for it goes beyond "capitalism" only through the paroxysm of the evils it begets.

Let me remark that Christians are confronted today, in the socio-temporal order, with problems quite similar to those their sixteenth- and seventeenth-century ancestors encountered in the area of the philosophy of nature. At that time modern physics and astronomy, then in their beginnings, were simply one with philosophies set against tradition. The defenders of tradition did not know how to make the necessary distinctions. They took sides against what was to become modern science, at the same time that they took sides against the philosophical errors which at the start were parasitic on science. It took three centuries to get rid of this misunderstanding, if indeed the world is yet rid of it. It would be a sad story if we should be guilty today, in the field of practical and social philosophy, of like errors.

In the words of Pope Pius XI, the great scandal of the nineteenth century was the divorce of the working classes from the Church of Christ. In the temporal order, the moral secession of the working masses from the political community was a comparable tragedy. The awakening in the working masses of what the socialist vocabulary calls "class consciousness" appears to us as a great gain, so far as we see in it man's becoming aware of an offended and humiliated human dignity and of a vocation. But it has been chained to an historic calamity, because this awakening has been spoiled by the gospel of despair and of social warfare which is at the bottom of the Marxist idea of class struggle and the dictatorship of the proletariat. And it was precisely into this *secessionist* conception, whose protagonist was Marx and whose demand is that proletarians of all countries should recognize no other common good than that of their class, that the blindness of the possessing classes in the nineteenth century precipitated the working masses.

Whoever has pondered on these fundamental facts and on the history of the labor movement understands that the central problem of our times is the temporal and spiritual problem of the *reintegration of the masses*. In my view, it is only an artificial and illusory solution of this problem when the attempt is made, as in the case of German National Socialism, to manufacture happy slaves through violence linked up with material ameliorations good in themselves but achieved in a spirit of domination, and with a psychotechnic solicitude vowed to satisfy and to benumb appetites. The fact is that one manufactures only unhappy slaves, robots of non-being.

However difficult, slow and painful it may be, the reintegration of the proletariat within the national community, not to exercise a class dictatorship in it, but to collaborate body and soul in the work of the community, will take place really, which means humanly, only by a recasting of social structures worked out in the spirit of justice. I am not naive enough to believe that this reintegration can be accomplished without knocks and sacrifices, on the one hand as regards the well-being of the privileged sons of fortune and on the other as regards the theories and the destructive instincts of fanatical revolutionaries. But I am persuaded that it requires above all else the free cooperation of the workers' leaders (élites) and of the masses who follow them, and this cooperation must go along with a better general understanding of historical realities and with an awareness, not wiped out but heightened, of the human being's dignity as worker and citizen. In like manner the return of the masses to Christianity will be brought about only through love, I mean love stronger than death, the fire of the Gospel.

We shall never give up hope of a new Christendom, a new temporal order of Christian inspiration. Now the means should correspond to the end, and already are the end itself as in the state of movement and preparation. If this is so, it is clear that in order to prepare a Christian social order we must use Christian means, that is to say true means, just means, and these are means animated, even when they are of necessity harsh, by a genuine spirit of love. In two books published in 1930 and 1933 [1] I have insisted at length on these axiomatic truths. Nothing is more serious or scandalous than to see, as we have for some years seen in certain countries, iniquitous and barbarous means used by men in the name of Christian order and Christian civilization. It is a truth embedded in the very nature of things that Christendom will be renewed through Christian means or it will be completely eclipsed.

The present state of nations obliges us to declare that never has the spirit been so profoundly humiliated in the world. And yet pessimism in the end always dupes itself. It disregards the great law which may be called the law of the double movement involving the energy of history. While the wear and tear of time naturally dissipates and degrades the things of this world and the "energy of history," and this means the mass of human activity on which the movement of history depends, the creative forces which are characteristic of spirit and freedom and are a witness to them, forces which ordinarily find their point of application in the effort of the few—who are thereby bound to sacrifice—improve more and more the quality of this energy. This is exactly the work of the sons of

---

[1] *Religion et culture; Du régime temporel et de la liberté.* English translation, *Religion and Culture; Freedom in the Modern World.*

God in history, it is the work of Christians if they do not belie their name.

People do not understand this work at all if they imagine that it aims at installing the world in a state from which all evil and all injustice would have disappeared. If this were the aim, it would be quite easy, considering the results, stupidly to condemn the Christian as utopian. The work the Christian has to do is to keep up and to increase in the world the internal tension and movement of slow and painful deliverance, a tension and movement due to the invisible powers of truth and justice, of goodness and love, acting on the mass which is opposed to them. This work cannot be in vain, it assuredly bears its fruit.

Woe to the world should Christians turn their back on it, should they fail to do their work, which is to heighten here on earth the charge and tension of the spiritual; should they listen to blind leaders of the blind who seek the means to order and to good in things which of themselves lead to dissolution and death. We have no illusions about the misery of human nature and the malice of this world. But neither have we any illusions about the blindness and malfeasance of pseudo-realists who cultivate and exalt evil in order to fight evil, and who take the Gospel as a decorative myth which cannot be regarded seriously without wrecking the machinery of the world. They themselves, meantime, take it upon themselves to ruin, to distract, and to torment this unhappy world.

The ferment of the pharisees, against which Christ put us on our guard, is a permanent temptation for the religious conscience. Undoubtedly, this ferment will not be altogether driven out of the world till the end of history. Meantime, in the social as well as in the spiritual order, we must never let up the fight against it. However great may be the mass of evil which a mass of pharisaism means to oppose, the latter is always as great an evil, because the good it sets against that evil is a good which does not give life but kills, as does the letter without the spirit: it is a good which leaves God without resources in man.

One of the gravest lessons afforded us by the experience of life is that, in fact, in the practical conduct of most people, all those things which in themselves are good and very good—science, technical progress, culture, etc., and even the knowledge of moral laws, and religious faith itself, faith in the living God (which of itself demands the love of charity)—all these things, *without love and good will,* serve to make men all the more evil and the more unhappy. So far as religious faith is concerned, this was demonstrated in the Spanish civil war by the inhuman feelings that surged up in the "crusaders" as well as in the "reds," but were confirmed in the former in the sanctuary of the soul. What happens is that, without love and charity, man turns the best in him into an evil that is yet greater.

When one has understood this, he no longer puts his hope on earth in anything less than that good will of which the Gospel speaks—it speaks of good will, not of good velleity; he puts his hope in those obscure energies of a little real goodness which persist in making life germinate and regerminate in the secret depths of things. There is nothing more destitute, nothing more hidden, nothing nearer to the weakness of the infant. And there is no wisdom more fundamental or more effective than that simple and tenacious confidence, not in the means of violence, deceit and malice, which certainly are capable of crushing men and of triumphing, but which a grain of sand is nevertheless enough to cause to be smashed one against the other—but simple and tenacious confidence in the resources of personal courage to give oneself, and of good will set to do as one ought the tasks of every day. Through this disinterested spirit flows the power of nature and the Author of nature.

INDEX OF NAMES